THE FOUR HUNDRED SONGS

OF WAR

AND WISDOM

Translations from the Asian Classics

THE FOUR HUNDRED SONGS OF WAR AND WISDOM

An Anthology of Poems from Classical Tamil

THE PUṞANĀṈŪṞU

Translated and edited by

George L. Hart

and

Hank Heifetz

COLUMBIA UNIVERSITY PRESS NEW YORK

Columbia University Press wishes to express its appreciation of assistance given by the Pushkin Fund in the publication of this anthology.

The preparation of this volume was made possible by a grant from the Translations Program of the National Endowment for the Humanities, an independent federal agency.

COLUMBIA UNIVERSITY PRESS
Publishers Since 1893
New York Chichester, West Sussex

Library of Congress Cataloging-in-Publication Data

The four hundred songs of war and wisdom : an anthology of poems from classical Tamil : the purananuru / translated and edited by George L. Hart and Hank Heifetz.
p. cm. — (Translations from the Asian classics)
Includes index.
ISBN 0-231-11562-8 (cloth)
ISBN 0-231-11563-6 (paperback)
1. Puṟanāṉūṟu. 2. War poetry, Tamil—Translations into English. 3. Tamil poetry—To 1500—Translations into English. I. Hart, George L. II. Heifetz, Hank. III. Series.
PL4758.6.F68 1999
894.8′1111080358—dc21 99-14021

Casebound editions of Columbia University Press books are printed on permanent and durable acid-free paper.
Printed in the United States of America
c 10 9 8 7 6 5 4 3 2 1
p 10 9 8 7 6 5 4 3 2 1

George Hart dedicates his work on this book
to the memory of Daniel Ingalls, mentor and guru of a generation of Indologists.

Hank Heifetz dedicates his work on this book
to Aaron St. John Heifetz
and
Samara Devi Heifetz
both writers

We would like to express our thanks to V. S. Rajam for her constant encouragement of this project and for her contributions to it—the extremely useful text she digitized with such care, her article on *tiṇais,* and the many suggestions that have significantly improved our translation. Our thanks are also due to N. Ganesan, who graciously supplied the rare text of some commentary that has been recently discovered.

CONTENTS

SHORT GUIDE TO TAMIL PRONUNCIATION

Tamil pronunciation is somewhat complex. The following guide is not meant to be complete, but it will allow the reader to pronounce most words with a modicum of correctness.

a is like the *u* in *but.*
ā is like the *a* in father.
i is like the *i* in *pill.*
ī is like the *i* in *machine.*
u is like the *u* in *put,* but final *-u* usually similar to
the German umlaut.
ū is like the *u* in *rule.*
e is like the *e* in *tell.*
ē is like the *a* in *fate.*
o is like the *o* in *no.*
ō is like the *ōa* in *boat* (longer than short *o*).
ai is like the *i* in *kite.*
au is like the *ow* in *now.*

Consonants are pronounced more or less as they appear, but Tamil distinguishes between retroflexes (with dots beneath them) and dentals (without). Retroflexes are pronounced with the tongue curled up so that one touches the top of the mouth with the top of the tongue (e.g. *t* in *part*), while dentals are pronounced with the tongue touching the front teeth (e.g. *t* in *stop*). Consonants with lines beneath are alveolars and are pronounced much as the dentals. When the single stops *ṭ*, *t*, *p* appear between vowels in the middle of a word or after *m* or *n*, they are voiced (*paṭam* is pronounced *paḍam*, aṉpu is pronounced aṉbu). Single *k* between vowels is like English *h* (only a bit harder): *akam* is pronounced as if it were *aham*. *ṅk* is like *ng* in *anger.* When *k*, *ṭ*, *t*, and *p* are doubled, they are pronounced as one would expect. At the beginning of a word, *c* is usually like English *s*, while when doubled it is like *ch* in chair. *ñc* is pronounced like *ng* in *tangerine.* The letters ṟ and ṉ are as one would expect, except that -ṟṟ- is like *tr* in train and -ṉṟ- is like *ndr* in Sandra. The letter *ḻ* is like *ir* in the American pronunciation of *sir.*

POET'S PREFACE

Hank Heifetz

In translating the public poetry of the ancient Tamils, George Hart and I have worked as we did in our earlier collaboration on *The Forest Book of the Kamparāmāyaṇam.* George—from whom I learned Tamil and whose knowledge of the language and culture is infinitely greater than mine—prepared careful prose translations with extensive notes and also translated passages from the principal commentaries. It was my job then to make the prose into poems in English. Occasionally I would offer a scholarly observation that George found useful, and he would comment sensitively on my verses but all credit for the scholarship of this book is due to George Hart, while I am fully responsible for the translations as poetry.

These are poems of "the public life," celebrating kings and war and the conventional values of ancient Tamil culture. They include powerful meditations on the core thematics of this warrior society: heroism, death, glory, stoicism. And there is a whole range of poems (many of the finest in the collection) about the conditions of the (upper-caste) poets and lower-caste bards and musicians, projecting their gross or sublime praise of rulers and implicitly (or very directly) of themselves:

> May you live long in this world as a refuge for poets! Without
> doubt, if you were not in this world, it would be empty,
> and poets would not endure! *(poem 375)*

and the plaints of creators who must live on the largesse of power:

who come here in need, leading this life of pleading,
to sow shining words in the ears of the generous
and so to gain what they wish for, with their strong
urges and anguished concern for dignity! *(poem 206)*

A series of poems about the wandering life of bards concludes the anthology, where the artist may receive his pay and acknowledgment:

He took the cymbals from my hand and he gave me roasted meat
and he gave me clear toddy to drink so strong it was like a snake's
rage! Then and there he made the hell of my poverty vanish
away! O lord, on that very night! *(poem 376)*

or in a profound moment of awareness that in a sense subverts the conventions of a praise poem and speaks directly to us through the force of poetry across the ages and beyond reductive, scholastic interpretations, the bard realizes that too great a closeness to power—even to its rewards—can be dangerous:

Happiness filled his heart and he showed desire for me to approach
him
and he gave me an elephant not yet calmed down after a kill,
sending out a stench from its tusks covered with blood, tossing
its body in anger! In terror I refused it, and he, ashamed, thinking
I felt it was too little, ordered an elephant brought to me that was
yet more immense! And so, because of that, even if my large family,
which has been burned dark under the sun, may suffer, I have realized
the gifts that he gives you cannot approach!
and I have never gone back to that land of his, with its hills.

(poem 394)

There is often as here a sense in these poems of the poem itself, the intrinsic power of an image, overturning a convention and speaking to us with an insight that perhaps the poet himself did not fully recognize.

As I once wrote elsewhere, the Tamil language "runs like a river"—long words, rapid speech, accumulating syllables—and these translations (sometimes straining against the bounds of English syntax) attempt to communicate something of the feel of these rolling rhythms, in war:

Drawn swords in their battle lust have swept forward
as they broke through the garrisoned walls and then went
twisting out of shape, buried in flesh. Spears,
conquering the fortresses of his enemies, have ravaged
the land densely fragrant with toddy
and have ruined themselves, the nails shattered
on their dark, hollowed shafts. *(poem 97)*

Enduring the troubles that have fallen upon him as king, cured
of his suffering from those noble wounds endured when weapons
on the field of battle tasted his flesh, the handsome scars have grown
together as if he were a tree with its bark stripped for use
in curing and his body is perfect! *(poem 180)*

in elaborate descriptions of nature as a reflection of human feelings and sentiments:

Lord! He rules Vaṭṭāṟu
of the rich waters where they frighten the birds with drums
sharply beaten in the growing fields
that are circled by the tidal pools
where the fish dart under the water
and the flowers blossom on the surface
like so many eyes and from the sand
heaped up by the great waters, birds
fly off on soft wings in cool wind. *(poem 396)*

or in the union of sensuality with the constant awareness of mortality:

When he holds
his lengthy audiences in the company
of bards wearing their lotus flowers
of gold and the singing women with their garlands of fashioned gold,
where his women of great purity and exemplary patience calmly carry
filtered and mixed toddy in gold pitchers and pour it out as if it were

amṛta for people to drink, his women whose glances are like those of
the deer,
whose brows bend like bows, whose tongues when they speak loudly
seem
to fear their teeth which are like little thorns and as they move,
their belt strings slide down, he does not forget, you do not have to
tell him
of the mutability of this world which does not endure. . . *(poem 361)*

Scholars of Tamil or those who already know these poems in the original may read these translations straight through from the beginning or search out our versions of specific poems. For the general reader of poetry, my suggestion is to browse. The praise of kings can be overpowering (and stifling and insincere at times) but if you browse, you are likely to encounter a sudden image, a moment when the door of vision opens into a deeper, more inner world—and that poem may be followed by others, elaborating, exploring, defining. George Hart in his introduction describes the practical and poetic context from which these poems arise (and much more) but, like all poetry worth reading, all art worth attending to, these poems composed two thousand years ago speak at their best not only to Tamils, or to Indians, but to our human race:

Every city is your city. Everyone is your kin.
Failure and prosperity do not come to you because others
have sent them! Nor do suffering and the end of suffering.
There is nothing new in death. Thinking that living
is sweet, we do not rejoice in it. Even less do we say,
if something unwanted happens, that to live is miserable!
Through the vision of those who have understood we know
that a life, with its hardship, makes its way like a raft
riding the water of a huge and powerful river roaring
without pause as it breaks against rocks because the clouds
crowded with bolts of lightning pour down their cold
drops of the rain, and so we are not amazed
at those who are great and even less do we despise the weak!

(poem 192)

INTRODUCTION

George Hart

THE *Puṟanāṉūṟu* is an anthology of 400 poems written between the first and third centuries C.E. by more than 150 poets, including at least 10 poetesses. The language is old Tamil, the precursor of modern Tamil and Malayalam. Comprising one of the eight "Sangam"[1] anthologies, the *Puṟanāṉūṟu* is among the earliest works in Tamil that we possess. It was written before Aryan influence had penetrated the south as thoroughly as it did later and is a testament of pre-Aryan South India and, to a significant extent, of pre-Aryan India. Consequently, the *Puṟanāṉūṟu* is extremely important to the study and understanding of the development of much of South Asia's history, culture, religion, and linguistics. But beyond this, the *Puṟanāṉūṟu* is a great work of literature, accurately and profoundly reflecting the life of Tamilnad 2,000 years ago. Its appeal is universal: it has much to say about living and dying, despair, poverty, love, and the changing nature of existence. The *Puṟanāṉūṟu* is one of the few works of classical India that confront life without the insulation of a philosophical facade; it makes no basic assumptions about karma and the other world; it faces existence as a great and unsolved mystery.[2]

The name of the work, *Puṟanāṉūṟu,* means literally "The Four Hundred [Poems] About the Exterior." Classical Tamil literature is divided into two overarching categories: *akam,* "interior," and *puṟam,* "exterior." The former are love poems, chronicling different situations in the development of love between a man and a woman. These poems are, in a sense, about life "inside" the family, especially about sexual relations between men and women. The "exterior" poems concern life outside the family, that is, the king and the king's wars, greatness, and generosity; ethics; and death and dying. Among the eight Sangam anthologies, only two contain exclusively *puṟam* poems: the *Puṟanāṉūṟu* and the *Patiṟṟuppattu,* which consist of one hundred poems (eighty are extant) to ten Chera kings. Of these two, the *Puṟanāṉūṟu* contains poems on a more varied assortment of themes, whereas the *Patiṟṟuppattu* is limited to poems glorifying the Chera kings. Of the four hundred poems of the *Puṟanāṉūṟu,* two have been lost, and some are missing several lines. The first poem is a traditional invocatory piece to Śiva, written by Peruntēvaṉār and probably later than the other poems. There are, then, 397 poems that are original *puṟam* poems of the Sangam period.

An excellent commentary for the first 266 poems of the *Puṟanāṉūṟu* has survived.[3] Included with each poem is a colophon that tells who sang it, to whom he or she sang it (if that is relevant), and other details. The colophon also gives a *tiṇai* and a *tuṟai* for each poem, literary categories that are discussed later in this introduction. Most of the poems are addressed to kings, more than fifty great kings (Chera, Chola, Pandya) and eighty-three small kings (*kuṟunilamaṉṉar*). And many poems were written by kings themselves.[4]

The *Puṟanāṉūṟu* is generally dated between the first century B.C.E. and the fifth century C.E. Zvelebil suggests that most of the earliest Tamil poetry, of which the *Puṟanāṉūṟu* is a part, can be dated between 100 and 250 C.E.[5] His evidence for these dates is both copious and persuasive. First, the poems do not mention the Pallavas, an important dynasty of Tamilnad that began in 350 C.E. Second, the Tamils' trade with the Greeks and Romans ("Yavanas") referred to in the anthologies could not have been significant after the second or third century. Third, linguistic evidence dates the *Puṟanāṉūṟu* to a period after the earliest parts of the *Tolkāppiyam* and the early Brahmi inscriptions, which can be dated to the first century B.C.E.[6] but before the *bhakti* literature that began to be composed in the seventh century. And finally, there is the famous Gajabāhu synchronism: the *Cilappatikāram,* a work of perhaps two centuries after the *Puṟanāṉūṟu,* mentions that Gajabāhu the First of Ceylon was contemporary with the Chera king Ceṅkuṭṭuvaṉ, who figures in the *Patiṟṟuppattu* and the *Puṟanāṉūṟu*. The date for Gajabāhu is approximately 171 to 193 C.E. An analysis of generations of kings, assigning 25 years to each generation, suggests that the main body of the early anthologies spans 120 to 150 years and that the Chera and Chola kings mentioned ruled between approximately 130 and 240 C.E.

Society: The King

The society that the *Puṟanāṉūṟu* describes had three basic features. First, it revolved around the king, who was thought to have important powers over the environment and to have the ability to neutralize and counteract dangerous magical forces. Second, the ancient Tamils believed—as they still do—in the power of a woman's purity, which they call *kaṟpu*. Because of this, the behavior of most women was severely restricted, and widows were supposed to undergo extreme austerities or to take their own lives as *satīs* at or after the funeral rites of their husbands. Finally, the ancient Tamils had a system of caste (*kuṭi,* now usually called *jāti*) not too different from what they possess today, a system that was not borrowed from the Aryans and that did not arise from the *varṇa* system first described in the Rig Veda. There were three great kings—the Chera, Chola, and Pandya—and many minor kings and chieftains. The Tamil area was in a state of incessant warfare, and men were supposed to fight with bravery and a reckless disregard of death. Consequently, many of the poems describe with hyperbole the "martial courage" (*maṟam*) of the warriors and the extraordinary strength of their women, who when their sons or husbands died in battle often wept with joy to see how brave their men had been.[7]

The *Puṟanāṉūṟu* is a treatise on kingship: what a king should be, how he should act, how he should balance his responsibilities, how he should treat his subjects, and how he should show his generosity. At the same time, it describes a society in which many kings were not generous or merciful and whose rule was merely a manifestation and exercise of power. Each king had certain accoutrements that reflected his legitimacy and were supposed to contain a kind of magic power that gave him strength. Among these were the tutelary tree, the royal drum, and the royal umbrella.[8] A few of the kings perform Brahmanical sacrifices, and some of them support Brahmins.

It is remarkable that so few of these poems show any clear Northern Indian attitudes toward kingship, but the era of the Hindu kings in the Tamil area came after these poems, beginning with the Pallavas and their attempt to "Sanskritize" and "Brahmanize" the society.[9] Later in South India and continuing until today, the ideal king has been a hybrid figure. His connection with the Hindu gods is a later development, whereas the requirements that he be generous and heroic (in the movies if nowhere else) are quite ancient.[10] Some of this process is self-creating, for most of the Hindu gods in South India were modeled after kings, and then later kings partly modeled themselves on Hindu gods.

The poems reveal kings locked in an interminable and vicious struggle for supremacy. Kings did not usually want direct power over the lands of their rivals; instead, they were happy if they could force their enemies to acknowledge their supremacy by paying tribute. What was important to the old Tamil kings was that they have the proper royal aura and that their subjects and others recognize this. It was crucial that they be treated with respect; otherwise, they could not function as kings, for they would not be acknowledged as such. It is no surprise, then, that we find the Tamil kings sparing no effort to prove their bravery and ferocity in war. At the same time, it was equally important that they show mercy and generosity toward their suppliants—especially poor bards, drummers, and poets—and the poems describe these attributes again and again.

The nature of the king was related to the ancient Tamils' belief system. For them, the world was precariously balanced between ordered, auspicious power and its disordered, dangerous analogue. The natural state of the world was dangerous and chaotic, as found in the forest (*kāṭu*), in the burial ground (also, not coincidentally, called *kāṭu*), and in any place where things are allowed to proceed in a natural way without intervention by human beings. The ordered analogue is found in a proper kingdom, one whose king is just, brave in war, and generous. Since the natural state of things is disordered, the function of human society is to change this state, to metamorphose dangerous power into auspicious power under human control. Only such a metamorphosis can guarantee the two things necessary for survival: rain and victory in war.

Central to this undertaking was the king, whose task was to take disordered power—from war, from the forest (hunting), and from low-caste bards and drummers—and to make it ordered. In a later time, the Hindu gods (who, in the south, were modeled after kings) also had this ability, which is why so many of their *sthalapurāṇas,* collections of foundation myths for sacred sites, involve blood and death.[11] To be controlled, dangerous power had to be contained and channeled; once controlled, power was thought to become auspicious and to bring fertility and good luck. This idea is clear in the way women were (and are) treated: a widow, tainted by death, is inauspicious, whereas a married woman is called a *sumaṅgaḷi* and is considered to bring good luck (as long as she is not barren or menstruating—conditions thought to reflect a disordered and natural state). What is intriguing about the king is that he does not seem to be in either an auspicious or an inauspicious state; rather, both conditions apply to him at once. Accordingly, the same poem shows him killing indiscriminately on the battlefield and then being generous, merciful, and careful of his kingdom's welfare.

It is impossible to overstate the importance of the king in ancient Tamil society. He is the main figure who makes possible the creation of an ordered condition of the world, and he does this by tapping the disorder, chaos, and death endemic to it. He kills in battle, drinks toddy and spirits (which connect him with the disordered world of the supernatural), and consorts with low castes (who are tainted by disordered power). Because of the king, the rains come, enemies are kept at bay, and the fields are fertile.[12] One common recurrence in the poems is the comparison of war to the harvest: the falling arrows are the rain; the flashing swords and spears are the lightning; the corpses with broken necks are the grain bending down ready for the harvest; the stacks of corpses are the stacks of paddy; and the elephants trampling the corpses are the buffaloes threshing the grain.[13] These metaphors show that the king is considered to be a sort of machine designed to metamorphose dangerous power—the killing on the battlefield—into its auspicious analogue—the production and harvesting of grain.

One of the more intriguing aspects of the king's power is that men can fight under his aegis and kill without being tainted by the dangerous power unleashed by their killing. Beyond this, if a king is legitimate, it does not matter what evil omens may appear, because he can counteract them.[14] As a result of the king's aura, his men are strongly attached to him—so much so that when he dies, some of them take their own lives.[15] This devotion has continued to the present in the Tamil country, both directed toward God and as loyalty to political leaders.[16]

Society: Women

The second important connection with the sacred in ancient Tamilnad was through women. Again, the king was in neither an auspicious or an inauspicious state but mediated between the two, whereas the low-caste person was always in an inauspicious state. Unlike these two figures, a woman could exist in either an auspicious or an inauspicious state. If she was married and had children, she was considered auspicious and imparted her positive aura to her husband. For this reason, many poems mention the chaste wife of a king—because such a woman was actually a source and sign of his power. Widows, however, were dangerous and were required to control this negative power through asceticism; that is, they were supposed to keep their heads shaved, to sleep on a bed of stones, to eat unappetizing food at the wrong times, to wear no ornaments, and to lead limited and miserable lives.[17] Furthermore, young widows were sometimes expected to take their own lives as *satīs.*[18]

The issue of woman's power is complex, often misunderstood in the modern West, where the worship of goddesses is erroneously seen as a sign of women's social empowerment. In the Tamil culture, a woman was (and is) supposed to observe *kaṟpu*—self-restraint, obedience, and chastity. The word comes from the root *kal,* "to learn," and signifies a state in opposition to nature, in which a woman's sexuality and conduct are theoretically unrestrained. Thus many folk stories attribute drought or other natural disasters to a woman's being unchaste.[19] Because uncontrolled sexual power—in the traditional Tamil, male-dominated ideology, the natural state of woman—is believed to be destructive, a woman must fit into very well defined (and restrictive) contours. Unless she is a widow, she must wear ornaments, tie her hair up (it is inauspicious to see a woman with her hair loose), remain chaste, perform various acts of self-denial and religious devotion to further her husband's welfare, draw a *kōlam* (an auspicious design usually made with rice flour) every morning in front of her house,[20] and engage in many other acts to subdue and channel her supposedly dangerous natural power toward beneficial ends. This dual role of woman in traditional Tamil society is expressed by a common proverb: *āvatum peṇṇālē aḻivatum peṇṇāḷē,* "Becoming is through woman, destruction is through woman."

Society: The Low Castes

Unlike the king and women, the low castes—drummers, leather workers, bards, washermen, and others—were always felt to be in a dangerous state, as they possessed a power that had to be contained and managed. This was done by regulating their behavior—making them live in certain areas, not allowing them into the houses of highborn people, and almost certainly not eating with them. The poems give much evidence for this, which I have summarized in an article showing that caste is indigenous to South India.[21] In the *Puṟanāṉūṟu,* low castes are said to be "of low birth,"[22] and they are clearly seen as possessing a special power over the world of the supernatural. Spirits are felt to be everywhere—as they are in modern South India—and they must be controlled so that they cannot cause harm. The low castes are people who have special powers to exercise this control, especially through their musical instruments, which are frequently described as containing or embodying dangerous spirits.[23] The most potent instrument was the royal drum, which was beaten during battle and was supposed to confer title to a kingdom. The royal drum was made of the wood of an enemy's tutelary tree and the skin of a bull that had defeated another bull in a formal fight.[24]

Among the ancient Tamils there were several very low castes, one of whose main functions was to make music. The three most prominent of these castes were the drummers, called Kiṇaiyaṉs (probably modern Paṟaiyaṉs), the bards, called Pāṇaṉs, and a group of drummers called Tuṭiyaṉs, who lived in wilderness villages and played the *tuṭi* drum. Of these groups, the Kiṇaiyaṉs and Tuṭiyaṉs seem to have had the lowest status and were not allowed in the houses of higher-caste families.[25] The bards, however, were allowed to live in the houses of the highborn and were supposed to sing songs appropriate to the time of the day. These songs were in different *rāgas,* called *paṇs* in old Tamil. The musical system was similar to Carnatic music of today and was clearly its precursor. Some of the bards managed on their own, and others banded together as dancers and performers. It is not clear whether each of these groups was considered a different subcaste, but it is likely that they were.

These performers served the king in several ways. They seem to have played the drum during battle—*Patiṟṟuppattu* 75 says that the drum-playing Kiṇaiyaṉs were actually the cause of the enemy's defeat. The instruments the Kiṇaiyaṉs played were thought to contain spirits that could be propitiated. Even today, some high-caste people believe that the goddess Sarasvatī is present in musical instruments. When the Kiṇaiyaṉs played, they invoked the spirits in their drums or lutes. Their playing thus was used both to contain dangerous forces during battle and to protect men lying wounded after battle. Drummers also would play during executions and would wake the king up in the morning.

Being of low caste, these bards and drummers were usually quite poor and always in need. To survive, they traveled around the countryside and attempted to attach themselves to the court of a king or chieftain. Upon arriving at a court, they would sing the greatness of the king's exploits, expecting some reward. No doubt, they also sometimes sang *akam* songs as well (although this may have been restricted to the Pāṇaṉs). In any event, the king often rewarded them with some of the booty he had captured from his enemies. In fact, one of the great requirements for being a good king was generosity: a king was supposed to give not only generously but beyond all reason (at least according to the poems).[26] The performers and the king drank toddy in great quantities and ate all sorts of meat. These performances by low-caste musicians were important to the king, as they were evidence of his legitimacy and connected him with the dangerous and disordered power he needed to function as a proper king, through their evocation of prowess and death on the battlefield and also through close contact with the low-caste performers, who embodied dangerous power. Indeed, several poems castigate kings for not being generous enough. The bards and drummers were obviously not above pressuring the king to give them lavish gifts.[27]

Poets

Writing reached Tamilnad from North India a few hundred years before the *Puṟanāṉūṟu* was composed.[28] A new group of poets was formed who called themselves Pulavaṉs, "people of knowledge," and who were from mostly high-caste backgrounds. These men and women composed poems modeled on the songs of the drummers and bards and, like them, traveled from the court of one king to another, reciting their poems and hoping for gifts.[29] Many of them became attached to the court of a king and were supported by him. The two most famous of these poets are Kapilar, a Brahmin whose patron was the chieftain Pāri, and Auvaiyār, a poetess who was supported by the king Atiyamāṉ.

The poems that form the Sangam literature—including the *Puṟanāṉūṟu*—come from this group of Pulavaṉs. In many of the poems, the poets pretend to be bards or low-caste drummers, but in others, they speak with their own voices, sometimes advising kings, addressing moral issues, or lamenting the instability of the world. The breadth of the subject matter in the *Puṟanāṉūṟu* is remarkable: it provides a mirror for the society that produced it and for subsequent life in South India.

Orality

The orality of the *Puṟanāṉūṟu* has been controversial. Kailasapathy suggested that since the *Puṟanāṉūṟu* has formulas and themes that, according to Parry and Lord, characterize oral literature, it must be oral.[30] I responded that the text is often far too complex to have been extemporized—the chief requirement for oral poetry—and that it must therefore have been written down as an imitation of truly oral poetry. This explanation fits the fact that the poems of the *Puṟanāṉūṟu* were composed by high-caste Pulavaṉs, or "poets," but that the material imitated was clearly extemporized orally by bards and drummers. Indian literature, however, does not fall as neatly into oral and written categories as does Western literature. Many old Indian texts contain many interpolations entered by literate scribes that cannot be differentiated by their style from truly oral sections.[31]

It is worth looking at the issue of orality in a little more depth. Parry and Lord, studying the oral songs of the Yugoslavian bards, found several elements to be characteristic of orally produced literature. Each is related to the fact that such works are not memorized but, rather, are created each time they are produced. The two most prominent features are formulas and themes. *Formulas* are set phrases that fit into a meter and are used over and over, such as "swift-footed Achilles" and "the wine-dark sea." *Themes* are set descriptions or episodes that the singer can use to construct his story, for example, a description of arming a hero or of fighting a battle.

The *Puṟanāṉūṟu* contains both these elements. For example, the final poems of the work are about a low-caste drummer (Kiṇaiyaṉ) who goes to a king in the morning, beats his drum, praises him, and is rewarded. The formula describing the drum is repeated several times. Examples are poem 373, "I also drum / on my black kiṇai drum with its handsome eye," and poem 374, "beating out a rhythm on my dark kiṇai drum / with its clear eye."[32] Formulas like these make clear the ultimate oral provenance of the poems. Nonetheless, fewer formulas are found in the *Puṟanāṉūṟu* than in many oral texts such as the *Iliad* and the *Odyssey, Beowulf,* and the *Mahābhārata.*

The *Puṟanāṉūṟu's* thematic content also is prominent. The poems are roughly grouped into thematic groups: the praise of kings, the *āṟṟuppaṭai,*[33] the highborn woman who has just reached puberty and whom local chieftains are trying to marry against the wishes of her people, and the king who is belittled when he does not give presents to poets.[34] These themes are even recognized and categorized by the tradition, although not as straightforwardly as the reader might like. Each poem also is given a *tiṇai* and *tuṟai,* described later.

I do not believe, however, that these poems are oral in the same way that the Homeric epics and the songs of the Yugslav bards are—they are too complex to be extemporized. Lord believes that oral poetry should be crafted in such a way that each line ends a thought. If more lines are added, they simply add to the thought that was essentially complete in the first line.[35] But the Tamil heroic poems often do not conform to this requirement. Sometimes we find a verb at the beginning of a poem and, many lines later, an object or subject, with an extraordinary complex structure intervening.[36]

Instead, the poems of the Sangam anthologies must have been written by literate poets who consciously imitated the oral works of illiterate Pāṇaṉs and the Kiṇaiyaṉs. When the poets emulated the works of these lower-caste oral performers, they did not produce oral poetry but poetry that contains some oral elements, even though it is too complex syntactically to have been extemporized in the way that true oral poetry is.[37] Some poems—like *Puṟanāṉūṟu* 89, in which Auvaiyār pretends she is a low-caste Viṟali visiting an enemy king, and like the last thirty poems of the *Puṟanāṉūṟu*—were careful imitations of the oral poetry of the bards and drummers. But some of the poems, like the great didactic poems 182 through 195, could scarcely have been modeled directly on the utterances of the low-caste performers.

Meter and Alliteration

Although this is not the place for a long technical discussion of Tamil meter, a basic introduction might be helpful to the general reader.[38] Meter in old Tamil is based on the line (*aṭi*), which, as in Western meters, is divided into components analogous to feet (*cīr*). Most lines in the *Puṟanāṉūṟu* contain four feet, although sometimes lines (or, more often, series of lines) of two feet alternate with lines of four feet. In all the poems, the penultimate line has three feet. Unlike Western prosody, Tamil metrics subdivides the feet into one or more subunits called *acai*. Syllables in Tamil are either short or long, and the *acai* is determined partly by length and partly by the number of syllables it contains.

An *acai* has one of two forms. One is simply a long syllable and is called a *nēr;* the other is two syllables, the first of which must be short, and is called a *nirai.* In Sangam literature, each *nēr* or *nirai* may be extended by a short *-u,* in which case it is called a *nērpu* or *niraipu.* The most common foot (*cīr*) is made up of two *acais;* feet of three *acai* (and, very rarely, of one *acai*) are also found in Sangam literature. In effect, this creates the following sorts of feet (not taking into account the *nerpu* or *niraipu*): — —; ⏑ ⏑ —; — ⏑ ⏑; and ⏑ ⏑ ⏑ ⏑. (These may occasionally be extended by another *acai.*) A line consists of either three or four of these feet. An example of how meter works in these poems can be seen in *Puṟanāṉūṟu* 112, a poem supposedly composed for the daughters of Pāri after their father was killed in the siege of his mountain fortress. The final -*u* of a *nērpu* or *niraipu* is indicated by "x":

On that day, under the white light of that moon,
we had our father, and no enemies had taken the hill.
On this day, under the white light of this moon, the kings,
royal drums beating out the victory,
have taken the hill. And we! we have no father.

The Tamil, scanned metrically, is as follows:

— — | — — | — — | ˘ ˘ — |
aṟṟait tiṅka ḷavveṇ nilaviṉ

— — x | ˘ ˘ — — | — — | ˘ ˘ ˘ ˘ |
entaiyu muṭaiyēmeṅ kuṉṟum piṟarkoḷār

— — | — — | — — | ˘ ˘ — |
iṟṟait tiṅka ḷivveṇ ṇilaviṉ

— ˘ ˘ | ˘ ˘ — | — ˘ ˘ |
veṉṟeṟi muraciṉ vēntarem

— — | — — — | — — x | ˘ ˘ — |
kuṉṟuṅ koṇṭāryā mentaiyu milamē.

The first and third line, which are identical except that "that" becomes "this," are made up of all long sounds, broken only at the end with the word for "moonlight." All the lines, with the exception of the fourth, contain many long syllables, producing a sort of mourning rhythm. This is achieved especially by a series of long syllables interspersed (in the second and final line) with a series of short syllables; this makes the rhythms seem forced and extreme, as in a state of grief. Then the mood changes suddenly in the fourth line, "royal drums beating out the victory," in which a staccato series of short syllables emulates a beating drum. This lasts only a moment and then modulates back to a rhythm of loss and mourning with the last syllable ("our"), which, by its meaning, belongs with the next line. This modulation is preceded and strengthened by the short "*ar*," the last syllable of "kings," which wants to be long but is forced to be short. The effect is extremely powerful:

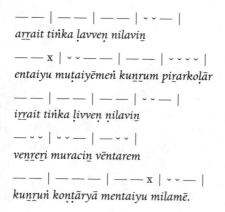

grief suddenly gives way to the raw sound of the war drum and just as suddenly returns, producing an effect of horror and great distress.

Throughout the *Puṟanāṉūṟu,* meter is used with skill and to good effect. The sort of alternation found in the preceding poem 112 is quite common, sections pertaining to war alternating with sections that do not. Usually, the rhythms of the war section are violent and staccato, and the other sections are closer to prose or normal discourse. Sometimes also, as in poem 112, some sections describing grief or mourning contain the sort of extended long and short sounds found in poem 112.

When the poems use lines of two feet, the feet are augmented by an extra *nēr* or *nirai.* Such lines are often used for description, and they have a feeling of relentless flow that we have attempted to capture in English. The beginning of poem 22 is an example:

. . . where the young elephants stand tied
to their posts, bursting with strength
as they shift in place, trunks swaying,
with high-stepping gait and the ripple of bells,
uplifted tusks, foreheads like the crescent moon
and angry stares, giant feet, huge necks,
the fragrant liquid of musth humming with bees
as if they were mountains flowing honey . . .

— — — — | — ˘ ˘ — — |

tūṅkukaiyā ṉōṅkunaṭaiya

˘ ˘ ˘ ˘ — | ˘ ˘ ˘ ˘ ˘ ˘ |

uṟaḻmaṇiyā ṉuyarmaruppiṉa

˘ ˘ ˘ ˘ — | ˘ ˘ — — — |

piṟainutalāṟ ceṟaṉōkkiṉa

— ˘ ˘ — | ˘ ˘ ˘ ˘ ˘ ˘ |

pāvaṭiyāṟ paṇaiyeruttiṉa

— ˘ ˘ — | ˘ ˘ — — |

tēṉcitainta varaipōla

˘ ˘ — — | ˘ ˘ ˘ ˘ |

miñiṟārkkuṅ kamaḻkaṭāt

˘ ˘ ˘ ˘ x | ˘ ˘ — — — |

tayaṟucōru miruñceṉṉiya

— ᵕ ᵕ — — | ᵕ ᵕ ᵕ ᵕ x |
maintumalinta maḻakaḷiṟu

— — — x | ᵕ ᵕ ᵕ ᵕ — |
kantucērpu nilaiivaḻaṅka . . .

Old Tamil also possesses an extremely complex system of alliteration, in which sounds from one foot are echoed by those in another foot. An example is the last foot of the first and third lines of the preceding poem: *nuyarmaruppiṉa* and *paṇaiyeruttiṉa,* in which the sounds "*aru*" and "*iṉa*" are repeated. A beginning rhyme or alliteration also can be found, although it is by no means as common as it became later. An example is in the last two lines of poem 112: *veṉṟeṟi* and *kuṉṟuṅ,* in which the *ṉṟ* sounds are echoed, or in several lines of poem 22, in which different feet begin with the same consonant. Another is in the last two lines of poem 112, in which alliteration ties the line echoing the war drum to the final line, modulating back to a tone of mourning.

Tiṇais *and* Tuṟais: *Conventional Categories and the Colophon*

The Sangam anthologies were put together rather late. The poet, Pāratam Pāṭiya Peruntēvaṉār, who wrote the invocation (*kaṭavuḷ vāḻttu*) of the *Puṟanāṉūṟu* and other anthologies probably lived in the middle of the eighth century C.E. The anthologies are not mentioned in Iṟaiyaṉār's *Akapporuḷ,* also dated about 750 C.E. Nor are they mentioned by Iḷampūraṇar, the earliest commentator of the *Tolkāppiyam,* who probably lived in the twelfth century. The anthologies are first mentioned in the thirteenth and fourteenth centuries by the commentators Mayilainātar, Pērāciriyar, and Nacciṉārkkiṉiyar. On this basis, Zvelebil concluded the anthologies were assembled—or at least that their compilation was finished—in the twelfth and thirteenth centuries.[39]

Each poem is assigned a *tiṇai,* defined by the Lexicon as "place, region, site," and each *tiṇai* corresponds to a tract of land, a time of day, a situation, and a *rāga* (which the Tamils called *paṇ*), in which it was sung. In the *puṟam* poems, the *tiṇai* is further subdivided into a *tuṟai* ("subject, theme"), discussed later. The *akam tiṇais* are named for flowers or flora (for the most part) found in the tracts of lands that the poems evoke, while their *puṟam* counterparts are named for a situation. Each *akam tiṇai* is characterized by people who live in a tract, animals, plants, a time of day, a season, and the like. Each is also connected with a conventionalized situation, although in fact the poet has a fair amount of latitude. For example, the *akam tiṇai* of *kuṟiñci* is named for a flower that grows in the mountains. The people mentioned in *kuṟiñci* poems usually are mountain dwellers who hunt and grow millet, and animals and plants that are found in the mountains often appear. The theme is frequently the surreptious meeting at night of an unmarried woman and her lover. Such specific associations are well developed in the *akam* poems,[40] but in the *puṟam* poems, specific *tiṇais* are far more problematical.

According to the *Tolkāppiyam,* there are seven major *tiṇais* for *puṟam* poems,[41] as follows (the description of the categories is Zvelebil's):

1. *Veṭci:* prelude to war, cattle raid; corresponds to the *akam* category of *kuṟiñci.* The time is night, the place a mountain.
2. *Vañci:* preparation for war, beginning of invasion. The *akam* counterpart is *mullai,* whose time is the rainy season and whose place is the meadowland.
3. *Uḻiñai:* siege. Its counterpart is *marutam,* and its place is the inhabited river valley.
4. *Tumpai:* pitched battle, corresponding to *neytal.* Evening and grief are often found in this *tiṇai.*
5. *Vākai:* victory, corresponding to *pālai.*
6. *Kāñci:* the transience of the world.
7. *Pāṭāṇ:* praise or elegy, as well as asking for gifts.

Unfortunately, these do not agree with the *tiṇais* we find in the *Puṟanāṉūṟu,* which are (1) *veṭci,* (2) *karantai,* (3) *vañci,* (4) *nocci* (defense of a fort), (5) *tumpai,* (6) *vākai,* (7) *kāñci,* (8) *pāṭāṇ,* (9) *kaikkiḷai* (one-sided love), (10) *peruntiṇai* (mismatched love), and (11) *potuviyal* (general heroism). All the love poems are about historical kings. An example of *kaikkiḷai* is poems 83 through 85, in which a woman describes her unrequited love for Cōḻaṉ Pōravaik Kōpperunaṟkiḷḷi. *Peruntiṇai* is applied to poems 143 through 147, which describe the abandoned wife of King

Pēkaṉ and urge him to take her back. Almost all the *potuviyal* poems are on the deaths of kings.

Tuṟais are subcategories of *tiṇais,* and the colophons of the *Puṟanāṉūṟu* give a *tuṟai* as well as a *tiṇai* for each poem. *Tuṟai* means "place, way, branch" and has come to mean a branch of knowledge and so a categorized subject or theme in literature. According to Iḷampūraṇar, one of the commentators on the *Tolkāppiyam,*

> When people, animals, grass, trees, earth, water, wind, etc. that are fit for the seven great *tiṇais* of *akam* or *puṟam* appear in a poem, they should be investigated according to the category they belong to and used with proper sensitivity and fitness to tradition. If they appear that way in their category to which they belong, it is a *tuṟai.*[42]

What the commentator seems to be saying is that the *tuṟai* centers on the people, plants, animals, and inanimate objects mentioned in the poem, whereas the *tiṇai* has more to do with the situation. The other commentators say similar things.[43]

The colophons of the *Puṟanāṉūṟu* list 67 different *tuṟais,* and the *Tolkāppiyam* enumerates 158. Of these 67 *tuṟais,* only 42 agree with the *tuṟais* enumerated in the *Tolkāppiyam;* 25 are entirely new. There is no example at all of 116 of the *tuṟais.* Moreover, the *tuṟais* of the *Puṟanāṉūṟu* often belong to *tiṇais* other than those prescribed by the *Tolkāppiyam.* As a result, V. S. Rajam concluded that the colophons of the *Puṟanāṉūṟu* were not following either the *Tolkāppiyam* or the *Paṉṉiru Paṭalam* (an ancient grammar that has been lost but was followed by a later work, *Puṟapporuḷ Veṇpāmālai*) but, rather, an unknown grammar or the anthologist's own notions of classification.[44] There is a reference to *tuṟais* in the *Puṟanāṉūṟu* itself, which seems at odds with all the other enumerations: in poem 152, the poet refers to 21 *tuṟais* that were appropriate to sing to a king. The old commentary says that this refers to themes in three pitches (high, low, and medium) that end on each one of the seven notes for each pitch (the author's meaning is unclear). Alternatively, he says, it could mean the *yāḻ,* which has 21 strings.

It seems, then, that it would be a mistake to pay too close attention to the categorizations of the colophons. After all, many centuries elapsed between the composition of the poems and their anthologization, and the colophons may have been added even later. The reader should be aware, however, that the poems are highly conventionalized: the themes, the tracts of land, and the juxtaposition of elements all are determined by a system that the poets must have interiorized and that must have seemed quite natural to them. The fact that this system does not wholly conform to the grammarians' exacting rules does not mean that it was not important to the poets. What is remarkable is that they were able to inject life and freshness into this rather rigid system, so that one rarely feels the literature is overly bound by rules and tradition.

North Indian Connections

The indebtedness of the early Tamil poems to North Indian culture has long been debated. Some scholars see the customs and lifestyles depicted by the poems—especially the more "civilized" or "cultured" manifestations—as clearly borrowed from North India.[45] Others have proposed the opposite: the poems represent a pristine Tamil culture, not significantly influenced by North India or any other outside culture.[46]

As with most extremes, the truth no doubt lies somewhere in between. Some elements in the poems are clearly of North Indian provenance, such as Brahmins, Brahmanical deities (Śiva, Viṣṇu); and mentions of the *Mahābhārata*, the *Rāmāyaṇa*, the Vedas, the Himālayas, and Buddhist and Jain ideas, especially regarding rebirth.[47] Yet for all this, the basic culture and outlook of the poems are apparently indigenous and only superficially influenced by North Indian ideas. The cultural structure we see in the poems, revolving around kings, women, and caste, must have already been very old in the Tamil area when the Sangam poems were written.

The same appears to be true for the poems' literary meters, forms, and themes, which were clearly taken from the oral literature of the bards and drummers. No doubt, the poets often embellished these themes and ideas, sometimes even creating something quite different. Occasionally, new themes appear that seem to have Jain or Buddhist origins.[48] Yet even these are treated in peculiarly Tamil ways—there is, for example, nothing remotely similar in Sanskrit to the great poem on karma (*Pur̲.* 192). The majority of the poems seem to owe little to the major traditions of North India. Their meters are utterly unlike Sanskrit meters, which are based on number of syllables rather than cumulative quantity,[49] and their flow is different (since Sanskrit pauses at the end of each stanza of four *pādas,* usually no more than 100 syllables or so and often many fewer).

Yet no one who knows the Sanskrit tradition well will find the poems of the *Pur̲anān̲ūr̲u* or the other Sangam anthologies alien. They share many significant elements with the Northern literature—conventions, figures of speech, and even cultural ideas that cannot be traced to Northern sources. I have tried to demonstrate that for the most part, these shared elements do not represent borrowings of the Northern tradition by the South. Rather, they fall into two classes: those that were present in a pan–South Asian context even before the advent of the Aryans and those that were borrowed by the Sanskrit tradition from the same Southern oral tradition that produced Sangam literature.[50]

The Pur̲anān̲ūr̲u *as Literature*

The *Pur̲anān̲ūr̲ū* represents a literary tradition that in its origins and its peculiar traits is separate from any other. It is a work that gives insight into the non-Aryan history of India and enables us to disentangle, to a remarkable extent, the strands of early Indian culture. It also is a significant and important work of world literature, treating universal themes in ways that are rather different from any other tradition. Like the Homeric epics and Greek lyric poems,the *Pur̲anān̲ūr̲ū* was among the first works of literature written down in its cultural tradition—and like its Greek counterparts, it is notable for its freshness and directness of expression. The *Pur̲anān̲ūr̲u,* unlike so many texts from premodern India, is not confined to the elite classes and their vision of the world. Rather, in its straightforward description of the lowest castes, of their poverty and struggle to survive, in its incessant and rather manic glorification of kings, in its delineation of the role of the king and his power, and finally in its search for ways to make sense of the suffering that it describes with such eloquence, the *Pur̲anān̲ūr̲u* stands out from other great texts of premodern India with an almost modern sense of the frailty and capriciousness of human existence.

NOTES

1. Zvelebil discusses the Sangam legend extensively in Kamil Zvelebil, *The Smile of Murugan on Tamil Literature of South India* (Leiden: Brill, 1973), pp. 45–49.

2. One of the most intriguing poems in the *Puṟanāṉūṟu* is poem 194, in which the poet blames the creator for making a world that is filled with pain.

3. We also possess the old commentary for five of the other poems (286, 300, 301, 305, and 315): see Irā Kavuṇṭar and Teyvacikāmaṇi, *Puṟappāṭṭurai* (Pollacci: Shanti Trust, 1976).

4. See *Kalaikkalanciyam* (1954), p. 519.

5. See Zvelebil, *The Smile of Murugan,* pp. 42, 28.

6. See Iravatham Mahadevan, "Tamil Brahmi Inscriptions of the Sangam Age," in *Proceedings of the Second International Conference Seminar of Tamil Studies,* ed. R. E. Asher, 2 vols. (Madras: International Association of Tamil Research, 1971), vol. 1, pp. 73–106.

7. The LTTE (Tamil Tigers) of Sri Lanka, a guerrilla group fighting for a separate Tamil homeland, have taken some of their practices and ideology from the Puṟanāṉūṟu. One example is the funeral for young men who have fallen in fighting, at which the mother is urged to express joy and is not supposed to cry. In addition, many of the phrases and terms they use to glorify war are drawn directly from this anthology.

8. For more on these, see George L. Hart, *The Poems of Ancient Tamil, Their Milieu and Their Sanskrit Counterparts* (Berkeley and Los Angeles: University of California Press, 1975), pp. 15–18. See also the notes to 23.9, 50.1, and 31.4.

9. See Burton Stein, *Peasant, State, and Society in Medieval South India* (Delhi: Oxford University Press, 1980). It seems quite likely to me that the Pallavas were imitating the Guptas, who ruled the first great and self-consciously Hindu kingdom.

10. Several modern politicians and movie stars have been treated like ancient kings. Chief among these are Annadurai, M. G. Ramachandran, and the LTTE leader Prabhakaran.

11. For a comprehensive survey and discussion of Tamil sthalapurāṇas, see David Dean Shulman, *Tamil Temple Myths: Sacrifice and Divine Marriage in the South Indian Saiva Tradition* (Princeton, N.J.: Princeton University Press, 1980).

12. The murderer Maṇikkuṟavaṉ is the subject of several folk songs and cults. In one song about him that I have collected, he is again and again referred to as a "king," even though his only notable pastime is murder. Indeed, a king must

demonstrate his power over life by killing, whether in battle, murder, or hunting. See George L. Hart, "The Maṇikkuṟavaṉ Story: From Ritual to Entertainment," in *Another Harmony,* ed. Stuart H. Blackburn and A. K. Ramanujan (Berkeley and Los Angeles: University of California Press, 1986), pp. 233–264.

13. *Puṟ.* 342, 369–371.

14. *Puṟ.* 20, 68, 105, 117, 124, 204, 384, 386, 388, 389, 395, 397.

15. *Puṟ.* 215–223.

16. One could cite the behavior of many people in Tamil Nadu when the chief minister, M. G. Ramachandran, was sick and subsequently died, as well as the treatment of the leader of the LTTE (Tamil Tigers), Velupillai Prabhakaran, by the members of that organization.

17. See *Puṟ.* 224, 253, 261, and especially 246 and 247.

18. This is the theme of the *Cilappatikāram,* recently well translated by R. Parthasarathy. See Ilankovatikal and R. Parthasarathy, *The Cilappatikāram of Iḷaṅkō: An Epic of South India* (New York: Columbia University Press, 1993)). In that epic, a young widow whose husband has been unjustly executed kills herself by tearing off her breast and is subsequently honored by having a stone brought from the Himalayas and erected to house her spirit.

19. See George L. Hart, "Woman and the Sacred in Ancient Tamil Nad," *Journal of Asian Studies* 32, no. 2 (1973):233–250.

20. *Kōlams* are the subject of a forthcoming dissertation from the University of California by Vijaya Nagarajan.

21. George L. Hart, "Early Evidence for Caste in South India," in *Dimensions of Social Life: Essays in Honor of David B. Mandelbaum,* ed. Paul Hockings (Berlin: Mouton Gruyter, 1987).

22. *Puṟ.* 82, 170.

23. *Puṟ.* 281, 285.

24. The royal drum is described in the following way in the *Patiṟṟuppattu* 30 (translated literally): "To worship with the resounding mantra the god [in the drum] whose strength is hard to endure, the high one raises the *piṇṭam,* which is so hard to obtain, and the demonness strikes her hands together and trembles from fear, and that sacrifice, covered with blood and oozing with toddy, not even attracting ants, is eaten by black-eyed crows and kites. With the voices that shake the earth of your warriors who have the resolve never to run, whose legs wear rings with shining designs, who disperse battles, who love fighting, your drum with its loud voice is beaten, king of cruel anger, and to its music the best of rice is given [to your fighters]." The *piṇṭam* was a ball of rice. Exactly what it signified and who the "high one" was are not clear. Presumably, he was some sort of priest from the very lowest caste, and the *piṇṭam* was some sort of terrible offering to the god in the drum. Even today, some village gods are worshiped by low-caste priests using blood offerings and liquor, or toddy.

25. The last poems of the *Puṟanāṉūṟu,* beginning with number 374, suggest that the Kiṇaiyaṉ was not allowed inside the palace.

26. For example, the great patron Pāri is supposed to have seen a jasmine vine with no support to climb on. Feeling sorry for the plant, he left his royal chariot to support it. See *Puṟ.* 200.

27. Kirtana Thangavelu studied a low caste in northern Andhra that sets up dolls outside an upper-caste house where someone has died. They refuse to remove their dolls—which are considered extremely dangerous and malevolent—unless they are paid. Her article, "Itinerant Images," will appear in a forthcoming issue of *MARG.*

28. This has been discussed extensively by Mahadevan: see Iravatham Mahadevan, "Tamil Brahmi Inscriptions of the Sangam Age," in *Proceedings of the Second International Conference Seminar of Tamil Studies,* ed. R. E. Asher. 2 vols. (Madras: International Association of Tamil Research, 1971), vol. 1, pp. 73–106.

29. This behavior was imitated by the later poet-saints called Āḻvārs and Nāyaṉmārs, who would travel from one temple to another, much as the earlier poets traveled from one court to another. The Hindu gods in Tamil Nadu (and other areas of South India) were modeled after kings.

30. See K. Kailasapathy, *Tamil Heroic Poetry* (Oxford: Clarendon Press, 1968); and Albert Bates Lord, *The Singer of Tales,* in Harvard Studies in Comparative Literature no. 24 (Cambridge, Mass.: Harvard University Press, 1960). I have discussed Kailasapathy's arguments in *The Poems of Ancient Tamil,* pp. 152–158.

31. This statement can be easily confirmed by glancing at the critical editions of the Sanskrit epics or of Kampaṉ's *Rāmāyaṇa.*

32. Each of the following (like the two examples in the text) is about beating the kiṇai drum:

70: "*nuṇ kōl takaitta teṇ kaṇ māk kiṇai*"
373: "*am kaṇ māk kiṇai atira oṟṟa*"
374: "*teṇ kaṇ māk kiṇai teḷirppa oṟṟi*"
378: "*arik kūṭu māk kiṇai iriya oṟṟi*"
382: "*teṇ kaṇ māk kiṇai*"
383: "*nuṇ kōl ciṟu kiṇai cilampa oṟṟi*"
387: "*teṇ kaṇ māk kiṇai iyakki*"
392: "*oru kaṇ māk kiṇai oṟṟupu koṭāa*"
393: "*mati purai māk kiṇai teḷirppa oṟṟi*"
394: "*oru kaṇ māk kiṇai teḷirppa oṟṟi*"
397: "*teṇ kaṇ māk kiṇai teḷirppa oṟṟi*"

33. Defined by the Lexicon as "a form of panegyric poem generally in akaval

metre in which one who has been rewarded with gifts directs another to the presence of the chief from whom the latter may also receive similar reward."

34. Many more examples of themes in old Tamil literature are given in my book *The Poems of Ancient Tamil,* pp. 285–290.

35. An example (composed by me) of one line would be "and then, he came, bearing gifts." An example of several lines in which the first line is amplified by the succeeding lines would be "then he saw her standing / her hair alight with the sun / her lips red and her forehead bright." The point is that each line of these quotations could be extemporized easily by a singer who does not have to think ahead very far.

36. For example, in *Puṟ.* 19, the verb "didn't I embrace" comes in line 6, and the object, "your chest" is in line 18. Between the verb and its object comes the detailed description of the battlefield. This structure is so complex that it cannot be rendered into English. In translating the poem, we had to separate out the parts of the poem so that they made sense. It is difficult to imagine a singer extemporizing a poem as complex as this one.

37. A good example of this in Western literature is Virgil's *Aeneid.* Although that work was modeled on Homer's oral model, it is, unlike Homer's, full of complex sentences that run for many lines.

38. For a detailed discussion of meter in Sangam literature, see V. S. Rajam, *A Reference Grammar of Classical Tamil Poetry: 150* B.C.*–Pre-Fifth/Sixth Century* A.D. (Philadelphia: American Philosophical Society, 1992), pp. 113–239.

39. See Zvelebil, *The Smile of Murugan,* pp. 25–26.

40. The five major *tiṇais* of *akam* poetry, are *kuṟiñci, pālai, mullai, marutam,* and *neytal.* These correspond to mountain land, desert (or forest), meadowland, paddy land, and the seashore. Each is associated with several situations in the *akam* poems. The most prominent are, in order, the secret rendezvous; the eloping of the couple or journey of the hero through the desert; separation; the triangle of the hero, his wife, and his courtesan; and secret meeting/grief at night. See George L. Hart, *Poets of the Tamil Anthologies: Ancient Poems of Love and War* (Princeton, N.J.: Princeton University Press, 1979), pp. 5–8.

41. See V. S. Rajam, "Caṅka Ilakkiyap Puṟappāṭalkaḷum Puṟapporuḷ Ilakkaṇamum," *Vaiyai* 4 (1974–75):54; and Zvelebil, *The Smile of Murugan,* pp. 103–105. For a full discussion of *tuṟais,* see John Ralston Marr, *The Eight Anthologies: A Study in Early Tamil Literature* (Madras: Institute of Asian Studies, 1985).

42. *Tolkāppiyam, Poruḷatikāram,* Cūttiram 510.

43. See Zvelebil, *The Smile of Murugan,* p. 106.

44. See Rajam's article "Caṅka Ilakkiyap Puṟappāṭalkaḷum Puṟapporuḷ Ilakkaṇamum."

45. This has been the position of many major scholars of South India. See, for example, S. Vaiyapuri Pillai, *History of Tamil Language and Literature; Beginning to*

1000 A.D. (Madras: New Century Book House, 1956); K. A. Nilakanta Sastri, *Aryans and Dravidians* (Ajmer [India]: Sachin Publications, 1979); K. A. Nilakanta Sastri, *The Culture and History of the Tamils* (Calcutta: Firma K. L. Mukhopadhyay, 1964); K. A. Nilakanta Sastri, *Development of Religion in South India* (Bombay: Orient Longmans, 1963); K. A. Nilakanta Sastri, *A History of South India from Prehistoric Times to the Fall of Vijayanagar* (Madras: Oxford University Press, 1976).

46. See, for example, Na Tevaneyan, *The Primary Classical Language of the World* (Ka[t]padi Extension, North Arcot Dt.: Nesamani Pub. House, 1966). This book has been used by politicians and others to support their idea that Tamil is the source of all true culture in India and, indeed, the world.

47. See Hart, *The Poems of Ancient Tamil,* pp. 51–80.

48. See, for example, *Puṟ.* 357, 367.

49. It is true that Pali, the Prakrits, and (later) Sanskrit also have some meters based on *mātrā,* or the total number of syllables in a line. These meters are not found in the oldest Sanskrit sources and are remarkably similar to their Tamil equivalents. See Hart, *The Poems of Ancient Tamil,* pp. 201–208.

50. In Hart, *The Poems of Ancient Tamil,* pp. 161–280, I have argued that many elements from this Southern Deccani culture entered the North Indian (and ultimately Sanskrit) literary tradition through Māhārāṣṭrī, the Prakrit that was spoken in Maharashtra, which belonged, like the Dravidian-speaking parts of South India, to the Megalithic Deccani culture in the first millennium B.C.

THE *PUṞANĀṈŪṞU*

1

Fragrant with the rains is his chaplet of laburnum. The garland
against the beautiful hue of his chest is of laburnum too.
He rides upon a pure white bull and it is said
his magnificent standard displays that same bull.
Poison has made his throat lovely. For that poison,
praise is chanted by the Brahmins who recite the Vedas.
Part of him has the form of a woman and that form
he can absorb, should he wish to hide it. And it becomes hidden!
The crescent moon shines on his forehead. For that crescent of the moon,
praises are chanted by his followers, the eighteen Gaṇas.
So he is, he who is shelter for all living beings,
in whose jar water never fails.
Resplendent with matted hair he practices arduous tapas.

2

Like the earth kept whole by its clay
and the sky raised up on the earth
and the wind that glides across the sky
and the fire sweeping up on the wind

or water that encounters fire, your nature
is that of the five great elements, for you endure
your enemies and your intentions are far ranging,
you have strength, destructive power, and you are merciful!
Rising from one of your oceans, the sun later descends
into your ocean of the west with the white surf of its waves.
You are king of a fertile country, with towns always prosperous!
You are bounded by the sky! O greatness! You who gave
heaps of food without stinting, of the finest rice,
till the time came when the hundred who were wearing their flower
garlands of golden tumpai and had seized the land perished in the field,
fighting furiously against the five whose horses wore waving plumes!
Even if milk becomes something sour, or the sun goes dark,
or the Four Vedas swerve from the truth,
may you shine on, with no loss, on and on with your unswerving
    ministers!
May you never be shaken, like Mount Potiyam, like Himālaya
with its golden peaks where long-eyed does sleep
on slopes in the faint dawn near fawns with tiny heads
under the glow of the three fires
in which the Brahmins offer ghee according to their difficult rites.

Murañciyūr Muṭinākaṉār sings Cēramāṉ Peruñcōṟṟutiyañcēralātaṉ. *Tiṇai: pāṭāṇtiṇai. Tuṟai: ceviyaṟivuṟūu* and/or *vāḻttiyal.*

3

A form like the full moon, your towering white umbrella
gives shade to the earth up to its border of timeless ocean.
Your royal drum, which is our protection, thunderously roars!
Born to the line of the Pandyas, whose hearts full of love turned
the wheel of the law, whose generosity was never exhausted!
Husband to a woman of stainless purity, whose ornaments are lovely!
Vaḻuti is your great name, in your strong hand a bright sword!
and you do not tire at the difficult work of Death
for whom there is no cure, as you ride the huge neck of your
    elephant

too fierce to approach, who batters the gates
of enemy walls with the weapons of his tusks, who has a massive trunk
and a spotted forehead bearing a golden frontlet, fragrant with the liquid
of musth, and running across him a rope dangles a bell down each flank.
Should the earth itself move, your words are immovable,
with your broad chest smeared with sandalwood
and your foot wearing your war anklet of gold!
In great suffering, through vast expanses,
without cities, without any water,
where bandits with keen eyes, marksmen with infallible arrow after arrow,
wait, intent, their hands shielding their eyes from the sun,
travelers already shot down lying under fresh piles of stones
where vultures are sitting, yearning, with even wings and hooked beaks,
there along forking trails, hard to reach, where umbrella thorn grows,
those who are in need come traveling, aching with desire for you because
you are capable of knowing, just from their faces,
what they want in their hearts and so you can heal their poverty!

Irumpiṭart Talaiyār sings Pāṇṭiyaṉ Karuṅkaiyoḷvāṭ Perumpeyar Vaḻuti. *Tiṇai: pāṭāṇṭiṇai. Tuṟai: ceviyaṟivuṟūu* and/or *vāḻttiyal.*

4

The blood splashed on swords that brought victory
makes them beautiful, like the red evening sky.
Their war anklets worn down on the battlefield, the legs
of conquerors are as smooth as the horns of killer bulls.
Shields spring holes from ringing arrows
as if they were mobile training targets.
While their riders gauge the time for attack

and urge them forward, horses bloody their mouths,
chafing at the bits, like tigers tearing throats.
Elephants assaulting gates, in ferocious action,
have blunted the points of their white tusks
and seem like Death himself devouring life!
And you in your splendor on your chariot decked with gold
and drawn by finely moving horses with waving plumes
are as wondrously radiant as the red sun when it rises
high into the sky out of the black ocean!
Because this is how you are,
the country of those men who have made you angry
wails without end, like a hungry motherless child!

Paraṇar sings Cōḻaṉ Uruvap Paḥrēr Iḷañcēṭ Ceṉṉi. *Tiṇai: vañci. Tuṟai: koṟṟavaḷḷai.*

5

Your land lies within a dense forest with elephants everywhere,
as if they were cows, and scattered black rocks that look
like water buffaloes. Greatness! Because you are the man you are,
I have something to say to you! You must be as careful
in watching over your country as you would be in raising children,
so that you may not become one of those who go to an endless hell
for their lack of compassion and love! How hard
it is to win command of a country and how vital is benevolence!

When he saw Cēramāṉ Karuvūrēṟiya Oḷvāṭ Kōpperuñcēralirumpoṟai, he said, "May you get your body"; this is the song of Nariverūut Talaiyār who got his body when he went and saw [that king]. [See the notes on this poem.] *Tiṇai: pāṭāṇṭiṇai. Tuṟai: ceviyaṟivuṟūu* and/or *poruṇmoḻik kāñci.*

6

Even north of the mountains that tower eternally frozen in the north,
even south of the river Kumari, river of terror, in the south, even east

of the ocean dug out of the earth at the eastern shore, even west
of the ancient ocean long set into place in the west, even below the earth
rising out of the body of the waters, the earth that is the lowest
level of the three-tiered universe, up
to the holy realm of the cows, the highest sphere,
may the glory and the fear of you travel, undiminishing! May you
be as free of bias in your judgments as the pointer of a balance
that measures huge quantities! May all that are yours flourish!
In the country of your enemies, when they showed resistance to your campaigns,
rapidly you advanced, your armies flooding like the sea, and you ordered
your elephants with their small eyes and densely spotted faces to charge ahead,
and you captured many strongholds that rose in green fields
near their cities and from those fortresses you took fine ornaments,
beautifully fashioned, which you apportioned, by rank, to those who asked them of you.
May your umbrella of victory bow down and circumambulate, in the auspicious direction,
the temple of the god with three eyes whom the Brahmins worship!
Greatness! Lower your head with respect before the hands raised in blessing
by those Brahmins who chant the Four Vedas! My king!
May your chaplet wither, assaulted by the sweet-smelling smoke
of flames rising from the lands of your enemies! And may
your anger vanish as you see your women wearing their pearl necklaces,
their faces glowing with the passing anger of lovers' quarrels!
Ah Kuṭumi! Worthy of your glory! Unfailing in your generosity!
You who once you have won them never boast of your victories!
Like the moon with its cooling rays and like the glowing sun
with the rays of its burning light,
O great ruler, may you long live here upon this earth!

Kārikiḻār sings Pāṇṭiyaṉ Palyākacālai Mutukuṭumip Peruvaḻuti. *Tiṇai: pāṭāṇṭiṇai. Tuṟai: ceviyaṟivuṟūu* and/or *poruṇmoḻik kāñci.*

7

Pressing him with your legs, you manage an elephant.
Your fine ankles seem smooth, the leg rings worn flat.
Your bow is so beautiful that it dazzles the eyes
as it rests in your hand curved to draw and release
your arrows in battle. Your chest is so broad the goddess Śrī forsakes
all others for it! You have the strength to drive back elephants! And whether
it is night or day matters nothing to your desire
for plunder and the sound of weeping, as your enemies scream
for their kin in the light of their blazing cities! O Vaḷavaṉ
riding your elegant chariot! In the countries of your enemies, nothing
of value remains throughout the vast spaces where there were cities always
shining with such fresh wealth they disdained earth
and used fish to block holes in dams where the cool water poured through, roaring!

Karuṅkuḻalātaṉār sings Cōḻaṉ Karikāṟ Peruvaḷattāṉ. *Tiṇai: vañci. Tuṟai: koṟṟavaḷḷai* and/or *maḻapula vañci.*

8

Kings who protect the earth praise him and obey him.
He desires his pleasures and will not bear to share dominion.
He is driven by the thought that he rules too little land.
His will is unrelenting! He is endlessly generous!
Circle of the sun eternally in movement! How you fail to resemble
Cēralātaṉ with his army that strikes always in open battle!
You only appear in the day! You turn your back to the moon
and leave! You advance from various directions! You vanish
behind your mountain and hide there till dawn
when glowing you spread your many rays through the enormous sky!

Kapilar sings Cēramāṉ Kaṭuṅkō Vāḻiyātaṉ. *Tiṇai: pāṭāṇṭiṇai. Tuṟai: iyaṉmoḻi* and/or *pūvai nilai.*

9

"Cows, and men who are Brahmins and share the holiness of cows,
and women, and you who are sick, and you who have had
no sons, precious as gold, to perform the demanding rituals
which protect the dead who are alive in the Southern Land, take
refuge! We are ready to shoot rapid volleys of arrows!"
he announces, since he is a champion of Righteousness.
May he with his Martial Courage, whose banners
mounted on murderous elephants throw shadows
across the sky itself, may Kuṭumi our king live for more years
than the grains of sand by the Paḫṟuḷi River whose waters are nourishing,
where his forefather Neṭiyōṉ ruled and celebrated
the festivals of the ocean and gave musicians reddish yellow gold!

Neṭṭimaiyār sings Pāṇṭiyaṉ Palyākacālai Mutukuṭumip Peruvaḻuti. *Tiṇai: pāṭāṇṭiṇai. Tuṟai: iyaṉmoḻi* and/or *pūvai nilai.*

10

Those who show you reverence you favor at once
and you dismiss the words of those who malign other men.
If you see evil done and are convinced it is evil,
you search out fitting penalties and impose them as is right.
If the guilty come, repent at your feet, and stand there in your presence,
you lighten your punishments and esteem them more than before.
Like a rainbow is the garland that hangs down against your chest
no warriors can confront, confronted only by your women
who live faultless lives and are endlessly gracious to guests,
giving them rice, fragrant with seasoning, bountiful, sweeter than amṛta!
Your actions trail no regrets! Your glory shines into the distances!
Great ruler of the city of Neytalaṅkāṉal!
I have come this far to see you with my desire to praise your many virtues.

Ūṉpoti Pacuṅkuṭaiyār sings Cōḻaṉ Neytalaṅkāṉal Iḷañcēṭ Ceṉṉi. *Tiṇai: pāṭāṇṭiṇai. Tuṟai: iyaṉmoḻi* and/or *pūvai nilai.*

11

The ruler of Vañci, city of victories
and of fame that reaches the heavens,
where the girls, who are without guile,
whose rounded forearms are covered with fine hair,
wear bright ornaments and pluck flowers
from curved branches for the dolls they mold
on the streaked sand, plunging then into the water
of the cool Porunai River—that king, whose victories
are sung in songs, has conquered fiercely resisting strongholds
and won the sight of his enemies' backs in flight,
and the singer who sang the Martial Courage
of that mighty king who won the sight of his enemies' backs
has won for herself a splendid ornament, shining
and heavy, and the husband of the woman who won the ornament,
a bard skilled in rhythmic song to the base note of the rāga,
oh he won
for himself a flower, a golden lotus
formed in glowing fire and strung on a silver thread!

Pēymakaḷ Iḷaveyiṉi sings Cēramāṉ Pālai Pāṭiya Peruṅkaṭuṅkō. *Tiṇai: pāṭāṇṭiṇai. Tuṟai: paricil kaṭānilai.*

12

Bards adorn themselves with lotuses of gold. And poets prepare
to mount gilded chariots and elephants with ornamented foreheads.
Is this justice? O Kuṭumi great with your victories!
There is nothing sweet in how you take the lands of others
but sweet are the things you give to those who ask you for favor!

Neṭṭimaiyār sings Pāṇṭiyaṉ Palyākacālai Mutukuṭumip Peruvaḻuti. *Tiṇai: pāṭāṇṭiṇai. Tuṟai: Iyāṉmoḻi.*

13

"Who is he?" you ask. He is riding an elephant and he seems
like the God of Death and his broad lofty chest
is savaged by the arrows shot against it which have torn
the bright fastenings of the tiger-skin armor that he wears,
as swordsmen swarm around him like a pack of sharks
and he moves along like a boat passing over the ocean
or like the moon among countless stars. The elephant
has gone into rut and cannot even recognize its keeper!
May he come back safe, that lord of a land where the farmers
collect feathers that peacocks have dropped in the fields,
as they gather up their sheaves of unthreshed paddy, a place
where the toddy is well aged, the fish delicious
and all around, like a wall, there lies abundant water.

When he saw Cōḻaṉ Muṭittalaik Kōperunaṟkiḷḷi going to Karuvūr, Uṟaiyūr Ēṇiccēri Muṭamōciyār who was on the roof story [? *vēṇmāṭam*] [of the palace] with Cēramāṉ Antuvañcēral Irumpoṟai sang this. *Tiṇai: pāṭāṇṭiṇai. Tuṟai: vāḻttiyal.*

14

Your mighty hands that reach to your knees have the power
to wield a well-made goad of iron that impels
your fierce murderous elephant forward to crash through
the bolts of guarded gates and power then to restrain
that elephant as needed, and your hands can rein
your brilliantly galloping horse the moment you judge
how deep the water is in a moat hacked
far down into the earth, and on your back you wear a quiver,
O king! so that from your chariot those hands can shoot arrows

and turn scarred from the strong string of your bow,
then grant precious ornaments to those who seek your favor.
A Murugan in your skills at war,
whose chest makes women suffer with desire and is
as immovable as the great earth for those who fight against you!
Soft are the hands of those who know no work
more difficult than eating rice and curry and chunks of meat
from new-killed flesh with its aroma of meat cooked
in the smoke of fire burning with the aroma
of flowers—the hands of those who celebrate you in song!

Taking [the poet] Kapilar's hand, Cēramāṉ Celvak Kaṭuṅkō Vāḻiyātaṉ said, "Your hand is soft." Then Kapilar sang this song. *Tiṇai: pāṭāṇṭiṇai. Tuṟai: iyaṉmoḻi.*

15

On their streets torn up by your swift chariots you yoked
lines of vile donkeys with white-frothing mouths and, plowing their noble,
spacious strongholds, made them wastelands!
You drove your chariot across the lands of your enemies
where the curving hooves of your horses, prancing with their white plumes,
hammered on the renowned, fertile fields resounding with birds.
You bathed your elephants, with necks
swaying and immense, giant feet and
raging glances and glittering tusks,
in the reservoirs those men had once guarded!
Given your fury, which of these then is greater in number
—your once eager enemies shamed and despairing after brandishing
their long spears that throw shadows and their beautiful shields
embossed with iron against the power of your swift vanguard
with its shining weapons, or else the number of spacious sites
where you have set up columns after performing many sacrifices
prescribed by the Four Vedas and the books of ritual,

fine sacrifices of an excellence that will not die away
and charged with a fame that is difficult to achieve,
oblations that rose rich in ghee and all the other
elements of the sacrifice? For you, which is greater,
O greatness! you whose might is a proper theme
for the odes that praise invasions and are performed by women
    singers
to the beat of the great drum
smeared with black paste and wrapped with strips of leather?

Neṭṭimaiyār sings Pāṇṭiyaṉ Palyākacālai Mutukuṭumip Peruvaḻuti. *Tiṇai: pāṭāṇṭiṇai. Tuṟai: iyaṉmoḻi.*

16

Destroying the land, your limitless army advances,
with its swift horses peerless in battle,
and it spreads out its shields like so many clouds,
moving forward, destroying the vanguard,
ravaging the rich fields, bathing elephants
in the waters of the reservoirs that had been guarded,
as the glare that rises up from the blazing fires
fueled by the wood of houses seems the red glow
of the sun when its rays are dwindling down!
You who win battles with no need of allies!
Your sword reeks of flesh, your chest of dried sandalpaste!
Chieftain who inspires fear! Ferocious as Murugan!
The land that had been defended you feed
to shining fire, devastating the wide and lovely fields
that know nothing of forest but sugarcane, fruiting
jacktrees, cool pakaṉṟai vines, bindweed mingling
with blossoming waterlilies! Greatness!
In fearful well-waged combat, your elephants fought as one!

Pāṇṭaraṅ Kaṇṇaṉār sings Cōḻaṉ Irācacūyam Vēṭṭa Perunaṟkiḷḷi. *Tiṇai: vañci. Tuṟai: maḻapulavañci.*

17

From Cape Kumari in the south, from the great mountain
in the north, from the oceans on the east and on the west,
the hills, the mountains, the woods, and the fields
in unison utter their praise of you! You
who protect us! You, who are descended
from those who ruled the entire world,
their gleaming wheels rolling free, you
who avoid cruelty and hold your rod erect,
are impartial and take only what is your due!
Murderous warrior who governs those living in cool
Toṇṭi, with its low-hanging coconut clusters, wide fields,
its mountain boundary and broad seashore where the sand
is like moonlight and there are flowers like fire
in the clear backwaters! As a killer elephant with long tusks,
very large, very strong, might disdain to notice
the cover over an elephant trap and be caught
in the deep pit and then destroy that hole
so that it cannot be used again, rejoining
his herd which is filled then with relief,
so, through your irresistible strength, you escaped,
overcoming your discomfiture, and many who had been
deeply despairing rejoiced! And praise of you
was sung on high before a multitude of nobles
of exalted family, while enemy kings served you,
calculating that they might gain rich land you had captured
or fine jewels that had come to you if only
your heart were gracious toward them, but more profoundly
they thought, "We will lose our high walls with the flags
upraised on them, we will lose our broad fortresses protected
with their outposts, should he glance at us in anger!"
and they serve you because of your might and your glory
which I have come to see and to praise, O greatness!
You whose army has so many shields that the people,
bewildered, see them as massed clouds, and so many
enormous elephants that the honey bees

take them for mountains, an army so hugely swollen
your enemies are terrified, so like the ocean that the clouds
try to draw water from it! You whose royal drum is like thunder
shattering the heads of snakes whose venom
is hidden within their fangs! Boundless benefactor ruling those of
the west!

Kuṟuṅkōḻiyūr Kiḻār sings Yāṉaikkaṭcēy Māntarañcēralirumpoṟai who, when he was caught by Pāṇṭiyaṉ Talaiyālaṅkāṉattuc Ceruveṉṟa Neṭuñceḻiyaṉ, escaped by force and ascended his throne again. *Tiṇai: vākai. Tuṟai: aracavākai* and/or *iyaṉmoḻi.*

18

You are of a lineage of strong men without equal
who through their efforts seized and ruled by themselves
the expanses of the broad earth wholly encircled
by the roaring waters and so established their fame!
May the days of your life be myriad, expanding
by ones and by tens toward the sum of ten million!
Powerful king of wealthy Mūtūr where the walls
are finely made and lofty, threatening the sky,
and schools of scabbard fish in the deep moats
snap up the small kāñci flowers that grow
at the surface of the water and there are tiny
sand eels, great murrels, lustrous keṭiṟu fish!
If you wish to be rich in your next birth, if you wish
to break the strength in the arms of the kings
of this world and rule alone, O magnificence! if you
wish to establish fine and glowing renown, only hear
what now you rightly should do!
No bodies woven of their parts can subsist without water.
Those who give these bodies food give them life.
The body massed together of food has food as its source.
That which men call food comes from water mingled with earth.
Those who bring together earth and water in union create

the means for bodies to exist in this world, for life to be!
Large but barren fields where men sow and stare at the sky
in no way serve the efforts of the king who rules there.
And so, O Ceḻiyaṉ, murderous in battle! you should not
disdain my advice but rather you should act quickly!
Those who construct dams so that the water collects
on low ground in the fields are assured, in this world, of glory!
Those who build none will have no renown enduring in this world.

Kuṭapulaviyaṉār sings Pāṇṭiyaṉ Neṭuñceḻiyaṉ. *Tiṇai: potuviyal. Tuṟai: mutumokikkāñci.*

19

Ceḻiyaṉ whose spear wins victories, how you displayed
the great abundance of lives and the singleness of Death
at Talaiyālaṅkāṉam where Tamils battled on this broad
mass of the earth surrounded by the roaring ocean!
where women of high birth said, weeping in their anguish,
"Like a flock of small birds startled up, then settling on a hill,
their arrows have flown and lodged in an agonizing elephant
brought down on the battlefield when they won the victory, swords high,
cutting off its mouth with the hollow trunk so that it rolled
across the earth like a plow! And our sons who were not old enough
to wear their hair groomed and oiled lie beside our husbands and now
is victory ours?" while Death, seeing them, felt shame
and felt pity on the terrifying battlefield where you defeated
the noble power of the seven chieftains! And I, as I
was thinking that it is like the enormous stone of a trap
set by a hunter who knows how to make such things work so as to catch
great tigers, didn't I, with fervor,
embrace your chest where the necklace of polished pearls shone!

Kuṭapulaviyaṉār sings Pāṇṭiyaṉ Neṭuñceḻiyaṉ. *Tiṇai: vākai. Tuṟai: aracavākai.*

20

Even if the depths of the vast waters,
and the expanse of the immense earth,
the directions traveled by the wind,
or space that lies empty, even if these
could be measured, you would remain beyond measure
for your knowledge, your kindness, and your great compassion!
Those who live under your shade
know nothing at all of burning other than the fire
that cooks their rice or the burning of the red sun!
They know of no bow that kills, but only the rainbow!
They know only of the plow and nothing of weapons!
Hero! you who consume the lands of your enemies while
those strangers perish along with their soldiers trained
in the tactics of battle! Your soil, so hard to conquer,
no enemies consume but only women with the cravings of pregnancy!
Under guard in your stronghold, arrows
rest. Righteousness rests in your just scepter.
Even if the evil omen is seen of new birds arriving and
the old birds leaving, your benevolent vigilance will endure
    unshaken!
Because this is the man you are,
all who breathe worry that some harm may come to you!

Kuṟuṅkōḻiyūr sings Cēramāṉ Yāṉaikkaṭcēy Māntarañcēralirumpoṟai. *Tiṇai: vākai. Tuṟai: aracavākai.*

21

Leader whose glory extends beyond the capacities of poets!
Vēṅkaimārpaṉ is grieving as he thinks, "With strong outposts
surrounding it and with its moats dug deeper than the limits
of the earth and its walls that seem to graze the sky, with
battlements that look like stars in the heavens and a forest
for protection which is so thick with trees not a ray

of sunlight can pierce it, my fortress Kāṉappēreyil
is as impossible for me to recapture as the water consumed
by iron a smith with black hands lowers into red fire!"
Victorious king! You who don a blossoming garland of tumpai
each and every day as you triumph in battle! You who have
exhausted the themes poets sing! May your spear flourish,
shining with glory, while those who show
scorn for you perish along with their good name!

Aiyūr Mūlaṅ Kiḻār sings Kāṉap Pēreyil Kaṭanta Ukkirapperuvaḻuti. *Tiṇai: vākai. Tuṟai: aracavākai.*

22

It is you who safeguard the wide,
sprawling camp and there is no need
to post guards across its spaces,
where the young elephants stand tied
to their posts, bursting with strength
as they shift in place, trunks swaying,
with high-stepping gait and the ripple of bells,
uplifted tusks, foreheads like the crescent moon
and angry stares, giant feet, huge necks,
the fragrant liquid of musth humming with bees
as if they were mountains flowing honey,
their enormous heads oozing pus as men
wearing no swords sleep safely beside them
below the shade of a white umbrella
hung with garlands like the moon resting
up near them in the sky and streaming rays;
and there are rows of roofs that are plaited
of soft sugarcane, covered with sprouts of the finest
swaying paddy, variously resplendent as if
we were at the site of a festival, a vast
place full of noise, where to the endless drumming of pestles,
maddened men dance the trance dance of the kuravai,
wearing green tumpai garlands with petals like gold, and thrust

within them are palmyra leaves, tall and swaying,
and the rustling rises and eddies like the waters of the ocean!
O killer king! You who rule those on high
Kolli hill and with the tribute humbly given you by kings
satisfy the families of those who come to you in need.
You have the glance of an elephant! You are like
Murugan, thirsting for victory! May you live long,
greatness! with your immeasurable wealth! Our king!
You have the power to give without stinting so that
shining, eloquent tongues sing of you and praise
no others! I heard that the land that is ruled
by Māntarañ Cēral Irumpoṟai is like the world
of the gods and I have come and with joy I have seen it!
Greatness! Untiring! Whose army roams abroad!
Because you never rest, you assure an abundance of rice!

Kuṟuṅkōḻiyūr Kiḻār sings Cēramāṉ Yāṉaikkaṭcēy Māntarañcēralirumpoṟai.
Tiṇai: vākai. Tuṟai: aracavākai and/or *iyaṉmoḻi.*

23

It was because I was thinking, "Your elephants, tired of ease in their sheds
where they were lashed to strong posts that are hard through and through,
have bathed and have drunk there and so the watering places are turbid.
Like the followers of Murugan, who slew Cūr and wears a garland
of green kaṭampu leaves that carry the fragrance of the monsoon,
your warriors, with their curved bows and fine, sharp arrows,
have taken whatever they wanted and what they have not taken,
so that no others may take it, they have destroyed—the grain no one
now will cook. Groves of trees guarded in honor of kings
have fallen in every town, chopped down by sharp axes.
Everywhere
wild fire is roaring so that fine, well-built houses
in great cities are consumed by the blazing flames! Each day he goes

there, and he shames his enemies as they see all this, and he does
far more, he whose insight surpasses that of any other man!"
Because of this, to see you, who showed the strength of Death
as you slaughtered and conquered in the battle of Ālaṅkāṉam where
your army assembled was so enormous the earth was twisted out of shape,
I have traveled through a wild wasteland where there are no people,
and a young doe racing, leaping, clinging to her young fawn, in that
fearful and barren place where the red silk-cotton trees loom over her,
feeds on the pale flowers of the vēḷai because
her handsome stag who had lost his horns has been caught by a tiger!

Kallāṭaṉār sings Pāṇṭiyaṉ Talaiyālaṅkāṉattuc Ceruveṉṟa Neṭuñceḻiyaṉ. *Tiṇai: vākai. Tuṟai: aracavākai* and/or *nallicai vañci.*

24

You have captured Miḻalai of the fine floodgates
which was ruled by the great Vēḷ Evvi,
whose generosity was limitless, and you have taken
its subject cities bursting with people past counting,
where brawny plowmen, as they grow tired cutting paddy
in the heat of the burning sun, leap into the waves
of the crystalline ocean and the strong fishermen, whose boats
are sturdy, drink their fiery toddy and begin to dance
to the rhythm of a slow kuravai; and wearing chaplets formed
of mastwood clusters, the soft flowers spread with pollen
flourishing under the spray of the ocean,
men take women with shining bangles
into their arms; and in cool fragrant groves
where bees swarm around the flowers,
women wearing glittering bracelets
and garlands of muṇṭakam mingle the juices
from the young fruit of great palmyras
and the sweet sap of flourishing sugarcane and the sweet water
from coconuts bunched on the high sand, then drink that beverage

of three flavors and leap into the water! And you have captured
Muttūṟu of the ancient, long-established Vēḷirs whose elephants
are decked with gold, where the reaped rice towers and cranes catch carp
in the fields and then fall asleep on the piles of grain! O Ceḻiyaṉ
with your tall umbrella of victory and your chariot and its banner!
May your stars remain and endure, but given over to destruction,
may the stars of your enemies not endure! As the force,
of your efforts, greatness! is praised by those of noble family
who live by the sword and are long linked to your victorious clan
as your life is long linked to you or your body is long
linked to your life, while those who come in their need to you
exalt your generosity, and rapt in pleasure you drink toddy
that is cool and fragrant and clear, brought to you by women wearing
shining bracelets who serve you in vessels of gold, may you act beneficently!
It is said that only by living in this way, one truly lives.
Many born in the wide world have never acted
to spread and firmly ground their fame but have merely existed and died!

Māṅkuṭi Kiḻār sings Pāṇṭiyaṉ Talaiyālaṅkāṉattuc Ceruveṉṟa Neṭuñceḻiyaṉ.
Tiṇai: potuviyal. Tuṟai: poruṇmoḻik kāñci.

25

It was as if the terrifying sun, which is swollen
with virulent anger and never abandons its usual course
as it soars up to disperse the darkness spread through the sky
glittering with stars, and the moon with its soft light
both fell to the earth when you fought against them and they died
on the battlefield where pain is endured—those two kings
of great, intractable force who had sworn an oath—and you
took their royal drums bound with straps of leather! But then,
O Ceḻiyaṉ! the firm joint of your spear was saved from breaking
and ruin through being hurled at enemies lingering around you,

when you saw the women with gleaming faces, anguished new widows
gone out of their senses, beating their lovely breasts into pain,
wailing without end, cutting off their masses
of soft black beautiful hair like dark glistening sand.

Kallāṭaṉār sings Pāṇṭiyaṉ Talaiyālaṅkāṉattuc Ceruveṉṟa Neṭuñceḻiyaṉ. *Tiṇai: vākai. Tuṟai: aracavākai.*

26

Like a boat driven by the wind
over the great depths of the vast ocean,
the elephant sundered the lines of combat
and within that broad swathe opened on the field,
you raised up your spear with its blade
shining! and you quickened the battle
so that kings fell, and you captured
their royal drums and spread your fame!
and then, with food you had created, you sacrificed on the killing field,
using an oven of crowned heads after pouring out a torrent of blood
into the cooking pot and stirring it with the ladle of an arm still
braceleted! Ceḻiyaṉ, murderous in battle! As Brahmins of the Four Vedas,
calm through the breadth of their knowledge, devoted to restraint,
surrounded you and kings carried out your orders, you completed
the sacrifice established by tradition! Ruler whose sword
prevails! Surely your enemies must have performed tapas,
for once they have won the fame of being your enemies,
though they cannot be victorious, they will live on in the world beyond!

Māṅkuṭi Kiḻār sings Pāṇṭiyaṉ Talaiyālaṅkāṉattuc Ceruveṉṟa Neṭuñceḻiyaṉ. *Tiṇai: vākai. Tuṟai: aracavākai.*

27

If you number those who have reigned, carefree in their majesty,
those who were born to fine, equally noble families, few of them
have gained glory and the songs like a row of hundred-petaled
flowers,
brightly shining colors raised by the lotus that grows out of the
mud.
O many are those who have vanished like the petals of the lotus!
They whose fame poets sing, when they have finished doing
everything they must do are said to gain for themselves
a flying chariot that needs no driver to guide it through the heavens.
So I have heard it said. My lord! Cēṭceṉṉi Nalaṅkiḷḷi!
In this world where the moon god turns and turns, making
even the ignorant aware that waxing truly exists, waning
truly exists, dying truly exists as does being born
truly exist, when you see the thin waists of those men
who come to you and are suffering with no regard to whether
they have talent or are just people without talent,
may it be possible for you to be generous, and may
an inability to give, an utter lack of generosity
mark those who stand opposed
in their enmity toward you whose strength is never diminished!

Uṟaiyūr Mutukaṇṇaṉ Cāttaṉār sings Cōḻaṉ Nalaṅkiḷḷi. *Tiṇai: potuviyal. Tuṟai: mutumokikkāñci.*

28

The eight sorts of monstrous births that people can suffer
have been described by wise men in the past as useless
and not of any worth—the blind whom no one favors,
the mass without form, the hunchback and the dwarf, the deaf,
the dumb, the creature that at birth looks like an animal
and the imbecile—but I have come here now and I have
something more to say as to what may be without worth!
Your enemies live in forests where wild cocks marked

with round red spots cry out, awakening men who guard the fields
of millet while you! you have a land where for the sake
of Righteousness, those who live in the city pluck and fling
stalks of sugarcane to people beyond the walls, and the stalks,
as they strike the ground, scatter the flourishing lotus blossoms,
and the earth looks like a stage where dancers have performed!
And so your wealth can nourish the three aims of life:
Righteousness, Prosperity, and Pleasure!
Greatness! When it does not, you neglect your own well-being!

Uṟaiyūr Mutukaṇṇaṉ Cāttaṉār sings Cōḻaṉ Nalaṅkiḷḷi. *Tiṇai: potuviyal. Tuṟai: iyaṉmoḻi vāḻttu* and/or *mutumoḻik kāñci.*

29

During the day, may the bards crowd around the festive
sessions of your court and their dark heads and tangled hair
turn radiant with fragrant garlands of gold, beautifully
crafted of thin plaques fashioned in the shape of lotuses
tempered in the fire and threaded onto fine pounded wires!
And when bards no longer surround you, then may your chest
where sandalpaste dries be encircled by the arms of your women!
And as the royal drum with its pleasing resonance is beaten
within your courtyard of which no one ever tires, may you be
    untiring
in your ceaseless attention to punishment for the evil and benefit
for the good, and may you never take the part of those who say,
"There is no good in doing good, nor any evil in evil!"
Happy are those who cleave to your weapon, who have received
a fine, flourishing land where those whose work
is chasing away the birds that light on fields of paddy
cook fish from the inlets on a fire of fallen palmyra leaves,
toss off strong toddy and, not yet satisfied, shake young coconuts
    down!
There is no need for them to live like your enemies
whom, out of your mercy, you permit to inhabit houses only
huts on four stilts with their thatched roofs of arrowroot!

May the virtue of compassion mark your actions, resulting
in easy giving by your people to those who may come to them!
In this world where they who take part pass through
as actors might at a festival, may those who surround you
be festive as they should be and may
the wealth that you protect be the source sustaining your good
name!

Uṟaiyūr Mutukaṇṇaṉ Cāttaṉār sings Cōḻaṉ Nalaṅkiḷḷi. *Tiṇai: potuviyal. Tuṟai: iyaṉmoḻi vāḻttu* and/or *mutumoḻik kāñci.*

30

There are those for whom it is as if they had gone
and established through measurement the path of the red sun,
the pace of movement of that sun and the sphere of the earth
around which the sun moves and the directions through which
move the waves of the wind and space that rests on nothing,
and they can describe exactly how these things always are!
Yet even the knowledge that knows all of this cannot know
you! because you make no outward show of yourself! Your strength
is hidden, like the stone missile an elephant may carry in its cheek!
So how can poets, through song, reveal who you really are?
O you have a country where many precious things that come
by sea are unloaded by lowly laborers onto great roads
near their own lands, out of great ships that have entered
the harbor without any need to lower
their masts or their soaring sails or to lighten their cargo!

Uṟaiyūr Mutukaṇṇaṉ Cāttaṉār sings Cōḻaṉ Nalaṅkiḷḷi. *Tiṇai: pāṭāṇṭiṇai. Tuṟai: iyaṉmoḻi.*

31

As in the proper course of things, Prosperity and Pleasure
are seen to follow in the wake of Righteousness, so it is with you

when your tall umbrella towering into the distance shines alone,
like the full lovely moon, and those two umbrellas follow behind.
With your intense desire to perpetuate your good name, you will
not rest
anywhere but in your camp where victories are won in battle!
Your elephants, their tusks blunted from thrusting, plunge them
into the guarded walls of your enemies and never cool down!
Your warriors wearing their war anklets exult at the sound of the
word
"War!" and they tell you that they will not hesitate to march
even into countries deep in the jungle and far distant! You linger
in the lands of your enemies, to the sound of festivals, and the
eastern
ocean is at your back while the white-capped waves of the ocean
of the west lap at the hooves of your horses. Kings
of countries to the north think, "He may circle the earth!"
and they feel bewildered, assaulted by pain
that makes their hearts shake, and their eyes do not close in sleep!

Kōvūr Kiḻār sings Cōḻaṉ Nalaṅkiḷḷi. *Tiṇai: vākai. Tuṟai: aracavākai* and/or *maḻapula vañci.*

32

You must know he would give away Vañci with its tall banners
so that we could fill the cooking pots for our families? And thinking
that women of the caste of bards, painted with colors, their arms
swaying like bamboo and their faces glowing, must be paid
for their flowers, he would give away Madurai with its many-storied
mansions!
Let us all sing his praises! Come, you people here in need!
Do you want to know who is master of this ancient country?
Like a weight of fresh clay arranged on a potter's wheel
by the potter's skillful children, it is his
to do with as he likes, this cool rice-growing land!

Kōvūr Kiḻār sings Cōḻaṉ Nalaṅkiḷḷi. *Tiṇai: pāṭāṇṭiṇai. Tuṟai: iyaṉmoḻi.*

33

In the good, southern land of the Pandya king
where in their spacious houses the wives of farmers
carry the white rice grown in the fields fed by reservoirs
and offer it to fill the basket in which a forest hunter
with fierce dogs presents his heap of venison and to fill the pot
from which a woman of the cowherd caste pours them yogurt,
so that those who came then leave happy, even there,
in your strength, you assaulted the gates in seven walls
and captured them and inscribed them with your great-jawed tiger!
Where you have taken your stand for war is a place of the highest beauty,
from which fiery battles stem! There singers sing the Odes That Praise
Invasions and the camp lanes smoothened with powdered cow dung
are resplendent with armed men! And the families of bards
are nourished with balls of rice and meat like closed
blossoms on garlands strung with fresh, green leaves!
Where you live is even lovelier by far than the festival
you celebrated, sacrificing male goats at every many-storied mansion
near the entrance of the compound with fresh flowers and thick sand,
where it is a pleasure to walk and where there are groves
of cool blossoms, and where no man strolls alone at night,
only pairs of lovers as close and quiet as puppets stilled
in their dance and skillfully fashioned and handsomely painted!

Kōvūr Kiḻār sings Cōḻaṉ Nalaṅkiḷḷi. *Tiṇai: vākai. Tuṟai: aracavākai.*

34

It is said that even those who are devoid of Righteousness
and slice off the udders of cows or those willing to abort
the fetuses of women wearing lovely ornaments or those
savage people who harm Brahmins may atone for their sins!
But even if the world should be shaken loose at its roots,

Righteousness affirms that no escape ever is possible
for those who through ungratefulness slay an act of kindness!
You whose wife wears choice ornaments! May the god of many rays
no longer rise for me unless, every morning and evening,
I sing of your great and forceful acts, chanting:
"He who assembled all the riches that never diminish
for bards who with honest hearts repeat their requests
in the large, open grove of towering jujube trees
and stuff themselves with balls of rich cooked rice
as does my family which mingles honey with grains of millet
large as the eggs of doves, though they were grown on poor land,
and boils the whole in milk and tears off good cooked meat
from small rabbits—long life to Vaḷavaṉ, our king!"
O greatness! I am nothing at all! May you live for more years
than the many tiny droplets borne in a huge cloud
carried to us by the east wind from the Himālayas where it formed
because of the good that noble men have done,
to pour down upon us with the sweet voices of its thunder!

Ālattūr Kiḻār sings Cōḻaṉ Kuḷamuṟṟattut Tuñciya Kiḷḷi Vaḷavaṉ. *Tiṇai: pāṭāṇṭiṇai. Tuṟai: iyaṉmoḻi.*

35

In this world massed together of earth that the wind
cannot penetrate, dressed in sky and surrounded
by the broad, vast sea, of the three who rule over
the cool land of the Tamils, those whose imperial drums
resound, it is your royalty that is truly royalty,
O greatness! And where the sugarcane with its swaying nodes
shows dancing white flowers that look like gathered spears
because of the flow of the cool and lovely Kāviri that breaks
into canals to feed the soil even if the sun's bright rays
should fill the four directions or the shining rays of the Silver
Planet

turn to the south, it is your country that is truly a country!
You are a king resplendent with the might of a country
so wealthy! Therefore hear me out as I speak of things
that concern you! When people wish for justice, fairly administered
as if Righteousness itself were the judge, then they find you
easily approachable, and asking only for drops of rain,
they receive showers! Is your broad umbrella, which rivals
the sky itself and in glowing blinds the eyes, a shield
against the sun as if it were a thick cloud in the midst of the vaulted
heavens blocking off the sun above? No! O Vaḷavaṉ
with your sharp spear! It is a shield for the suffering people!
On the broad field of battle where divisions of elephants
struggle and then lie scattered here and there like chunks
of the hollow palmyra tree, when your armies in combat
withstand oncoming forces, then rail at their retreating backs,
even the victories accomplished stem from what grows in the
    furrow
pierced by the weapon of the plow! If the rains should fail,
if the harvests lessen, if in the work of men things happen
that go against nature, this vast world blames its kings!
If you really understand this, if you will not attend
to people who with no foundation at all spew slanders,
if you will protect those weighed down with dependents, those
who care for the oxen that plow, if you will protect
the castes, even your enemies then will praise your feet!

Veḷḷaikkuṭi Nākaṉār sings Cōḻaṉ Kuḷamuṟṟattut Tuñciya Kiḷḷi Vaḷavaṉ and is absolved of old taxes [or an old debt]. *Tiṇai: pāṭāṇṭiṇai. Tuṟai: ceviyaṟivuṟūu.*

36

Whether you have him killed, whether you let him go free,
is something you yourself will judge, knowing which choice
will bring you renown. Within the high walls of the king's city,
within his guarded palace grounds, a sound can be heard from all

the groves outside, as they chop down the trees that had been protected
and the long branches fragrant with flowers lie isolate,
their former glory lost, cut off by the ax with the long handle
and handsome blade filed sharp by a smith with blackened hands;
and the white sand by the cool Āṉ Porunai River flies up as they fall,
while women with elegant anklets and small bracelets exquisitely turned
play on a dais with beans made of gold. And that king sits there,
taking his ease. To bother fighting against him here
to the sound of your drum with its garland like a rainbow would be shameful!

Ālattūr Kiḻār sings Cōḻaṉ Kuḷamuṟṟattut Tuñciya Kiḷḷi Vaḷavaṉ when he was besieging Karuvūr. *Tiṇai: vañci. Tuṟai: tuṇai vañci.*

37

You descend from Cempiyaṉ with his fierce army and his shining spear,
who freed a bird of its anguish—and you with the power of thunder
blasting into a cave where a five-headed cobra lives with the venom
in its white fangs, a fiery and savage enemy upon a huge
mountain where green vines grow while the lightning zigzags
across the sky, O greatness! you had the force in battle
to destroy the ancient capital, with its walls shielded
in bronze, its cavernous moats crowded with alligators,
its pools of deep water where vicious crocodiles collect
in the dark ranges of the bottom and rush up and snap
at reflections of the lights that men who are standing guard
hold high in the middle of the night! But you did not
consider how wondrous all this was but only
that the king with a harnessed elephant could be found within the city!

Māṟōkkattu Nappacalaiyār sings Cōḻaṉ Kuḷamuṟṟattut Tuñciya Kiḷḷi Vaḷavaṉ. *Tiṇai: vākai. Tuṟai: aracavākai* and/or *mutal vañci.*

38

Victorious king, you who ride a mountain
of an elephant and lead a vast army
with flags of many colors that flutter
as if they were brushing the sky clean!
Fire breaks out where your angry glances fall!
Gold springs up wherever you look kindly!
If you wish that there be moonlight in the red sun
or the blaze of the sun within the white moon,
you have the power to make it so, whatever you will!
And I, born in your shadow, raised in your shadow,
how far may my mind go? People in need believe
that even for those living in the blessed world where one
is at ease among groves of trees with their flowers of gold
and what has been earned through karma is duly received,
something is missing because the rich there need not give
nor the poor request. But since the pleasures there can be found
here as well, even in enemy countries those
in need turn their thoughts toward your land because it is yours!

Āvūr Mūlaṅkiḻār sings Cōḻaṉ Kuḷamuṟṟattut Tuñciya Kiḷḷi Vaḷavaṉ when he asked, "Did you think of me? What country are you from?" *Tiṇai: pāṭāṇṭiṇai. Tuṟai: iyaṉmoḻi.*

39

Since you were born in his lineage, he who dispelled the pain
of a dove by climbing upon a scale with its fixed pointer
white at the ends because tusks of an elephant with spotted feet
had been cut off and set there, your generosity cannot increase
your fame! And when I think of how your ancestors destroyed
those walls hanging in space, immensely strong and resistant,
which enemies feared to approach, your skill at killing in battle
cannot increase your fame! And since Righteousness has been
established
and abides in the court of the city of Uṟantai of the Cholas

who are imbued with Martial Courage and never suffer harm,
governing with justice cannot increase your fame! Vaḷavaṉ!
you who won the battle kindled by courage, whose thick arms
are like crossbars, whose chaplet is blinding, who ride a proud horse!
How may I describe you, since you made Unwithering Vañci
wither and destroyed the Chera king with his lofty chariot
so finely built, who had inscribed his symbol of the bow to adorn
Himālaya with its immeasurable heights, its towering
summits of gold, how can I sing of your great and powerful acts?

Māṟōkkattu Nappacalaiyār sings Cōḻaṉ Kuḷamuṟṟattut Tuñciya Kiḷḷi Vaḷavaṉ. *Tiṇai: pāṭāṇṭiṇai. Tuṟai: iyaṉmoḻi.*

40

You do not respect the fortresses protected by your enemies
where Martial Courage resides but you rush at them and you
destroy them! With the fine gold that had formed their crowns,
you in your virile manhood had war anklets fashioned
and they glitter on your legs! O powerful king! Today
we have seen you and we would wish to see you always,
and may those who sing ill of you have their necks bowed down
while those flourish who sing of your glory! O greatness!
May you, with your kind words, be easy to approach,
who rule a land where the small space
a cow elephant lies down upon can feed seven elephant bulls!

Āvūr Mūlaṅkiḻār sings Cōḻaṉ Kuḷamuṟṟattut Tuñciya Kiḷḷi Vaḷavaṉ *Tiṇai: pāṭāṇṭiṇai. Tuṟai: ceviyaṟivuṟūu.*

41

Even Death must wait for his due time but you
do not wait but whenever you want you kill, my king
who triumphs in battle, destroying the finest of men

in armies dense with spears! While awake and in dreams,
men see sights that are hard to endure: shooting stars
falling in all the eight directions; long branches,
without any leaves, of great trees seized by drought;
and the sun with its blazing rays looming very near;
bird calls that are terrifying shrieks; teeth falling out
and onto the ground; pourings of oil through hair;
men riding on boars; people stripping off their clothes;
powerful weapons, the color of silver, on a table overturning;
and then, when they see you are approaching, O strength in battle!
they cannot protect their homes, and bewildered, they kiss the eyes
like flowers of their sons and they hide the pain from their wives;
and there is massive confusion among those troubled men in the
country
that has incurred your anger, O Vaḷavaṉ
mighty in war, you who advance like fire on the wind!

Kōvūr Kiḻār sings Kuḷamuṟṟattut Tuñciya Kiḷḷivaḷavaṉ. *Tiṇai: vañci. Tuṟai: koṟṟavaḷḷai.*

42

Endless in your charity, death-dealing in battle, our leader!
Greatness! Your elephant is like a mountain! Your army resounds
like the ocean! Your spear with its sharp blade shines
like lightning! You are strong enough to make the heads tremble
of the lords of the earth, and so what you do is never wrong!
I say nothing special. This is no new thing for you!
With your righteous, faultless scepter you offer protection
as a tiger protects a cub, and those whom you rule listen
only to the sound of cool water, never even in their
dreams hearing the noise of your army advancing
to cause your enemies suffering, to make them cry out, "Vaḷavaṉ!
May you live long but please, now, halt!" You are the ruler of a fine
country,
eminently prosperous, of cities with rich fields whose people
in hospitality give their relatives from arid lands gifts:

scabbard fish that rice cutters pluck from the last sluice,
tortoises overturned by plowmen's blades, sweet sap
harvesters take from the sugarcane, and waterlilies gathered
by women who come to draw water at the great source!
Like the many rivers that descend from the mountains and flow
down from higher land toward the sea, every poet flows
toward you! And like Death when he is enraged, when he whirls
his ax against which there is no cure and the living
suffer, you flow with force
toward the lands of those two kings who oppose you!

Iṭaikkāṭaṉār sings Kuḷamuṟṟattut Tuñciya Kiḻḻivaḷavaṉ. *Tiṇai: vākai. Tuṟai: aracavākai.*

43

You are a descendant of that powerful man who was generous
without end and who because he was afraid a dove might die
that had come to him for shelter, escaping with its tiny steps
from the swoop of a kite with sharp claws and curving wings,
entered the scale, and at the act, even among the holy men
with their glowing masses of tangled hair who to relieve
the pain of those living on earth eat only the air,
endure the scorching rays of the sun's heat and seek the sun,
even among them there was amazement! Younger brother
to Tēr Vaṇ Kiḻḻi, you whose great wealth stems from your ferocity
in conquering your enemies! Chieftain of warriors with curving bows
and long arrows! Master with strong hands of a swift horse!
In words that merited hatred, I said to you, "I have my doubts
as to your origins! None of your ancestors who wore the garlands
of mountain ebony flowers made Brahmins suffer! How can you?"
I had wronged you and was mistaken but you were not only
    unoffended
but deeply ashamed, as if the fault were yours! You whose power
is a thing to be seen! You have shown that the high virtue
of forgiving those who have wronged them comes with ease
to those who have been born into this clan and so it was surely

I who was wrong! May the days of your life be wonderful
and more numerous than the sand heaped
in dunes by the Kāviri with its sweet, abundant waters!

Cōḻaṉ Nalaṅkiḷḷi's younger brother Māvaḷattāṉ and Tāmaṟpalkaṇṇaṉ were playing dice [vaṭṭu], and [Māvaḷattāṉ] concealed [the dice] [and, when found out,] grew angry and threw the dice [at Tāmaṟpalkaṇṇaṉ]. At that, [Tāmaṟpalkaṇṇaṉ] said, "You are not the son of the Chola [king but a bastard]," and [Māvaḷattāṉ] felt shame. Thereupon Tāmaṟpalkaṇṇaṉār sang this song. *Tiṇai: vākai. Tuṟai: aracavākai.*

44

They cannot go bathing in the huge reservoirs with their herds
of dark-skinned females, nor have they been given their rice
trampled down and rolled into balls mixed with ghee and so
the elephants strain against their strong upright posts and bend them.
Their trunks sweep the ground. Their breath is hot. Constantly shifting,
they trumpet like thunder. With no milk, children cry. Women cover their heads
that are bare because they are without flowers. Wailing voices
are heard in the fine, well-fashioned houses that have no water.
It is a painful thing how you linger here at your ease, O lord
of a powerful horse whose strength can hardly be equaled!
If you live by Righteousness, open your gates and say, "The city
is yours!" If you live by Martial Courage, open them and fight!
But if you are without Righteousness, without Martial Courage and all
you do is hide on your own grounds within your high walls
while your massive gates stay closed
and never open, do you realize how much cause for shame there is in this!

Kōvūrkiḻār sings Neṭuṅkiḷḷi when Cōḻaṉ Nalaṅkiḷḷi besieged Āvūr and he was locked inside [that city]. *Tiṇai: vākai. Tuṟai: aracavākai.*

45

He does not wear the pale leaf of the great palmyra palm
or a garland from the margosa tree with its black branches.
Your chaplet is dense with laburnum and he who fights against you
wears a chaplet dense with laburnum! If one of you is defeated,
your lineage is defeated, and it is not possible that both
of you can win! So what you do is no good thing
for your lineage! And yet, this battle will give such joy,
making their bodies swell with pride,
to kings who are like you, with their chariots waving banners!

Kōvūrkiḻār sings Cōḻaṉ Nalaṅkiḷḷi who was besieging Uṟaiyūr and Neṭuṅkiḷḷi, who was besieged [by him]. *Tiṇai: vañci. Tuṟai: tuṇaivañci.*

46

You were born to the line of him who relieved the pain of a dove
and wiped away many other sorrows besides! And these descend
from men who in their lives gave cool shade and shared
what they had, fearing that those who eat by plowing the fields
of knowledge might suffer! They are children, still wearing their hair
unoiled, and when they see the elephant they forget their tears! Then,
confused, they look around the field and feel
terror they never imagined! If you have heard me out, then do as you wish!

When Cōḻaṉ Kuḷamuṟṟattut Tuñciya Kiḷḷivaḷavaṉ was having the children of Malaiyamāṉ [crushed to death] by elephants, Kōvūrkiḻār sang this and saved them. *Tiṇai: vañci. Tuṟai: tuṇaivañci.*

47

Does this life of a bard in need of favor harm anyone else
as he grows lean in search of reward, thinks about patrons,

moves along like a bird, crosses many rugged wastelands
and does not think them long, sings the best that he can
with his tongue that isn't perfect, and is happy with whatever
he receives, feeding his family and eating without saving,
and generous as well, holding nothing back? No, this life harms no one
other than by the shame it causes rivals in the disciplines of song
when he walks off, with his head held high, and there and then
he is happy! His is a life as fine as yours,
you who have gathered wealth from ruling the earth and whose fame soars!

When a poet named Iḷantattaṉ [came] from Cōḻaṉ Nalaṅkiḷḷi [who was besieging Kāriyāṟṟut Tuñciya Neṭuṅkiḷḷi in Uṟaiyūr] and entered Uṟaiyūr, Kāriyāṟṟut Tuñciya Neṭuṅkiḷḷi thought he was a spy and was going to kill him. Kōvūrkiḻār sang this and saved him. *Tiṇai: vañci. Tuṟai: tuṇaivañci.*

48

Tōṇṭi, lovely with its groves along the sea,
fragrant with nectar from the garland Kōtai wears
across his chest and from the garlands of the women who embrace
Kōtai and from the waterlilies blooming in the dark
salt pans—that is our city and he is our king!
If you should go to him as he is, remember me as well,
you who are in need of favor and speak the language
of wisdom, and say, "I have seen the man
who raised your fame on high when you towered in battle!"

Poykaiyār sings Cēramāṉ Kōkkōtai Mārpaṉ. *Tuṇai: pāṭāṇṭiṇai. Tuṟai: pulavarāṟṟuppaṭai.*

49

Shall I call him a mountain king? Shall I call him a king of the plains?
Or a king of the lands by the sea, by the cool roaring ocean?
Kōtai, with his sword on high! how can I place him in words?

When men of the mountains strike their noisemakers, from nearby then,
from the fields where bending blades of rice are swept by wind
and from the ocean rich in waters, as one all the birds take flight!

Poykaiyār sings Cēramāṉ Kōkkōtai Mārpaṉ. *Tuṇai: pāṭāṇṭiṇai. Tuṟai: pulavarāṟṟuppaṭai* and/or *iyaṉmoḻi*.

50

Before they returned from bathing the awe-inspiring drum
which hungers for blood and is decorated with golden shoots
of balloon vine and a garland the color of sapphire, fashioned
of long dense peacock feathers, their bright spots shining,
lending a glow to the dark wood of the drum's sides
where thongs cut lengthwise are tied without flaw, I
climbed up on its bed, all covered with flowers and as soft
as if a froth of sesame oil had been spread over it.
You turned away the edge of your sword that would have,
had you been enraged, cut me in two! That was enough in itself
for all the fine Tamil people to know! But you did even more!
You approached me and raised your strong arm
big around as a concert drum and fanned me to keep me cool!
Is it because you have clearly heard that only for those
who gain fame in this world, making it spread far and wide,
can there be a place there, in the world
of exalted existence, victorious hero? Is that why you just did this?

When Mōcikīraṉ climbed unknowing on the bed of the royal drum of Cēramāṉ Takaṭūreṟinta Peruñ Cēralirumpoṟai, [the king] did not make a mistake, but when he rose from sleep, he took a chowry and fanned him. Mōcikīraṉār then sang this song to him. *Tuṇai: pāṭāṇṭiṇai. Tuṟai: iyaṉmoḻi.*

51

When there is too much water, there is no dam against it!
When there is too much fire, no shadow can shade the living!

When there is too much wind, no strength resists it! Like all these
is Vaḻuti, fierce in battles, with his great radiance!
When they say the cool Tamil land is ruled in common,
he will not bear it and he dissents in battle! If he wishes
tribute, kings who say "take what you want!" and give things to him
do not tremble. But to be pitied, to be pitied are those
who lose his grace! Like the white-winged ants from the red mound
raised up with so much labor and hardship
by the many tiny ants, they whirl around alive for only a day!

Aiyūr Muṭavaṉār sings Pāṇṭiyaṉ Kūṭakārattut Tuñciya Māṟaṉ Vaḻuti. *Tiṇai: vākai. Tuṟai: aracavākai.*

52

A male tiger, in his cave on a high peak where evil spirits roam,
stretches and rises, full of his strength, and with his heart moved
by a hunger for meat, taking whatever direction he may wish,
sets out ravenously in search of his prey. You are like him,
with your intent to kill and obliterate the kings of the north,
Vaḻuti whose chariot is well fashioned, whose warfare is fierce
and blazing! Since you have willed your war, who are these kings
of the wide earth? They are surely to be pitied, on whose lands
long streamers of smoke that smelled of flesh rose once from the fish
cooking in every town, to wreathe around the curving branches
of marutam trees in the fields of paddy. But now those lands
are ruined, their fine wealth lost, turned to forest where the wild hens
streaked with spots lay their eggs to fill the handsome gambling halls
pitted by the pieces slammed down in play by white-haired old men
in huge public squares that are barren now, where sacrifices
no longer are performed, so that the gods
once worshiped with uproar have left their pillars behind!

Marutaṉiḷanākaṉār sings Pāṇṭiyaṉ Kūṭakārattut Tuñciya Māṟaṉ Vaḻuti. *Tiṇai: vākai. Tuṟai: aracavākai.*

53

You removed the anguish constricting glittering Viḷaṅkil where the young women
who wear bright bangles leave the mansions embedded with sapphires that shoot out
rays to dazzle the eyes and then they go and dance on a stage of sand
raised high and stretching straight out and as white as pearls from the long
ripe shells, O Poraiyaṉ with your swift horses and with your elephants
taking the field! If our songs are long, then they are too long! If they are short,
they say too little! And so it is that in our hearts we come to feel bewildered!
By men like us, with muddled minds, your glory can never be sung through to its
entirety! And yet into this great world, towering poets have been born and how
can we refuse to live on and continue the tradition? We hear you saying, "If only
Kapilaṉ were alive today, he whose fame was radiant and whose learning was immense,
he who with his eloquent tongue could produce, on the instant, a taut
and complete poem, how truly wonderful that would be!" But yet I will sing
in a way that will be worthy of your might
upon the field of battle, I will sing of how you overwhelmed your enemies!

Poruntiliḷaṅkīraṉār sings Cēramāṉ Māntarañcēralirumpoṟai. *Tiṇai: vākai. Tuṟai: aracavākai.*

54

To those who like us live in need the time can be anytime
for easily approaching the ancient city full of sound

as if we owned it, there where our king lives, where we can enter
his great formal audience in daylight with our heads held high!
So smooth the approach for those who come in need but should I think
of those kings who have made their joint resolutions and risen up
against Kōtai of the swift horses, the cup of whose hand never
desists from giving gifts to those who have come to him,
who holds back nothing, who shames the generosity of the clouds,
and chooses to protect us, then that land of his—he who holds power
within his strong hand—seems like the territory a shepherd who wears
a garland of branches strung with fresh leaves, his clothes soiled,
his mouth pursed, dares not even skirt
with his flock, their heads so small, because it is the wide range of a tiger!

Kōṉāṭṭu Eṟiccilūr Māṭalaṉ Maturaik Kumaraṉār sings Cēramāṉ Kuṭṭuvaṉ Kōtai. *Tiṇai: vākai. Tuṟai: aracavākai.*

55

You surmount the two kings just as upon the forehead of that god
with the blue black throat one eye glows alone very near
the new moon that he bears in his hair, he who brought victory
to the gods of great power when he shot a single arrow at three walls
from his bow of a soaring mountain strung with a snake, O Māṟaṉ you who wear
a garland of flowers! Yes, it is true that triumph grows out of the four
divisions of an army: ferocious elephants fiercely raging; horses, haughty
and of swift, varied gaits; tall chariots with their rising banners;
and foot soldiers with strength in their hearts and the passion for battle,
yet his pursuit of the high road of Righteousness is still the root cause

of victory for a king! And so for that reason, do not allow your rod of office
to be twisted out of shape by thinking of some as "my people," nor reduce
your own virtue by doing harm to others as "mere foreigners!" but instead
in your blazing strength be as virile as the sun, in your gentleness
be as large and as cool as the moon, and be as generous as the clouds!
Great being, possessing these three virtues may you live a long life
so that no longer will there be any men who own nothing! As on the broad
and beautiful bay where Neṭu Vēḷ rules at Centil washed by the white crests
of waves flowing in from the deep waters there lie all the grains
of fine black sand in the dunes raised
and amassed by the rushing wind—may your life last even more days!

Maturai Marutaṉiḷanākaṉār sings Pāṇṭiyaṉ Ilavantikaippaḷḷit Tuñciya Naṉmāṟaṉ. *Tiṇai: Pāṭāṇṭiṇai. Tuṟai: Ceviyaṟivuṟūu.*

56

There is the god whose neck is the color of sapphire, on whose banner the bull
spells out victory, whose matted hair spreads like fire, whose ax is irresistible;
and there is the god who carries a palmyra palm on his banner, whose body is white
as a conch twisting upward under the ocean, who kills with his murderous plow;
and there is the god who longs for triumph, on whose flag which towers up high
into the sky stands a bird, and who is the color of lovely blue sapphire polished

to a high sheen; and the shining Red God who rides a peacock, he who is never
defeated, and a deep blue peacock flutters upon his banner—among these four
whose power shields the world, who bring on destruction, whose fame cannot perish,
you are to be ranked, for with your anger that cannot be opposed, you are
like Death! With your overwhelming force, you are like the stark white god!
With your great fame, you resemble the god who slays those that scorn him!
And you are like Murugan, because whatever you may embark on you complete in full!
Since you so much resemble each and every one of them, how can there be anything
anywhere that you could not secure? May you live on, with a sweet life,
giving away precious ornaments to all those who come to you in need
and never running out of them, while every day you take your pleasure as women
wearing their shining bangles bring you the cool and fragrant wine
carried here in their excellent ships by the Greeks and the women pour it
for you out of pitchers made of gold that have been fashioned with high
artistry, O Māraṉ, you whose sword is raised on high, like the sun
with its rays of heat driving away the darkness that has filled in
the spaces of the beautiful sky, like the moon that spreads
out its cool rays in the west, may you live
long and as firmly established as they are together with the world!

Maturaik Kaṇakkāyaṉār Makaṉār Nakkīraṉār sings Pāṇṭiyaṉ Ilavantikaippaḷḷit Tuñciya Naṉmāraṉ. *Tiṇai: Pāṭāṇṭiṇai. Tuṟai: Pūvainilai.*

57

Whether they have learning or whether they have no learning at all,
in the eyes of those who sing of your glory, you are like Viṣṇu!
Māṟaṉ,
praise for whom has the virtue of so often having come to be
the subject of description! I am going to tell you something!
When you conquer others' lands, let your men plunder the fields
where the heavy stalks of paddy bend down low, and let the fire
eat great vast cities! And should your long and glittering spear
that flashes like lightning across the sky show the wish
to kill enemies, well then let it kill! But do not cut down
so much as a single one of his sacred trees,
since they cannot serve even as hitching posts for your tall
elephants!

Kāvirippūmpaṭṭiṉattuk Kārikkaṇṇaṉār sings Pāṇṭiyaṉ Ilavantikaippaḷḷit Tuñciya Naṉmāṟaṉ. *Tiṇai: vañci. Tuṟai: Tuṇaivañci.*

58

You are ruler over the Kāviri River with its cool waters! And that
man
is a bull born of the great lineage of the Pandyas and because his
ancestors
have now all vanished, he is the support that never weakens of his
ancient clan
with its noble reputation, as a root might hang down from a banyan
tree
and sustain an overarching limb that offers dense shade so that,
without flowering,
fruit still burgeons, though its main trunk has died! And he, though
young,
is a bull among the war-wise Pandyas. Like the white lightning that is
irresistible
when it strikes at the snakes and their children, he will not bear his
enemies! And you

are the lord of the city of Uṟantai, which is an abode of Righteousness. He is
the king of Madurai which is famous for Tamil, where he rules with his cooling
rod of office; and presiding there he commands the three royal drums that possess
their resounding voices, in that city which draws sandalwood from the mountains
and pearls from the ocean waves, since for him the wealth that comes from paddy
and water is commonplace, available to any and all! As if the god who carries
a palmyra palm on his banner and whose skin is as white as milk and the one
who wields the discus, the dark-colored god, those two great beings
were to stand together, so do you two seem, shining such that you spread
terror with your fearsome forms! Could there be anything sweeter, since you
two lords are as you are! Listen to me as I go on! May your glory grow and may
it last long! May your aid, each to each, the one supporting the other,
be reciprocal! And if neither the one nor the other proves false to your alliance,
then men will have spoken the truth when they say that you will win this wide
and flourishing world circled around by the sea with its roaring waves!
And so, paying attention to what is of benefit and paying attention to what
is right, and paying attention to the paths on which your ancestors traveled,
may this your unity continue as it is today, with your hearts filled with love
while you pay no attention to the vulgar words of those strangers who may
attempt to force themselves between you! In victory following after victory,

may your spears be brandished upon the field where men kill! And in the lands
of others, where there are mountains rising, may the summits be incised
with the sign of the tiger showing the curving
of its stripes and with the sign of the carp who rises from the deep waters!

Kāvirippūmpaṭṭiṉattuk Kārikkaṇṇaṉār sings Cōḻaṉ Kurāppaḷḷit Tuñciya Perun Tirumāvaḷavaṉ and Pāṇṭiyaṉ Veḷḷiyampalattut Tuñciya Peruvaḻuti when they were together [i.e. were allies]. *Tiṇai: pāṭāṇṭiṇai. Tuṟai: uṭaṉilai.*

59

Vaḻuti! Your beauty glows, as befits you! Your strong
arms reach to your knees and a necklace hangs down low
upon your handsome chest! You know, at your own free will,
how to show your grace! You do not take lies for truth!
You are, great being, like the sun that rises from the ocean,
never relenting in your burning ferocity
toward your enemies, but you are like the moon to men like me!

Maturaik Kūlavāṇikaṉ Cīttalaic Cāttaṉār sings Pāṇṭiyaṉ Cittiramāṭattut Tuñciya Naṉmāṟaṉ. *Tiṇai: pāṭāṇṭiṇai. Tuṟai: pūvai nilai.*

60

In the sky arching above us, with the Red Planet flickering there
like a lantern on a ship in the middle of the ocean, we saw
the full moon that had swung to its height! Then my dancing woman,
wearing her few bangles, like a wild peacock in that wilderness,
and I along with her paid homage to it at once, bowing down again
and again as we thought to ourselves, doesn't it resemble the white
umbrella all hung with garlands of our king, that which
is fine and fearsome and shields us from the heat of the sun, he

whose sword never fails, whose royal drum roars in triumph, Vaḷavaṉ,
our king! a man like a great ox who when there are wagons filled with salt
collected from the salt pans near the sea
with axles sunk into deep holes can pull them out and drag them up the mountains?

Uṟaiyūr Maruttuvaṉ Tāmōtaraṉār sings Cōḻaṉ Kurāppaḷḷit Tuñciya Perun Tirumāvaḷavaṉ. *Tiṇai: pāṭāṇṭiṇai. Tuṟai: kuṭai maṅkalam.*

61

There in the watery fields where the eels go flashing and the women
weed out the small and lovely patches of blue and white waterlilies
where the harrow has passed and has killed and cut up scabbard fish
so that the fat pieces can be taken and eaten right from the pools
by the laborers with strong arms, fathers of children too young
to dress their hair who after growing tired of the taste of great coconuts
climb up on the growing stacks of grain their fathers are raising and
leap up into the air trying to bring down fruit from the palmyra palms—
in that good land prosperity is born again every day, where with his spear
gleaming, with his elegant chariot and his powerful hands, the lord
Ceṉṉi rules! And when the laborers have finished their fish, they take
glowing white rice from the freshly cut paddy and eat until their ribs
bulge out and then they walk heavily back to the fields and the sheaves
near the high-piled grain! If any men exist who believe they can oppose
his chest crossed by its garland like a rainbow, they should know what
will happen to them! We have never seen any living being succeed against

his arms like iron gate bolts! Even less do we see
sorrow in those who could instantly take refuge at his handsome feet!

Kōṉāṭṭu Eṟiccilūr Māṭalaṉ Maturaik Kumaraṉār sings Cōḻaṉ Ilavantikaip Paḷḷit Tuñciya Nalaṅkiḷḷi Cēṭceṉṉi. *Tiṇai: vākai. Tuṟai: aracavākai.*

62

How can the war flare up now and soldiers brace against advancing troops?
Demonesses, garishly glowing, plunge their hands into the wounds of warriors
who have died there in battle and smearing their hair red with the blood,
they dance then to the sad throb of the paṟai drums beaten in slowed pain.
Vultures are feasting on the army and the two kings too have perished
along with their soldiers, those kings who with Righteousness on their side
in furious battle fought a valiant war. Their umbrellas of majesty
droop down and their drums, whose power has drawn praise, stand ruined.
In that enormous camp, where there were hundreds of men speaking in varied
languages, so many of them gathered together that all the space was consumed,
now there is no one with strength left to triumph on the battlefield
and so the uproar of combat has suddenly stopped and that silence
is terrifying! As yet their women, the widows, do not eat green leaves
nor do they bathe themselves in cool water. Lying there on the ground,
they embrace the chests of their fallen men. While those who always dine
on the most fragrant food, who wear garlands of flowers that never wither,
whose eyes do not blink, attend to welcoming the new

arrivals entering and filling up the other world
that is so hard to attain! May the glory of both of you shine on!

Kaḻāttalaiyār sings Cēramāṉ Kuṭakkō Neṭuñcēralātaṉ and Cōḻaṉ Vēṟpaḥṟaṭakkaip Peruviṟaṟ Kiḷḷi when they fought on the battlefield and fell. *Tiṇai: tumpai. Turai: tokainilai.*

63

The many elephants of the army, unable under the anguish of the arrows
to charge on in battle have died there! All the many horses
of fine breed and famous for their victories have fallen there
along with men of Martial Courage! All the noble warriors
who rode to war in their chariots have fallen now and their eyes
are covered over with their shields! The drums of the kings,
beautifully fashioned, with their knotted straps and hairy eyes,
have been abandoned, without any one to carry them, and are ruined!
Smeared with sandalpaste, the chests of kings have been pierced
by the long spears as they fought and died on the battlefield!
And now what of their land that used to be filled with unending
fertility, where the women twining themselves armlets of waterlilies
plucked in the fields had filled their mouths with well-parched rice
and plunged into cool refreshing waters!
What will become now of that vast and lovely land they ruled?

Paraṇar sings Cēramāṉ Kuṭakkō Neṭuñcēralātaṉ and Cōḻaṉ Vēṟpaḥṟaṭakkaip Peruviṟaṟ Kiḷḷi on that battlefield [see poem 62]. *Tiṇai: tumpai. Turai: tokainilai.*

64

Shall we go, my dancing woman, you who wear your sparse bangles?
Shall we pack up the good yāḻ and the ākuḷi drum and the patalai drum

and visit him who in his majesty spends his time on the lands of enemies
within his own large camp after his ranks of elephants have waged war
and the white-headed, red-bodied vultures stop short in the air
above the fresh flesh? If we go to see Kuṭumi
the king, our food will no longer be gruel stewed with far too much water!

Neṭumpalliyattaṉār sings Pāṇṭiyaṉ Palyākacālai Mutukuṭumip Peruvaḻuti.
Tiṇai: pāṭāṇṭiṇai. Tuṟai: viṟaliyāṟṟuppaṭai.

65

The drums have forgotten their drumming clay. The yāḻs have forgotten their rāgas.
The giant pots lie over on their sides and have forgotten how to hold the ghee.
His followers have forgotten the pure toddy around which the bees would gather.
The plowmen have forgotten how they used to raise an uproar and the villages
with their broad streets have forgotten how to carry out their festivals!
Just as on the great day when the moon has grown full and the two spheres of light
stare one at the other and then one of them vanishes over the mountain out
into the empty evening, so in shame after having taken a wound in the back,
although from a worthy opposing king who had thought to take aim at his chest,
that ruler of imposing Martial Courage now is seated next to his sword. He has chosen
to sit on the ground, facing the north! And here by day,
when the sun is shining, time does not go by as the time of day once did before.

Kaḻāttalaiyār sings Cēramāṉ Peruñ Cēralātaṉ when he fought with Cōḻaṉ Karikāṟ Peruvaḷattāṉ, was ashamed of a back wound [he suffered] and faced north [to starve himself to death]. *Tiṇai: potuviyal. Tuṟai: kaiyaṟunilai.*

66

One of your ancestors mastered the movement of the wind
when his ships sailed on the dark and enormous ocean!
Karikāl Vaḷavaṉ, you who master rutting elephants!
You did march off and you did win the victory and you displayed
your power, since you were the one who triumphed in combat but yet
on the battlefield of wealthy Veṇṇi didn't he surpass you,
gaining great fame across the world when ashamed
at a wound in the back, he sat turned northward and starved himself to death?

Veṇṇik Kuyattiyār sings Cōḻaṉ Karikāṟ Peruvaḷattāṉ. *Tiṇai: vākai. Tuṟai: aracavākai.*

67

Gander! I call out to you! Gander! I call out to you!
Here I stand idle in the evening when things become unclear
and the blossoming light of the moon once it has united
its two horns shines out like the glowing face of that hero
triumphant, murderous in battle, bestowing grace upon his own land!
If you, after feeding on loaches from the great bay of Kanyakumari
should fly off to the mountain of the far north and stopping on your way
in the fine land of the king of the Cholas you should go to the towering
mansion at Kōḻi accompanied by your youthful beloved and enter that palace
without even stopping at the gate and if you should say, loud enough
for the great king Kiḻḻi to hear you, "Āntai of Picir is your

humble servant!", then when you have done that he will give you
the gift of a fine ornament he treasures
so that your beautiful mate may wear it and she will be filled with delight!

Picirāntaiyār sings Kōpperuñcōḻaṉ. *Tiṇai: pāṭāṇṭiṇai. Tuṟai: iyaṉmoḻi.*

68

Their ribs stick out at their sides as if they were lizards that have been skinned,
for your family is starving and wherever you may look, you see no one who could lift
away their hunger! Since over and over you mourn that there are so few
ears here to hear you, why do you linger, bard! in this land? In a fine country
where the people are nourished by the overflowing water of the Kāviri River
undermining trees and streaming out like milk from the breast offered to a child
once the impurity of the time of birth has ended, there is a lord, a great man who wears
an ornament dotted with red on his broad handsome chest, who bows gently to his women,
but who fiercely locks away warriors into his prisons and because he does not command
his men to move against an enemy when the omens are bad and clearly indicate subversion
may exist within his land, those warriors of endless Martial Courage shout out
"We will die here!" and in a street handsomely built for the passage of chariots
they slap their swelling arms to the rhythm of a drum meant to quiet them down
and some men drinking strong toddy let the cups fall from their unsteady hands

while elephants, although no one rides on their heads, dance in the mud rendered
fragrant by that splashing toddy as they listen, with rapt attention, to the sound
of a muḻā drum that is being beaten somewhere within a towering mansion
in the city of Uṟantai, where he reigns as ruler!
If you forget about the gates of other kings and go to him, he will be generous!

Kōvūrkiḻār sings Cōḻaṉ Nalaṅkiḷḷi. *Tiṇai: pāṭāṇtiṇai. Tuṟai: Pāṇāṟṟuppaṭai.*

69

In your hand is a yāḻ accustomed to the playing of a master. On your body
your hunger shows, because you can find no one to be your patron.
Around your waist you wear some rags soaked in sweat, patched together
with many different colors of thread and you have no choice but to move
carefully lest you rip open the new seams! Bard! As empty of strength
as the body of a man who lacks the will to act when he must, so
is the state of your large family burned black under the sun!
Since now you have traveled everywhere and you calmly ask
this of me, then I will tell you! Where the murderous elephants of kings
moan with their wounds in a camp of fluttering banners while other elephants
have been cut down and lie in their pools of blood, there, turning
the battleground into a field of flesh, his fighting army has passed,
the troops of the lord of Uṟantai with its tall shining mansions! It is he
who raises his spear against oncoming warriors and he is always ready to march
at once into the lands of his enemies! If you choose to go and visit

that Kiḻḻi Vaḷavaṉ, who wears a fine garland and a handsome gold ornament
flashing like fire, you will not have to wait before his tall gateway and once
you have seen him, once you have gazed and gazed till you have had your fill
of gazing at how he gives away chariots in the middle of the day, you can be most
certain you will not fail to gain an ornament in the form
of a lotus that the bees can never taste, though they move toward it past the flowers!

Ālattūrkiḻār sings Cōḻaṉ Kuḷamuṟṟattut Tuñciya Kiḻḻivaḷavaṉ. *Tiṇai: pāṭāṇṭiṇai. Tuṟai: Pāṇāṟṟuppaṭai.*

70

You who travel seeking gifts! You whose words are full of wisdom!
Over and over you repeat, "Bard with your small yāḻ, the strings as sweet
as honey! Rest here a while and enjoy, beaten on its clear eye,
the music from the big drum balanced upon its thin sticks
like a turtle drawn from a reservoir and impaled on an iron rod!"
If you bring to your mind the fine reputation of Kiḻḻi Vaḷavaṉ,
lord of a prosperous country where the two healers of hunger,
rice and water, abound and the spacious residences know nothing
of the fire of war but are aware only of the kitchen fire so filled
with rice it does not matter how much may be taken out for use, since
the rice never grows any the less—as if it were water in a cool
reservoir in the moist month of Tai—and if you travel to him,
quietly and leisurely, with your dancing woman and her glowing face
and her lovely smile and her hair fragrant with trumpet flowers
from a village ruled by Paṇṇaṉ who gives with open hands
and where the six-legged bees searching around the many sweet smells
sip at the blossoms of small white waterlilies, then you will be rich!
Unlike gold earned by bringing firewood into a city

and depending on the chance of sale, his generosity is certain! May his efforts prosper!

Kōvūrkiḻār sings Cōḻaṉ Kuḷamuṟṟattut Tuñciya Kiḷḷivaḷavaṉ. *Tiṇai: pāṭāṇṭiṇai. Tuṟai: Pāṇāṟṟuppaṭai.*

71

Raging like lions, kings with relentless armies and hearts
of leonine unrestraint have formed a federation and pronounced
that they will go into battle against me! If I do not assault them
so that I can hear them scream in the uproar of a combat they will not
be able to endure and then see their backs as they go fleeing in their chariots,
let me give up the touch of my woman whose eyes, shadowed with collyrium
and worthy of her face, are large and lovely! And in my court where benevolence
exists and justice is never abandoned, let me grant authority to someone
unworthy of it and twist my rod of office out of shape by wandering
from the right path! And may I lose the pleasure of joyous laughter
in the company of my friends who are as near to me as my own eyes:
Māvaṉ who is the ruler over Maiyal where the riches are never-ending
and the cities prosper encircled by the far-famed Vaiyai River,
and Āntai of long established Eyil, and Antuvaṉ Cāttaṉ of broad
renown and Ātaṉaḻici and Iyakkaṉ, that fierce man, and all of my
other friends! And let me no longer reign as king over this land
of the south, distinguished for its ancient lineage that has offered
its protection to mankind! Let me be
instead reborn to rule as protector over the dry lands of foreigners!

The song of Ollaiyūr Tanta Pūtappāṇṭiyaṉ. *Tiṇai: kāñci. Tuṟai: vañcinak kāñci.*

72

How they sicken me when they trumpet, "Those who claim that his land
is a power are laughable. He is too young!" and when they add,
"We have fine tall elephants with enormous legs and imposing feet
who wear tinkling bells that hang down either flank and we have chariots
and we have horses and we have warriors well skilled in the handling
of their weapons!" And so they show no fear of my immense strength
but swollen full of the fury of their enmity to me in their rage
they speak their tiny speeches! If I do not come upon them all gathered
together and drive them to destruction on the stern field of battle
and obliterate their drums, then may those who live under the protection
of my shadow no longer see any shade to which they may turn!
Let them weep and cry out about the cruelty of their king and let
those subject to me rain insults upon my rod of office! And the poets
praised for their great skill, Māṅkuṭi Marutaṉ with his vast and lofty
range of learning as well as all the others as firmly established
as the earth, let them leave my land and sing no more about it! And may
I suffer the loss of my wealth and be unable to help
men who come to me begging, so that those dependent on me are pierced with pain!

The song of Pāṇṭiyaṉ Talaiyālaṅkāṉattuc Ceruveṉṟa Neṭuñceḻiyaṉ. *Tiṇai: kāñci. Tuṟai: vañcinak kāñci.*

73

If they would come quietly and bowing down before my handsome feet
plead with me to give them things, then for me it would be as
nothing to grant them my kingdom and the right to it embodied

in my fine drum! And even if they were to ask for my precious life,
I would grant it to them in this world! But that fool who makes
a joke of my resolution, he who ignores power in the powerful
is like a blind man who stumbles on a sleeping tiger, even though
everyone else has seen him very clearly. Never will that man
escape and return to his own! If I do not march against him and make him
suffer where he stands as if he were a tall trunk of bamboo, strong
and thick but trapped under the feet of a fierce elephant who feeds
on bamboo, then may my garland wither away in the embraces
of many women with thick black hair who do not
respond to me, who carry no love for me within their pure hearts!

The song of Cōḻaṉ Nalaṅkiḷḷi. *Tiṇai: kāñci. Tuṟai: vañcinak kāñci.*

74

If a child was stillborn or what emerged was only a mass of flesh,
though they thought it not yet human my ancestors treated it as such
and as they should, they cut it with a sword! Has it come down
to their descendant sitting and suffering like a dog in chains, unable
to restrain himself, begging to be given a little water through the magnanimity
of people without generosity or to be granted
food that may calm the fire within his belly within this world?

Cēramāṉ Kaṇaikkālirumpoṟai fought with Cōḻaṉ Ceṅkaṇāṉ on the field of Tiruppōrppuṟam, was captured, imprisoned at Kuṭavāyiṟ Kōṭṭam [fortress], asked "Give me water," did not get it, then [when he asked again] did get it, kept it in his hand without drinking, and died. This is his song as he died. *Tiṇai: potuviyal. Tuṟai: mutumoḻikkāñci.*

75

One who is barely a man may think he has gained the right to a kingdom

through the victories of the ancients and that destiny has passed on
sovereignty to him after death has taken all of his ancestors.
And now he towers over other men and implores his subjects
to pay him their taxes. For a ruler like that, the wealth of royal rule
truly is a heavy burden. But with a great man, the riches of his kingdom
seem as light as a dry twig in the hot season on a white, near-weightless
cork tree with its small branches growing by a reservoir where deep water
has dried away, for he has become king through his own efforts, enduring
the thick of battle and he has taken his riches on his own from kings,
ah! with their drums, with their
white umbrellas of royalty rising up stainlessly pure to the sky!

The song of Cōḻaṉ Nalaṅkiḷḷi. *Tiṇai: potuviyal. Tuṟai: potumoḻikkāñci.*

76

For a man to be defeated or slain by another man, one to one,
is nothing at all new. It is the ordinary way of this world.
But we have never heard before today of anything like this!
Because they were ignorant of the might and majesty of Ceḻiyaṉ,
who is beautiful to see as he wears his chaplet and garland
flowing with honey, which is close-woven of strands of the long
balloon vine and of glowing shoots from the large branches
of the margosa tree whose thick trunk grows in the courtyard
and who has his ornament of gold and the riches of his land
and the sweet resounding sound of his clear kiṇai drum,
the seven who wear the anklets of war thought they would unite
and fight him, but when they came against him, he overcame
their fine strength and slew them, by himself on the field of battle!

Iṭaikkuṉṟūrkiḻār sings Pāṇṭiyaṉ Talaiyālaṅkāṉattuc Ceruveṉṟa Neṭuñceḻiyaṉ. *Tiṇai: vākai. Tuṟai: aracavākai.*

77

Standing there in the high chariot with his hand on the resplendent support
formed in the shape of a lotus, with the war anklets shining on his legs
that have shed their anklets of bells, wearing the bright shoots
of margosa strung with the long balloon vine on his head from which
the hair tuft of youth has just been cut, holding a bow in the hand
that has barely lost its tiny bracelets, who is he? May his chaplet flourish!
Though he wears a garland, he has not removed the amulet of childhood
from his neck. Only today is he weaned from milk and begun
on solid food! As new warriors come at him, in fury, one,
then another, he shows no pride, no contempt. And for the fact that
he can grip them tightly, break their balance and bring them down
to the earth and then kill them as the sound of it rises
into the vast sky, he neither rejoices nor does he think it any great thing!

Iṭaikkuṉṟūrkiḻār sings Pāṇṭiyaṉ Talaiyālaṅkāṉattuc Ceruveṉṟa Neṭuñceḻiyaṉ.
Tiṇai: vākai. Tuṟai: aracavākai.

78

They showed no respect for the chest of my lord, which is
as difficult to oppose as a powerful tiger living in a cave
who stretches himself, gets to his feet and emerges after prey,
my lord who is hard to harass, whose strong feet glowing
with their curving joints do not retreat in battle, whose might
is ferocious! They rose up roaring, "We are the best! We are
great! He is very young to fight against us! The spoils will be rich!"
Contemptuous of him they advanced, warriors without worth!
But when they scattered on the battlefield, with their eyes glazing,

he did not kill them there, but before their finely ornamented women
dying of shame, in the cities of their fathers,
to the clear beat of the kiṇai drum, there he went and killed them there!

Iṭaikkuṉṟūrkiḻār sings Pāṇṭiyaṉ Talaiyālaṅkāṉattuc Ceruveṉṟa Neṭuñceḻiyaṉ.
Tiṇai: vākai. Tuṟai: aracavākai.

79

He has bathed in the cool pond at the gate of his ancient city
and has donned bright shoots of margosa from the inner meadow,
and walking, like an elephant, behind the clear beat of the kiṇai drum,
Ceḻiyaṉ has come, he who is ferocious in battle! Against him
stand many warriors without worth.
Will some of them survive, given there is so little daylight left?

Iṭaikkuṉṟūrkiḻār sings Pāṇṭiyaṉ Talaiyālaṅkāṉattuc Ceruveṉṟa Neṭuñceḻiyaṉ.
Tiṇai: vākai. Tuṟai: aracavākai.

80

There in Āmūr, where the toddy is potent and sweet,
one of his legs squeezes the chest of the powerful wrestler
and crushes his vigorous strength while the other leg wrapped
around the back stifles his attempts to break free.
How I wish that Tittaṉ, so difficult to oppose, a winner
of battles, could see this, whether or not it would please him!
Like a famished elephant trying to gobble down bamboo,
at head and foot he twists and snaps the body
of the wrestler who has taken the field, and triumphing, he is killing him!

Cāttantaiyār sings Cōl̲an̲ Pōravaik Kōpperunar̲kiḷḷi when he fought Mukkāval Nāṭṭu Āmūr Mallan̲ [the wrestler/warrior from Āmūr in the land of Mukkāval] and stood there killing him. *Tiṇai: tumpai. Tur̲ai: erumai mar̲am.*

81

There is an uproar louder than the sound of the swelling sea!
The trumpeting of his elephants lasts longer than the monsoon's thunder!
If the warrior who wears a chaplet of laburnum strung tightly on a thread,
whose hand is a cup for giving gifts,
lays his hand on anyone, how that man is to be pitied!

Cāttantaiyār sings Cōl̲an̲ Pōravaik Kōpperunar̲kiḷḷi. *Tiṇai: tumpai. Tur̲ai: aracavākai.*

82

In the hand of a low-caste leather worker stitching a cot,
with a festival impending and his wife in labor and the sun
descending while the rain comes pouring down, as he
pulls thread through and again through, the needle flies!
When the warrior tried to take the city,
the lord who wears a chaplet of laburnum fought with that speed!

Cāttantaiyār sings Cōl̲an̲ Pōravaik Kōpperunar̲kiḷḷi. *Tiṇai: tumpai. Tur̲ai: aracavākai.*

83

Because of the young warrior who wears war anklets on his legs
and whose beard is the color of collyrium, the bangles hang loose

on my arms and I am afraid of my mother. Yet if I should embrace
those shoulders of a warrior, I may be shamed before the assembly!
May this bewildered city tremble as much
as I do, forever, not able to choose, divided between two minds!

Peruṅkōḻi Nāykaṉ Makaḷ Nakkaṇṇaiyār sings Cōḻaṉ Pōravaik Kōpperunaṟkiḷḷi. *Tiṇai: kaikkiḷai. Tuṟai: paḻiccutal.*

84

Though he is forced to live on gruel, my lord has broad shoulders,
and I, though I sit here by his house, am as pale as gold.
If my lord will accept the challenges and will step
onto the fighting field, then in our large and noisy city,
for the warriors who blithely approach him
at the festival, he will be like a road that daunts the merchants of salt!

Peruṅkōḻi Nāykaṉ Makaḷ Nakkaṇṇaiyār sings Cōḻaṉ Pōravaik Kōpperunaṟkiḷḷi. *Tiṇai: kaikkiḷai. Tuṟai: paḻiccutal.*

85

This is not the city here that belongs to my lord!
This is not the land here that belongs to my lord!
And so there are some who are saying, "Victory! Victory!"
And so there are some who are saying, "No victory for him!"
Good then! Two fine opinions voiced by many people!
I ran, to the tinkling of my lovely anklets, and I stood
by my house, leaning on a palmyra tree with its trunk large
as a muḻā drum, and I saw it, that the victory was his!

Peruṅkōḻi Nāykaṉ Makaḷ Nakkaṇṇaiyār sings Cōḻaṉ Pōravaik Kōpperunaṟkiḷḷi. *Tiṇai: kaikkiḷai. Tuṟai: paḻiccutal.*

86

You grasp the fine pillar that holds up my small house
and you ask me "Where is your son?" I do not know
where my son may be. Like a cave of rock
that a tiger inhabited and then abandoned
is this womb which gave birth to him!
You will find him out there somewhere on the battlefield.

The song of Kāvaṟpeṇṭu. *Tiṇai: vākai. Tuṟai: ēṟāṇ mullai.*

87

You, our enemies! Think twice before you come on to the field!
We have a warrior among us who will go against you in battle.
He is like a wheel fashioned with great care
over a month by a craftsman who creates eight chariots a day!

Auvaiyār sings Atiyamāṉ Neṭumāṉ Añci. *Tiṇai: tumpai. Tuṟai: tāṉai maṟam.*

88

Whoever you may be, think twice before you say, "We will fight
and defeat his vanguard and the rest of his army!" That is, before
you have seen my lord who has capped fine battles with festivals,
whose broad and lovely chest shows an elegant ornament from which rays
shoot out—the chief of the young, overpowering warriors
whose long spears glitter and sparkle, with his shoulders like great drums!

Auvaiyār sings Atiyamāṉ Neṭumāṉ Añci. *Tiṇai: tumpai. Tuṟai: tāṉai maṟam.*

89

"Woman of the caste of bards! With your shining forehead and your eyes
darkened by collyrium, with your simple manners and your sloping mons
glowing with a string of jewels, are there any who can fight in your
broad land?" you ask me over and over, king of an army that does battle!
Yes, there are warriors, young and strong, who are like snakes without fear
when struck with a stick and also there is he who whenever he hears
the resonance of the wind striking against the clear-voiced eye
of the taṇṇumai drum wrapped with leather straps
and hanging in the courtyard shouts "To war!" and he is my lord!

Auvaiyār sings Atiyamāṉ Neṭumāṉ Añci. *Tiṇai: tumpai. Tuṟai: tāṉai maṟam.*

90

If a fierce tiger is raging on the slope of a hill
fragrant with leafy jasmine and white lilies blossoming
like broken conches, can a herd of deer linger there?
When the sun begins to blaze, is it possible for darkness
to exist, collected in a quarter of the tangled sky?
Is there any road that can resist the progress of proud oxen,
scattering wet sand and splitting apart rocks as they haul
a wagon of merchandise out of the deep hole in which
it had sunk, the crossbar clashing and grinding on the axle?
Your hand that reaches to your knees is like a crossbar
of strength that cannot fail, O foremost of warriors!
Could anyone throughout this vast earth
take your land and exult, once you have entered the field?

Auvaiyār sings Atiyamāṉ Neṭumāṉ Añci. *Tiṇai: tumpai. Tuṟai: tāṉai maṟam.*

91

King in the line of Atiyaṉs! You who pour out the toddy that makes men roar!
You whose powerful hand with its sliding bracelets triumphs and brandishes
an infallible sword that brings you victory, cutting your enemies down
on the field! Añci of the golden garland, rich in murderous battle!
May you live as long as he lives on whose head the crescent moon
glows, whose neck is as dark blue as sapphires! O greatness!
Without considering how difficult it is to obtain the sweet fruit
of the myrobolan plant with its tiny leaves, which has to be plucked
from a crevice on the summit of an ancient mountain hard to climb,
you kept silence in your heart about its powers,
and so that you might rescue me from death, you gave me that fruit!

Auvaiyār sings Atiyamāṉ Neṭumāṉ Añci after getting the nelli fruit [from him]. *Tiṇai: pāṭāṇṭiṇai. Tuṟai: vāḻttiyal.*

92

Their tenses all wrong and no way to know their meaning,
they are no match for music played on the yāḻ, but yet
the babbled words of a son will still fill a father with love.
O Neṭumāṉ Añci, you who have seized many fortresses, their walls
guarded by soldiers, just like those words
are the words that come out of my mouth, since they make you feel love!

Auvaiyār sings Atiyamāṉ Neṭumāṉ Añci. *Tiṇai: pāṭāṇṭiṇai. Tuṟai: iyaṉmoḻi.*

93

In the forward march of battle, with the royal drum enwrapped in thongs

roaring, how can there be any victory left to be won? They came
but could not stand against your vanguard. They scattered and they ran!
Kings without majesty, they evaded what would have been done
had their deaths come naturally, of sickness, and their bodies taken
to be laid out on ever green grass of the finest kind by Brahmins
schooled in the Four Vedas and the principles of Righteousness,
who would have then chanted, "Go to where the great warriors go!
those who wear their splendid war anklets, those who have died
in a good battle and kept faith in their manhood!" and forgetting
any love they may have had for them, they would have then wounded
the bodies with the sword so as to free them of sin and buried them.
But no! Because you, great and wonderful! slaying, scattering the battle
around you as elephants fell on the killing field, the juices of their musth
flowing into their mouths where dragonflies
were humming, you sustained a noble wound while you were charging forward!

Auvaiyār sings Atiyamāṉ Neṭumāṉ Añci when he fought and received a wound. *Tiṇai: vākai. Tuṟai: aracavākai.*

94

As is a great elephant settling into the water to clean
his white tusks at a bathing site for the little children
of a town, so sweet you are for us, O greatness! But like
that elephant when he has entered into rut,
dangerous to touch, O greatness, you are other than sweet to your enemies!

Auvaiyār sings Atiyamāṉ Neṭumāṉ Añci. *Tiṇai: vākai. Tuṟai: aracavākai.*

95

These are adorned with feathers of the peacock and encircled by garlands
and have strong, thick, well-fashioned shafts and are anointed with ghee
while they repose in a sprawling, well-guarded palace; but those spears,
with their blades and joints broken when they pierced enemies, are always
to be found in the blacksmith's small shed, for he who is lord
and chieftain of those who gather in need,
who grants food when there is plenty
and when there is not will share his own,
our king owns those spears that are tipped with sharp blades!

Auvaiyār, sent by Atiyamāṉ Neṭumāṉ Añci as an envoy to Toṇṭaimāṉ, sang this when he showed her his armory. *Tiṇai: pāṭāṇṭiṇai. Tuṟai: vāṇ maṅkalam.*

96

For my lord's son around whose handsome, powerful chest
are strung opening blossoms of the tumpai flower, he whose hands
are strong and heavy, two enemies have been aroused. The first
are the women who gaze at him entranced until their arms
grow slender, and the flowers of their eyes darkened with collyrium
pale. And for the other—because they fear that his elephants
may drink water from their reservoirs and because his retinue, even
when there are no festivals, eats the meat of sheep
and expects cooked food, the cities he visits hate having him linger there!

Auvaiyār sings Atiyamāṉ Neṭumāṉ Añci's son Pokuṭṭeḻiṉi. *Tiṇai: pāṭāṇṭiṇai. Tuṟai: iyaṉmoḻi.*

97

Drawn swords in their battle lust have swept forward
as they broke through the garrisoned walls and then went
twisting out of shape, buried in flesh. Spears,
conquering the fortresses of his enemies, have ravaged
the land densely fragrant with toddy
and have ruined themselves, the nails shattered
on their dark, hollowed shafts. Charging
at gates bolstered by crossbeams, his elephants, shaking loose
the heavy ornamental rings tightened around their tusks, have battered
their way into the fortress against troops of enemy elephants.
Spread across the field, his horses attack and they destroy
the golden garlands of the warriors who stand massed against them,
while their hooves, laboring on the battleground, are stained with blood.
He himself, with his army like the ocean that encircles the earth,
wears a garland of golden tumpai blossoms and carries a shield
pierced by arrowheads that leave marks like leg rings and like tiny bowls.
How can those who draw his anger escape? Let me tell you
that if you wish to hold your fine and ancient city
where the ears of thick-stemmed paddy intertwine,
you must go and pay him tribute. Should you refuse,
he who is a conqueror in battle will not let it pass.
If you will not believe me, then do not wonder when you
will have to leave the arms of your tender women who wear small bangles
and a cluster of braids hanging down curled by a twisting jewel
in the shape of a fruit. Now that you have learned this, fight your war!

Auvaiyār sings Atiyamāṉ Neṭumāṉ Añci. *Tiṇai: pāṭāṇṭiṇai. Tuṟai: iyaṉmoḻi.*

98

When they saw your elephants moving, battling
and blunting their tusk tips in quenching
the furious bravery of frontline enemies,
they set new gates and crossbars in their walls.
When they saw your thoroughbred horses, laboring to advance
on stained hooves that tore at the bodies trampled
on the field, they blocked up the paths in their forests
with forked stakes. When they saw your spears, never
at rest in their scabbards of hide but flying through
the chests of men, they strengthened the handles
on the shafts of their shields. When they saw the Martial
Courage of your raging soldiers covered with sword wounds,
they thrust into quivers arrows still bloody from recent hits.
You who do not even protect yourself with the smoke
of mustard seed, you are like Death who will always move swiftly
from behind and will strike in an instant to carry away the life!
Those who do not praise you, will they not be plunged into grief
when their far-flung territories flowing with abundant water
and the paddy dipping and trembling as far
as the farthest ridges of the fields are turned to wasteland?

Auvaiyār sings Atiyamāṉ Neṭumāṉ Añci. *Tiṇai: vākai* and/or *vañci. Tuṟai: aracavākai* and/or *koṟṟavaḷḷai.*

99

As did the ancient lineage of your ancestors who served the gods
and offered oblations and secured the gift, hard to gain, of sugarcane
for this world and rolled the wheel of their power around
the earth that is surrounded by the ocean, you inherited by right
the war anklet of fine gold you wear on your leg, the garland
of flourishing palmyra, your garden filled with flowers, the long
spear

stained from recent passage through flesh, the seven symbols, and your
precious, immutable title to the land. But these were not enough for you
and you advanced against the seven kings with their great drums
resounding! Eager for war, you attacked and you showed your power
in victory on that day. The singers could not sing at the height
you warrant! But Paraṇaṉ now has sung of you, of your arms
with which you held the discus that destroys
strongholds and that demolished fiercely inimical Kōvalūr!

Auvaiyār sings Atiyamāṉ Neṭumāṉ Añci when he attacked Kōvalūr. *Tiṇai: vākai. Tuṟai: aracavākai.*

100

In his hand he holds a spear. On his legs he wears war anklets.
On his body there is sweat. On his neck is a fresh wound.
Shining on the curls of his black hair are needlelike leaves
from the height of a young palmyra palm and he wears them entwined
with huge blossoms of veṭci and with flowers of the vēṅkai tree.
His enemies flee the sight of them! It is as if he were
some mighty elephant that has just come back from battle
with a tiger, so that the rage he has felt has not yet
left him. Ah! For those who aroused his anger,
there was no escape! The eyes that saw
his enemies still are crimsoned even though they see his small son!

Auvaiyār sings Atiyamāṉ Neṭumāṉ Añci when he saw his beloved son born. *Tiṇai: vākai. Tuṟai: aracavākai.*

101

Not for one day did we go to him, not for two days did we go to him,

but though we brought many along with us and stayed for many days,
he seemed as eager to welcome us as he was on the first day!
When we receive gifts from Atiyamāṉ who owns fine chariots
and elephants adorned with ornaments, no matter whether he takes
more or less time to give, the presents are already there, they
are in our hands! as if a ball of food had been left
between an elephant's tusks! He will not fail us. O my heart,
you who worry about food! No more
need for you to suffer! May all his efforts prosper!

Auvaiyār sings Atiyamāṉ Neṭumāṉ Añci. *Tiṇai: pāṭāṇṭiṇai. Tuṟai: paricil kaṭānilai.*

102

Those who sell salt carry a spare axle with them lashed
to the wood underneath because they think about oxen
who are young and unacquainted with the yoke, about a heavy load
in the wagon which must pass over heights and travel low ground
and who knows what might happen? You, so bright with glory are like
that axle, your hand a cup for giving to others! Greatness!
You are like the moon at the time when it is full!
How can there be darkness for those living under its radiance?

Auvaiyār sings Atiyamāṉ Neṭumāṉ Añci's son Pokuṭṭeḻiṉi. *Tiṇai: pāṭāṇṭiṇai. Tuṟai: iyaṉmoḻi.*

103

Woman of the caste of bards, you whose bangles are so few
in the wasteland! You carry a patalai drum slung to one side
and on the other side hangs a small muḻā drum, hollow
within, while you wonder who can turn this dish right
side up? If you will go to him, he is not far away!

He is in the land of his enemies where from the burning
battle zone, a mass of black smoke surrounds
the young elephants, like a cloud around mountains!
Añci of the many spears, even when times are hard,
can keep dishes so moist with rich fat it looks as if
they hold soft meal cakes baked of wax
and they never have any time to dry! May all his efforts prosper!

Auvaiyār sings Atiyamāṉ Neṭumāṉ Añci. *Tiṇai: pāṭāṇṭiṇai. Tuṟai: viṟaliyāṟṟuppaṭai.*

104

You warriors! Take care of yourselves! Let us tell you
my lord is like a crocodile who in shallow water muddied
by the playing of children from the city, can drag in, bring down,
and slaughter an elephant, with the water only knee deep! If you forget
his many resourceful acts and despise him
as "no more than a young man," then victory will come hard for you!

Auvaiyār sings Atiyamāṉ Neṭumāṉ Añci. *Tiṇai: vākai. Tuṟai: aracavākai.*

105

Woman of the caste of bards, whose face glows! When trailing
down in a cascade from all the peaks of a mountain where
rope ladders hang and running through canals in the wide fields
plowed for horse gram, so that it does not matter if it fails to rain
or does rain, to leave cool drops on the fresh flowers of blue waterlilies,
their dark petals swarming with bees at the surface of mountain pools—

water is less sweet than the grace of Vēḷ Pāri
from whom you will win a crimson ornament if you go to him and sing!

Kapilar sings Vēḷ Pāri. *Tiṇai: pāṭāṇṭiṇai. Tuṟai: viṟaliyāṟṟuppaṭai.*

106

The gods will not disdain whatever people bring them,
even the erukkam flower, a middling thing, neither good
nor bad, with its tight clusters and its brownish leaves.
And so if there are soft, foolish people
who go to lord Pāri, he will reward them because he is a generous man!

Kapilar sings Vēḷ Pāri. *Tiṇai: pāṭāṇṭiṇai. Tuṟai: iyaṉmoḻi.*

107

"Pāri! Pāri!" they say, and with their eloquent tongues
the bards praise one man and sing of his many strengths.
But more than only Pāri matters.
The monsoons too are here to preserve the world!

Kapilar sings Vēḷ Pāri. *Tiṇai: pāṭāṇṭiṇai. Tuṟai: iyaṉmoḻi.*

108

Since dried ends of sticks have been set out by a Kuṟavar woman
and they are of sandalwood, their fragrant smoke is spreading
through the branches of flowering vēṅkai on the slope near Paṟampu,

which belongs to those who sing. Nor will Pāri, Righteousness
his mantle, refuse to submit to them if only
their request is respectful, as if they were coming to him in need!

Kapilar sings Vēḷ Pāri. *Tiṇai: pāṭāṇṭiṇai. Tuṟai: iyaṉmoḻi.*

109

Of course, Pāri's city of Paṟampu is a miserable place!
Even if you three with your great royal drums should all
besiege it, four crops flourish there with no need of farmers!
For the first—from bamboo, with its tiny leaves, a rice springs up,
and the second, with its sweet pulp, is the ripening jackfruit,
and third, thickly growing, is the vaḷḷi root with its luxuriant vine,
and the fourth is honey, with its lovely darkness pouring out,
the color overwhelming the peak of the tall mountain dense with
vines!
Like the sky is his mountain and in that sky the springs
are like stars! Though you have your elephants tied up
to every tree there, though your chariots are spread across
every field, he will not be overcome through any
of your efforts! Swords will not force him to yield.
But I do know how you can capture his land! If you should just
play on a small yāḻ with its tensed, polished strings
while your women of the caste of bards, with their rich, fragrant
hair,
follow you, and you come dancing and singing,
he will yield his country to you then and his mountain!

Kapilar sings Vēḷ Pāri. *Tiṇai: nocci. Tuṟai: makaṇ maṟuttal.*

110

Though the three of you with your murderous and victorious armies
unite in your enmity, Paṟampu will be very difficult to take!
There are three hundred villages in the good land

of cool Pa̲rampu, and all three hundred belong to those who have
come to him in their need! But if you will go
and you will sing to him, you win us and Pāri and his mountain!

Kapilar sings the three kings [Chera, Chola, Pandya] when they laid siege to Parampu. *Tiṇai: nocci. Tuṟai: makaṇ maṟuttal.*

111

Of course the great dark hill is a miserable place!
To conquer it by the spear would be hard for kings
but easy to win for a woman with a drum, her blackened eyes
like two blue waterlilies, if she comes to it singing!

Kapilar sings Vēḷ Pāri. *Tiṇai: nocci. Tuṟai: makaṇ maṟuttal.*

112

On that day, under the white light of that moon,
we had our father and no enemies had taken the hill.
On this day, under the white light of this moon, the kings,
royal drums beating out the victory,
have taken the hill. And we! we have no father.

The song of Pāri's daughters. *Tiṇai: potuviyal. Tuṟai: kaiyaṟunilai.*

113

Once there was friendship in you, and a profusion of wealth
to be used for giving rice when asked and fried and stewed meat,
cooked and never ending, while jars of liquor were opened
and male goats were slaughtered; but now, since Pāri is gone,
I am bewildered and there is nothing I can do. My eyes
stream with tears and I bow down to you and salute you,
far-famed Paṟampu! and I go, and as I go I wonder

what men will have the right to touch the black
fragrant hair of the girls who wear long rows of engraved bangles?

The song of Kapilar as he took leave of Paṟampu as he went to entrust Pāri's daughters to the care of Brahmins. *Tiṇai: potuviyal. Tuṟai: kaiyaṟunilai.*

114

It rises up for those standing here, and if you walk
a little way and stand there, O how sadly it rises,
where once the courtyards flowed with the fermenting
sap from masses of sugarcane fiber pressed out
as if they were balls chewed by elephants,
the hill of the lord who used to freely give away chariots!

The song of Kapilar as he stood looking at Paṟampu while he took Pāri's daughters [away from there]. *Tiṇai: potuviyal. Tuṟai: kaiyaṟunilai.*

115

On one side, the sound of a waterfall. On the other,
filtered, clear, sweet toddy, eager to fill the bowls of bards,
poured out and spilling and flowing, carrying along stones!
All that, as it was, is gone now on the hill
of the kindly lord who was ferocious
to kings who commanded many spears and mighty elephants.

Kapilar sings Vēḷ Pāri. *Tiṇai: potuviyal. Tuṟai: kaiyaṟunilai.*

116

Skirts of waterlilies sway across their thighs, made of full-blown
blossoms that grew in large, deep springs where the water is sweet.
With their cool and beautiful eyes, their light laughter, the girls

climb up on a heap covered with dwarf date palm, where sponge gourd
has rooted and calabash has spread, near a hut that has cotton
growing in the front yard, and there is a fence of thorns and near it
are twisting paths choked up with grass, and standing there on the mound,
they count the wagons that carry the salt for the salt merchants.
I feel pain and how I wish that my life were over! There was a time
when they would climb the highest peak on the wide mountain
where prosperity was unending and the peacocks would rise up
and dance in gardens of cultivated flowers while on the great slopes
planted with crops, there were monkeys that were swinging and leaping,
and trees gave fruit in and out of season, so many that the monkeys
could not take them all; and as the kings with their great armies
came against the hill in war, ignorant of how difficult it would be
to prevail against their father Pāri, he who wielded a sharp spear,
he who was the master of abundant toddy,
from the peak the girls would count the proud horses bearing the iron weapons of kings!

Kapilar sings Vēḷ Pāri. *Tiṇai: potuviyal. Tuṟai: kaiyaṟunilai.*

117

Even if the Black Planet turned the color of smoke or a comet should appear,
or the Silver Planet were to pass across the sky of the south,
still the fields were full of grain, the bushes blossomed with flowers,
and in a long line, wild cows with their huge eyes
who had calved right alongside the houses were grazing
on good grass, and the rains never failed because there were
so many noble men attracted by benevolent government,
even though the land lies in a dry zone, where jasmine with its green leaves

blooms like the sharp teeth of a kitten,
there where the father of the girls with fine bangles was king!

Kapilar sings Vēḷ Pāri. *Tiṇai: potuviyal. Tuṟai: kaiyaṟunilai.*

118

That small reservoir with its clear water and its sloping
shore like a half moon running along hills and knolls
now is shattered in the land that was once governed
from cool Paṟampu by Pāri who gave
chariots away and whose massive arm held a sharp spear.

Kapilar sings Vēḷ Pāri. *Tiṇai: potuviyal. Tuṟai: kaiyaṟunilai.*

119

Where, during the time sweet to the eyes when the monsoon rains poured down
and the flowers of the teṟuḻ vines bloomed like ornamental paint
on the faces of elephants, and there was curry with tamarind and sweet
buttermilk and termites from their red mounds and a wealth of soft millet,
there where the generous lord gave more than other kings with royal drums
to those who came in need to him, he who was like
a single tree on a long shadowless road—is that land ruined?

Kapilar sings Vēḷ Pāri. *Tiṇai: potuviyal. Tuṟai: kaiyaṟunilai.*

120

In the fields on the red hills where the monsoon has brought
abundant moisture, though vēṅkai trees had grown there before

in the intense heat, they plow many furrows and mix in the dust
and do their planting, and when the many stems spring up mingled
with palli weed, they root out those weeds so that the ears
flourish and grow big, and then when the dark stalks rise high,
the color of a peahen that has just given birth, and are dry
at top and base, they cut the fresh common millet that has grown
so very well and they cut the little millet, and then when the green
sesame seed blackens, it becomes time to reap the white pods
of the densely growing bean vines and in every household, in the huts
roofed with grass, they share the clarified toddy that had been buried
and matured in liquor jars, and frying kaṭalai seeds in fragrant ghee,
they cook their rice. And the woman of the house with her long arms
serves out the food so that people can mix it up together and eat it
from large plates, in that land ruled by the man who resembles Murugan,
the man who longs for war, who has listened to the clatter
of the war anklets of his enemies running from him, the man used to being sung
without end by poets, the father of the girls with luxuriant black hair,
his land where waving bamboo rustles on the peaks,
is his land of such wealth that no one ever feels pain now destroyed?

Kapilar sings Vēḷ Pāri. *Tiṇai: potuviyal. Tuṟai: kaiyaṟunilai.*

121

Thinking of one man, one direction to go, many men
come to you in their need, from the four directions!
Greatly generous lord, it is hard to know how deserving
they may be and giving gifts is an easy thing to do.
But once you really weigh their worth,
then you will stop judging all poets as somehow the same!

Kapilar sings Malaiyamāṉ Tirumuṭik Kāri. *Tiṇai: potuviyal. Tuṟai: poruṇmoḻikkāñci.*

122

The sea cannot overwhelm it nor your enemies try to seize it!
Kāri! You who wear the anklets of war on your handsome feet!
Your land belongs to the Brahmins who tend the sacred fires!
If ever one of the three kings requires your alliance,
presents brought to you then by his emissaries with their
wishes that your power may flourish become the property
of those who come to you in need and praise your ancestry!
Other than the arms of your woman who speaks so softly,
who is as faithful as Arundhatī,
there is nothing you call your own, and you are the greater because of it!

Kapilar sings Malaiyamāṉ Tirumuṭik Kāri. *Tiṇai: pāṭāṇṭiṇai. Tuṟai: iyaṉmoḻi.*

123

If someone takes his seat every morning in his court
and drinks himself blissfully drunk, it's a simple thing
then to give away chariots! But Malaiyaṉ, whose good name glows
and is never diminished, even without getting delightfully drunk,
gives away more lofty, ornamented chariots
than the drops of rain that fall on fertile Muḷḷūr Mountain!

Kapilar sings Malaiyamāṉ Tirumuṭik Kāri. *Tiṇai: pāṭāṇṭiṇai. Tuṟai: iyaṉmoḻi.*

124

Even if they go on the wrong day, even if evil omens
harass them, even if they enter at a bad time and say things
they should not say, they will not return with empty hands
if they sing their praises of him
who has a great mountain with roaring, evenly descending waterfalls!

Kapilar sings Malaiyamāṉ Tirumuṭik Kāri. *Tiṇai: pāṭāṇṭiṇai. Tuṟai: iyaṉmoḻi.*

125

So that we may, again and again, drink down
great jars of toddy after eating succulent chunks of meat
layered with fat that calms raging fire and looks like the cotton
women spin, for that I have come to see you, my lord!
And may the toddy you yourself then swallow
with such gusto in your happy home, like a strong ox
eating its hay after plowing, O powerful hero who overcomes
the power of your enemies! may that toddy be the finest amṛta!
The victor who slew and who triumphed as the elephants
fell dead like so many mountains praises you
when he says, "He gave us victory!" and the defeated—
as he thinks that had it not been for Malaiyaṉ with his strong spear
who came swiftly onto the field, his handsome legs glowing
with the anklets of war and turned the fighting around,
O how easy it would have been for them to win the battle!—
he praises you as well when he says, "It was he
who made us lose!" and so, O greatness!
like holy Murugan on whose high mountain
the great rain clouds make their home,
for whoever has any stake in you, you are always one and the same!

When Cēramāṉ Māntarañcēral Irumpoṟai and Cōḻaṉ Irācacūyam Vēṭṭa Perunaṟkiḷḷi were fighting, Tērvaṇ Malaiyaṉ [i.e. Malaiyamāṉ Tirumuṭik Kāri, according to D.] aided the Chola king. Vaṭama Vaṇṇakkaṉ Peruñcāttaṉār sang this song to him. *Tiṇai: vākai. Tuṟai: aracavākai.*

126

You are descended from the lord whose steadfast rule was never
to run away, that man of eminence who seized gold from the
ornaments
on the foreheads of enemy elephants and then made the foreheads
of bards glow, adorning them with golden lotuses that do not fade!
Lord of Muḷḷūr, where the waterfalls roar like drums of war
and a small forest seems to be sleeping through nights with its

dense darkness, though the Brahmin Kapilar, he of purest knowledge
among all the people of the world, already has sung about you
so that your wide-spreading fame will endure, so that you will become
ever more prosperous along with your family that can never be destroyed,
and there is really no room any more for bards who have come to you
in their need—nevertheless on the instant we sing your praises!
And therefore we are like boats in the western ocean that belong
to some lord other then Cēraṉ who commands his raging armies
and runs his ships that carry gold so that no other vessels dare
to travel those waters! Spurred by our need and invited by
your glory, we take on the task of singing about your virtues,
beginning with your generosity. You who attack as the drums
resound like the thunder that destroys snakes with their fangs
like thorns, you who demolish bitter onslaughts while kings
die on the field of battle together with their finest elephants,
you who repel the assaults of enemies
who won't join you, lord of the land that holds the lovely Peṇṇai River!

Māṟōkkattu Nappacalaiyār sings Malaiyamāṉ Tirumuṭik Kāri. *Tiṇai: pāṭāṇṭiṇai. Tuṟai: paricirruṟai.*

127

The bards who sing their honeyed songs to the small yāḻ
with its body round and dark like a berry on a kaḷam bush
have left now, and beside the high hitching stakes, flocks
of forest peacocks linger as the elephants are all gone!
They say Āy's women retain no ornaments except their marriage tālis,
which cannot be given as gifts, that his palace falls into disrepair
unlike the palaces of those who have no renown spreading

across the world, those who fill their bellies with spiced rice
sweet to the tongue, those
kings with their war drums who give nothing away to others!

Uṟaiyūr Ēṇiccēri Muṭamōciyār sings Āy. *Tiṇai: pāṭāṇṭiṇai. Tuṟai: kaṭainilai.*

128

On Poti Mountain, the realm of Āy who wears sliding bracelets,
in the giant branches of the jack tree growing in his courtyard,
a monkey, thinking it a fruit, beats on the clear, sweet-singing
eye of a drum left hanging there by some who traveled to him
in their need and a wild goose calls out as if keeping time!
Unless a woman will approach it dancing,
mighty kings have no hope of ever coming near that hill!

Uṟaiyūr Ēṇiccēri Muṭamōciyār sings Āy. *Tiṇai: pāṭāṇṭiṇai. Tuṟai: vāḻttu* and/or *iyaṉmoḻi.*

129

He is the lord of the great mountain where jack trees grow
with their sweet-pulped fruit, where Kuṟuvaṉs turn blissful
on aged liquor poured out for them through curving bamboo tubes
within their huts with eaves barely overhanging and then out
in a courtyard beside a vēṅkai tree they dance the kuravai dance. If
for Āy Aṇṭiraṉ who leads in murderous war, the unclouded sky were
to blossom
into stars without end, turning all white, the black holes vanishing,
it would be like the elephants he has granted
those who came to him in need or would at the least bear some
resemblance!

Uṟaiyūr Ēṇiccēri Muṭamōciyār sings Āy. *Tiṇai: pāṭāṇṭiṇai. Tuṟai: iyaṉmoḻi.*

130

Āy, you whose curving necklace glitters with its sapphires!
Within your land do the young elephant cows give birth
to ten calves at once? When I try to number the fine elephants
you have given away with an open, smiling face to those who came
singing of you and your mountain, they sum up to even more
than the spears that were thrown down
on the day you routed the Koṅkaṉs up to the shore of the western ocean!

Uṟaiyūr Ēṇiccēri Muṭamōciyār sings Āy. *Tiṇai: pāṭāṇṭiṇai. Tuṟai: iyaṉmoḻi.*

131

Did it sing praises for the hill of Aṇṭiraṉ with his chaplet
of vaḻai flowers, whose spear never fails, who is lord
of the great mountain where massed clouds come
and settle, that this small and lovely forest holds so many elephants?

Uṟaiyūr Ēṇiccēri Muṭamōciyār sings Āy. *Tiṇai: pāṭāṇṭiṇai. Tuṟai: iyaṉmoḻi.*

132

First I thought of others and only then I thought of him
and so may my heart sink, may my tongue be cut out
and my ears be stopped up like wells in a deserted city!
If it were not for Himālaya touching the sky in the north
where in the cool shade of a takaram tree a yak is sleeping
with his beloved after having fed on bitter oranges and sweet-smelling grass
and drunk from a fresh spring that is filled with waterlilies—
in the south if it were not for the lineage of Āy,
surely this wide world would slide loose and turn upside down!

Uṟaiyūr Ēṇiccēri Muṭamōciyār sings Āy. *Tiṇai: pāṭāṇṭiṇai. Tuṟai: iyaṉmoḻi.*

133

Dancing woman, delicate by nature, only with your ears
have you heard of his great fame, but you have never seen him!
Should you wish to catch sight of him, then walking so you seem
a peacock with its spreading feathers, the mountain wind
blowing through the fullness of your sweet-smelling hair,
go and see Āy who has chariots
and generosity like a cloud that releases its rain!

Uṟaiyūr Ēṇiccēri Muṭamōciyār sings Āy. *Tiṇai: pāṭāṇṭiṇai. Tuṟai: viṟaliyāṟṟuppaṭai.*

134

Āy is no businessman trading in virtue for his own profit,
thinking what he does in this birth will serve him in his next,
but because before him other noble men
have followed this right path, his generosity is what it is!

Uṟaiyūr Ēṇiccēri Muṭamōciyār sings Āy. *Tiṇai: pāṭāṇṭiṇai. Tuṟai: iyaṉmoḻi.*

135

With my wife, the dancer decked with bangles following after me
and struggling to climb the narrow paths, their crevices hard to cross
in the high mountains where tigers wander, her body stooped over
and taking only short steps because she has already walked too
much,
I have come, my king! since I have thought of your great fame
that has spread far, and at my side, with my heart uneasy,
I have cradled my small yāḻ, its strings like stretched wires of gold
tightened, full of singing melody when I play the rāgas across
all the landscapes but more than any other the paṭumalai rāga that
firmly

resides upon this instrument through whose full use I live!
Lord of the mountain! Āy! Great descendant of the Vēḷir lineage!
Whenever you notice within your court those who have come to you
in need, you give them crowds of elephants with feet large as mortars
and you also give them the calves. I do not want an elephant
nor a horse nor a chariot harnessed to a horse with shining
golden fittings! When such as bards and singers and those who have come
in their need to you gather in your gifts and make them their own,
you who truly know how riches bear fruit never consider thinking
that those things are yours and taking them back! I have come for nothing
but to see you! lord of a land widely praised,
you who have the power to overcome the onslaughts of enemies.

Uṟaiyūr Ēṇiccēri Muṭamōciyār sings Āy. *Tiṇai: pāṭāṇṭiṇai. Tuṟai: pariciṟṟuṟai.*

136

The lice are an enemy! They're all over us,
their eggs securely laid within the hollows
of the seams of our clothes that have been sewn
and resewn with so many threads they might as well be
the bowls of our yāḻs, where the strings hang down!
And hunger is an enemy, a ferocious one,
pursuing me and pursuing my family,
so that we sweat and our eyes water,
our flesh wastes away from lack of food!
And the bandits, men who steal like monkeys,
fierce and greedy and spread throughout
the coolness of the mountain dense with trees,
they are one more enemy, oblivious to our state,
who demand what we may have and blight our lives!
But praising you we have filled our mouths with your name,
believing that Āy will understand who are

our enemies! We have trusted in your glory!
We have climbed up through the wasteland
under the blazing sun and we have come to you
with great desire! Those who give to such
as us truly give away their wealth while
giving to others is only giving back to themselves!
All that I have to say has been said. You now determine
what is right for you. Give us gifts and send us
away! "May your years outnumber the grains of fine sand at the ford
of Tuṟaiyūr where the sluices run with cool water!"
every day we will sing, in praise of you, and consume the plenty that
you grant us!

Tuṟaiyūr Ōṭaikiḻār sings Āy. *Tiṇai: pāṭāṇṭiṇai. Tuṟai: paricilkaṭānilai.*

137

I no longer have any will to sing of the three kings,
of their victories, their territories along the shores of the ocean,
of their herds of elephants and their roaring royal drums.
But you are still the same man I knew before. The lord of Nāñcil!
on whose land there are handsome mountains where seeds
sown in reservoirs full of water do not die of drought
but spring up like sugarcane stems, and where the rains
open flowers as wide as the eyes of women
even under blazing summer sun and where every day the flowing
of the river, clear as a pearl, bears the blossoms
of golden vēṅkai on their black stalks to the sea!
And in your land there are small cascades
of white water falling and one towering mountain!
May you live a long life! May that
father and mother who gave birth to you live a long life!

Oruciṟaip Periyaṉār sings Nāñcil Vaḷḷuvaṉ. *Tiṇai: pāṭāṇṭiṇai. Tuṟai: iyaṉmoḻi* and/or *pariciṟṟuṟai.*

138

Bard with your clothes torn to rags, old man
carrying your small yāḻ with its resounding voice
who were so intent on coming here, who moved across
many paths dense with cattle, passed over so many
mountains dense with deer and waded through many fords
filled with their fish, you have the fine idea of leaving
to seek out the king! But your lord won't just say "Come again."
Like tall ears of millet in a broad field where on trees
the parrots sit and wait is that husband of women
with lush dark hair and adorned with costly ornaments!
Who will even know you when you return?

Marutaṉ Iḷanākaṉār sings Nāñcil Vaḷḷuvaṉ. *Tiṇai: pāṭāṇtiṇai. Tuṟai: pāṇāṟṟuppaṭai.*

139

Though I have to make a living for the many
young girls who wear their double braids,
whose shoulders are scored from all their carrying,
and for my dancing women too, waists as thin
as vines and their feet aching from the long climb,
I will tell you the truth and not lie to you!
You, lord of Nāñcil mountain with its towering summit, whose lineage
counts men of power who were never false to their commitments!
Conscious of the need to grant me a gift, your heart maintaining
that will, there is no time for you to wait for just
the right moment! Because you have no fear at all of dying
for the good of your king, he who is always generous!
And since that is so, suppose a time of terrible battle
comes one day like the world
torn out of place? My family as it suffers with hunger would mourn!

Marutaṉ Iḷanākaṉār sings Nāñcil Vaḷḷuvaṉ. *Tiṇai: pāṭāṇṭiṇai. Tuṟai: paricil kaṭānilai.*

140

Poets whose tongues sing with eloquence! Isn't the lord
of Nāñcil Mountain where giant jackfruit grow a fool?
What I asked of him was only a little bit of rice
so that my dancing women adorned with their bangles
might cook it with the leaves they plucked in the rear yard.
But he knew of my value and he knew his own stature
and he gave me a giant elephant like a hill that towers
over vast surrounding wasteland! Can one so much as imagine
a more lopsided gesture of liberality?
Don't great men when they are generous show any proportion?

Auvaiyār sings Nāñcil Vaḷḷuvaṉ. *Tiṇai: pāṭāṇṭiṇai. Tuṟai: paricil viṭai.*

141

You who are in need, who travel seeking help, with your
fierce hunger and your family burned black under the sun,
you keep asking us over and over, "Who are you who halt
in this wasteland as if it were home, unhitching
tall chariots from fine horses while the garland
of the bard shines with new gold and the garland
of the dancing woman who wears rich ornaments glitters?"
We were worse off than you before we visited the lord
whose spear wins victories. And look at us now!
Our king, Pēkaṉ, who has horses, who has elephants
flowing with musth, once gave a garment to a peacock
in the rain, though he knows they don't wear clothes!
Because he feels the poverty of others, because it is
a virtue to give what one can, he is generous

and not at all for the sake of a better birth in his next life!

Paraṇar sings Vaiyāvik Kōpperum Pēkaṉ. *Tiṇai: pāṭāṇṭiṇai. Tuṟai: pāṇāṟṟuppaṭai* and / or *pulavarāṟṟuppaṭai.*

142

Like the clouds who form part of an endless family
raining down on the dry reservoirs, on the wide fields,
even on arid salt flats rather than where they might be useful,
with his elephants in rut, war anklets on his feet, this is
Pēkaṉ! Ignorant though he is of how to grant gifts,
marching against an enemy army no ignorance marches with him!

Paraṇar sings Vaiyāvik Kōpperum Pēkaṉ. *Tiṇai: pāṭāṇṭiṇai. Tuṟai: iyaṉmoḻi.*

143

Lord of a land where on the slopes the Kuṟavaṉs offer a profusion
of sacrifices so as to draw the clouds around their mountain
and when those clouds will not stop pouring rain they pray
to their god to drive the clouds away and then, contented
at the vanishing of the rain, consume millet in their fields!
Pēkaṉ of the swift horses! you who rage in war, you who generously
grant gifts! Who may that poor woman be? When yesterday
because of the suffering of my family who had been wandering
in their hunger through the wasteland, I came to your door
in this town upon a great towering mountain where a waterfall
roars like a royal drum of war being struck with sticks,
where I praised you and sang of you and your mountain,
she was there, not able to hold back a fierce flowing of tears
and her breast turned wet from the sobbing
as she went on crying and crying with a sound like a sad flute!

Kapilar sings Vaiyāvik Kōpperum Pēkaṉ because of [his wife] Kaṇṇaki, whom he abandoned. *Tiṇai: peruntiṇai. Tuṟai: kuṟuṅkali* and/or *tāpata nilai.*

144

How can you be so coldly cruel, so without compassion?
As we were playing our small yāḻs in the cevvaḻi rāga of longing
and singing of your forest, the look of it during the monsoon!
we saw a young woman in grief that seemed to have no end,
her darkened eyes glowing like dusky, fragrant waterlilies but overflowing
with tears that fell to wet her breasts adorned with their ornamentation.
Bowing down to her, we asked of her, "Young woman! Are you
some relation to the lord who wants us to be with him?"
With her fingers like budding red kāntaḷ flowers she brushed
away her tears and then said to us, "I am no relation of his!
Hear me out! Pēkaṉ, whose fame glows, hungers for the beauty,
they say, of another woman who resembles me and in his resounding
chariot he pays his frequent visits
to the lovely city that is all encircled with jasmine!"

Paraṇar sings Vaiyāvik Kōpperum Pēkaṉ because of [his wife] Kaṇṇaki, whom he abandoned. *Tiṇai: peruntiṇai. Tuṟai: kuṟuṅkali* and/or *tāpata nilai.*

145

With your elephants in rut, with your proud horses, with your fame
that does not fade, Pēkaṉ, you who gave clothing to the dark
mindless peacock in compassion because it was shivering with the cold!
I come to you not because I am hungry, not because of the burden
of my family! But the gift for which I beg is that tonight
you may mount your chariot strung with bells and free her

of the anguish she lives with, and for that I sing "May those
who love mercy act with justice!" while I play on my small yāḻ
black as a kaḷam berry, keeping
those who love the music swaying to the rhythm.

Paraṇar sings Vaiyāvik Kōpperum Pēkaṉ because of [his wife] Kaṇṇaki, whom he abandoned. *Tiṇai: peruntiṇai. Tuṟai: kuṟuṅkali* and/or *tāpata nilai.*

146

We don't want your wealth! We don't want your precious gems!
Pēkaṉ who kills in battle! If you would show me your favor
and grant me a gift while, playing in the cevvaḻi rāga of longing
on my small yāḻ, I sing of your fine, mountainous land,
then lord! hitch the horses to your towering chariot
of great speed so that upon that pitiful young woman
grown thin through your cruelty, wasting away
with gnawing grief, a sight of suffering, they may
with sweet smoke perfume the hair lush as the tail
of a peacock lifted by the wind
and then adorn it with a cool and fragrant garland.

Aricilkiḻār sings Vaiyāvik Kōpperum Pēkaṉ because of [his wife] Kaṇṇaki, whom he abandoned. *Tiṇai: peruntiṇai. Tuṟai: kuṟuṅkali* and/or *tāpata nilai.*

147

Because I have come to you crossing many mountains where the falls
of the water plunge down from caves in the stone and I have played for you
on my small yāḻ in the cevvaḻi rāga of longing, you should grant me the gift
of yourself setting out today so that the woman, beautifully dark with eyes
that are cooling and proud and streaked with red lines that are lovely,

may have her hair black as collyrium washed until it shines like a polished
sapphire gem and let that hair left dry too long be decorated with flowers
that are fresh, she who was standing in solitude yesterday listening
beside your house to the sweet sound of the monsoon, O king of the Āviyars!

Peruṅkuṉṟūrkiḻār sings Vaiyāvik Kōpperum Pēkaṉ because of [his wife] Kaṇṇaki, whom he abandoned. *Tiṇai: peruntiṇai. Tuṟai: kuruṅkali* and/or *tāpata nilai.*

148

Naḷḷi with your glowing mountain where the waterfalls roar down
from the summit! I praise the wealth you desired and gained
through unrelenting effort! To those who have come to you in need,
surrounding you in your sprawling city glittering with its rice bins,
you have been magnanimous, and each and every day you bring and dispense
fine gems and elephants! And we do not have the will to praise insignificant kings,
or sing about things that they never did.
We will not exalt men of that kind with our small but elegant tongues!

Vaṉparaṇar sings Kaṇṭīrak Kōpperunaḷḷi. *Tiṇai: pāṭāṇtiṇai. Tuṟai: paricirruṟai.*

149

Naḷḷi! May your life be long! Naḷḷi! With the soft lilt of low notes
in the evening my people sang marutam poems of unfaithful love and playing
on the yāḻ in the morning, they sang songs in the mode of cevvaḻi
where lovers yearn for their lovers in the evening, and so they violated

all due order! And why? Because you not only defend but you give!

Vaṉparaṇar sings Kaṇṭīrak Kōpperunaḷḷi. *Tiṇai: pāṭāṇṭiṇai. Tuṟai: iyaṉmoḻi.*

150

As I was resting against the root of a jackfruit tree and my clothes
in tatters looked like the ruffled black wing of a kite
in the cold, wet season, as I was utterly worn out and in pain from my
wearisome going to and fro through the varying lands and I was not thinking
of myself at all, a chieftain saw me. He was a man of great wealth,
a hunter who was holding a powerful bow in his hand, on his head
a glowing diadem of blue sapphires shooting out brilliantly clear rays,
his feet with their fine anklets flecked with blood from the slaughter
of a whole herd of deer! I rose to my feet and I bowed to him
but he put out his hand and he sat me down. And before his young men
off wandering through the forest could come and catch up with him,
he made a fire where rapidly he cooked tender meat with fat on it
as pure as ghee and he gave all of it to me, saying, "You eat this,
along with your large family that has been burned black under the sun!"
We ate it as if it were amṛta and we sated the gnawings within us
of our hunger and we drank cool water from a cascade descending
down the side of a mountain flourishing with lovely trees!
Then when I began to take my leave of him, suddenly he said to me,
"I am a man of the forest! I have with me no other precious
ornaments to give!" and to me he gave the shining necklace
of pearls he was wearing around his neck, along with a dense
armlet complete with its clasp! Then I asked, "What is your country?"
but he would not tell me his country. When I asked him, "What
is your name?" he would not tell me his name! But on the road
I asked and I heard from many others who he was, that he was Naḷḷi,
the protector of handsome, far-famed Tōṭṭi Mountain, of that towering

hill. It was him! the lord of the soaring mountain
from which the sweet water flows down glittering like cut crystals!

Vaṉparaṇar sings Kaṇṭīrak Kōpperunaḷḷi. *Tiṇai: pāṭāṇṭiṇai. Tuṟai: iyaṉmoḻi.*

151

Because in that land over which he ruled, so that bards might over
and over be overcome with joy in days gone by, if the master of a house
on the slope of a mountain that touches the sky had gone traveling
to a far country, his women would put on their ornaments and taking
heavy-witted elephant cows with hairs scattered across their heads to serve
as presents, they would give them away, filling the place of their lord, and so
I closely embraced Kaṇṭīrakkōṉ, famous for his magnanimity. You as well
would merit my embrace were you not descended from the race of Naṉṉaṉ
who owned many chariots of gold! My people avoid singing of you
because on your high, sweet-smelling mountain where the clouds,
whirling, rain down on the lower slopes infested
with spirits, your doors are bolted against men who sing beautiful words!

[Once], when Iḷaṅkaṇṭīrakkō and Iḷaviccikkō were together, Peruntalaic Cāttaṉār went there. He embraced Iḷaṅkaṇṭīrakkō but did not embrace Iḷaviccikkō. When [Iḷaviccikkō] asked, "What did I do so that you did not embrace me?" the poet sang this song. *Tiṇai: pāṭāṇṭiṇai. Tuṟai: iyaṉmoḻi.*

152

I spoke of the man with the great bow, master of the hunt, who aimed

his arrows with the utmost precision, bringing down an elephant, slaying
a tiger with gaping jaws, dropping a hollow-horned spotted stag,
felling a boar with a head heavy as a mortar, burying
his point in a lizard that had taken refuge near him in a deep hole,
he who was widely famed for his skill at killing, consummate in the art
of archery, but just who was he? He who had been killing did not
seem to be someone who made his living in that way but he appeared
to possess immense wealth. Was it that lord of a richly yielding mountain
with a waterfall cascading down its side, was it Valvilōri
on whose broad and handsome chest dried sandalpaste rests
or was it someone else? Still I decided that I would sing a song
and I said to my dancing women, "Now I will sing. You spread the clay
over the mṛdaṅgam drum, pluck the rāga on the strings of the yāḻ
and blow on the trumpet that is open at one end like an elephant's trunk,
play on the ellari drum, play on the ākuḷi drum,
softly beat on one of the eyes of the patalai drum,
place in my hand the black staff that foretells the future,"
and I approached him. When we had sung all the twenty-one themes
of song before him as it was right for us to do since he was a lord
and then addressed him as "King!" he was embarrassed, for the title
surely was his and when we told him though we had wandered across
every country there was no hunter anywhere who might be compared
with him, he would not even let us ask for whatever we wanted!
He gave us boiled fatty meat from the deer he had killed in the hunt,
he gave us toddy that was like melted ghee and right there,
in the wasteland, he said to us "Take this!" and gave us
fine, faultless gold mixed in with heaping piles of blue sapphires
all from his mountain, he who is the lord of the mountain
of Kolli which is majestic and lofty, which has caves

around its summit, he who has the will
for victories, he who gives without ever holding anything back!

Vaṉparaṇar sings Valvilōri. *Tiṇai: pāṭāṇtiṇai. Tuṟai: paricil viṭai.*

153

Only to witness the generosity, like a rain cloud, of Ātaṉ Ōri
who never ceases to wage murderous war, on whose wrist a bracelet
curves, whose ornaments of gold shoot out rays of light, lord
of the hill that is adorned with clouds, he who each and every day
gives away a decorated elephant to those who have come to him in need,
only for that my family of dancers traveled across great distances!
They were granted a waterlily inset with blue sapphires, one that never
blossomed in cool water and a chaplet strung on a silver cord
and ornaments and an entire herd of elephants and then they departed.
Is it because they are hungry no longer that they don't dance
even when the sweet instruments play
that are held together with string and why they have forgotten how to sing?

Vaṉparaṇar sings Valvilōri. *Tiṇai: pāṭāṇtiṇai. Tuṟai: iyaṉmoḻi.*

154

People who go to the shore of the sea with its waves still ask
those who know where water can be found to quench their thirst.
In the same way wise men, though in the company of kings,
will seek out those who are generous and without flaws!
Nor do I think, "What is this worth?" about whatever wages
I gain! With my mind on you I have come here
because I am poor. It is hard for me to beg and say

"Give to me!" Whether you grant me things or not,
I can easily sing of your manhood which is such
that you could never run before weapons thrown in war
and I sing of your mountain, Koṇkāṉam of the many cool waterfalls
that descend in their streams close
together from the summit, like the spotless spreading out of a
robe!

Mōcikīraṉār sings Koṇkāṉaṅkiḻāṉ. *Tiṇai: pāṭāṇṭiṇai. Tuṟai: paricirruṟai.*

155

To your side withering away with hunger you, a bard, press
your small curving yāḻ and briefly, with a few choice words, you ask
where are those caring people, alert to relieve your suffering?
Listen to me now! As in an abandoned city, cow's-thorn flowers
swing their pure golden blossoms toward the sun as it is rising, so
the dining dishes of poor poets turn toward the chest crossed
with a cool garland of the master of great
Koṇkāṉam Mountain, he whose fame glows, and then the dishes
blossom with food!

Mōcikīraṉār sings Koṇkāṉaṅkiḻāṉ. *Tiṇai: pāṭāṇṭiṇai. Tuṟai: pāṇāṟṟuppaṭai.*

156

Mountains mastered by other kings have but one power
while towering Koṇkāṉam has two! For it can surround itself
with those people who have come to it in their need, craving for
the food that they expect to receive, and it has the other virtue
as well of repelling the formidable armies
of those kings who march against it and exacting tribute from them!

Mōcikīraṉār sings Koṇkāṉaṅkiḻāṉ. *Tiṇai: pāṭāṇṭiṇai. Tuṟai: iyaṉmoḻi.*

157

To endure it when your own followers do you wrong,
to see due cause for shame in the poverty of others,
to be so powerful that enemies cannot escape your army,
and to come striding proudly into the courts of kings,
of such virtues your own people are not truly worthy!
But there is a man I follow with a chest that opens out
like a flower when he draws the bow, whose spear kills,
he who wears a chaplet of kāntaḷ flowers, king of the Kuṟavars,
lord of the great fertile mountain that blocks the moving clouds, where
in a cave as the sun descends, a massive tawny male tiger attends
to a fine stag trumpeting for his young and bewildered doe because he is
lost in the forest, separated from his family, unable
to find his way home—my lord Ēṟai is worthy of those virtues!

Kuṟamakaḷ Iḷaveyiṉiyār sings Ēṟaikkōṉ. *Tiṇai: pāṭāṇtiṇai. Tuṟai: iyaṉmoḻi.*

158

There was Pāri, the chieftain who fought his combats with kings
while the sticks beat down on the royal drums and spotless
bright conches were sounded, the lord of Paṟampu where a white fall
of water rolling stones in its flow thunders down a tall mountain,
and there was Ōri with his powerful bow who ruled Kolli's shining summit
and Malaiyaṉ, mighty in war, who was as generous as a rain cloud
and who won his victories in battle astride his stallion Kāri
and Eḻiṉi, who reigned astride his towering Stallion Mountain
wearing his chaplet of kūviḷam and his curving necklace, with his sharp spear,
and there was Pēkaṉ, who ruled over a great mountain with towering summits
watched over by an unassailable god, on its cold slopes caves full of darkness,

and there was Āy, whom Mōci, whose words are the truth, has sung,
and there was Naḷḷi, who made his enemies flee from him, whose generosity
was truly noble, who took it upon himself to utterly remove the poverty
of those who came to him with desire—these seven dead,
thinking of you now I have come here swiftly, for in your mind you maintain
the thought that you will relieve the suffering of those who arrive
singing to you in their need so that a feeling of pity is stirred,
and to others as well you give gifts! O lord of Mutiram mountain
where there is unending prosperity, where on the slope of the hill,
bamboo grows that reaches up to touch the sky, and where a monkey
hungry for some jackfruit made even more lovely for him by its surroundings
of tall breadfruit and curapuṉṉai trees, succeeds in taking a fruit
with a thorny shell, well matured, and with his hand he summons
his mate to him, she whose fur is as soft as cotton! You, Kumaṇaṉ,
whose might shines throughout this world, you with your finely fashioned
chariots and your far-famed generosity,
triumphant over your enemy I pray will be the spear you raise!

Peruñcittiraṉār sings Kumaṇaṉ. *Tiṇai: pāṭāṇṭiṇai. Tuṟai: vāḻttiyal* and/or *paricil kaṭānilai.*

159

My mother is old. Over and over she complains about how many years
have passed and she is still alive and her life will not end. Hobbling
with so many small steps, a stick for an extra leg, her hair like
spread string, her eyesight gone, she cannot even walk to the verandah.

And my love wears her one meager, filthy garment and she is
hungry and as she thinks of how things stand with her she grieves.
Her body is faded, her breasts withered as the many children moving
beside her squeeze them and suck at them. In despair she plucks a young,
half-grown shoot sprouting on a kīrai plant on a garbage heap that others
have picked near clean and she throws it into a pot without any salt
and sets it on the fire. She does not even remember when she ever
had rice and without any buttermilk she eats the green leaves
and complains about the Order of the World. Now you should make
the hearts of these two people happy as I praise you for the fame
of your generosity, which is like a cloud coming with lightning
and roaring thunder as it sheds its rain down on millet not yet
sprouting its ears of a lovely dark color, after it has been planted
among wild rice on a wide space of land new to cultivation
but burned over by men of the forest and transformed into a field.
You should make my family happy, all of them, because they are
shriveled up, consumed now by hunger. Yet should you even
give me a ferocious elephant with its upraised tusks, I will not
accept it if it is offered without goodwill. But if you should offer,
with joy and to please us, even a tiny crab's-eye seed, then
I will willingly take it! Kumaṇaṉ, you who wield a spear,
sharp pointed! Greatly glorious lord! Famed for your victories!
Born into a flawless, towering lineage!
I ask you to be gracious and satisfy us! I who sing about you!

Peruñcittiraṉār sings Kumaṇaṉ. *Tiṇai: pāṭāṇṭiṇai. Tuṟai: paricil kaṭānilai.*

160

So that the coolness may be granted to our scored, twisting, shrunken guts
and to our bodies covered with sweat, baked down and eaten up by our hunger
because no rice has entered them like the drops of rain that come pouring down

with the thunder whose voice makes us quiver with pleasure as they consume
the glowing rays of the fearsome sun and the wilderness where the grass
has been burned dry begins to flourish—to do that for us he will set out small
golden bowls, marked by much use, around the great silver salver! And they will be
like stars circling around a moon that has been all filled up with rice and ghee
and pieces of meat spiced to taste and then he will say, "The families of singers
must never be in need!" and as if it were nothing important to him at all,
he will distribute rare and precious ornaments of gold!
I have been told that if I go to Kumaṇaṉ, he who rules
the city of Mutiram, where the streets are flowing with strong drink, he who
has the noble reputation of being more of a friend to us singers than he is
to his own friends, he will then be deeply generous to us. This is how people
have spoken of your towering fame! and so I have come here as fast as I could
with my heart urging me on! Since my house is empty of food, and my son who has a sparse
topknot on his head, his stomach turning, seems to have forgotten that his house was
ever there to feed him and he tries many times to suck at an empty breast where
there is no milk and from it he draws nothing! Craving rice and porridge,
he opens the empty jars in the house, one after another, and when he is done with that,
he bursts out crying. When she sees him like this, my wife will tell him
a story, to frighten him, about a ferocious tiger, and in her pain she will try

to distract him by pointing at the moon. She tells him to think about his father
and pretend to be angry with him while she herself goes on grieving
under the full light of day! I ask that she may become rich through your giving me
now, at once! wealth in masses that cannot fade away and be lost. And we will
lavishly sing our praises for your vast fame and we will cause it to rise
up everywhere across the earth surrounded
by the waters of the ocean washing against it with their rolling waves!

Peruñcittiraṉār sings Kumaṇaṉ. *Tiṇai: pāṭāṇṭiṇai. Tuṟai: paricil kaṭānilai.*

161

In the season of the heat the rains that are the source of wealth do not fall
nor do the swiftly scudding clouds loom up like great mountains that have come
to term after drawing up their water from the roaring ocean so that
it is shrunken, then to gather together wherever they may wish to complete
their duty of pouring down the rain along with the thunder and the lightning.
Nevertheless water in abundance will fill the Ganges
and will go beating against its shores so that all beings
can come there and drink! And this is an image of you who are the king
for me just as much as you are for other men! So I would like to return
home in pride, seated high on an elephant stretching up like a mountain,
a splendid ornament glowing on its forehead, the bells hanging down

its flanks ringing in alternating rhythm, its full grown tusks raised
high so that pearls can roll down them from its temples, its trunk
like a palmyra tree. And my wife who has been weeping for me will be amazed!
She who had lost her strength, her power of sight out of grief, will stare
over and over at the wealth that you have gained through your energies, she
who had been thinking, "My life is gone along with this day, gone away
with him who had no love left for me, to have gone off across that arduous,
never-ending wilderness where the strong stag stands and chews his cud
and ruthless bandits on the routes maraud and murder!" Lord whose victories
are many! I have come to you driven by my need, invited by your fame!
Listen to me with favor as I fashion my verses in honor of your generosity!
Do not fix your mind on whether I have the skill for such an achievement
or whether I do not, but recognize at once how worthy I am and think only
of that which you already must know, the range of your own excellence!
My lord! Let me leave here so endowed that the three great kings will feel
endless shame! We will sing many times over in praise of your rich wealth,
of your army which has labored in the battle of spears so that your women
with their fine ornaments may feel delight each time they embrace your broad,
massive chest smeared with sandal paste and marked with the numerous signs
of good fortune, so that those you live within your cooling

shadow may don many ornaments as your royal drum roars out in
the morning!

Peruñcittiraṉār sings Kumaṇaṉ. *Tiṇai: pāṭāṇṭiṇai. Tuṟai: paricirrurai.*

162

You don't care about those who may come to you in need
but no one can say there aren't those who do care for them!
Raise your eyes! There are those who come in need and those
who are generous to them! Look at the gift given to us of a handsome,
towering elephant that we have brought here and have lashed
to your sacred tree and the tree
groans with it! Lord of a swift horse, I leave you now!

When Peruñcittiraṉār went to Veḷimāṉ, Veḷimāṉ was resting [literally, sleeping]. He told his younger brother to give the poet a present. He gave only a little, and the poet, not taking it, went and sang Kumaṇaṉ. Kumaṇaṉ gave [him] an elephant, and the poet brought it and tied it to Veḷimāṉ's tutelary tree. Then he went [to that king] and sang this song. *Tiṇai: pāṭāṇṭiṇai. Tuṟai: paricil viṭai.*

163

To your friends, the women who love you! to your friends, the women
you love! to the elder women of your family with all their virtues
and their purity! to those who gave to you so that the fierce hunger
of our family might be soothed, expecting repayment only whenever we could!
without thought of who they may be, without asking me, without a thought
of us living as well as we can, you also, mistress of the house!
should give, to everyone! the wealth that has been granted us

by Kumaṇaṉ of the straight spear,
who is the lord of Mutiram where the fruit hangs down on the trees!

Peruñcittiraṉār sang Kumaṇaṉ, received a gift, brought it [home], and said [this] to his wife. *Tiṇai: pāṭāṇṭiṇai. Tuṟai: paricil.*

164

Mushrooms are growing on my clay oven because it has never been worn
down! It stands as high as ever! It has utterly forgotten how to cook!
I have seen my wife suffering, anguished by the gnawing of her hunger.
Her eyes with their moist lashes are like rain, filled with her tears
as she looks at the face of her infant, who cries each and every time
he tries to suck at her empty breast, ugly now with no milk,
its teat closed up and the skin dry as leather! I have considered
all this and I have come to you, Kumaṇaṉ skilled in battle! Once
you have learned how I stand, what state I am in, I will never leave
until I have been given something, even if I have to force you!
For you were born into a line that lightens the poverty of dancers
who carry fine yāḻs, their rows of strings tuned to rāgas,
and their covers of hide and drums smoothened with clay to be struck!

Peruntalaic Cattaṉar sings Kumaṇaṉ after his country was taken from him by his younger brother and he went to live in the forest. *Tiṇai: pāṭāṇṭiṇai. Tuṟai: paricil kaṭānilai.*

165

In the world which does not endure, men who have sought to endure,
have made their own fame firm and then they have vanished!
Men of immense wealth, of unapproachable eminence, have failed
to create an awareness of any lasting connection with their ancestors,

since to those in need who made requests of them, they gave nothing!
While I stood and sang of that leader, who owns strong horses,
who has a radiant and flawless reputation, who grants to singers
murderous elephants with lovely foreheads, bells dangling to their feet
ringing in alternating rhythm, he spoke and what he said to me was,
"I can't bear being so weak! When I see a great being in need, for him
to go away without anything would be worse than losing my land!"
So he handed me his sword and he offered me his head for there was nothing
better for him to give me than himself! I have come here to you now
overwhelmed with joy as if from a victory
for I have seen your elder brother and his unyielding determination!

When Peruntalaic Cāttaṉār saw Kumaṇaṉ, whose country had been taken from him by his younger brother and who had gone to live in the forest, [that king] gave him his sword. [The poet] brought it, showed it to Iḷaṅkumaṇaṉ [the younger brother] and sang this. *Tiṇai: pāṭāṇṭiṇai. Tuṟai: paricil viṭai.*

166

You who are descended from men renowned
for their superb learning, men who
performed to perfection all twenty-one
kinds of sacrifice, who confirmed
the truth, never thinking it false,
who understood lies that resembled truth,
thus defeating those who would contend
with the one ancient work of six sections
and four divisions, focused on Righteousness,
never swerving from the well-chosen words
of the Primal Being with his long, matted hair!
You glow in your black antelope skin
from dry forest land, needed for the ritual,
worn over the thread around your shoulder!
Your beloved wives, worthy of your high

station, flawlessly faithful, free of harshness,
renowned for their virtue, donning the sacred ornaments,
their foreheads small, their hips and thighs large and wide,
of few words and rich abundant hair, request their ritual
    responsibilities!
Whether in settled land or jungle, omitting
none of the fourteen sites, you pour out
more ghee than there is water, sacrifice
more times than there are numbers, spread
your fame wider than the earth, and at
the great moment when a difficult sacrifice is completed,
may we always see you in your high and perfect state, offering
    hospitality!
Once I have eaten, devoured the food and mounted
a chariot, I will celebrate my luck and then go off
to our city with its cool bathing places ever renewed
by the fresh waters of the Kāviri River spread
with flowers when above the tall gold-bearing mountain
in the west, the thunder roars! May you be
as firmly established over the earth
as Himālaya where the bamboo grows and rising mountains block
    the clouds!

Āvūr Mūlaṅkiḻār sings Cōṇāṭṭup Pūñcāṟṟūrp Pārppaṉ Kauṇiyaṉ. *Tiṇai: vākai. Tuṟai: pārppaṉa vākai.*

167

You when you confront a war win that war as you take
your stand routing their armies, your body slashed over
with the scars of wounds from their swords, and you become then
a grim sight to the eyes but a sweet thing to hear about!
But they, because when they see you they race away, their backs
turned away from you and so their bodies show no wounds, they
remain a sweet sight for the eyes yet a grim thing to hear about.
So you are sweet in one respect and they are sweet in another!
Where is there any difference then, master of swift horses

with the war anklets on your handsome feet, Kiḻḻi! victorious
in battle? Yet it is you that this world
honors! Greatness! Why should that be? Now tell us why!

Kōṉāṭṭu Eṟiccilūr Māṭalaṉ Maturaik Kumaraṉār sings Ēṉāti Tirukkiḻḻi. *Tiṇai: vākai. Tuṟai: aracavākai.*

168

Ruler of Stallion Mountain which no one mounts, where Kuṟavaṉ
men of the hills have planted the tiny thick-sheathed millet
without any need to plow on a wide slope grown with bamboo as
a waterfall roars, as pepper plants grow where the dry earth was plowed up
by fierce boars and their sows and offspring so that the rich tubers
of flowering kāntaḷ shone uprooted, and now choosing an auspicious day,
the Kuṟavaṉs harvest the fresh growth so that they may eat well. They pour
sweet foaming milk from a wild cow into an unwashed pot that smells
of boiled venison, its broad sides white with fat, and they set
the pot on the fire. Then, in the open, where it is lovely
with wild jasmine and nightshade flowers, they eat their rice
cooked over sandalwood branches, sharing it out on the wide
leaves of plantain trees that grow dense clusters of fruit!
O master of bowmen who carry sharp spears, who wear handsome
chaplets of vēṅkai flowers that are woven together with fibers
from the naṟai vine, bowmen whose arrows are accustomed to being
resharpened after use! Magnanimous Koṟṟaṉ of the swift horses!
They say that those who come in need sing of you, praising you
so intensely that their eloquent, honest tongues ache, making
their words heard in order that your bright, flawless glory
may spread, undiminished, to the farthest
limits of the Tamil land. And kings who are miserly men will be ashamed!

Karuvūrk Katappiḷḷai Cāttaṉār sings Piṭṭaṅkoṟṟaṉ. *Tiṇai: pāṭāṇṭiṇai. Tuṟai: paricirruṟai* and/or *iyaṉmoḻi* and/or *aracavākai.*

169

When your army moves forward, you advance before the army
opposing you as they brandish arms and fling their missiles but when
their army advances, you shift to the rear of your army, supporting it,
taking your stand there like a mountain damming up a broad river!
For these reasons, O greatness! it is always hard to catch
any sight of you! and the anguish of my family is a great anguish!
Please grant a gift to me right now! May your power prosper
for a very long time! May it never fall before your enemies!
May it be like a towering pole made of the murukku tree
with its broad leaves and raised up to serve as a target
for many young Kōcars as if they were its enemies,
to launch their conquering spears and learn the art of glittering weapons!

Kāvirippūmpaṭṭiṉattuk Kārikkaṇṇaṉār sings Piṭṭaṅkoṟṟaṉ. *Tiṇai: pāṭāṇṭiṇai. Tuṟai: paricil kaṭānilai.*

170

You who are his enemies, be careful when you come anywhere near
Piṭṭaṉ of the sharp spear, lord of the mountain that holds a village
where fences of gooseberry thickets are gnawed apart and eaten
by wild cows and the yards are rough with berry seeds, where
the fearsome tuṭi drum with its clear eye is beaten by a lowborn drummer
as hard as he can strike, his powerful hand reddening, among
those good people who eat by using their bows as plows, men who live
without learning and hunt throughout the day, and the boom of that drum

merges with the hooting of owls on the high mountain where a tiger
is sleeping! To the dancing women that lord gives shining pearls
from the white tusks of small-eyed elephants and to the families
of bards who play rāgas on their good yāḻs he passes out
strong clarified toddy that has been filtered through fiber! Even though
that powerful man is gentle toward those who seek him,
toward his enemies he is as potent as the anvil which combats
the hammer brought down on it with great force
by a blacksmith with his strong hands trying to mold iron!

Uṟaiyūr Maruttuvaṉ Tāmōtaraṉār sings Piṭṭaṅkoṟṟaṉ. *Tiṇai: vākai. Tuṟai: vallāṇmullai* and/or *tāṉaimaṟam.*

171

Today if we should go to him he will give us gifts! Should we wait
for a little while and then go to him again, he will give us gifts!
and should we make a habit of going to him, he would not even think
he has given to us before but then every single day, without
fail, he would fill our empty plates to our hearts' content!
May Koṟṟaṉ with the handsome spear complete, just as he wishes,
his difficult labor of combat, so that his king may be happy!
If you want many herds of fierce bulls, with sheds to hold them,
if you want heaps of paddy piled up in the fields, if you want
valuable ornaments and elephants, that great man is capable
of granting them! And this worth of his raised on Righteousness
is valid for others just as it is for his own people! Because this is
how he is, may my lord not even suffer the pain of a thorn
in the sole of a foot! May all his efforts
prosper so that people may live on in this world where the generous are rare!

Kāvirippūmpaṭṭiṉattuk Kārikkaṇṇaṉār sings Piṭṭaṅkoṟṟaṉ. *Tiṇai: pāṭāṇṭiṇai. Tuṟai: iyaṉmoḻi.*

172

Put the cooking pot on the fire! Set out the rice! Serve toddy
without stinting! Let the dancing women who wear glittering
ornaments, who are skilled at song, don their garlands!
Do all the other things that go along with these!
There is no cause at all for anyone to be sad! Piṭṭaṉ
who has swift horses is master of a fertile country
where should a fire go out, kindled during the night
by guards in the millet fields to protect the future food,
perfect jewels flashing light will dispel the dense
darkness! Long life to his spear victorious
in arduous battles, to vastly generous Kōtai, even to his enemies the kings!

Vaṭamavaṇṇakkaṉ Tāmōtaraṉār sings Piṭṭaṅkoṟṟaṉ. *Tiṇai: pāṭāṇṭiṇai. Tuṟai: iyaṉmoḻi.*

173

May Paṇṇaṉ live long for all the days that I am alive!
Singers! Will you look at how this man's family suffers!
The sound of people who are eating can be heard like birds
chirping in a full-grown tree that is filled with fruit!
Like scattered lines of little tiny ants setting
off toward the high ground and carrying their eggs,
mindful that the time is coming when the rains that
do not fail will fall, children in large families go
here and there carrying rice in their hands. We see them
and having seen them, over and over again we ask,
"Give us a straight answer, is the house
of that physician who cures hunger nearby or far away?"

Cōḻaṉ Kuḷamuṟṟattut Tuñciya Kiḷḷi Vaḷavaṉ sings Ciṟukuṭikiḻāṉ Paṇṇaṉ. *Tiṇai: pāṭāṇṭiṇai. Tuṟai: iyaṉmoḻi.*

174

When the harassing Asuras had massed together and hidden away the sun
and human eyes were damaged by the darkness because they could not see
the sun's far-shining eminence, he whose form of fierce force is
as dark as collyrium reclaimed it. And he set it in its place to relieve
the anguish of the round world! Your father gained his fame by doing
the same for the Chola king Vaḷavaṉ, who had won great victories but now
was grieving for his lost kingdom. Flourishing the king's white umbrella
of power that seemed like the moon, he set it firmly in its place again
to soothe the suffering of the fine and fertile Chola land where the great
Kāviri River descends, dashing against its shores and wearing them away,
the roaring flood of its waters breaking their own path, and your father
quieted the pain then of the palace with its field for training horses
where the royal drum would rise and resound. The king had been hiding
in a place very hard to reach upon that high mountain adorned with clouds,
for which Kapilar, whose tongue never told a lie, sang the praises
—the mountain of Muḷḷūr far too great for ridicule, since it has seen
the backs of enemy warriors who had hungered for battle swiftly running away!
Your father whose fortress was carved with the mark of the tiger
that lives within caves, he who wore glittering ornaments and a chaplet
humming with bees and a great name, your father has left us behind
to go to the world of the gods, there to enjoy the rewards of beneficent actions
he performed in this world, and so you instead have come here
and your purpose is to relieve the misery of those whose hearts now

are troubled, around whom the directions of space wheel, who have lost
their direction, O lord with a flourishing garland! Like you, in the season
of the long summer stripped of all green, when the rocks crumble,
when the forests blaze up and the many reservoirs filled with water
dry away to their shores, a cloud gathers roaring
with thunder and lightning and pours down rain to form pools in the earth!

Māṟōkkattu Nappacalaiyār sings Malaiyamāṉ Cōḻiyavēṉāti Tirukkaṇṇaṉ. *Tiṇai: vākai. Tuṟai: aracavākai.*

175

Ātaṉuṅkaṉ! My lord! May you live long! Those
who open my heart would see you there! Should I forget you,
it could only be when my life is leaving my body!
I would have to forget myself to forget you,
who are like the broad sphere of the sun when it settled
into the mountain cleft that the Mauryas—with the banners
and lofty umbrellas of their chariots touching the sky, their spears
victorious—cut as a path to the world for their
strong-spoked wheels! You who take
the duty to protect everyone upon yourself throughout the day and the night!

Kaḷḷil Āttiraiyaṉār sings Ātaṉuṅkaṉ. *Tiṇai: pāṭāṇṭiṇai. Tuṟai: iyaṉmoḻi.*

176

Yours is the chieftain of great Māvilaṅkai where girls
with shining bangles dig up the black earth in play
where a boar has scored it and discover tortoise eggs
with their meatlike aroma and tubers of the waterlily
that smell like honey in that land where the sluices
are roaring! Yours is that Nalliyak Kōṭaṉ who wears words

of praise sung for him by poor men who play upon
their small yāḻs and so, my destiny, may you flourish!
When my heart considers the days I spent not seeing him as if
someone in Pāri's city of Paṟampu were to ignore the clear water
of those cool springs only because they rise within
the selfsame city, then it feels uneasy for the days to come,
thoughtful whenever it senses his supremely gentle benevolence.

Puṟattiṇai Naṉṉākaṉār sings Ōymāṉ Nalliyakkōṭaṉ. *Tiṇai: pāṭāṇtiṇai. Tuṟai: iyaṉmoḻi.*

177

For us, after wasting away for many days and straining
our eyes with all the searching, to be granted an elephant
adorned with gold in exchange for our songs in the lofty, radiant
palaces of kings with their glittering swords means far less
than the great coming of dawn in the western land dense
with forests that is ruled by Āti, whose fame is immense,
where any friend may be admitted but even the moon, should it seek
battle, could not enter, where the turrets for the archers
are furnished with machines of war, and in many outlying,
close-set fortified points, men with reddened eyes exchange
swigs of toddy and after drinking themselves full crave
something sour, and stuff themselves with jujube fruits
and the sweet-sour kaḷam berries, then climb the handsome
dunes along the river flowing with honey and pluck black plums
which they sit and eat. There, we who have come receive, set out
on palmyra-leaf baskets, endless portions of rice
and meat, thick with fat, from fierce boars caught for us by hunters!

Āvūr Mūlaṅkiḻār sings Mallikiḻāṉ Kāriyāti. *Tiṇai: pāṭāṇtiṇai. Tuṟai: iyaṉmoḻi.*

178

Cāttaṉ whose fame ranges far is a man of dulcet benevolence,
for he has vowed that he will never eat if ever his urgings

cannot persuade noble men to do so once they have entered
his courtyard with its expanses of sand where elephants
sigh because they hate being tied to posts, where horses
swift as the wind neigh with their hatred of stables!
But when in terrifying battle, the various swirling weapons
are launched by his enemies and strapping young men
who had drunk their cups of liquor forget the vows
they swore within the city and break
in their fright, then it is he who stands before them, shoring them
up!

Āvūr Mūlaṅkiḻār sings Pāṇṭiyaṉ Kīrañcāṭṭaṉ. *Tiṇai: vākai. Tuṟai: vallāṇmullai.*

179

"Since all those who are generous in this world have perished,
who is there to turn my bowl right side up, now face down
and worthless for any pleading because no one is giving?" When I
have asked this question, the answer offered to me has been the lord
of Nālai whose great fame never lessens, a warrior serving
the Pandya king who has seized much territory and the drums,
tightly laced, of his enemies and who wears finely fashioned
ornaments Śrī might envy, the lord of Nālai who if that king
needs an army, aids him with the sword and should he require
counsel, gives him wise advice—whatever he needs! Persevering as
an ox
whose yoke never slips, he whose straight spear
of fine battles feeds the vultures! Nākaṉ! Many answer me with his
name!

Vaṭaneṭuntattaṉār sings Nālai Kiḻavaṉ Nakaṉ. *Tiṇai: vākai. Tuṟai: vallāṇmullai.*

180

He doesn't have the wealth that every day he would lavish on others
nor the pettiness to say that he has nothing and so refuse!

Enduring the troubles that have fallen upon him as king, cured
of his suffering from those noble wounds endured when weapons
on the field of battle tasted his flesh, the handsome scars have grown
together as if he were a tree with its bark stripped for use
in curing and his body is perfect! Not a scar! In Īrntai he lives
and practices generosity! He is an enemy to the hunger of bards!
If you wish to cure your poverty, come along with me, bard whose lips
are so skilled! If we make our request of him, showing our ribs
thin with hunger, he will go to the blacksmith of his city
and will say to that man of powerful hands,
"Shape me a long spear for war, one that has a straight blade!"

Kōṉāṭṭu Eṟiccilūr Māṭalaṉ Maturaik Kumaraṉār sings Īrntūr Kiḻāṉ Tōyaṉ Māṟaṉ. *Tiṇai: vākai. Tuṟai: vallāṇmullai* and/or *pāṇāṟṟuppaṭai.*

181

The calf of a black forest elephant and the well-loved son
of a dark-eyed mountain woman rush together toward a fruit
fallen into the yard from a wood-apple tree growing in the common land
of the city of Vallār with its sweeps of hills and its large,
encircling forts where the arrows are smeared with flesh
and the guarded forests are hard to conquer and Paṇṇaṉ rules,
he whose sword cannot fail. If you want to rescue your poor
and starving family, go there now. Go before
he moves against the enemy and display
your poverty so that you will gain a gift that is the enemy of hunger!

Cōṇāṭṭu Mukaiyalūrc Ciṟukaruntumpiyār sings Vallārkiḻāṉ Paṇṇaṉ. *Tiṇai: vākai. Tuṟai: vallāṇmullai* and/or *pāṇāṟṟuppaṭai.*

182

This world exists because men exist who even if they
were to win the divine drink of the gods would not drink it
by themselves only thinking of its sweetness, men without

hate, without slackness in action though they may have fears
like the fears of other men, who would even give their lives
for fame but would not accept fame with dishonor were it
to gain them all the world, men who have no regrets, and with virtues
so exalted, never exert their powerful energies
for themselves but only for others. It is because they exist that we do!

The song of Kaṭaluṇ Māynta Iḷamperuvaḻuti. *Tiṇai: potuviyal. Tuṟai: poruṇmoḻikkāñci.*

183

Learning is a fine thing to have if a student helps a teacher
in his troubles, gives him a mass of wealth and honors him
without ever showing disdain! Among those born from the same belly,
who share the same nature, a mother's heart will be most tender
toward the most learned! Of all who are born into a joint family,
a king will not summon the eldest to his side but instead he will
show favor to the man among them who has the greatest knowledge!
And with the four classes of society distinguished as different,
should anyone from the lowest become a learned man,
someone of the highest class, reverently, will come to him to study!

The song of Pāṇṭiyaṉ Āriyappaṭai Kaṭanta Neṭuñceḻiyaṉ. *Tiṇai: potuviyal. Tuṟai: poruṇmoḻikkāñci.*

184

If you reap ripe paddy and mash it into balls for the feeding
of your elephants, less than what grows on a mā will be enough
for many days. But an elephant let loose to feed by itself

will trample a thousand mās of grain that will never touch its
mouth!
When a wise king is conscious of the right path and he then taxes
as he should, his country will offer him as much as ten millions
and it will still flourish! But if he is a ruler without backbone,
who has no idea of the right and each day desires things which
he simply takes without love while his corrupt followers do the same,
then as if he were the field that an elephant
invades, he will not even feed himself and the world will collapse!

The song of Picirāntaiyār when he went to see Pāṇṭiyaṉ Aṟivuṭai Nampi. *Tiṇai: pāṭāṇṭiṇai. Tuṟai: ceviyaṟivuṟūu.*

185

When a cart that is well guarded has a driver who is skilled,
it will move through the world, with wheels and shaft joined,
and it will roll on smoothly without meeting any obstacles!
But if the driver does not know how to handle it, then every single
day
he will sink the cart into dense and hostile mud
and it will create nothing but immense, fierce suffering over and
over!

The song of Toṇṭaimāṉ Iḷantiraiyaṉ. *Tiṇai: potuviyal. Tuṟai: poruṇmoḻikkāñci.*

186

Rice is not the life of the world nor is water the life!
The king is the life of this world with its wide expanses!
And so it is incumbent upon a king who maintains an army
wielding many spears to know of himself: "I am this world's life!"

The song of Mōcikīraṉār. *Tiṇai: potuviyal. Tuṟai: poruṇmoḻikkāñci.*

187

Whether you grow rice or whether you are a forest,
whether you are a valley or whether you are a mountain,
if they are good men who inhabit you,
then you are good, land! and may you long flourish!

The song of Auvaiyār. *Tiṇai: potuviyal. Tuṟai: poruṇmoḻikkāñci.*

188

Piling up wealth and possessions, a man can feed crowds of people,
but unless he has children coming to him in the middle of his meals,
who cross the floor with their tiny steps, stretch out their small
hands for the food, setting it down then, kneading it, chewing it,
stirring it and smearing themselves all over with rice and with ghee
in a way that enraptures their father,
then he will have won nothing throughout all the days of his life!

The song of Pāṇṭiyaṉ Aṟivuṭai Nampi. *Tiṇai: potuviyal. Tuṟai: poruṇmoḻikkāñci.*

189

Between that lord of tenacious purpose, who with his white umbrella
of royalty shades the earth that is encircled by the cool ocean,
sharing it with no one, and the lowly man without learning
who goes sleepless in the middle of the night or in the day hunting
the swift animals, there is everything in common: the possession
of a measure of food and two sets of clothes and all the flow of life!
The worth of wealth is that it can be given
away! If you think of nothing else but enjoying it, many things fail!

The song of Maturaik Kaṇakkāyaṉār Makaṉār Nakkīraṉār. *Tiṇai: potuviyal. Tuṟai: poruṇmoḻikkāñci.*

190

May your days lack the friendship of those men without soul
who hold the wealth they have inside their closed fists
and try to cling to things, like the rat that waits
for the brief time between maturation and harvest
to take the grain that hangs low and with it stuff his hole!
But may your days have the friendship of those with strength
and undiminishing resolution like the hungry tiger
who will not eat a fierce boar then and there because
it fell to his left, but will on the next day
wake up famished on a great mountain and leave
his cave empty behind him to bring
down to his right side a massive bull elephant!

The song of Cōḻaṉ Nalluruttiraṉ. *Tiṇai: potuviyal. Tuṟai: poruṇmoḻikkāñci.*

191

"How can it be you that don't have any gray hair, though you have lived
for many years?" You have asked the question and I will give you an answer!
My children have gone far in learning. My wife is rich in her virtue!
My servants do what I wish and my king, who shuns corruption, protects us!
And in my city there are many noble men who through their deep knowledge,
have acquired calm, have become self-controlled,
and the choices they make in their lives are built on the quality of restraint!

When Kōpperuñcōḻaṉ was facing north [starving himself to death in the rite of vaṭakkiruttal], Picirāntaiyār went to see him. The good men [cāṉṟōr] there asked him, "We have heard of you for many [years], yet you have no gray hair." [This] is what he said to them. *Tiṇai: potuviyal. Tuṟai: poruṇmoḻikkāñci.*

192

Every city is your city. Everyone is your kin.
Failure and prosperity do not come to you because others
have sent them! Nor do suffering and the end of suffering.
There is nothing new in death. Thinking that living
is sweet, we do not rejoice in it. Even less do we say,
if something unwanted happens, that to live is miserable!
Through the vision of those who have understood we know
that a life, with its hardship, makes its way like a raft
riding the water of a huge and powerful river roaring
without pause as it breaks against rocks because the clouds
crowded with bolts of lightning pour down their cold
drops of the rain, and so we are not amazed
at those who are great and even less do we despise the weak!

The song of Kaṇiyaṉ Pūṅkuṉṟaṉ. *Tiṇai: potuviyal. Tuṟai: poruṇmoḻikkāñci.*

193

Surely as if someone were hunting you across the breadth
of a white salt-flat stretching out like a flayed skin
thrown down to dry, one could run like a deer
and flee, but life with a family binds up your feet!

The song of Ōrēruḻavar. *Tiṇai: potuviyal. Tuṟai: poruṇmoḻikkāñci.*

194

In one house the funeral drum rattles. In one house
the wedding music of a concert drum booms out pleasure!
Women who have their men with them don ornaments of flowers!
Women whose men have gone off pour down their falling tears.
Surely a god who has no virtues is the creator of this world
which is so filled with pain!

May those who comprehend its nature see their way to bliss!

The song of Pakkuṭukkai Naṉkaṇiyār. *Tiṇai: potuviyal. Tuṟai: peruṅkāñci.*

195

All of you many noble men! All of you many noble men!
Your cheeks are wrinkled with age! Your white hairs
stick out like bones on a carp! Your years are fruitless!
All of you many noble men! When that god of death, he who has
a sharp ax and ferocious power will come to tie you up, then
you will feel your regrets. If you are unable to act for the good,
at least stay free of anything that is wrong. If you can do this,
then all will be happy for it and beyond that,
you will be on a way that leads you along the good path.

The song of Nariverūuttalaiyār. *Tiṇai: potuviyal. Tuṟai: poruṇmoḻikkāñci.*

196

If you say you will give what you can and when you cannot give
to anyone, explaining that you have nothing, you say no—
these are the two modes of benevolence proper to manhood!
If you say you will give when you cannot, or claiming that you
have nothing, you say no when really you could give—these,
at once! are two ways you injure those who come to you in need,
though they are also the means to destroy the good name of
    benefactors!
But let that be as it may! Even if we have never seen this before,
those of our clan are now seeing it here for the first time!
But we hope your children stay free of disease! I will not
lose heart and give up because of the sun's heat! I will not
turn torpid because of the cold. Thinking of my delicate woman
with her glowing face, who shows her purity only in her modesty,
    living
in a house that merely wards off the wind due to my poverty

which seems made of rock, I will move on! May you enjoy fine days!

Āvūr Mūlaṅkiḻār sings Pāṇṭiyaṉ Ilavantikaippaḷḷit Tuñciya Naṉmāṟaṉ when he was slow in giving him a gift. *Tiṇai: pāṭāṇṭiṇai. Tuṟai: paricil kaṭānilai.*

197

When we think, "This king has chariots with banners fluttering
at their heights, with horses that gallop like the rush of the wind!"
and "That king has elephants which fight as if they were ramming mountains
while his army glowing with weapons could as well be the ocean!"
or "This is a conquering king, who triumphs in his wars
with his drums that are as awesome as the roaring of thunder!"
the wealth of such rulers does not astonish us, they who are shaded
by white umbrellas, who wear bright ornaments, whose armies hold lands!
But there is a kind of man who does astonish us, though he may
only be king of a village that grows no more than millet
from dry fields, the small leaves sprouting from the living joints
of the tiny fragrant muññai plants that sheep have grazed down
within the enclosures fenced with thorns, if that man only shows
the virtue of knowing how to treat us as we should be treated!
Even when we are overwhelmed by suffering, we do not turn our minds
to the wealth of those who are utterly without awareness,
but we think of the poverty, O greatness!
of those who are truly aware, and over and over we feel happy!

Kōṉāṭṭu Eṟiccilūr Māṭalaṉ Maturaik Kumaraṉār sings Cōḻaṉ Kurāppaḷḷit Tuñciya Peruntirumāvaḷavaṉ when he was slow in giving him a gift. *Tiṇai: pāṭāṇṭiṇai. Tuṟai: paricil kaṭānilai.*

198

"May your sons live long who wear their sounding anklets,
whose mouths are as lovely as coral, who were born of the woman

with fine ornaments, with divine purity, on whose breasts
a shining necklace lies like a waterfall descending
a great mountain, your woman who desires you!" With words like
these,
I have praised and celebrated you, my lord whose chariot is strong!
While my uneasy heart, due to its abundant longing, speaks of you
even in my dreams because it is happy, overjoyed to have seen
your riches like those of the god who rests on the banyan tree,
lord of the spear! I say my farewell. May your garland flourish!
Throughout the entire breadth of the cool land of the Tamils,
you make your enemies bow down and you take what they have
as your spoils and enjoy it, you whose fierce strength is hard
to subdue! And your sons are just like you! May they possess
the great generosity of their ancestors who always cut down
their enemies and seized their finely fashioned ornaments
and with them filled your great city already bulging with gold!
May you live long, with your days and your years increasing more
than the water of the great ocean dense with waves, than the sand
in that ocean, than the drops of the rain in the trailing,
lofty clouds! May you prosper to the fullest! May you be happy with
your
good name and all the wealth you wish for, as time and time again
you look upon your grandchildren! O great being! I feel anguish
because of my desire for your kindness! I am like a bird craving
drops of water, in a distant country where I have no kin at all!
I am accustomed to the shade your feet offer and even living
here I am there every day! Do not forget me! Hero with your swift
horses!

Vaṭama Vaṇṇakkaṉ Pēricāttaṉār sings Pāṇṭiyaṉ Ilavantikaippaḷḷit Tuñciya Naṉmāṟaṉ when he was slow in giving him a gift. *Tiṇai: pāṭāṇṭiṇai. Tuṟai: paricil kaṭānilai.*

199

A flock of chirping birds never will stop to think,
"Yesterday we ate all the many fruit growing

on that huge branch of the sacred banyan tree!"
If they have gone to it once, they keep on going there.
Just like them are those who come in need. The men
of noble acts who welcome them own what they own
only for them. The need of men who come to them becomes their own need!

The song of Perum Patumaṉār *Tiṇai: pāṭāṇṭiṇai. Tuṟai: paricil kaṭānilai.*

200

Lord of a mountain where the slopes rise so high that the summit
cannot be touched by the clouds and a male monkey with black fingers
plucks and eats fruit from a green-leafed jackfruit tree towering
upon that mountain, handsome with his red-faced mate, a sight glowing
into the distances and then he settles to sleep at the top of a bamboo!
Viccikkō whose long spear with its fierce tip is proud of eating human fat,
whose ferocious elephants blaze as they take the field, who wears curving
ornaments that bear radiant jewels! These are the daughters of that Pāri
whose lofty virtues were known far and wide, who gave away a tall chariot
with sonorous bells, saying, "Take it!" to a jasmine vine adorned
with flowers, so that it might climb, though the vine had never
put scars on its tongue through singing that king's praises!
And I who am a firmly respectable Brahmin come to you in my need!
You who are a master of the sword which makes your enemies bow down
to you in due and right order! Accept these girls I am offering you,
O lord who overcomes any recalcitrant
opponents, ruler of a country where the harvests never fail!

The song of Kapalir when he took Pāri's daughters to Viccikkōṉ. *Tiṇai: pāṭāṇṭiṇai. Tuṟai: paricirruṟai.*

201

If you want to know who they are, they are his daughters,
he who granted whole cities to those who had come to him in need
nor will the noble renown fade for his act of giving a chariot
for the jasmine to climb, he who owned elephants with jingling bells,
the lord of Paṟampu, the most high Pāri! As for me, I am a friend
of their father. These girls are mine. And I am a Brahmin
and a poet and I have brought them with me! Among the generous
caste of Vēḷirs you are the most generous, most a Vēḷir
of the forty-nine generations of Vēḷirs who gave gifts
without limit, who ruled distant Tuvarai with its long
walls that seemed to be formed of bronze, the city that appeared
in the sacrificial pit of a northern sage! You who reign
over victories in battle! Great king with your garlanded
elephants! Pulikaṭimāl with your chaplet of blossoming flowers!
You know what a man should do and so you can do, for bards, what
you should do! I offer you these girls! Accept them! Lord
of the great mountain that yields gold! You whose strength
cannot be matched on the earth overarched by the sky and encircled
by the ocean, whose army puts fear into enemies
with conquering spears! O ruler of a land that can never be ruined!

The song of Kapilar when he took Pāri's daughters to Iruṅkōvēḷ. *Tiṇai: pāṭāṇṭiṇai. Tuṟai: paricirruṟai.*

202

Now listen to how Araiyam was destroyed, the long-established city
which had been of help to your ancestors through its gold treasured
in tens of millions of pieces! It was an ancient city that instilled
fear! Known by two names, it was famed for its constant victories

up there, on the tall mountain, where a wild bull being pursued
by hunters in the forest of veṭci trees races on never
finding any refuge, leaving the traces of his flight
in sapphires sprung clear on the slope and the scattered sheen
of gold! Pulikaṭimāl with your chaplet in flower! You who received
your wealth wholly inherited from your father! There was a man
among your ancestors who was wise, like you, and showed contempt
for Kañāa Talaiyār who had composed celebrated poems and the destruction
of his city resulted from it! O king with your chariot
finely fashioned! Pardon those vile and muddied words of mine
when I said, "May these daughters of Pāri who gave generously
find their protection among the ancient line of Evvi!" Greatness!
I take my leave of you! May your spear win its victories!
You who rule a land with villages perched on tall hills
where the dark petals of the black-stemmed vēṅkai flowers
when they have blossomed drift down over
the rocks that look then like the striped backs of huge tigers!

The song of Kapilar when Iruṅkōvēḷ would not take Pāri's daughters. *Tiṇai: pāṭāṇṭiṇai. Tuṟai: paricirruṟai.*

203

If the clouds thought, "We've rained other days!" and stopped raining,
if the fields thought, "We've grown food before!" and stopped growing,
there would be no life at all then for any being that draws a breath!
If people like me make requests, if we say, "Give me something again!"
it is cruel for a person like you to refuse them with the answer that
"You have gotten gifts from us before!" King whose chariot is handsome!
Those who are approached with the confidence that they will give—and who

do not—disappoint far more than those who do not have anything to give.
You are not that kind of man! You are generous! You do your duty
to bards! With the words "These are yours!" you grant them fortresses
difficult to conquer, even while they are still
in the hands of your enemies! My lord, be faithful to your duty of sheltering bards!

Ūṉpoti Pacuṅkuṭaiyār sings Cēramāṉ Pāmuḷūreṟinta Cōḻaṉ Neytalaṅkāṉal Iḷañcēṭ Ceṉṉi. *Tiṇai: pāṭāṇṭiṇai. Tuṟai: paricilṟuṟai.*

204

It is a stain on one's honor to make a request, saying "Give me something!"
but to answer with "I will give nothing!" is a still greater stain!
To offer someone a gift, saying "Take this!" is a lofty act and yet
it is even more lofty an action to respond, "I will not accept it!"
People in need of water will not drink from the great ocean where
an expanse of limpidly clear water spreads out roaring with waves,
but when a site has drinkable water, even if it may be small and muddy
and roiled by the horses and cows who make their way there to drink,
many paths will lead to it. When those who are in need think of kings
and go to them, then they cannot insult them. It is the times and the omens
that are to be blamed! And so I will not hate you. May your life,
Ōri! be a long one! You who are a generous man, you who give
gifts without setting any limits as if you
were some cloud filled with thunder and lightning in the sky!

Kaḻaitiṉyāṉaiyār sings Valvilōri. *Tiṇai: pāṭāṇṭiṇai. Tuṟai: paricilṟuṟai.*

205

Even from the three kings with all their wealth, we
want nothing unless it is given with love! Enemies
with swift horses, though they may be men who live enraged
at anything short of victory, will still go to you for refuge!
And your army swollen with swords breaks the spirit of aggression
in your other enemies! O lord of Kōṭai Mountain which is
surrounded
by white flowers! O hunter with a great bow and swift, fierce dogs
who destroy the herds of deer, big and small, that block their way.
May you be free from illness! As the finest of clouds, to gather
their new roaring wealth, plunge downward and collect
together by the ocean and do not leave without water,
so the families of those who come to you in need, do not
leave without fine elephants
who raise their gleaming tusks nor without chariots!

Peruntalaic Cāttaṉār sings Kaṭiyaneṭuvēṭṭuvaṉ when he was slow in giving him a gift. *Tiṇai: pāṭāṇṭiṇai. Tuṟai: paricirrurai.*

206

You who are the gatekeeper! You who are the gatekeeper!
Gatekeeper who never closes the gate against those
who come here in need, leading this life of pleading,
to sow shining words in the ears of the generous
and so to gain what they wish for, with their strong
urges and anguished concern for dignity! Does the lord
Neṭumāṉ Añci, whose horses are swift, not know himself
or not know me? This is no empty world and all the wise
and famous men are not dead. And so we will swing our ornaments
on to our shoulders and pack up our instruments in their cases.
Like the children of a carpenter who cuts trees, their hands skilled
at wielding the ax, when they roam the deep forest—
whether we go this way or whether we go that way, we will have
rice!

Auvaiyār sings Neṭumāṉ Añci when he was slow in giving her a gift. *Tiṇai: pāṭāṇṭiṇai. Tuṟai: paricilṟuṟai.*

207

Rise up now, my heart! We are leaving. Those men who
do not truly exercise their skills may well wish for the rewards
offered by someone who scowls at them and feels no happiness
within him and acts as if he did not know you were standing
right there in front of him—a king without the enraptured
goodwill a benefactor should feel! One ought to say, "Come forward!"
to people who have worth! This world is a large one! Those
who care are legion! Get up, the force within you unrestrained,
as untamed as an āḷi with ferocious strength!
Who would choose to linger shriveling up inside,
ignored in public, to win a piece of raw fruit from an uncaring person!

When Veḷimāṉ was sleeping [or "after he had died"], Peruñcittiraṉār asked his younger brother Iḷaveḷimāṉ ["the young Veḷimāṉ"] to give a gift. When he gave only a little, [the poet] did not accept it and sang this song. *Tiṇai: pāṭāṇṭiṇai. Tuṟai: paricilṟuṟai.*

208

While I was standing there and had said, "I have crossed many hills
and mountains to come to him and win some reward," he spoke
with a will to show me love and grace, saying to his men,
"Let him take what I have given him and go on his way!" But
what did he know of me, this king his enemies cannot withstand?
I am not a man who traffics in gifts, willing to accept
something he offers without so much as seeing me! If he would give me
no more than a single seed of millet

but with love, and knowledge of my true worth, how sweet that would be!

Peruñcittiraṉār went to Atiyamāṉ Neṭumāṉ Añci. [The king] would not see him but gave him a gift with the words "take this and go." [The poet] did not accept it and said this. *Tiṇai: pāṭāṇṭiṇai. Tuṟai: paricirruṟai.*

209

You are the lord of a fine land where in the towns that are surrounded
by rice farms, the laborers who reap the paddy drink their toddy
from the broad leaves of waterlilies with buds spreading open their petals
within the lovely fields full of white waterlilies and herons
from the reservoirs asleep on the stacks of hay and those men then
sway to the soft beat of waves breaking in the cool ocean!
Like a flock of birds winging through their home in the empty air,
hungry for a profusion of fruit, the noise of them resounding
through the caves of a great mountain but disappointed then and returning
with nothing because the fruit has been exhausted on a tall tree,
must I go back with my hands empty? O master of the sword!
Should you even give me nothing, I will not grieve because of that!
Greatness! May you always be well! You who resemble Murugan
with his thirst for war! You who have a chest that is like a mighty
mountain and day after day women long for the hour when
they can press themselves against it and their hair is fragrant
and perfect and abundantly flowing and they speak sweetly
and wear their finely crafted ornaments! May
the court which surrounds you happily by day realize how close we two are!

Peruntalaic Cāttaṉār sings Mūvaṉ when he was slow to give him a gift. *Tiṇai: pāṭāṇṭiṇai. Tuṟai: paricil kaṭānilai.*

210

Men like me might as well not be born in this world if men
like you turn into this, renouncing affection, looking on
without compassion, turning forgetful of your great duty
to protect humanity! Because my wife, my beloved, with her faultless
purity, yearns for me, and her frail life is in the balance,
it is impossible for her not to think of me! She grieves,
her suffering so intense it deserves to be sung as she wonders
whether death that knows no order has fixed on me out of turn,
and whether I am gone forever so that she should wish for death.
And because of this I take my leave, going away from here to lighten
the lingering pain of my wife! Leader! May your life be a long one!
But look there now! As I move on with a sad heart, my poverty
precedes me and I can do no more against it than the fortresses,
well guarded and hard to assault,
of your enemies on their front lines can do against you!

Peruṅkuṉṟūrkiḻār sings Cēramāṉ Kuṭakkōccēralirumpoṟai when he was slow to give him a gift. *Tiṇai: pāṭāṇṭiṇai. Tuṟai: paricil kaṭānilai.*

211

Ruler of renown! You who win your victories as the kings
die before you and your oncoming army while your royal
war drum surges and roars like the fiercely raging thunder
with its formidable onslaught that shatters the fearsome
heads of terrifying snakes and capsizes tall mountains
that seemed to stand surveying the earth, then rushes on
to shatter hills! I am a man of rank and I have come
to you in my need, thinking that because of your munificence
you would do me honor! When I told you how kings had cruelly
refused to receive me, surely you did what came into your mind
on that day and cupped your hand as if with an intent to give
but on the next day you showed no shame at my anguish over your
change of mind! You were false to your word but even so I spun

my language to make you feel ashamed. Praising you until my tongue,
eloquent and subtly skilled, feels the pain, I bow down to
and extol your broad, always victorious chest, ever more famous
as I sing and sing of it till its fame draws forth renewed singing.
I am going. And I think of her as she lingers, a pauper, in our house
with the old walls undermined by mice who, finding no food,
skitter here and there while she holds my son who having sucked
at it many times without getting milk, forgets
even how to take the breast, O my woman with her glowing face!

Peruṅkuṉṟūrkiḻār sings Cēramāṉ Kuṭakkōccēralirumpoṟai. *Tiṇai: pāṭāṇṭiṇai. Tuṟai: paricil kaṭānilai.*

212

If you ask me who my king is, my king lives in a land
rich and fertile, always producing fresh crops, where laborers
drink the strong, dizzying liquor filtered and aged for them
and as much cooked tortoise as they want and then bulging
their handsome cheeks full of juicy pieces of roasted lamprey,
they feast in perpetual festival and forget their occupation.
His name is Kōpperuñcōḻaṉ and he comes from Uṟaiyūr. He is
an enemy to the hunger of the suffering families of bards!
And he delights in laughter with the poet Potti, in their
perfect friendship, in true abounding happiness every day!

Picirāntaiyār sings Kōpperuñcōḻaṉ. *Tiṇai: pāṭāṇṭiṇai. Tuṟai: iyaṉmoḻi.*

213

Victorious king with your potent, powerful energies, you who
kill in ferocious battle, whose white umbrella lightens the world!
If you will weigh these two men who are advancing against you
in this world surrounded by raging waters, they are no

ancient enemies of yours with long-established strength!
Their eyes straining for the sight of battle, they've changed
their ways and risen up to confront you! As well, if you look
at yourself, you are not like them, lord of murderous elephants!
You have now gained a noble, wide-ranging reputation!
and after you go to the world where the great abide, your title,
relinquished then, will be theirs by right! Now once you
have realized that this is the way things are, listen
yet more closely to me, listen to more, you who long for glory!
These young men who have launched themselves against you
with their relentless intentions, with their thoughtless designs—
if they lose, to whom will you leave your imposing wealth?
And if you should lose to them, O ruler hungry for battle!
you will leave only shame and those who hate you will rejoice!
So restrain your Martial Courage! Rise up now and may the resolve
within you long flourish! You must act well so that the shade
afforded by your feet, a refuge for those who endure suffering,
not lose respect, so that they who abide in that world
hard to attain, where the gods live,
will receive you among them with desire as an honored
guest!

Pullā̲r̲r̲ūr Eyir̲r̲iyan̲ār sings Kōpperuñcōl̲an̲ when he went against his sons.
Tiṇai: vañci. Tur̲ai: tuṇaivañci.

214

You men without will! Your hearts still cling to their perspectives
stained with flaws! You live with instability and always you
wonder whether or not you should perform a righteous act!
A man who goes out hunting for an elephant will find it!
A man who hunts for a small bird will return with empty hands!
And so if those noble men who hunt for exalted goals should gain
what is merited by their karma, then in the world where the good
and the bad karma no longer accumulate they take their pleasure!
And if they do not savor pleasure in that world without karma,
they may never have to be born again! And if they are never

to be born again, then clearly while establishing one's fame
as solidly as a summit in the Himālayas,
it becomes of the utmost importance to die with a purified body!

What Kōpperuñcōḻaṉ said as he sat facing north [and starving himself to death in the rite of vaṭakkiruttal]. *Tiṇai: potuviyal. Tuṟai: poruṇmoḻikkāñci.*

215

They tell me that Picirōṉ lives in the good land of the southern king
where a woman of the cowherd caste makes porridge, dropping into white
curds white petals of the vēḷai flower whose blossoms grow
in their profusion along the streets strewn with cow dung
and then she cooks up a cereal of forked-eared pounded millet,
boiled with fine tamarind mash so that laborers who pick beans
may eat them both and to their heart's content. That news keeps me alive.
At a time when I was rich, he remained
there, distant! but he will not stay away in my time of pain.

Kōpperuñcōḻaṉ [who is starving himself to death in the rite of vaṭakkiruttal], speaking to the good men [cāṉṟōr] who said, "Picirāntaiyār will not come," says, "He will come." *Tiṇai: pāṭāṇṭiṇai. Tuṟai: iyaṉmoḻi.*

216

Don't speak of your doubts to me, saying, "Yes we may have heard of him
but we've never seen him at all though many years have passed.
Yes, he has the right to sit beside you as your familiar friend
of faultless conduct, but lord! it is not possible that he will act
on that friendship now!" O you are full of wisdom! But he, he
has never slighted me! He is kindness itself! He is my intimate friend!
He has no use for the kind of faithless behavior that would ruin

his renown! Whenever he offers his name, he says "My name
is that of simple Cōl̲an̲!" He has the right. It has been
given to him by his flawless love. And there is more! He will not
stay there, away from me, at a time
like this! He will be coming. Now. Keep a place free for him.

Kōpperuñcōl̲an̲, who is facing north [and starving himself to death in the rite of vaṭakkiruttal] tells [his comrades who are also starving themselves to death] to make a place for Picirāntaiyār [to sit so that he can join them]. *Tiṇai: pāṭāṇtiṇai. Tur̲ai: iyan̲mol̲i.*

217

Consider what a miracle is this courage that he has, to sit
here starving, a man of so many magnificent qualities!
And even more miraculous that a high nobleman of splendor,
who loves him and lives in another land, a man mighty in renown,
with friendship his walking staff, should come to him here at such a
time!
The majesty of the king who said that his friend would come
and the insight of the man who has come so that he may remain
a friend without fault lead one to wonder and wonder again
and then pass beyond wondering! When it has lost
a king of such long-standing glory who owned the heart
of a nobleman living in a land where the king's rod
of office did not reach, what then will
become of this world! It will be a place, I know, to be pitied!

The song of Pottiyār when he saw that Picirāntaiyār had come to be with Kōpperuñcōl̲an̲ who was facing north [and starving himself to death in the rite of vaṭakkiruttal]. *Tiṇai: potuviyal. Tur̲ai: kaiyar̲unilai.*

218

Though they arise far away from one another, gold and coral
and pearls and the lovely sapphires generated on a great

and immovable mountain form a fine ornament that has
inestimable value once they have been all fastened
together in a single place—and so are noble men
always found in the company of other men
who are noble and vile men are set next to vile men!

The song of Kaṇṇakaṉār when he saw Picirāntaiyār facing north [and starving himself to death in the rite of vaṭakkiruttal]. *Tiṇai: potuviyal. Tuṟai: kaiyaṟunilai.*

219

Warrior! You who are wasting away all the flesh on your
body under the speckled shade, on this island in the river!
Are you angry with me? For those
summoned by you who have sat down beside you are many!

The song of Karuvūrp Peruñ Catukkattup Pūtanātaṉār when he saw Kōpperuñcōḻaṉ facing north [and starving himself to death in the rite of vaṭakkiruttal]. *Tiṇai: potuviyal. Tuṟai: kaiyaṟunilai.*

220

The way a keeper who has lost his elephant after feeding it
sumptuous food and after caring for it many years may weep
with grief when he looks at the empty post in the mournful stall
where once it lived, didn't I shed tears when I looked out
on the empty public square of the ancient city where Kiḷḷi
the generous would pass, he who wore a golden garland
and whose fame was great and who used to give away gifts of
chariots?

After he went [and saw] Kōpperuñcōḻaṉ facing north [and starving himself to death in the rite of vaṭakkiruttal] and then returned and saw Uṟaiyūr [the Chola capital], Pottiyār wept and sang this song. *Tiṇai: potuviyal. Tuṟai: kaiyaṟunilai.*

221

He was widely renowned for giving gifts to singers!
He showed his great kindness in generosity to dancers!
He used his rod of power only with deliberate forethought
praised by the righteous! His firm friendship was praised
by the discerning! He was gentle with women! Powerful with
the powerful! He sheltered the high masters of the faultless Vedas!
But death did not stop to think what he was, did not
value that worthy man at all but seized on his sweet life!
Embrace your grieving families and come forward, poets
whose words are honest, and let us berate Death, let us say,
"As mourning swings through the wide world, the man who
sheltered us, who took on
undying glory, now has become a deep-rooted stone!"

The song of Pottiyār when he saw the memorial stone of Kōpperuñcōḻaṉ [who had died after facing north and starving himself to death in the rite of vaṭakkiruttal]. *Tiṇai: potuviyal. Tuṟai: kaiyaṟunilai.*

222

"After the glory for parents that is a son has been born to your
    beloved wife,
she who never leaves the shade of your body and her body glows
with radiant ornaments burnished in fire, come back then!"
you said and you were heartless to send me away from here!
You must know how much I feel for you!
You who long for renown! Where shall I take my place?

The Pottiyār when he returned after his son was born said, "Give me a place." *Tiṇai: potuviyal. Tuṟai: kaiyaṟunilai.*

223

They offered shade to many and the world spoke well of them!
Then because they could not achieve their goals they sat down

in a tiny space and became enduring and deeply rooted stones.
If someone goes to him with as much desire as sweet life
has for a body, someone with long-standing love,
someone who has the right, he will make a place for him even here!

Kōpperuñcōḻaṉ, even though he had become a [memorial] stone, gave Pottiyār a place. As [the poet] faced north [to starve himself to death in the rite of vaṭakkiruttal], he sang this. *Tiṇai: potuviyal. Tuṟai: kaiyaṟunilai.*

224

He won his victories in war, never sparing strong fortresses!
Together with his friends, he threw down whole pots of liquor!
He offered his shelter to the large families of bards!
Surrounded by his faultless women extolled for their purity,
for their immaculate nature, he performed the Vedic sacrifices
in the court of Righteousness where justice is well practiced
after those conversant with proper custom stand up and show
their knowledge, within the circling many-layered wall where
the towering post of sacrifice rises next to the kite to be fed!
He who had all that knowledge, how wise a man he was
who has died now and how this world is to be pitied!
Like vēṅkai trees that cowherds strip of their branches,
cutting them with sharp swords to feed their precious
herds who are hungry in the fearful drought of summer
when the waterfalls dry up and as the branches of flowers fall,
the vigor of the trees is shattered,
so the sweet and tender women shed their ornaments!

Karuṅkuḷavātaṉār sings Cōḻaṉ Karikāṟperuvaḷattāṉ. *Tiṇai: potuviyal. Tuṟai: kaiyaṟunilai.*

225

Listen if you want to know what has become of the majesty
that led an army of raised spears which destroyed the power

of kings, which circled the wide world in the proper direction
and was so vast that the front of the army ate palmyra seeds,
the center the ripe fruit and the rear ate the tuber
matured so that it split open with its fibers and was cooked
on a fire! That majesty lies now in a broad, thorny forest
upon salty land crowded with weeds! The conches of war
with their curled mouths that once hung solidly together
like the dangling nests of weaver birds lest the king
Cēṭceṉṉi Nalaṅkiḷḷi might hear them can now be heard
in the morning and as they are sounded at the doorways
of the protectors of the earth
with melodious drums announcing victories, I stand here in
mourning.

Ālattūrkiḻār sings Cōḻaṉ Nalaṅkiḷḷi. *Tiṇai: potuviyal. Tuṟai: kaiyaṟunilai.*

226

If Death had come to him in hatred, or shown anger
or so much as touched him, there would have been no escape
for Death! He must have joined his palms together in respect
as a singer would and praised him and begged to take
Vaḷavaṉ who wore a garland of gold,
whose chariot was powerful, whose army won victory in dense
battles!

Māṟōkkattu Nappacalaiyār sings Cōḻaṉ Kuḷamuṟṟattut Tuñciya Kiḷḷivaḷavaṉ.
Tiṇai: potuviyal. Tuṟai: kaiyaṟunilai.

227

You, Death! you who show no mercy are a total fool!
Because you had no grain you have gone and cooked
and eaten up the seeds! You will see how true this is!
Since you have taken Vaḷavaṉ, that man whose chaplet
swarmed with bees, who wore thick golden ornaments

and who was just like you, he who each and every day
could calm the hunger that consumes you with his flawless
force through the daily slaughter of his victories
on the field of battle where water is rich red with blood
of horses, elephants, men with shining swords,
all of them falling, whom do you have now to calm your hunger?

Āvaṭuturai Mācāttaṉār sings Cōḻaṉ Kuḷamuṟṟattut Tuñciya Kiḻḻivaḷavaṉ.
Tiṇai: potuviyal. Tuṟai: kaiyaṟunilai.

228

O potter who fires pots! Potter who fires pots
in a kiln which shoots up a mass of blackened smoke
across the vast sky as if all darkness had been gathered
into the broad and ancient city, potter who fires pots!
You are to be pitied! How can you do what you must do?
He who had elephants with swaying tusks, he who was born
in the line of Cempiyaṉ, he whose massive army poured
over the earth, whose majesty was far famed, whose
fine, undying glory has been praised by the poets
and has spread far across the sky as if it were the sun
with its expanding rays, the great Vaḷavaṉ has reached
the world of the gods and now you want to fashion an urn
large enough to enclose him! With great Mount Meru
for your clay and the wide earth
for your wheel, will you be able somehow to throw that vessel?

The Aiyūr Muṭavaṉār sings Cōḻaṉ Kuḷamuṟṟattut Tuñciya Kiḻḻivaḷavaṉ.
Tiṇai: potuviyal. Tuṟai: āṉantappaiyuḷ.

229

At midnight crowded with darkness in the first
quarter of the night when the constellation of Fire
was linked with The Goat and from the moment

the First Constellation arose, formed like a bent palmyra,
and the one shaped like a reservoir was glittering
at the farthest limit, during the first half
of the month of Paṅkuṉi, when the Constellation
of the Far North was descending and the Eighth
Constellation was rising and the Deer's Head
sinking into the sea, a star fell from the sky! Not slanting east or north,
like a light for the earth surrounded by ocean, a star fell as roaring,
spreading fire stirred and swollen by the wind! When we saw this,
I and many others who had come to him in our need thought, "May the king
who rules a good land with a waterfall whose music is like a drum, may he
live without illness!" A feeling of despair spread throughout our
troubled hearts and we were afraid! Now the seventh day has come and
as great elephants lie sleeping on their trunks and the royal drum
tightly bound with its straps has burst its eye and rolls across
the ground and the white umbrella of protection is snapped off
at the base and ruined and the proud horses swift as the wind stand
stock still, he has reached the world of the gods! Has he
who was the lover desired by women who wear shining bangles
forgotten those women who were his companions? He was a man
the dark color of a mountain of sapphires! His strength bound up
his enemies and killed them. And to those
who wished him well he was munificent beyond measure!

Kūṭalūrkiḻar, fearing that Kōccēramāṉ Yāṉaikaṭcēey Māntarañcēralirumpoṟai would die on a certain day, sang this song when [that king] died. *Tiṇai: potuviyal. Tuṟai: āṉantappaiyuḷ.*

230

With his glittering sword and dazzling feats of war, the man
who never spoke a false word, whose rod of justice never trembled,
who warded off intruding enemies so that the herds of cows

tender to their calves could be at peace in the forest and travelers
with their aching feet could rest wherever they pleased and heaps
of paddy might stand unguarded in the fields, E̱lini has fallen,
fighting on the battleground! Everywhere you look, the people
that he loved are in anguish like a child who has been abandoned
by the woman who gave birth to it but you, Death!, you who have
no virtues, you have lost more than the world which stands
plunged into grief, the heart of it filled with a pain
heightened by hunger! Like a farmer whose family has fallen
into hard times and so he forgets the good of the fields
which are the source of life and eats his own seeds, if you
had not eaten up this man, how you would have grown
fat wolfing down the lives of his many enemies on the killing field!

Aricilkiḻār sings Atiyamāṉ Takaṭūrpporutu Vīḻnta Eḻiṉi. *Tiṇai: potuviyal. Tuṟai: kaiyaṟunilai.*

231

Should his body wish, let it advance to the shining cremation fire
piled up of sticks with singed black tips like those a Kuṟavaṉ
of the hills cuts on a burned-out field, or if it does not wish
to advance toward the fire, let it go and rise on its own to touch
the sky! That man was like the glowing sun
with the cool-rayed moon of his umbrella and his fame will never die.

Auvaiyār sings Atiyamāṉ Neṭumāṉ Añci. *Tiṇai: potuviyal. Tuṟai: kaiyaṟunilai.*

232

May there be no morning anymore! May there be no evening
anymore!
Let the days I have left in my life not have any more meaning!
As the feathers of peacocks adorn his memorial stone of a hero,
when the small cup of clear toddy filtered through fiber is poured
down upon it, will he accept it, he who would not

accept an entire country of high mountains with soaring summits?

Auvaiyār sings Atiyamaṉ Neṭumāṉ Añci. *Tiṇai: potuviyal. Tuṟai: kaiyaṟunilai.*

233

Let it be a lie! Let it be a lie like the story of the discus
fashioned of fine iron supposed to be owned by Akutai
who performed strong and noble feats, who gave away elephants
with their huge feet to those who came to him in their need!
Let it be a lie, that in the chest of Evvi, on which the huge
pendant hangs, whose weapons were murderous in war, overlord
of a great gathering of bards, there are many
impressive wounds, as the insistent voice proclaims in the morning!

Veḷḷerukkilaiyār sings Vēḷ Evvi. *Tiṇai: potuviyal. Tuṟai: kaiyaṟunilai.*

234

Do I feel my grief? May the duration of my life end!
How is it possible that he can accept a small, bland
memorial ball of rice set down on grass by his dear wife
once she has cleared and smeared smooth with cow dung a tiny
spot the size of an elephant's footprint, he
who took his meals with throngs, his door open for the world to enter!

Veḷḷerukkilaiyār sings Vēḷ Evvi. *Tiṇai: potuviyal. Tuṟai: kaiyaṟunilai.*

235

When he had only a little toddy, he would give it to us. But now no longer!
When he had ample toddy he would give it to us

and then happily drink what was left to him as we sang. But now no longer!
When he had a little rice, he would set it on many dishes. But now no longer!
When he had heaps of rice, he would put it out on many dishes. But now no longer!
Wherever he came upon bones full of meat, he gave them away. But now no longer!
Wherever arrows and spears crossed the battlefield, there he stood. But now no longer!
With his hands that were fragrant with orange scent,
he stroked my hair with its stench of meat. But now no longer!
Piercing holes through the wide bowls of great, towering bards,
through the hands of those who came to him in need and through
the tongues of poets with their elaborate skill at shaping words,
dimming the pupils in the leaden eyes of all their dependents,
the spear ran that flew
through his chest and only then
it fell to earth! Where now is that lord who has been our support?
Now there are no singers any more! Now there are none who are generous to singers!
Like the giant pakaṉṟai flower that flows with nectar and grows
in a cool watery place but is never worn by anyone,
many lives pass away without ever having given a single thing to other men!

Auvaiyār sings Atiyamaṉ Neṭumāṉ Añci. *Tiṇai: potuviyal. Tuṟai: kaiyaṟunilai.*

236

Master of a mountain where a huge fruit chewed at by monkeys
so that it looks like a torn up drum is food for many days
to the hillmen Kuṟavars armed with bows! Most generous Pāri!
No matter how closely we cared for each other, you did not
let it win you over! Surely you must have been angry with me!
When you did not let me come with you, you denied
our rich friendship, the many years that you watched over me!

You told me I had to stay here. Because you behaved
in that way, I could not be as near you as my love for you
could reach! May I be with you, may I see you without a moment
apart in the next life, just as
in this life! May this be granted to me through some great destiny!

After Vēḷ Pāri died, [and] entrusted his daughters to Brahmins, Kapilar sat facing north [to starve himself to death in the rite of vaṭakkiruttal] and sang this song. *Tiṇai: potuviyal. Tuṟai: kaiyaṟunilai.*

237

On a day of hunger, as I came near to the high gate and wishing
long life for its overlord stopped there to sing, I was thinking
"When song was planted in the ear of that strong man who never
could lie, who was like soothing shade in summer, then it would
bear fruit! But now the desire I treasured is worthless!
It is like empty fire blazing up in a cooking pot. It has
no value now! Death has been brazen enough to take life without
making any distinctions, without caring if the poor are fed!
Now without any rest the women beat their breasts in pain
and fragments of bangles are scattered like plantain flowers.
Those with eloquent tongues who came here in need are grieving
together with their families! Because the hero, he who wielded
his sharp spear, is gone to the salt land of the burning ground
overgrown with spurge and he has disappeared. May there be a curse
on Death!" If a tiger has spied out and brought down his prey
of an elephant on a high mountain but that elephant escapes,
the tiger will not search for a rat to catch! We will
instead go away from here as rapidly as the water of a river
rushing into the many waves of the ocean
and we will win good gifts! Rise up, my heart, and follow your
resolve!

When Peruñcittiraṉār went to Veḷimāṉ, he had [already] died. [His younger brother] Iḷaveḷimāṉ ["the young Veḷimāṉ"] gave only a little. [The poet] did not accept it and sang this song. *Tiṇai: potuviyal. Tuṟai: kaiyaṟunilai.*

238

He has gone to the burial ground in the forest where the male
of the kite with its red ears and the pokuval bird and the crow
with its strong beak and the owl perch without fear near the curving
surface of the red burial urn set down into the earth,
and then move wherever they please in the company of a pack
of ghouls! He who once loved to drink toddy! Like his women
whose bangles are gone, the families of bards have lost
their former glow and the beauty they had has withered away!
On the massed royal drums, the eyes have been torn open!
Elephants like mountains have lost tusks and no one rides them.
I did not know that Death with his blazing strength was savagely
marauding and that my lord, ah! he was the pitiful victim!
Because I have come, I am miserable! What will happen to those
who depend on me? As if I were someone dumb and blind
whose boat has overturned on a rain-swept night and his heart
is swollen with intolerable suffering and he sinks without hope
into the ocean, it would be best that I die in the spiraling
of this whirlpool of pain, this flood
of irresistible waves, measureless and unfathomable! It would be just.

The song of Peruñcittiraṉār after Veḷimāṉ had died. *Tiṇai: potuviyal. Tuṟai: kaiyaṟunilai.*

239

He embraced women wearing bangles on their arms
and in a guarded forest he adorned them with flowers!
He smeared himself with cool, fragrant sandalpaste.
He destroyed his enemies along with their families
and his friends he praised to the skies!
He never flattered anyone for his strength
nor lorded over someone because he was weak.
Never did he beg from others but never
would he refuse any who begged from him!
In the courts of kings, he displayed his towering glory.
He repelled the armies bent on invasion,

and he saw the backs of armies in retreat.
He drove his horses with prodigious speed
and sent his chariot down long roads.
He rode out on noble elephants!
He emptied jars of toddy, thick and sweet,
and he made bards happy, freeing them of hunger,
and he would never use bewildering words!
Since he did all that he should do, you can
cut off and fling away his head or burn
the head of the man who sought such glory! Do as you will!

Pēreyil Muṟuvalār sings Nampineṭuñceḻiyaṉ. *Tiṇai: potuviyal. Tuṟai: kaiyaṟunilai.*

240

He who gave away horses with gaits of various rhythms
and elephants and whole territories and cities with unending revenue
ceaselessly to singers, Āy Aṇṭiraṉ has gone to the world
of the gods accompanied by his women with their tiny bangles
and their high-sloping mounds of love, when Death who has
no mercy took them away. At the side of a burning ground
where sedge grows, where a wide-mouthed owl settled into the space
of the hollow of a tree hoots to the dead his message
that they must burn and be added to the ashes, his body
rested, and vanished as the glowing fire consumed it. The eyes
of poets have been dimmed. Nowhere do they see anyone
who can shelter them. Their families clamor but they
can do nothing for them and they go off
shrunken with hunger now, away to the countries of other kings!

Kuṭṭuvaṉ Kīraṉār sings Āy. *Tiṇai: potuviyal. Tuṟai: kaiyaṟunilai.*

241

"He who wears a cooling garland of flowers, he who gave gifts
of sturdy chariots to those who went to him in need, Aṇṭiraṉ

is coming!" roars the drum covered with skin within the palace
of Indra whose great hand wearing glowing bracelets
holds the lightning bolt, and the music of it soars into the sky!

Uṟaiyūr Ēṇiccēri Muṭamōciyār sings Āy. *Tiṇai: potuviyal. Tuṟai: kaiyaṟunilai.*

242

Young men do not don them. Women with their bangles do not
pluck them. The bard does not gently bend the branch down
with the tip of his yāḻ and then adorn himself with the flowers.
Nor do the singing women wear them now. Cāttaṉ who overwhelmed
warriors with his powerful spear and was a man has died
and do you, jasmine! still blossom in his land of Ollaiyūr?

Kuṭavāyiṟ Kīrattaṉār sings Ollaiyūr Kiḻāṉ Makaṉ Peruñcāttaṉ. *Tiṇai: potuviyal. Tuṟai: kaiyaṟunilai.*

243

How sad it is to think about it now! When I was young I would
take the hands of girls at play near the cool pond as they plucked
flowers on the dense sand to decorate a doll they had made
of mud and when they hugged me I hugged them, when they swayed
with me I swayed with them, and the boys who were my friends
    would never
betray me or even know the meaning of deception! And I would
    climb out
on a branch of a marutam tree with its high boughs growing
near the water so that it sagged toward the pond, so that
it curved down to the water and gracefully while the people
watching on the shore were filled with wonder, I dove
to the bottom of the deep water and brought up a handful of sand
in my ignorant youth! Where is it gone? Trembling, propped
on a strong cane with a metal knob, the few

words I speak wracked with coughs, how miserably old I have
    become!

Toṭittalai Viḻutaṇṭiṉār sings Ollaiyūr Kiḻāṉ Makaṉ Peruñcāttaṉ. *Tiṇai: potuviyal. Tuṟai: kaiyaṟunilai.*

244

Bees do not come here to hover around the heads of bards;
their bangles gone, the arms of dancing women glow no longer;
and those who have come here in need . . .

Tiṇai: potuviyal. Tuṟai: kaiyaṟunilai.

245

Though it is so immense, does my grief nonetheless have
its limits, since it is not fierce enough to finish with my life?
On the salty earth all overgrown with sedge, on the burning ground,
my wife has gone her way to the other world, her bed
the shining fire of the pyre whose wood yields its glow
of blazing fuel! And I am
still alive! What kind of a place is this world?

The song of Cēramāṉ Kōṭṭampalattut Tuñciya Mākkōtai when his [wife] Peruṅkōppeṇṭu had died. *Tiṇai: potuviyal. Tuṟai: kaiyaṟunilai.*

246

All of you noble men! All of you noble men!
You do not let me go, you do not allow me to put
an end to my life! All you noble men with your perverse planning!
I am not a woman to endure eating a ball of boiled rice
squeezed within a hand and left lying overnight on a leaf
without a touch of fine fragrant ghee pale as the seeds

from a curving cucumber striped like a squirrel and split
open with a sword, or to eat food of steamed vēḷai leaves
cooked in tamarind and a paste of white sesame seeds,
nor am I one to sleep, without a mat, upon a bed of stones!
To you the pyre of black branches that has been raised
on the burning ground may well be fearful but to me,
now that my husband with his powerful arms has died,
a lake flowing with water where lotuses
open their luxuriant petals and the fire are the same!

The words of Peruṅkōppeṇṭu, the wife of Pūtapāṇṭiyaṉ, when she was entering the fire. *Tiṇai: potuviyal. Tuṟai: āṉantappaiyuḷ.*

247

In the zone where spirits roam, at the light of a fire
hunters have kindled by scraping up a spark on the dry wood
dragged in by elephants, where a female monkey has startled
a large herd of gentle deer and then digs at earth, there a woman
wanders toward the burning ground, her hair streaming wet
and falling loose down her back while her large eyes are filled with grief!
Though she, in the vast well-guarded palace of her husband
where the eye of the concert drum never is silent, has only
been alone for a little while,
she is fleeing her young years that make her tremble with the sweetness of life!

The words of Maturaip Pēralavāyār when he saw [Peruṅkōppeṇṭu, the wife of Pūtapāṇṭiyaṉ,] entering the fire. *Tiṇai: potuviyal. Tuṟai: āṉantappaiyuḷ.*

248

The small white waterlily is a paltry thing.
When we were young, we wore them but now
since our lord with his great strength is dead, its seeds
are the miserable food we have to eat

at the wrong hours and together with our suffering.

Okkūr Mācāttaṉār sings. . . . *Tiṇai: potuviyal. Tuṟai: tāpata nilai.*

249

There was a time when in the wide-ranging country of that lord
where fishermen wielding their nets suddenly stir up the lake
in which the flowers are bright as fire and a sand eel burrows
into the mud, its nose sharp as a weaver's spindle, and a whiskered
scabbard fish leaps above the surface and a tortoise is overturned
suddenly as when a sharply beaten taṭāri drum stops short, and the fishermen
catch a dense school of carp glowing like swords and they take murrels
with feelers like the folded young leaves of palmyra trees,
there was a time when food was meant for sharing and that lord fed
many people in one place, but now it is over! His wife with her lovely
forehead and restrained purity, as he enters the world of exalted
being . . . . wishing to give him food, clears off a small dusty space
the size of a winnowing fan, her eyes endlessly
weeping, and cleanses it with cow dung mingled with the water of her tears.

Tumpaic Cokiṉaṉār sings. . . . *Tiṇai: potuviyal. Tuṟai: tāpata nilai.*

250

You at whose gateway those coming in need were halted
by the rice and the best of meat crackling with the sound
of frying spices, you whose cool and fragrant pavilion
halted the weeping of bards, O wealthy, mighty palace!
You have lost everything, you and the wife who has cut off
her hair and shed her small bangles and eats nothing
but waterlily seeds, now that the father of sons who would
refuse white rice because they wanted it only

mixed with sweet milk has gone to the lonely burning ground!

Tāyaṅkaṇṇiyār sings. . . . *Tiṇai: potuviyal. Tuṟai: tāpata nilai.*

251

We have seen a warrior who made the bangles of his women loosen
with their longing for him, women lovely as dolls wearing
their tiny bracelets in the mansion as elegant as a building depicted
in a painting. Now he bathes in a waterfall on a high mountain
overgrown with bamboo and dries the curling, matted hair that falls
low on his back, and the red fire, strong and raging,
fueled with wood brought in by forest elephants is what he yearns
for.

Mārippittiyār sings. . . . *Tiṇai: vākai. Tuṟai: tāpata vākai.*

252

His matted hair wan as new leaves of a tillai tree, bleached
by the white roaring waterfall, he plucks the leaves from a dense
growth of tāḷi bushes, who to capture the woman that now lives
in his house, and is as lovely as a peacock
without guile, would go hunting with a net of words in days
gone by!

Mārippittiyār sings. . . . *Tiṇai: vākai. Tuṟai: tāpata vākai.*

253

You do not feel my pain now. Because you have died, I cannot
rejoice with the young men who wear chaplets bound with strong
cord
as they celebrate. Must I go and tell your people of your death
while I lift my hands empty of bangles, showing whitened bands
as when the bark is stripped from sprouts

of bamboo that have never seeded? Tell me what I must do!

Kuḷampantāyaṉār sings. . . . *Tiṇai: potuviyal. Tuṟai: mutupālai.*

254

The young men and the old men have left for another place.
When I embrace you, young warrior, you do not rise,
with your chest pressing the earth, you who have fallen
in the wilderness! While I show my arms that are pale
and wear no bangles, if the word that their young man is now
only this should reach your family, what will happen
to his mother who praises him every day, ceaselessly
repeating "For me the strength and majesty of my son
are like the fresh fruit growing in front of the city
on a ripe banyan tree that is all
filled with birds"? You should feel deep pity for her!

Kayamaṉār sings. . . . *Tiṇai: potuviyal. Tuṟai: mutupālai.*

255

If I start to scream, I fear that tigers may come for you!
If I hug you and try to lift you up, I cannot raise
your broad chest. May unjust Death, who brought you pain,
shiver till he is exhausted, just as I do. Take my hand
which is still dense with bangles and we
will go into the shadow of the mountain. Only walk a little while.

Vaṉparaṇar sings. . . . *Tiṇai: potuviyal. Tuṟai: mutupālai.*

256

O potter who makes pots! Potter who makes pots!
Like a small white lizard caught on the spoke of a turning wagon
wheel,

I've come with him across wasteland after wasteland. Take pity
upon me as well! And on this wide earth spreading out
in far-ranging expanses, fashion him a burial urn, one
that will be large, potter
who makes pots in the ancient town spreading out in great expanses.

Tiṇai: potuviyal. Tuṟai: mutupālai . . . .

257

Who is that man with the bow, his legs strong, his belly
elegant, his chest wide, with angry eyes, his beard
the deep shade of kucci grass, with full sideburns growing
down low from his ears, the one who is like a pebble
in the sandals of his enemies? Must we feel sorry for him?
You should consider that he rarely leaves his city. He does not
fortify the forest to defend himself. Early in the morning,
he surveys sites where the herds of cows that belong
to his enemies have gone and he points at them and he counts them
and then he attacks and seizes them with his bow. As many
as they are then, of what use are they to him, he who does not
whiten his own bowl with milk and never hears
the sound of churning sticks spattering drops of milk by the light of
day?

Tiṇai: veṭci. Tuṟai: uṇṭāṭṭu . . . .

258

Seizing cows from the city of Kantāram where the liquor
ferments well, like the ripened fruit of the kārai bush
with its thorny stalks, he traded them for toddy,
which he drank. Then he ate fresh meat and wiping his hand
still moist with spit on the body of his bow,
he went off to the field of battle, the young man
with the meager beard! Before these warriors have had their meal,

he'll bring back cows and he'll fill the squares of their city
with the herds! Don't let anyone touch those jars of drink
that have been sweetly aged, because the man
will be dusty and tired from raiding and he will want that liquor!

Ulōccaṉār sings. . . . *Tiṇai: veṭci. Tuṟai: uṇṭāṭṭu* . . . .

259

Though the large herd moves on behind its leading bull, they do not.
They are there, hanging back. You cannot see the warriors who hold
powerful bows as they crouch in hiding within the great
leaf-shrouded forest. Do not go! Do not go after the cows
that leap and gambol as if they were low-caste women whose bodies
have been possessed by a god,
you who wear war anklets and by your side a shining sword!

Kōṭaipāṭiya Perumpūtaṉār sings. . . . *Tiṇai: karantai. Tuṟai: cerumalaital* and/or *piḷḷaippeyarcci* . . . .

260

You tried to play a forceful melody but the strings of your yāḻ
altered at your touch to sound the viḷari mode of grief.
Your heart felt weak and you set out. Then, on seeing the omen
of a housewife spreading her hair to dry, you paid your homage
to the god who lives in the shadow of prickly pear trees on salty land.
Bard! You are coming now with hunger in your stomach, sadly
joining
your palms together in respect and you keep asking over and over,
"Will I see him?" Listen to how well we stand! Accept the fields
he has granted you and eat your fill or else wake up at night
and feel your anguish. Either of these two things you can do
at once. They are so simple. He was renowned for defeating
the brave men who used to appear in battle before his walls
and seize great herds to take back to their own city. He crossed

the flood of arrows they had loosed at him upon the raft
of his war drum and he killed them and he freed his herds.
Like the moon which escapes from between the sharp fangs
of the devouring serpent as the whole world grieves for it,
he would return with fame, with a herd of many cows
and calves that he had wrested from the warrior Maṟavars.
Like a snake when it sheds its skin, he has gone off now
to the world which is so difficult to attain. On the shore
of a small stream in a forest, in an inaccessible place,
his body has fallen, pierced by arrows as if it were a target
collapsing, quivering upon its fixed base. But the name
of that hero with his great renown is inscribed on a stone
under a pavilion raised up of cloth, on a small site
no one else can fill, and that stone
is adorned with the beauty of a guileless peacock's feather.

Vaṭamōtaṅkiḻār sings. . . . *Tiṇai: karantai. Tuṟai: kaiyāyunilai* and/or *pāṇpāṭṭu*. . . .

261

O the sadness! O mansion of my lord, where the doors were never closed!
The raised verandah with its worn floor where the finest of rice was given
away without end and cups of liquor were never left empty, the bees
hovering over them—it is now like a boat in the bed of a dried-up river!
O I have seen it! May my eyes be ruined! Within you there was the sizzling
of lamb's meat cooking in a pot with heated ghee, like the pained moaning
sound of an elephant in rut in the royal palace overflowing with wealth
of the Protectors of the World, so that the tired eyes of strangers
arriving would open wide, in the old days! But they have vanished now!

The lord who harried the cattle raiders, those primitive and powerful archers,
so that the owl's harsh voice called his kin of other owls to a feast
on the dead, the lord who returned from raids wearing fragrant basil
that hangs down like the udders of heifers, the proper ornament
as the learned well know, he who returned right here with the herd,
that hero with his victorious spear is gone and now he has become
a memorial stone. Because of this, like his wife who mourns
all alone, who has shaved off her hair in the anguish of widowhood
and had her ornaments stripped away,
you too have turned wan and you have lost all that at one time adorned you.

Āvūrmūlaṅkiḻār sings. . . . *Tiṇai: karantai. Tuṟai: kaiyāyunilai* and/or *pāṇpāṭṭu*. . . .

262

Strain the toddy! Slaughter a male goat! In a pavilion
with pale columns, roofed over with green leaves,
spread the fresh sand everywhere that has been
carried here by the waters! My lord is approaching now
with a herd, but more tired than he is are the men
who take their stand beside him behind
the cattle and they ward off the vanguard of the enemy!

Maturaippērālavāyār sings. . . . *Tiṇai: veṭci. Tuṟai: uṇṭāṭṭu* and/or *talaittōṟṟam*. . . .

263

You who come in need, carrying your large drum with its single eye
like the foot of a giant elephant, if you should travel in that direction
do not fail to bow down when you pass the memorial stone! Then
for sure this desolate path will turn fertile, and attract the bees!
He was the man who won back a huge herd of cows that had been

seized and when his ignorant young men fled, he did not,
but like the shore of a river in flood time,
he drove the enemy back and sank among fierce arrows loosed from their bows.

Tiṇai: karantai. Tuṟai: kaiyaṟunilai . . . .

264

Now they have raised a memorial stone and set it up on a mound
erected on stony ground and they have circled it with a garland
of red flowers strung on split hemp and they have placed a feather
from a lovely peacock there and inscribed his name on the stone.
Ignorant of the death of that noble man who brought in
cows and calves and drove off
his enemies, will the families of bards come here still?

Uṟaiyūr Iḷampoṉ Vāṇikaṉār sings. . . . *Tiṇai: karantai. Tuṟai: kaiyaṟunilai.*

265

On worn down land, barren and rocky, far away from the city,
you have turned into a stone adorned with leaves by cowherds who tend
many cattle and who tie glowing fragrant clusters of vēṅkai flowers
from the tall trees and palmyra fronds with them to your stone,
O lord of fast horses! Not only the wealth given to those
who came to you in need and then lived out their lives
in the shadow of your feet when you were like thunder in the sky
but also the sure victories of kings
who had their swiftly running elephants have vanished with you!

Cōṇāṭṭu Mukaiyalūrc Ciṟukaruntumpiyār sings. . . . *Tiṇai: karantai. Tuṟai: kaiyaṟunilai.*

266

Lord of great victories! Master of a land where the fields gleam
with water and even though it is summer when no huge, bountiful
cloud
has poured down rain and the mud is still drying at the bottom
of the reservoirs, nevertheless in the broad shade of a waterlily
with its hollow stalk, a snail who has a spiraling face
and horns like spindles is mating in broad daylight
with a female conch! You whose lofty umbrella reaches the sky!
Ceṉṉi with your strong horses! As if listening to the cry for help
of a man who has presented himself in a meeting hall where noble men
are assembled, please, right now, grant me relief for this poverty of
mine
that muddies my thoughts, within my body with all of its senses
whose life has turned so twisted
that I hide myself whenever I feel that guests are thinking of visiting
me!

Peruṅkuṉṟūrkiḻār sings Cōḻaṉ Uruvappaḥrēr Iḷañcēṭceṉṉi. *Tiṇai: pāṭāṇṭiṇai. Tuṟai: paricil kaṭānilai.*

267, 268 [missing from text]

269

Wearing a garland of wild jasmine full of seeds and a few blossoms
and buds as sharp tipped as a kuyil's beak resplendently
bedecking your thick black hair, you drank once, and again,
of liquor as amber as a tiger's eyes poured out in a new cup,
and then because a tuṭi drummer wearing a chaplet of dried leaves
and drumming the call to battle on his drum had come,
you refused to praise and accept the filtered, intoxicating
toddy they then offered you but instead took up this sword,
they say, into your powerful hand and with it after tracking
bowmen who had seized the many long lines of cattle in combat

where the warriors wore fragrant basil, you cut down
those enemies while the red vultures screeched, sailing on their
curving wings!

The song of Auvaiyār. *Tiṇai: veṭci. Tuṟai: uṇṭāṭṭu.*

270

They who roll their wheels of the law across the earth,
they who master elephant herds, whose royal drums roar
like the clouds in the sky where the many stars glitter,
they are all grieving together on the battlefield. Mother
of children! Woman of a noble house! You whose hair
is gray and now without fragrance, unperfumed! I too
am grieving! You must look! On the fearful battlefield
where men of bravery, indomitable, listened to the sweet
sound resound of the taṇṇumai drum as it summoned up
the warrior armies with its booming voice, where they met
in a great battle to dominate the center of the field,
there they mourn that man of valor
who fell by the sword, like a tree cut through with a giant ax!

The song of Kaḻāttalaiyār. What he said to the mother as he saw [the dead hero]. *Tiṇai: karantai. Tuṟai: kaiyaṟunilai.*

271

We used to see garments of nocci flowers, dark bunches grown
on fields which never knew of a lack of water and their colors
worn across the broad and lovely mounds of love of women
with filigreed ornaments would fill one's eyes! But now
we see a kite taking flight after it has snatched up
a torn garland of nocci flowers all changed and covered
with a fearful smear of blood

because it had been worn by that man whose goal was courage.

The song of Veṟipāṭiya Kāmakkāṇiyār. *Tiṇai: nocci. Tuṟai: ceruviṭai vīḻtal.*

272

Nocci tree with your dark clusters that are like so many masses
of sapphires! Of all the trees that bear their flowers, you
are the most beloved! You rest across the mounds
of love of women wearing bangles who bring their beauty
into the broad, well-guarded city! And you have the honor
of being worn upon the mighty head of the noble man who refused
to surrender his city but stood his ground
and broke the resistance of his enemies before the fortified wall!

The song of Mōcicāttaṉār. *Tiṇai: nocci. Tuṟai: ceruviṭai vīḻtal.*

273

His horse is not coming back! His horse is not coming back!
Everyone else's horses have come back! The one that belongs
to the man of wealth who fathered the son of our house, his boy
who wears a topknot like a dull-colored mane, that horse
has not come back! Like a huge tree that might have been caught
at the meeting place of two rivers
of great size, has the horse that he was fighting on fallen?

The song of Erumaiveḷiyaṉār. *Tiṇai: tumpai. Tuṟai: kutiraimaṟam.*

274

The warrior of great worth, who wears a purple waistband and a garment
covered with designs of flowers and a chaplet of the feathers
of peacocks, has hurled his spear at an elephant that was charging

against him and now he is dangerously hard pressed, he who had
caught in his hands the javelins that enemies hurled at him
from ranging horses, had clasped and seized
fierce hold of their chief, dashed him down and then held up the dead body!

The song of Ulōccaṉār. *Tiṇai: tumpai. Tuṟai: kutiraimaṟam.*

275

This man bends three things, a curving chaplet for his hair,
his garment curving around him and wrinkled from wear, and a king
by saying whatever he wants to say. He has pierced the rear guard
so that the cohort besieging him cried out in fear and he stretches
his long, sharp spear toward the army. Men shout, "Stop him
here! Stop him!" but that means nothing at all to him! Like an elephant
in chains, he is hindered only by the guts that are entangling his feet!
As if he were a cow that loves her calf,
he advances toward his friend who is fighting against the front ranks!

The song of Orūuttaṉār. *Tiṇai: tumpai. Tuṟai: kutiraimaṟam.*

276

He is the much loved son of that old woman with her white hair
free of fragrant oils and her dried-up breasts with their nipples
shriveled like the fruit of an ironwood tree, she who has
so many virtues, and as if he were a few drops of curd
young herder women flick into a pot of milk
with their sharp nails, he pervades the enemy's army with pain.

The song of Maturaip Pūtaṉ Iḷanākaṉār. *Tiṇai: tumpai. Tuṟai: tāṉai nilai.*

277

When she learned that her son had fallen slaying an elephant,
the old woman whose hair was as white as the feathers
of a fish-eating heron felt even more joy than the time
she gave birth to him. And the tears that she shed then
were more than the drops that hang
from sturdy bamboo after they collect there in the rain.

The song of Pūṅkaṉ Uttiraiyār. *Tiṇai: tumpai. Tuṟai: uvakaik kaluḻcci.*

278

When she heard the many voices saying, "That aged woman with dry,
veined arms where the soft flesh hangs down, she whose belly
is wrinkled like a lotus leaf—her son was afraid of the enemy army
and he showed them his back and ran!" then rage overcame her and she said,
"If he fled in the furious battle, I will cut off the breast
at which he sucked!" and she snatched up a sword and she
turned over every body lying there on the blood-soaked field.
And when she found her son who was scattered
in pieces, she felt happier than she had been the day she bore him.

The song of Kākkaipaṭiṉiyār Naccel̤l̤aiyār. *Tiṇai: tumpai. Tuṟai: uvakaik kaluḻcci.*

279

May her will be broken! What she has decided on is so cruel
but yet it is fitting for a woman descended from an ancient line!
Her father, the day before yesterday in battle, brought down
an elephant and then fell dead on the field! Yesterday
her husband drove back a long rank of warriors and then

was cut down in the fight! And today she heard the sound
of the war drum and she was overwhelmed with desire! Her mind
whirling, she put a spear into the hand of her only son and she wound
a white garment around his body and smeared oil upon the dry
topknot of his hair and having nothing
but him said "Go now!" and sent him off into the battle!

The song of Okkūr Mācāttiyār. *Tiṇai: vākai. Tuṟai: mūtiṉ mullai.*

280

In the chest of my lord, there are mortal wounds.
Bees are swarming in the bright middle of the day.
Within the great mansion, lights keep flickering out.
My eyes have not slept and they long for sleep.
The hooting of the owl is heard, making men afraid.
The words of the worthy old woman are not finished,
she who scatters water and rice and listens
to the bodiless voice of an oracle! Tuṭi drummer!
Bard! Dancing woman who sings! You deserve
pity! For you to stay alive in this world
is hard! But far harder it is for me to think
of going on living like the widows who have shed
their ornaments, water trickling down my close-shaven
head caked with mud, and for food the seeds
of the small white lily that was his garland of war!

The song of Māṟōkkattu Nappacalaiyār. *Tiṇai: potuviyal. Tuṟai: āṉantappaiyuḷ.*

281

In the towering house we will set out margosa flowers and branches
of the ironwood tree with its sweet fruit. We will play the curving
yāḻ and many other instruments. Moving your hand gently,

spread mai paste, and scatter the white mustard seed around
the house. Playing a flute of bamboo, singing a Kāñci song
of the passing of things, striking sweet-sounding bells,
lighting fragrant incense everywhere, come my good friend,
we will guard the wounds of that noble man,
his anklets incised with flowers, who drove off the threat to the king!

The song of Aricilkiḻār. *Tiṇai: kāñci. Tuṟai: toṭāk kāñci.*

282

If you ask me, "Where is he?" the man of imposing actions
who carried out his duty, who made his advances across
the broad field of battle while the spears ran through him
. . . .
because warriors, doing what they had to do, unleashed
their spears at his chest with its glittering garland where
the weapons hung as they reached him, his body is not anywhere
to be found and his life has been drained away.
His enemies, quieted, their enmity exhausted
. . . .
except for his broken shield, which has lost its power
to protect but lies on the battlefield and has not been destroyed.
He has established his good name shining into the distances
and he is alive in the mouths of bards with their eloquent tongues.

The song of Pālaipāṭiya Peruṅkaṭuṅkō. *Tiṇai. . . .*

283

The man from Aḻumpil—where in the morning an otter seizes its prey
of a scabbard fish, its leap scattering the bright red kurali vine
through the cool reservoir, and must then fight off a hungry
crocodile for whom a snake is no more than a shrimp and finally

darts away—it seems that the man would not give up his struggle
and so among the mass of the Kōcars gathered together and thirsting
for victory,
he would devastate the battlefield . . . . while
spears bristle on his friend's chest like spokes on a wheel's hub
and upon the thick sand women with soft arms who had been
playing
with dolls on their verandah now care for him, that man—before
his friend's life ends—is filled with fury and puts upon his own head
the garland twined of tumpai flowers
with long green leaves, as the bees go buzzing above its fragrance!

The song of Aṇṭarnaṭuṅkalliṉār. *Tiṇai: tumpai. Tuṟai: pāṇpāṭṭu.*

284

When he hears the cry "Come at once! Come at once!" called out
by royal messengers of noble birth who travel here and travel there,
the man of ancient lineage dons his garland
looped with a string and goes on foot alone
and turns the difficult battle around, then straightens the bent blade
of his sword on the tusks of an elephant he had cut down
facing it straight on, and he laughs
at the man who in flight shows his back to him!

The song of Ōrampōkiyār. *Tiṇai: tumpai. Tuṟai: pāṇpāṭṭu.*

285

All you men who live in the camp! All you men who live in the
camp!
In the hand of the drummer is a spear! In the hand of the bard
who carries a small yāḻ with a body curving downward and strings
that sound sweet is a shield! A sight to see, like densely packed
close-set sacks filled with new rice. . . . .
The hero who around his hair is wearing a withered garland because

the king arrived at his mighty palace encircled by the noble entourage
that does his labors, that hero with his shining, powerful shoulders,
enemy arrows swarming around him, shed his blood—O how the field
turned to mud with it!—when a long spear hurled with furious
rage entered his chest and then fell to the ground alongside
his anklets dripping human fat. . . . .
All the men around him said when they saw it, "Because no more
villages where the farms have fields of grain with ears twining together
and waving in the wind were left to give away, he gave a village
with barren land, the only one remaining, to the chief
of that poor family." As they praised him, he bowed down his head.

The song of Aricilkiḻār. *Tiṇai: vākai. Tuṟai: cālpumullai.*

286

Like white goats, the young men surrounded him
and a cup was passed above the heads of many
to my son and yet it did not lead to his
being laid out on a legless bed
and covered with a pure white cloth.

The song of Auvaiyār. *Tiṇai: karantai. Tuṟai: vēttiyal.*

287

Pulaiyaṉ beating on your tuṭi drum,
low-caste man with your throbbing drumsticks!
Those mighty warriors will never retreat even if arrows
shoot down like monsoon rain, even if spears fly through the air
like the small carp through a reservoir, even if massive elephants
wearing their golden forehead ornaments lower their heads
and gore with the tips of their white, glowing tusks!

What does it matter to them if they win farming villages
where scabbard fish leaping in reservoirs full of water
dart out onto the paddy fields that belong to towering
mansions! And should they die, they will have flawless women
for their wives in the highest world!
Stand here and look at the coming, rampaging enemy king!

The song of Cāttantaiyār. *Tiṇai: karantai. Tuṟai: nīṇmoḻi.*

288

In the middle of the battlefield, as the drum is beating,
tightly bound with its leather straps, covered with the unfinished skin
of the victor in a bull fight between two fine animals with horns
ending in sharp tips and streaked from their goring thrusts
into the mud, on that fierce field with a heart throbbing in shame
pierced through and through by a long spear hurled in fury,
swaying with blood . . . . around him
vultures crowd in so tightly, they leave
no room for anyone who might want to embrace his chest heaving
blood.

The song of Kaḻāttalaiyār. *Tiṇai: tumpai. Tuṟai: mūtiṉmullai.*

289

Though when the field is wet, all of them will do their work,
a plowman will look over each of his oxen with great care to
determine
which are the best he has! So among all those men of ancient lineage,
all those men of greatness, those men with their exalted dignity,
when he takes the vessel of new gold filled up with toddy
and brought to him with reverence and he says "Give this to that
man,"
do not be surprised at it! Bard, don't you hear the message
"Now is the time for you to wear flowers for battle!"
spoken by the voice of the drum,

its mouth covered in the hands of the low-caste drummer?

The song of Kaḻāttalaiyār.

290

Give him liquor and then drink yours! O lord of raging
war and of herds of elephants and of handsome chariots!
The father of your father and the father of his father together—
like the hub set by a carpenter at the center of a wheel—
stood their ground on the field where men raise and hurl spears
and there, without blinking, perished. He too is a man of might, famed
for his courage. Like a palm-leaf umbrella
when it is raining, lord! he will ward off the spears they aim at you.

The song of Auvaiyār. *Tiṇai: karantai. Tuṟai: kuṭinilaiyuraittal.*

291

You of lower caste! And drummers! And people skilled in song!
Come to the dark man wearing clothes that are pure white!
Fend off the sound of the great birds! And I, with the whirling
melody of viḷari, will keep away the white foxes. May the king
shudder, as I do, for he took the garland woven with jewels
which he was wearing and placed it on the head of that man
eager to die for no reason while
on his own head he set that man's garland, of a single strand.

The song of Neṭuṅkaḷattupparaṇar. *Tiṇai: karantai. Tuṟai: vēttiyal.*

292

Don't be angry at him because when we offered the sweet,
cool toddy to him at his proper place in the order of honor,
though it had been brought for the king, he refused it

and took up his sharp sword and leaped to his feet, you small
men of no worth! If on the battlefield he chooses to behave
as he has here, then he is no one who will tell you to call him
when it happens to be his turn, but he will take
his stand to block the route of a great surging army, as suits a man!

The song of Viricciyūr Naṉṉākaṉār. *Tiṇai: vañci. Tuṟai: peruñcōṟṟunilai.*

293

On the elephant that cannot be controlled with a goad the man beats
the drum of warning for the battle to be fought with local chieftains
and it roars out for those people who feel shame. Since she has lost
more things of beauty and value than we have, since the war
has broken out, the girl who sold flowers
is off to another home. You should feel compassion for her!

The song of Nocciniyamaṅkiḻār. *Tiṇai: kāñci. Tuṟai: pūkkōṭkāñci.*

294

He fought and stood aside and shouted, "If any of you are done with the days
allotted to you and wish to vaunt the majesty of your king and your own glory—
then come at me!" on the field of battle where combat was so close you could not
distinguish who was ours and who were the enemies of our men all doing
Death's work as they embraced the weapons they had brought virgin
from the camp where the men had seemed an ocean flooded by the descending light
of the moon like a white umbrella. But as if facing a jewel
dropped by a snake, no opponent dared
approach your husband who wore the row of garlands on his chest!

The song of Peruntalaic Cāttaṉār. *Tiṇai: tumpai. Tuṟai: tāṉai maṟam.*

295

When she contemplated the majesty of that handsome man
who in the middle of a battlefield that was like the ocean
rising, had advanced, his sword forged in fire stretching out
ahead of him, leading his troops into the battle where hurled
missiles fell men, shouldering into the oncoming army,
cutting open space until he died between the two hosts,
that warrior's mother, with her inflexible will,
was overcome by love then and again her withered breasts gave milk.

The song of Auvaiyār. *Tiṇai: tumpai. Tuṟai: uvakaik kaluḻcci.*

296

There is a clamor through all the houses as branches of margosa
are broken off and Kāñci songs of evanescence are sung
and the people, their hands smeared with ghee, burn mustard seed,
the smoke rising. That noble man must be cutting
down the king who enraged him. For his chariot is late returning.

The song of Veḷḷaimāṟaṉār. *Tiṇai: vākai. Tuṟai: ēṟāṇ mullai.*

297

As our reward in this place we do not want those villages
where sambur deer sleep with their fawns on the densely strewn husks
of a green cereal with long, handsome nuts curved like the massive
horns of buffalo who show their easy saunter and their longing
for expanses of water. As we praise and refuse, drinking the sweetly
aged liquor strained through fiber and afloat with flowers, it is proper

for us to receive farming villages along the rivers where waterfowl
lay their eggs near the fords, it is right for us who stand in battle
as the long spears with their sharp tips pierce
our chests so that we seem like palmyra trees all filled with jagged stems!

Tiṇai: veṭci. Tuṟai: uṇṭāṭṭu . . . .

298

He offers us the unfiltered toddy and he is himself content
to drink it clear. That king is hardly a cruel man!
Though he is now besieging the fortress of his enemies,
difficult to conquer, still he does not
bite his lip and roar at us to move ahead of him to the attack!

The song of Āviyār. *Tiṇai: karantai. Tuṟai: neṭumoḻi.*

299

The horses—though moving unsteadily because they had been fed
only husks of black gram from the ruler of a village hedged in
with cotton bushes—like ships cutting through the ocean split
open the front of the army! The horses of the rulers of riverine cities,
though they eat paddy mashed with ghee and are close curried and garlanded,
stand frozen in fear, like women in their time of the month, when
they must not even touch dishes, who have entered the temple of avenging Murugan!

The song of Poṉmuṭiyār. *Tiṇai: nocci. Tuṟai: kutirai maṟam.*

300

You shout, "Bring me my shield! Bring me my shield!" If you hold
your shield and you shelter yourself behind a rock, then maybe

you may escape. In the light of day yesterday you killed a man
whose younger brother with his eyes rolling like crab's-eye seeds
on a dish will now search you out as if
you were a pot of liquor brewed in one single house within a giant
city!

The song of Aricilkiḻār. *Tiṇai: tumpai. Tuṟai: tāṉai maṟam.*

301

All you many noble men! All you many noble men! Fenced round
for the sake of war with impenetrable bushes of thorns like the hair
of virgins, you live in the camp filled with uproar! All
you many noble men! Attend to your king with the roaring drum
in the midst of his army! Attend to your elephants with their
raised, glowing tusks! However many days your war may last,
how can we, on any day, attack those who do not attack us?
And when men attack our king, he will not go out to meet the attack
unless your king is there too! Who knows what he is planning?
You should be careful not to say, contemptuously, "There are so many
of us!" Look over there! In celebration of the exalted
virtues of his horse moving with all speed and without any delay
along minor roads, he came here during the night as if
he were measuring the earth! And he will never brandish
his spear with its glowing tip except
before the elephant ridden amidst the clamor by your king!

The song of Āvūr Mūlaṅkiḻār. *Tiṇai: tumpai. Tuṟai: tāṉai maṟam.*

302

Like bamboo which has been bent in two and let
shoot up, horses are running and leaping. Flowers
are twisted into the hair of women with gleaming bangles.
Villages on poor land where roads barely exist are granted
to bards wearing fragrant, many-stranded garlands of bitter orange
while their fingers pluck the strings of small yāḻs

with curving necks as they softly beat time. If you
were to try to count the elephants cut down in exultation
by the spear of that warrior who destroys those who dare
stare at him, neither the stars in the sky
scattered with clouds nor the drops of the cool rain would suffice!

The song of Veṟipāṭiya Kāmakkāṇiyār. *Tiṇai: tumpai. Tuṟai: kutirai maṟam.*

303

On a horse so swift it breaks the spirit of those who watch it,
with the hooves cutting the earth as if pushing it backward,
the young warrior who torments and destroys those who make
light of him, piercing chests with his long and strong
and raging spear—you can see him coming, he who yesterday,
before the famous kings, forced warriors aside like a boat
sailing the ocean that washes between its shores and brought
down bull elephants with shining tusks
whose young cows, their heads so tender, mourned for them.

The song of Erumaiveḷiyaṉār. *Tiṇai: tumpai. Tuṟai: kutirai maṟam.*

304

You put garlands on your women adorned with their long earrings.
You drink down filtered toddy to drive away shivers and chills.
You hurry to caparison a fast horse whose speed of foot
outruns the wind. They were told you were putting no food
in your stomach and that you were choosing among your
many horses and that you had said you would battle the man
who killed your elder brother and also take on the man's
younger brother both of them together! Hearing of this,
the sprawling, glowing camp of the king with a victorious
war drum who has won his triumphs in combat
trembles, knowing that your word will be no different from your
deeds.

The song of Aricilkiḻār. *Tiṇai: tumpai. Tuṟai: kutirai maṟam.*

305

A young Brahmin walking on the tips of his toes, his waist
become as thin as a vayalai vine, came and entered
the camp by night and without halting there he said only
a few words. At that they threw away their siege ladders,
and defense-gate stakes and stripped
the bells from their elephants that had fought well in many wars.

The song of Maturai Vēḷācāṉ. *Tiṇai: vākai. Tuṟai: pārppaṉa vākai.*

306

The woman with soft, bright hair and a shining face from a village,
where there are lovely families and thorny hedges of kaḻal vines and where
the reservoirs muddied by wallowing elephants are hard to use for drinking,
surely pressed her palms together in respect to the huge, immovable rock
and prayed to it: "May guests come to me, and may my lord
. . . .
struggle along with his king against great enemies, the way to win land!"

The song of Aḷḷūr Naṉmullaiyār. *Tiṇai: vākai. Tuṟai: mūtiṉmullai.*

307

Where is my king, he who was my support? There is a warrior
fallen with the mountainous elephant he was attacking, a man
who it seems we do not know—look there! Clusters of aging flowers

have dropped from the nightshade bushes of the forest and drifted
till they rest on the curls of his strong head like the tails
of spotted squirrels in the summer. He had been taking
the lives of his enemies like a buffalo bull, gone lame,
doomed, abandoned without water or grass by salt merchants
in a lonely place. Having seen him, the king who is riding
a raging elephant decides there is nothing better
than to die on the field of battle and being profoundly aware
of how hard it is to become a man whose fame will be
sung, he shows the stature of a warrior
perishing in battle without any wish to continue in life!

Tiṇai: tumpai. Tuṟai: kaḷiṟṟuṭaṉilai. . . .

308

Worthy bard who rouses longing in us through your small yāḻ
with its strings like twisted gold drawn out into wires
and its body that gleams like lightning and its voice that hums
like bees! The small-bladed spear of the king of the village
has pierced the towering face of the elephant the enemy king
is riding and that king's spear launched in anger has torn the chest
smeared with sandalwood of my lord! But when our great hero
plucked out the shining weapon that had ripped his chest open
and brandished it and threw it back, the elephants of his enemies
all showed their backs and went running away
and their innocent mates, whose heads are tender, were ashamed of
them!

The song of Kōvūrkiḻār. *Tiṇai: vākai. Tuṟai: mūtiṉmullai.*

309

For someone to kill his enemies is not difficult, blunting the iron tips
of spears and winning victories in the fierce battles,

but when they know my lord is in the camp, which then becomes
like a hole where a cobra lurks or like the yard where
a murderous bull roams to and fro, then enemies though their strength
is imposing feel fear before
his flashing fame, he who raises his long spear in victory!

The song of Maturai Iḷaṅkaṇṇik Kōcikaṉār. *Tiṇai: tumpai. Tuṟai: nūḻilāṭṭu.*

310

O my heart, in pain and in anguish for him to whom I used to bring
milk and feed it to him and when he wouldn't drink, though I wasn't angry,
I would threaten him with a tiny stick and he would show fear!
But now that descendant of strong men who fell in earlier days
has slain painted elephants over and over and says he does not feel
either the wound or the arrow within it. The tuft of hair
on his head is like the mane of a horse
and his beard is still sparse as he lies now on his shield.

The song of Poṉmuṭiyār. *Tiṇai: tumpai. Tuṟai: nūḻilāṭṭu.*

311

His pure white garment now soiled with the filth of streets
strewn with pollen, though it had been washed every single day
by a washerwoman at a well dug in salty land, the lord
who wears a flowering garland, who had met the needs of many,
has no one to be of aid to him on the field of battle.
His handsome, reddened eyes blazing,
he is powerful enough to ward off weapons with his own sole shield!

The song of Auvaiyār. *Tiṇai: tumpai. Tuṟai: paṇpāṭṭu.*

312

It is my duty to bear him and to raise him. It is
his father's duty to make him into a noble man. It is
the duty of the blacksmith to forge and give him a spear.
It is the king's duty to show him how to behave rightly
and the duty of a young man is to fight
indomitably with his shining sword, kill elephants, and come back home.

The song of Poṉmuṭiyār. *Tiṇai: vākai. Tuṟai: mūtiṉmullai.*

313

The great warrior of the land with the rough roads
has no wealth ready at hand. But when there are those
who come to him in need with their desires for lofty chariots
and for elephants, he will do his duty by them. Like a hill
on a wild shore near a salt pan, now undermined by the waves
from which the traders in salt
have hauled away their wagon loads, his goodwill is not to be belittled.

The song of Māṅkuṭikiḻār. *Tiṇai: vākai. Tuṟai: vallāṇmullai.*

314

The husband of the woman with a glowing face who is light to his house,
the man of virtues, the forward edge of the army, whose spear wins
victories, hails from a village in the wastelands where the myrobolan plant
grows with its dun-colored seeds and there are deserts scattered
with sprays of dry leaves and many are the memorial stones raised for heroes.
If his king is threatened, he will block

the enemy army sweeping ahead in its onslaught, raising high its flags!

The song of Aiyūr Muṭavaṉār. *Tiṇai: vākai. Tuṟai: vallāṇmullai.*

315

If he has much food, some will be left for himself. He'll give more
to those who come to him in need than to those whom duty binds him to feed.
He is a good companion who enjoys dining with ordinary people.
This is Neṭumāṉ Añci. Like a stick of kindling set into the eaves
of a house, he can hold his place without displaying his strength
but like the huge fire that surges
from that stick, suddenly he can show himself with his full power!

Auvaiyār sings Neṭumāṉ Āñci. *Tiṇai: vākai. Tuṟai: vallāṇmullai.*

316

He has praised liquor, he has praised liquor, the man asleep
from the stupor of the morning's drunkenness, in an unswept yard
full of straw and he is our king—and we are his bards! Yesterday,
to feed those who came to him as guests, he pawned the sword,
ancient and large, that was hanging at his side. Today I will pledge
my small yāḻ with its black body to back up the truth of my words!
But do not suppose that because of this he will not give gifts!
Go to him, and your woman with a waist as slender as a vine
will put on glowing ornaments. And we will drink from vessels
filled with liquor and feel bliss. Then you will come home
with your mouth red from the drinking, because
an enemy king riding a small-eyed elephant has died, falling before him!

The song of Maturaik Kaḷḷiṟ Kaṭaiyattaṉ Veṇṇākaṉār. *Tiṇai: vākai. Tuṟai: vallāṇmullai.*

317

The man with a victorious spear . . . . for
the drunken man, who has come, who lies stretched out
in the yard, if you have a skin or if you have a mat
or if you have anything else, then give it to him quickly!
To free us of desire . . . .
. . . . to us,
to others, to everybody he gave gifts and now he is sleeping.

The song of Vēmpaṟṟūrk Kumaraṉār. *Tiṇai: vākai. Tuṟai: vallāṇmullai.*

318

The leaves plucked to make the curry will wither. The wood
carried in for fuel will dry out. The city now ruled
by that great being whose dark wife is as soft and lovely
as a peacock, that rich city where a small bird, beside his mate
with her colorless crest, a black-throated male living in the eaves
of a house eats rice from paddy that was grown in a broad field
while resting in his nest made of shavings from the lute strings
of bards and the hair of lions that seems
like frayed peacock feathers—that city will go hungry should the
king perish!

The song of Peruṅkuṉṟūr Kiḻār. *Tiṇai: vākai. Tuṟai: vallāṇmullai.*

319

I know that down at the bottom of a pot with a flaking mouth
in front of our small house, there is a little bit of water
from a red place, from a well dug into red-soiled ground
in a ravine, and the water is fit to drink. Since the day
is too far gone for us to set a handful of dried millet out
in the front yard full of thatch-leaved pens so that the doves

and the partridges may take it as bait, all we have now is some
cooked rabbit, but we will give it away! Bard with your
well-trained mouth, come in and stay with us! From this village
where children whose heads are easily hurt hitch up a calf
to a toy chariot as if it were an ordinary calf—though
it tosses its head because its mother is a cow of the forest
with curving horns—the lord went off to do work for his king.
When
he returns he'll garland the dancing woman
who is your wife and give you a garland of gold, forever unfading.

The song of Ālaṅkuṭi Vaṅkaṉār. *Tiṇai: vākai. Tuṟai: vallāṇmullai.*

320

In the shade of hanging jackfruit, where no pavilion is needed
because there are dense stands of teak and bindweed in that yard,
an elephant hunter is lying fast asleep. And so a single stag
mates with the doe set out to entice him and takes his pleasure
with nothing else on his mind. Seeing the sweetness of them
joined together, the hunter's wife, afraid that the stag may run away
from the doe and fearing too that she may wake her husband,
stands
motionless in her house. Cackling loudly, a partridge and a cock
of the forest peck up and swallow some handfuls of millet
drying on a deerskin. She catches them and prepares them on a fire
of sandalwood. With your large family burned black under the sun,
bard! you should blissfully consume that meat cut up for you
into pieces, fragrant with the smell of sand eels cooked along with it,
and then rest here a while before going on your way,
in this town ruled by the man who is noble and far famed,
who is so generous that every day he gives away gifts to those
who have come to him in their need, holding back
nothing of the great, limitless wealth granted to him by his king!

The song of Vīrai Veḷiyaṉār. *Tiṇai: vākai. Tuṟai: vallāṇmullai.*

321

Protected by the chieftain who rages in battle, whose head
is resplendent with a sword wound, the town is in the wastelands
where a male quail with spots on his back, one who has been
trained to be a powerful fighter, waits for the right moment
and snatches some sweet white sesame seed, newly husked
and drying on a winnowing pan, then suddenly tries to kill
a field rat with lovely ears curving like the inner petals
of a kōṅku flower in the summer, and the rat runs off to hide
among the tender, glittering ears of abundant millet . . .
. . . . fruit that is wolfed down. Go! Bard!

The song of Uṟaiyūr Maruttuvaṉ Tāmōtaraṉār. *Tiṇai: vākai. Tuṟai: vallāṇmullai.*

322

Where near the parched trunks of prickly pear with its thorns
like horns on an ox that moves slowly along for the plowing,
children whose heads are easily hurt search out wild rats
through the stubble of freshly cut millet and snatch up
their bows and cause an uproar that startles a small hare
with big eyes that jumps into the courtyard and shatters
black pots and if the sugarcane press makes a loud noise,
scabbard fish with thick necks leap up nearby, there can be found
a city in the wastelands and it is ruled by
a spearman who grants no sleep to kings of cool cities by the waters.

The song of Āvūrkiḻār. *Tiṇai: vākai. Tuṟai: vallāṇmullai.*

323

Where an old wild cow, showing no fierceness, takes as its calf
the fawn of a doe that has been slain by a tiger and gives it

suck . . . .
the city of the spearman who grants whatever they may wish,
holding nothing back, to those who come to him in need,
and if there is war, the white spears raised,
draws his sword only against an elephant with feet huge as mortars!

The song of . . . kiḻār. *Tiṇai: vākai. Tuṟai: vallāṇmullai.*

324

Children with their large heads, close friends whose glances
when angry are like those of male wildcats, whose soft mouths
smell of the flesh of birds that they have eaten, whose fathers
are foul-mouthed hunters, these children make arrows
by setting the hollow white thorns of the umbrella thorn tree
into slender sticks of broomstick grass and bend their bows
of small branches and hunt for wild rats in the cotton plant hedges.
In that village with handsome families, where there is wasteland,
where the dung of white sheep that have eaten kumiḻ fruit
is spread out like nuts, under a pavilion with strong pillars
by the light of a little fire kindled by a cowherd, the modest
man of great worth who sits down with bards is a friend
who knows his friend's heart and will give
his life if harm threatens that king whose armies win victories.

The song of Ālattūr Kiḻār. *Tiṇai: vākai. Tuṟai: vallāṇmullai.*

325

In a place defended by forests hard to cross—where men whose words
can be trusted kill porcupines, men who live lives of struggle and take
turns at drinking the water that oozes up after a cow and her calf
have dug at mud and then drunk whatever liquid may have collected in holes

once the fresh torrential rains have poured to their finish and ceased
in the wasteland where wild boars root in the dust and these men, when
they want to share slices of lizard flesh, cut up in the courtyard
of a small house with shelters for cattle made of branches
of oṭu, put them on the fires so that a smell of rich fat spreads
along the street to the spot where, below the shade of a sturdy
jujube tree with a dried top in a front yard, children whose heads
are easily hurt play with bows and arrows—the city is there
ruled by that man of great virtue, whose generosity never
halts but who can halt attacking armies
even when they are led by a king with a spear that has won victories!

The song of Uṟaiyūr Mutukaṇṇaṉ Cāttaṉār. *Tiṇai: vākai. Tuṟai: vallāṇmullai.*

326

The town is defended by forests that are difficult to cross
where a young hen frightened by her enemy—a wildcat
stalking within an old hedge there in the dark—trembles
for her life and clucks so loud it seems to tear the flesh
inside her throat; and then by the light of a small fire kindled
by a woman spinning cotton who rises to clean off the area
with its piles of seeds, the hen turns calm when she sees
her cock with his crest like the red flower of a coral tree.
The woman wants to apportion to guests and to bards who are with them
a stew cooked of a lizard with its short legs that was captured
only a short distance away on the shore of a pond by the children
of hunters and she makes the stew with yogurt, pouring on oily fat,
mixing in other good things. And a forehead ornament of gold that was worn
by a lordly elephant in a mighty battle where it charged
and won the fierce fight will be given away, a mighty gift, by her husband!

The song of Taṅkāṟ Poṟkollaṉār. *Tiṇai: vākai. Tuṟai: mūtiṉmullai.*

327

After he gave what he owed to the creditors who besieged him,
whatever was left to him of his small low-yielding harvest
of millet that required only the stamping feet of boys
rather than buffaloes for its threshing was eaten up
by hungry bards. Then, since no one came to his gate,
in order to soothe the poverty of his family he told
low men what he needed and borrowed millet—
that man of worth has the strength to repel advancing kings!

Tiṇai: vākai. Tuṟai: mūtiṉmullai. . . .

328

. . . The villages of the wastelands do not yield rice
with their forest tracts where neither trunks nor leaves flourish
but the two kinds of millet are all they have and all
of that is gone, given away to those who came to him in need
. . . . he is satisfied.
Though that is how he stands, bard, after you have eaten
curds poured into milk in a pot with a jujube fruit . . . . . .
and strong toddy sour as a kaḷavu berry . . . .
. . . . and savory pieces of dried meat
together with grains from plucked ears, cooked with a pouring
of ghee and pulpy white rice stirred with a ladle
and you're happily sitting . . . .
. . . . he will give
gifts if you go to him and you sing of the king of a village
where a hare comes to chew the small
fragrant muññai vine spreading at the foot of a palmyra palm in a courtyard.

Tiṇai: vākai. Tuṟai: mūtiṉmullai. . . .

329

There, at dawn, they set the offerings before the stones
memorializing heroes outside a village with only a few families,
who brew liquor in their houses, bathe in their good water and light
lamps fueled with ghee, so that their streets are sweetened by the cloud
of abundant smoke. Though that territory is secure and dominating, it seems
like a hole where snakes with striped necks live! Each day,
ignoring the suffering of kings, the noble man whose fame
is celebrated gives gifts generously
to bards within that city he protects. And he holds back nothing!

The song of Maturai Aṟuvai Vāṇikaṉ Iḷavēṭṭaṉār. *Tiṇai: vākai. Tuṟai: mūtiṉmullai.*

330

As the hostile onslaught bent on destruction beats at the front ranks
of the army of his king, he alone, sword raised in his right hand,
blocks the enemy from surging on and so he is like a shore
to a great ocean, that man whose lineage, like him, has shown
preeminent generosity, the ruler of a village which other than always
feeding those who come to it singing
does not even create enough income to merit being taxed by a king!

The song of Maturaik Kaṇakkāyaṉār. *Tiṇai: vākai. Tuṟai: mūtiṉmullai.*

331

The strong man of the village where men live by plowing
with their bows and the wells are hacked out of stone to hold

heavily brackish water will be able—even when he is
impoverished—
to come up with what he knows he doesn't have—as if he were
an ignorant cowherd in extreme cold kindling a small fire
in the faded evening. When he has something, though very little,
he does not worry about there being many who come to him
in need, but like a woman who is the light of her house,
who deals out food, in due order, within a long, high pavilion,
he can give away a bit here, a bit there according to worth.
But when times go well for him, as with the white rice of sacrifice
poured out in front of their doors by kings
who protect the world, he can, when he is needed, shower down his
gifts!

The song of Uṟaiyūr Mutukūttaṉār. *Tiṇai: vākai. Tuṟai: mūtiṉmullai.*

332

The spear that belongs to the warrior from this city is not
like the spears of other men but its worth is immense.
It may rest in the eaves of a hut, its long back
gathering dust. It may travel, garlanded, in procession
around the streets and reservoirs of pure water while
the sweet voices of virtuous women mingle with the notes
of yāḻs that had been stored in large sacks. Or it may advance
so that the entire land of the enemy reels! Should the spear do that,
then it never stops thrusting into the faces
of the massive elephants of kings with their armies like the vast ocean!

The song of Viriyūr Nakkaṉār. *Tiṇai: vākai. Tuṟai: mūtiṉmullai.*

333

Poets! If you should go to where little rabbits with big ears
and black necks and eyeballs like buds—like the bubbles that rise

when a hard shower falls on water—are playing and leaping near a bush
in a pitted courtyard within the city, you should stay a good while,
even though the misery there is such that no one conceives of the worth
that accrues from feeding poets and so no one will tell them to eat.
Then take your leave. Because you are leaving, the woman of the house
will feel a desire to feed you and since she has willingly given away
all the common millet and the little millet as food
to those who have come in need, because she has nothing left
worth giving to you poets in return for your visit to the city,
she will set out on the surface of a mortar the millet
that they have left dry on the stalk as seed and she will never
let you go away empty. Assembled at every hunter's house in the city. . .
. . . . if kings
should come, with their elephants encircled by girths and ridden
by strong men, with lofty chariots, wearing their gloves made of the skin
from the backs of lizards, the food will be just the same
and the gifts that hero gives will be what he has seized from the enemy!

Tiṇai: vākai. Tuṟai: mūtiṉmullai. . . .

334

Little rabbits with long ears, tiny feet, hair as fine
as the elephant grass growing in the beautiful reservoirs,
hide in the haystacks on a lovely field where children
whose heads are easily hurt begin to make noise in a courtyard
. . . . Afterwards . . . . city.
As she feeds bards and offers shelter to those who have come in need,
the wife does not turn from her work while the noise
of eating is heard nor the warrior with a strong sword from his work

of granting gifts to those who have come in need . . . .
a forehead ornament of gold
worn on the spotted face of an elephant with towering tusks.

The song of Maturait Tamiḻakkūttaṉār. *Tiṇai: vākai. Tuṟai: mūtiṉmullai.*

335

Of strength hard to overcome . . . .
. . . . Other than the bottle flower,
the golden jasmine, the wild lime, and the wild jasmine,
there are no flowers. Except for the common millet with
its black stems, and large-eared millet and the small vine
of horse gram and the spotted bean plant, there is no food.
Other than the Tuṭiyaṉ drummers and the Pāṇaṉ singers
and the Paṟaiyaṉs and the Kaṭampaṉs, there are no castes.
Except for memorial stones revered for the men who stood
their ground before oncoming enemies and repelled them, slaying
elephants with high gleaming tusks, and then died,
no gods are to be worshiped with paddy poured out before them.

The song of Māṅkuṭikiḻār. *Tiṇai: vākai. Tuṟai: mūtiṉmullai.*

336

The king with his desire for her is in a burning rage.
Her father, though it is his duty, will not let her go.
The elephants, great rings ornamenting the tusks set high
on their shining faces, have been unleashed from the sacred tree.
Warriors of both factions have shut their mouths and raised
their gleaming swords. The range of instruments sounded surpasses
the knowledge of musicians! It is sad how this ancient city, well protected,
hard to conquer, has fallen into such turmoil! This mother is evil
and surely has no principles for she created this quarrel, blithely

raising those young, erect breasts until they reached their present beauty.
Not as yet full grown, they are as lovely as the buds
of a flowering red cotton tree on Vēṅkai Mountain, which are emblems of victory!

The song of Paraṇar. *Tiṇai: kāñci. Tuṟai: makaṭpāṟ kāñci.*

337

How the king of the Chola country is roaring with anger!
His wealth from ruling the earth he thinks of as nothing.
Like the cool spring on Pāri's mountain of Paṟampu,
whose heart opens like a flower when men approach him
as bards would, their hands poised to receive gifts,
surrendering the strength of their swords, singing his praises
while his hand in its might, with its glittering bangles, endlessly
grants gifts, like that spring is the girl with a glowing face, a glory
among women, so hard to catch a sight of, hidden in the great brown mansion
fragrant with the smoke of cooling agar that has softly settled there
and there she trembles like a fine cloth washed and hung
on a line to dry. Because she is as she is, the kings do not
stop coming, though all they can do is care for their fierce-eyed elephants
stationed in every grove and keep them fed with mouthfuls of rice
from bowing plants while everyone watches them attend
to their animals. Terrifying, long spears that have won their victories
on the battlefield are flourished by her brothers and their heads
are frightening, smeared with blood! Because those men are steeped
in such Martial Courage, will she, who is adorned with handsome ornaments,
come to feel her young breasts—that are as lovely as the tusks
of elephants and now are scattered
with the spots of puberty—pressed within any man's hands ever?

The song of Kapilar. *Tiṇai: kāñci. Tuṟai: makaṭpāṟ kāñci.*

338

Even if the three victorious kings were to come here, their bows
tensed, wearing margosa with its black branches or the yellow laburnum
or palmyra leaves on their foreheads, he would not give his only daughter
in her innocence away to anyone who does not bow down and offer him
proper homage—that king of a city where, in the midst of a field
with ears of grain enfolding each other and handsome gardens, a single wall shows
which looks like a ship sitting dry and safe on the shore of the sea—
because the wealth she owns, based on her father's plunder, is equal
to Neṭuvēḷātaṉ's city of Pōntai, with its plowed fields
and its rice paddies spread over with water and its houses
full of rice and its streets full of gold
and its groves full of flowers where the bees buzz and settle!

The song of Kuṉṟūrkiḻār Makaṉār. *Tiṇai: kāñci. Tuṟai: makaṭpāṟ kāñci.*

339

In that place where the huge bulls with their many cows
spread over a spacious grassy field chew their cud in the rich shade
of flowering trees, and the cowherds pluck wild jasmine
from the bushes full of blossoms and small long-eared rabbits
when they are chased with little sticks jump like scabbard fish
in deep water and women with belted hips and braceleted arms
play in the ocean, then leap
into a reservoir, and they gather
waterlilies by the salt pans and their dresses of green leaves sway
densely on the fields . . . . like an ornament
she must steadily continue to grow. Wishing for arduous war
to be joined, she has seized and she has hidden away
the brave hearts of courageous kings,

masters of elephants with ears as large as winnowing fans!

Tiṇai: kāñci. Tuṟai: makaṭpāṟ kāñci. . . .

340

That young, dark girl who is plucking the beautiful clusters
of crab's-eye flowers, the seeds red as rubies with their black spots,
and as she runs, her leaf skirt sways. . . . .
If you ask whose daughter she is, listen! If they should take up
    weapons, he
will not take up. . . . .
. . . . The father of those warriors
has destined her for kings of great worth, such as bring down
elephants with trunks like huge
palmyra palms on the battlefields lovely with fragrant basil!

The song of Aḷḷūr Naṉmullaiyār. *Tiṇai: kāñci. Tuṟai: makaṭpāṟ kāñci.*

341

The father of the young girl whose sloping mons is covered
with a lovely skirt of leaves and flowers, whose anklets
are painted with red dots, will not give her to the king
even though he begs for her! A strong gate locked shut
with a crossbar, walls of pounded clay, where a flag always flies
. . . .
Together with his followers ferocious as a band of tigers,
he will not be false to his vow. He is spoiling for a fight.
He has ordered his men to don flowers and has bathed in a reservoir.
And the chieftain, while laying his hand on his weapon, has spoken:
"Either tomorrow I will marry that girl who is resplendent
with glittering ornaments, whom no man has ever had, who is
yielding by nature and has the spots of puberty spreading

across her beautiful breasts; or else my body scarred by the cutting
edges of long spears, my strength fired by my Martial Courage
used to hard fighting, I will go to the world from which no one
returns!"
This cool city by the river with its fertile tracts of land,
will surely lose its great beauty,
like a cool reservoir roiled into motion by a combat of elephants!

The song of Paraṇar. *Tiṇai: kāñci. Tuṟai: makaṭpāṟ kāñci.*

342

Noble man with the victorious spear! Wondering, you ask,
"The young woman who wears a chaplet of mayilai flowers
whose shoulders are as long as the flowing wing of a forest crow—
can she be the daughter of anyone other than a warrior?"
Her loveliness, so choice as to merit the envy of Lakṣmī,
is for no one but fighting men! Her father is the overlord
of cool, riverine lands where the young of a yellow-legged crane,
when it forages and eats with its long beak near the shore
in the soft mud, finds eggs like mustard seed laid by sand-eels
and the babies of fine prawns! And should the kings begin
a great war just because they cannot have her, her brothers
will display their greatness by plowing every single day,
as is right, with their spears, and for them their stacks
of hay will be the dead corpses
and war elephants their buffaloes for threshing the harvest!

The song of Aricilkiḻār. *Tiṇai: kāñci. Tuṟai: makaṭpāṟ kāñci.*

343

"In Muciṟi with its drums, where the ocean roars,
where the paddy traded for fish and stacked high
on the boats makes boats and houses look the same
and the sacks of pepper raised up beside them

make the houses look the same as the tumultuous
shore and the golden wares brought by the ships
are carried to land in the servicing boats,
Kuṭṭuvaṉ its king to whom toddy is no more
valuable than water, who wears a shining garland, gives out gifts
of goods from the mountains along with goods from the sea
to those who have come to him. Even if you humbly bring
and bestow as much fine and copious wealth as that city possesses,
she will not marry someone who is unworthy of her." So says
her father and will not grant her hand. Think! Will the tall city
suffer where sighing kites sleep on the middle wall of the fort,
the roads hard to conquer are filled with weapons,
but ladders have been thrown up by men who have come to force
their way in!

The song of Paraṇar. *Tiṇai: kāñci. Tuṟai: makaṭpāṟ kāñci.*

344

Either they will bring in fine and massive wealth—cities
where full-feathered peacocks who have eaten the best of rice
rise up and fly and come to settle in a marutam tree near the water
when girls whose arms are dense with bangles call out to them—
or else they will bring on Martial Courage without principles—
the hostile spread of piercing fire and dense smoke—
one of these will surely come to be because of the lines
spreading on her mons, she who wants vēṅkai
pollen for her body . . . a chaplet of sandalwood and cool kāñci
leaves. . . .

Aṇṭar Naṭuṅkalliṉār sings . . . *Tiṇai: kāñci. Tuṟai: makaṭpāṟ kāñci.*

345

Elephants have been tied to the sacred guardian trees,
devastating them! The streets are filled with dust

as the chariots hurry along them. The roadways are
in confusion as the horses go galloping down them.
The fords have turned all muddy because there the weapons
have been washed. Since warriors are gathered there—men
who will fight—many new kings have come so that the earth
bends under the great weight! They are to be pitied
who must think of how the vast space filled with pain
is guarded as if by the iron mouth of a bellows that pants
like an elephant cow, while they feel desire for the girl who has full,
burning breasts tipped with black nipples, who has a glance
which entrances men! Her brothers will not give her to any man
who is not their equal. They have no wish for wealth. Their only
wish is to enter battle. Though the city has warriors with shields
woven of strips and though they have swords that deal out wounds,
though their unwashed heads flash with bits of meat and smell
of blood, though they have long black spears well fashioned
through being turned on a lathe, what
will become of this fine city along the river with its hedges of cotton?

Aṇṭar Naṭuṅkalliṉār sings. . . . *Tiṇai: kāñci. Tuṟai: makaṭpāṟ kāñci.*

346

Her former nurse feeds the daughter and tells her, "You're not grown
even now. You must still drink milk. And I have some here!" Her mother
does not object. Her older brother, a brave young boy, claims he has
some learning. Her father, powerful in battle, holds his shining spear.
But her beauty will be wasted with no one to desire it so that this lowly
place will turn barren. Once those who must die are gone,
no one will remain to protect the families of the living. How certain it all is!

The song of Aṇṭarmakaṉ Kuṟuvaḻutiyār. *Tiṇai: kāñci. Tuṟai: makaṭpāṟ kāñci.*

347

She is like the city of Kūṭal surrounded by deep waters,
ruled by Akutai who is courageous in war, whose chest
is smeared with sandalwood paste, the cutting edge of whose spear
is scarred, the blade cracked from all its assaults, he who wears
a crushed garland of green tumpai while his bright, glittering
sword kills, like a man's tongue when it reddens as it covers
his teeth and tries to pry out the bits of fine food he has eaten
while drinking fragrant toddy, her growing breasts
reddening, with her luxuriant black hair, ...
What will become of the trees of our city? Though their massive trunks
can be seen from far away—they are weakening
at the roots because elephants fit for the warring of kings are tied there!

The song of Kapilar. *Tiṇai: kāñci. Tuṟai: makaṭpāṟ kāñci.*

348

She is like the city of Ūṇ, ruled by Taḻumpaṉ whose words
are always true, where bards who catch little fish live
on one street and on another potters who gather honey after the bees
fly off frightened by the taṇṇumai drum that is beaten by harvesters
of the white paddy, leaving their sweet hive on a jagged branch
growing from the node of a palmyra palm. If her mother had never given birth
to this girl whose darkened eyes look like blue waterlilies, then none of this
would ever have happened! The trees of our spacious harbor are suffering,
long chariots standing wherever
there is shade, and elephants with red-painted foreheads tied up everywhere!

The song of Paraṇar. *Tiṇai: kāñci. Tuṟai: makaṭpāṟ kāñci.*

349

The king wipes the sweat from his forehead with the tip
of his spear and speaks words that are fierce. Her father
says nothing to ingratiate himself but only mouths curses.
So they stand, and the lovely dark woman with her sharp teeth,
her proud eyes lined with beautiful red lines and as cool
as rain clouds, like a small fire kindled
with wood against wood, brings sorrow now to her native city.

The song of Maturai Marutaṉ Iḷanākaṉār. *Tiṇai: kāñci. Tuṟai: makaṭpāṟ kāñci.*

350

With its moats filled and its breastworks fallen down
and its walls crumbling, our scarred and ancient
city cannot withstand a war! What will become of it?
Kings with fast horses and their royal drums roaring
like the thunder when the rain comes, have arrived at dawn
and they roam around our towering gate! Her brothers,
with their power to confront and kill, won't be satisfied
without a fight! Over the lovely, well-formed breasts
of the young girl with red-lined, darkened eyes like the sharp
blade of a spear flourished in the work of battle,
as the bracelets dance on her wrists, the spots of her puberty are
    spreading!

The song of Maturaik Kaṭaikkaṇṇampukuttārāyattaṉār. *Tiṇai: kāñci. Tuṟai: makaṭpāṟ kāñci.*

351

With their royal drums that are sounded when they win victories
and their vast armies that resemble the roaring sea and their
    elephants
with massive feet who wear bells that dangle down along their flanks
and with their chariots, flags fluttering above them, and their horses,

crowded together in a great uproar with their warriors and their weapons,
the kings will never be satisfied because her father will never
give away that beauty of hers which is like that of the city of Vākai,
ruled by generous Eyiṉaṉ! With its defenses, with its fields
along the rivers and a reservoir of clear water where a crane
streaked with red hunts fish but now tired of the flowering
pollen-laden branches of a marutam tree
sleeps perched on the limb of a lovely kāñci, what will happen to this city?

The song of Maturaik Paṭaimaṅka Maṉṉiyār. *Tiṇai: kāñci. Tuṟai: makaṭpāṟ kāñci.*

352

Within a white cup that is filled with toddy,
full udders, ... give milk.
Under a sagging, green umbrella, flowers
growing on a jasmine bush are plucked.
Young girls who wear bracelets of lily stems on their wrists
climb up on a hill and dive into a reservoir
so that water runs out of the outlet . . . .
. . . . in Uṟantai
surrounded by white paddy, ruled by the munificent Tittaṉ
who trades in toddy. Even if you offer fine and valuable gifts,
objects with great fame of their own just like that city, the man
of imposing virtues will not accept them. Her breasts with their black
nipples blossom and she has many lovely glowing spots of puberty that shine
like a young vēṅkai tree with clustered flowers on its spreading branches,
and her brother with his horse pained by a small stick . . .
. . . . who?

The song of Paraṇar. *Tiṇai: kāñci. Tuṟai: makaṭpāṟ kāñci.*

353

Your eyes half closed with desire, you bring your chariot to a halt
and stare at her tender beauty while she walks on the sand
swept in by the ocean, resplendent in a golden garland
and her belt-string of gold studded with many jewels and wrought
faultlessly by a master smith, O lord of victorious battles!
and you ask and you ask and you do not stop asking,
"Whose daughter is she?" I will tell you now if you will listen.
She is a daughter to a king of ancient lineage, who always
gives food daily to his young men with strong bows, the rice
drawn from towering mounds that are threshed in the early morning
through leveling the many stacks that rise up like mountains.
To great kings of ancient lineage who came and yesterday asked
. . . .
. . . . with their sharp-tipped spears, scars
on the blades after they have killed with them on the battlefield
where they made blood flow, and their wounds
cotton cannot staunch, fearsome are her older brothers!

The song of Kāvirippūmpaṭṭiṉattuk Kārikkaṇṇaṉār. *Tiṇai: kāñci. Tuṟai: makaṭpāṟ kāñci.*

354

The spear with its heavy shaft is plunged into water and her father,
though kings advance against him, will not yield. Since his foremost
warriors have gathered, he sends them on ahead so that he may bathe.
The elegance of this city where the young girls play in the water
of a reservoir at the entrance to all the fields of paddy and then return
to their wealthy homes carrying scabbard fish which leaped from that water
because of their fear of a crane catching carp—will it be destroyed
by the innocent and joyful gaze of the woman whose arms are as graceful

as bamboo with its large joinings, whose high breasts
rise in their beauty and are spread over now with the spots of puberty?

The song of Paraṇar. *Tiṇai: kāñci. Tuṟai: makaṭpāṟ kāñci.*

355

The wall is without a rampart. Because it holds no water,
the moat has calves grazing and frisking in it. So the city
stands. Her father does not think about this, since he
is deluded. And her brothers—Kiḷḷi of the swift horses
who wears a chaplet lovely to look at
. . . .

Tiṇai: kāñci. Tuṟai: makaṭpāṟ kāñci. . . .

356

Across it spreads the jungle. Upon it thick spurge grows.
There in broad daylight the owls cry out and demon women open
their mouths wide. The cremation fires glow and clouds
of smoke cover that fearful burning ground. Hot, white
ashes on the earth littered with bones are quenched by tears
of lovers, weeping, their hearts full of longing.
It has seen the back of every human being, all the people
living in this world as they go away,
but no one has ever seen it turn its back and go away.

The song of Kataiyaṅ Kaṇṇaṉār. *Tiṇai: kāñci. Tuṟai: makaṭpāṟ kāñci.*

357

Though this world linked together by mountains joined with hills
is thought to be shared in common by the three kings,
there have been those who alone held power and yet their years

have passed until all their wealth could not help them
but only the righteous actions they had sown could be
of any aid to them at all. As Death seizes lives
and the relatives assemble and weep, such help is hard
to gather for those who have given up
that raft which carries one from this to the other shore!

The song of Piramaṉār. *Tiṇai: kāñci. Tuṟai: maṟakkāñci* and/or *peruṅkāñci.*

358

This vast and flourishing earth around which the sun
circles may give rise to seven leaders in a single day!
If you balance the world against the practice of tapas,
this world is not worth even the weight of a mustard seed.
So lovers of liberation have renounced the earth, which shows
that the goddess of good fortune does not renounce
those who renounce her. But those who won't renounce her she
renounces!

The song of Vāṉmīkiyār. *Tiṇai: kāñci. Tuṟai: maṉaiyaṟam, tuṟavaṟam.*

359

Even the rulers of countries go to the burning ground
where the land is waste and desolate and filled with dry thorns,
and owls are there with blazing mouths and undulating shrieks,
and small foxes, their glistening teeth smeared with fat,
chew at corpses; where demonesses, grasping and embracing the
dead,
dance swinging their legs on that salty land in terrifying movement
by the light of the pyres, their bodies sending out the stench
of hot meat because they have consumed the bloodless flesh.
And that day will come when you must go there as well,
but your bad reputation will remain, and your good reputation.
Shunning a bad name, seeking a good one,

you should not favor avarice but your words
should be impartial. If you are endlessly generous
and say to those who come to you in their need:
"Take these!" and give them many elephants with tusks
glittering and also horses caparisoned in gold and high,
ornamented chariots, then after all have seen you go
to the other world your fame will remain here, shining and
enduring!

Kāviṭṭaṉār sings Antuvaṉkīraṉ. *Tiṇai: kāñci. Tuṟai: peruñkāñci.*

360

They barely eat and they are rarely angry.
Their words are few but they listen attentively.
They have sensitive feelings and they give much away:
clear toddy and toddy that has not been filtered,
rich, juicy meat seasoned with spices!
Meeting men humbly, speaking agreeable words,
and acting for the greater good of the many,
O greatness! there are few kings who have ruled
the world with such beneficence! Listen to me now.
Many understand nothing of these things! The riches
of such men do not last. Even at this very moment,
their wealth is unstable. And therefore, always,
you should act in the way it is right for you to act.
Take care that those who come to you for your largesse
have their needs satisfied! When people have been carried on the bier
to the burning ground, that fearful place of desolation,
that salty wasteland overgrown with spurge, site of what
is other than life, and they lie there on grass, receiving toddy
and a few grains of rice at the command of outcaste Pulaiyaṉs,
and then they have entered the mouth of fire,
for many of these who ate and grew fat no fame has flourished!

Nākaraiyar who is called Caṅkavaruṇar sings Tantumāṟaṉ. *Tiṇai: kāñci. Tuṟai: peruñkāñci.*

361

You roam around searching for lives, Death with your roar
as loud as monsoon thunder, you who can never be sated!
That man of majesty has no fear of your coming, he who poured
the ritual water as he gave away vessels of value to Brahmins versed
in the many noble sacred texts as they perform the sacrifices,
he who gave more generously than a mother
to many men, who gave an abundance of elephants
and crisply gaited horses to those who sing
of his munificence, who with fondness granted many rolling chariots
to those who sought shelter at his feet
which had put an end to enemies! When he holds
his lengthy audiences in the company
of bards wearing their lotus flowers
of gold and the singing women with their garlands of fashioned gold,
where his women of great purity and exemplary patience calmly
carry
filtered and mixed toddy in gold pitchers and pour it out as if it were
amṛta for people to drink, his women whose glances are like those of
the deer,
whose brows bend like bows, whose tongues when they speak loudly
seem
to fear their teeth which are like little thorns and as they move,
their belt strings slide down, he does not forget, you do not have to
tell him
of the mutability of this world which does not endure, you do not
have to tell him
because he has studied all of it, all that he already knew . . .
. . . . he has knowledge!

. . . Kayamaṉār sings. . . .

362

Across their chests the necklaces are swaying as if they were
half moons inlaid with the choice gems that resemble suns!

The royal drum to which sacrifices are offered resounds
within the camp and throughout the army in its multitudes that looks
as if a god had been provoked—the white flags of victory raised up
high in lust for war, the warriors whose feats have been monumental
spreading across the earth! Brahmins! Listen to the uproar
produced by the assault, its force as hard to withstand as Death himself!
This has nothing to with your Four Vedas! This is not a matter
for mercy. It has nothing to do with Righteousness but rather Acquisition!
Abandoning bewilderment, throwing delusion aside,
giving away lovely towns surrounded by paddy fields,
so that the ritual water flows like the ocean
from their hands, giving away heaps of cooked rice,
giving away finely fashioned ornaments because they feel sure
that they should not stay at home where the chatter
of their relations obscures the existence of the burning ground—
that broad place where on the wan, salty earth stretching out and covered
with tiny white bones, the strong-voiced crow and the owl shriek
even in broad daylight—they slip away to escape from home,
fearful of being confined to this
small world, so that they may reach heaven with their very bodies!

Ciṟuveṇṭēraiyār sings [the same king who was the subject of the previous poem—part of the colophon of that poem has been lost]. *Tiṇai: potuviyal. Tuṟai: peruñkāñci.*

363

Blissful kings who have protected and ruled over the vast earth
encircled by the dark ocean so that not even a speck of land as large
as the center of an umbrella thorn leaf belonged to others
have gone away to their final home on the ground where corpses burn,
more of them than the sand heaped up by the waves. All of them

have gone there and have perished as others took their land.
And so you too should listen! There is no life that endures
with the body and does not vanish! Death is real and not
an illusion! Before the grim day comes when on the burning ground
where thorn bushes grow wound together with spurge
on that broad site where the biers rise up and a man of a caste
that is despised picks up the boiled,
unsalted rice and does not look
anywhere around him and gives it
to you so that you accept a sacrifice for which you have no desire
with its dish the earth itself, before that
happens, do what you have decided to do
and utterly renounce this world whose farthest boundary is the sea!

Aiyātic Ciṟuveṇṭēraiyār sings. . . . *Tiṇai: potuviyal. Tuṟai: peruñkāñci.*

364

The singing woman is wearing a garland that will not fade
and on the head of the bard a large lotus flower that never
blossomed in a lake shines like a flame. We'll throw
a big black male goat upon the red fire and we'll have a feast,
  eating
solid chunks of succulent meat rendered even richer
by the spices and as our tongues reddened from drinking liquor
move the meat around in our mouths we'll give away gifts
to those in need who approach us. Come you are fierce
in war, let us be happy! Such things will be hard to have,
O greatness! on the day we go to the broad burial ground
with its urns, where a male owl never stops shrieking
perched in the hollow of an ancient tree
whose many fallen roots have split the earth and sway in the wind!

Kūkaikkōḻiyār sings [the same king who was the subject of the previous poem—part of the colophon of that poem has been lost]. *Tiṇai: potuviyal. Tuṟai: peruñkāñci.*

365

Her face is like the sky marked with the immense confusion
of a storm and her eyes are like the two huge moving spheres
as the earth goddess weeps, she who is so virtuous, crying out,
"I do not pass away as former kings have done, their power
so immense they found no new enemies, as they rolled their chariot wheels
that are beautiful, of gold, with sapphire spokes and hubs of diamond
over the ocean so difficult to cross, where even the shifting
wind does not go! No, I remain here like a whore,
while many who praise me wish that I may long endure!"
The Kāñci odes of grief and mourning
have even reached that far those say who know these things!

The song of Mārkkaṇṭēyaṉār. *Tiṇai: kāñci. Tuṟai: peruñkāñci.*

366

Those great men to whom no other men can even be compared,
whose royal drums with the mighty voices beaten out
by fine small sticks, like the thunder when it strikes down
serpents, roared aloud a single command to heroic warriors,
even they, their fame left safely behind them, have vanished!
And so, son of a righteous man, chieftain among those men who are courageous!
I am going to tell you one thing, and listen to me!
Don't let others know how strong you are
but learn what they are saying, and help those who take action
like men while the sun is up, and when night falls, you should
consider what will happen next, and then, lord, speak out!
Just as a massive ox will plow and then devour his hay,
you may feel disturbed by the women with lovely red lines
in their eyes who pour out choice filtered toddy
into a fine-fashioned vessel, lord of endless
wealth! . . . . killing a male goat and tearing off the roasted meat,
you should have it set out on leaves and given without stinting

to those people who are hungry for that food that is like an oblation
and grant a place to those who want boiled rice and then you yourself
should eat! As with the goats collected for sacrifice who fill all the space
of the enclosures laid out for ecstatic dancing within every grove
along the water where the shores are heaped
with flowing sand, death is real, not in any way is it illusion!

Kōtamaṉār sings. . . . *Tiṇai: kāñci. Tuṟai: peruñkāñci.*

367

Though the world, as fine as sugarcane syrup and no less wonderful
than the world of the Nāgas, was theirs, it did not pass on with them
but went to others, though they were foreign kings who struggled for it.
You should give away flowers and gold and sanctify your gifts with water
so that the moistened hands of Brahmins who come to you in need
are filled. You should drink pure toddy filtered through fiber
and served in golden vessels by richly ornamented women
and you should get yourself drunk and give away treasures
to those coming to you in need! So you ought to live through the days
allotted for you in this world. You will have no other boat
when drowning but your good deeds as your source of life!
You kings who ride in chariots with banners, you who own
the white umbrellas of victory, enthroned in your beauty
which is like the three fires of the twice-born Brahmins
who have subdued their senses through one-pointed will!
What I have said is all that I know. May you live your days in splendor!
May they be loftier than the stars that rise and move
through the sky, more numerous than raindrops from a dark thundering cloud!

Auvaiyār sings Cēramāṉ Māvaṇkō, Pāṇṭiyaṉ Kāṉappēr Tanta Ukkirapperuvaḻuti, and Cōḻaṉ Irāyacūyam Vēṭṭa Perunaṟkiḷḷi, when they were all gathered together. *Tiṇai: pāṭāṇṭiṇai. Tuṟai: vāḻttiyal.*

368

If I think that I'll receive an elephant and go home,
all the elephants like hills on which glowing clouds
are caught have been shot full of arrows and have died.
If I think that I will take away a tall chariot decorated
with a lotus-shaped support for one's balance, the fine horses
with elegant gaits exhausted from circling have lost
their force and fallen to the earth. If I think
I'll take horses with cropped manes, they have died,
wounds covering their bodies and like ships when there is
no wind, they lie in their great numbers in a handsome pool of blood.
You who labor with the plow of your sword so that men
are stacked like hay! On the broad, savage field where
those who have come in need, stripped of joy, grieve
for there is nothing to bring away, I sang and beat out sharp rhythms
on the clear eye of my taṭāri drum which is like the bottom
of a rutting elephant's foot, so that I may carry home that necklace
shaped like a snake that you wear between your shoulders
big around as the concert drum of dancers, above your armlets
studded with sapphires!

Cēramāṉ Kuṭakkōneṭuñ Cēralātaṉ fought Cōḻaṉ Vēṟpakaṟaṭakkaip Peruviṟaṟkiḷḷi on the battlefield and fell. His life not leaving, he lay there with a necklace on his neck, and Kaḻāttalaiyār sang [of] him. *Tiṇai: vākai. Tuṟai: maṟakkaḷa vaḻi.*

369

The elephants with their dark trunks and their handsome tusks
raised on high and tipped with iron are the clouds.
The swords of warriors who swore oaths as they flourished them

for the attack form the lightning. The royal drums that received
a sacrifice of blood are with their glowing drumsticks
the thunder that makes those snakes, the enemy kings, tremble
and feel deep anguish. The fast horses are the driving wind
on the wide field where arrows shower down like rain released
by the mighty strings of the strong, swift bows. On the drenched
battlefield, chariots are the plows. In the long and fresh
furrows scored and then turned over by your weapons
of battle after you had arrived at dawn, white spears
and clubs that were seized and hurled have been planted.
And the terrible new crop, with the handsome heads bending low,
has been the many towering stacks of corpses with female
ghouls crowding around them. Demons and herds of foxes
thresh the field while evil spirits take up their guard posts.
Great lord who sits in session for singers! On that field which is
resplendent, I drum fiercely on my taṭāri drum with its strong voice,
with its new skin as flawlessly white as a stick of sandalwood powder
and bound with straps of leather. I have come here singing,
O greatness! Give me a gift of elephant bulls along with their cows
and their calves, with their feet like tuṭi drums, bulls who would
never shrink back, who wear golden ornaments to decorate their foreheads
so that they resemble Himālaya with its towering summits of gold
which rise up to touch the clouds that are filled with an uproar,
there where waterfalls roar. You who wish to be
famous, as you should be, for your generosity which knows no end!

Paraṇar sings Cēramāṉ Kaṭalōṭṭiya Vēlkeḻu Kuṭṭuvaṉ. *Tiṇai: vākai. Tuṟai: maṟakkaḷa vaḻi* and/or *ērkkaḷa uruvakam.*

370

I have seen no generous men and I try to think of how I can escape
from my troubles. I pack my things and carry the fiber and soft shoots
of palmyra with me and because I have nothing to eat, I search

the directions, trying to find a wealth of food for my large family
burned black under the sun and drooping as hunger devours them.
I have come, dried out from the sweat of fatigue, with my stomach
withered and shrunken! Behind me I leave a wilderness where the cry
of an owl harsh as a tuṭi drum resounds across the wasteland
and a vulture is heard calling out for his mate from his perch
on the lovely forked branches of an uḻuñcu tree within a vastness
full of drought where bamboo dies scorched and dries away
and the ridged fruit of the bowstring hemp shrivels. I have come
like a bat, its mind filled with the thought of a tree in fruit.
I have come here, to the field where the gurgling blood rises
and spreads across the earth, since a cloud of glowing weapons
has rained down the ripe, wished-for fruit and when the rich
curving grain is cut, the stems heap up and elephants circle
like buffaloes to thresh and reduce the many piles of fallen corpses,
driven along by the palmyra whip of the sword. Beating out
my clear rhythms on my large-eyed taṭāri drum, singing praises
of the broad field of violent valor, to show its glory, I have come
in search of a gift that will be like a mountain with high, lovely,
iron-tipped tusks. O greatness! you who are lord of the fearful field
where a female demon finds and snatches a powerful braceleted arm
severed by an ax and weeps from exhaustion because her legs are tangled
in the coils of the ridged guts
of fearless men, as the vulture and the red-eared eagle wheel in the sky!

Ūṉpoti Pacuṅkuṭaiyār sings Cōḻaṉ Ceruppāḻiyeṟinta Iḷañcēṭceṉṉi. *Tiṇai: vākai. Tuṟai: maṟakkaḷa vaḻi* and/or *ērkkaḷa uruvakam.*

371

I saw no one throughout the vast world who would be my patron
as I sat by the foot of a tree, resting there, hungry,
when I threaded a garland of blossoming flowers for myself
on a string and donned it to make my bright black hair

gleam. With me were my drum and my carrying bag
and I picked up my cooking pot, holding it in my hand with care,
since it was chipped at the mouth, and because I had no rice
I felt desire that overcame all my other desires for things
I must have while in the courtyard the shining margosa blossoms
were falling. I had pushed through difficult country, thinking of you,
of your good name, you who plow with the plowshare of your bow,
living in your camp of wide renown where your thundering drum
resounds . . . . attacking mercilessly, as great sharp-edged weapons
follow their whirling paths, arrows arrive. And I beating on the
    wide eye
of my tightly strapped taṭāri drum which resembles the moon
so that it quivers and playing my ākuḷi drum, for the sake of a gift
with a spotted face and a massive wrinkled trunk and giant feet
like kettledrums, I have come to you, greatness! to the field
where headless corpses are stacked and to destroy those stacks,
elephants are the buffaloes, lifted swords the palmyra whips, so that
driven to the threshing, the elephants dismember the corpses!
Where a terrifying demoness, with teeth shining like a boar's tusks,
chews and relishes white fat mixed with flesh and weaves a garland
of intestines and wears it on her head and dances and sings,
"May he who gave us such profusion, to eat and stuff ourselves full,
live more years than the many stars shining in the sky!"—
that is your field, lord, where a dust of dried blood swirls!

Kallāṭaṉār sings Talaiyālaṅkāṉattuc Ceruveṉṟa Pāṇṭiyaṉ Neṭuñceḻiyaṉ. *Tiṇai: vākai. Tuṟai: maṟakkaḷa vaḻi* and/or *ērkkaḷa uruvakam.*

372

To take home with me your necklace that glows like the moonlight—
that is the whole reason I came here, singing your praises, loudly
beating my tightly bound taṭāri drum! Within your crowded camp
where the glistening light of flawless swords flashed like lightning
and brought victory, where the rain of arrows poured down,
you made the field of flesh radiant with your sacrifice
on an oven of severed heads obtained with toil from enemies

who opposed you, with kūviḷam wood the fuel, with ridged guts
tumbling, as a barren sacrificial priestess stirred and turned them
with severed skulls set upon sticks and cooked them up into a ball
of food that even animals would refuse and the male cook then
intoned:
"May the fresh water poured from the burning mouth
suffice as if for all the guests at a wedding!" And he lifted it on high!

Māṅkuṭi Kiḻār sings Cēramāṉ Kaṭalōṭṭiya Vēlkeḻu Kuṭṭuvaṉ. *Tiṇai: vākai. Tuṟai: maṟakkaḷa vēḷvi.*

373

You who have won the victory, with your great army of warriors
who are happy to suffer the anguish of being wounded as if
they were being squeezed tight by an uplifted sword
glowing and dripping with blood, O king with your vast camp
where the royal drum roars like thunder, where the elephants,
well trained in combat, are clouds, the horses and chariots
falling are drops pouring down to break apart at the touch
of earth, and the fearsome arrows are a whirling wind! . . .
. . . As if they were peahens with huge circles on their feathers
and innocent eyes who walk around bewildered, women with their
soft arms
wander, leaving their long-walled mansions empty, each by herself,
yet do not enter the courtyard to take their own lives but thrill
at the wounds! . . . . They wished long life to the horses
with decorated manes and came under your shade, finding the shade
of fame nowhere else! Children with wisps of hair on their heads
and fine chest ornaments, if they lose their play arrows, not seeing
the faces of their fathers and elder brothers. . . . On the field of battle
where the kings fled and fell and died, he did not charge with the
sword
but he, a killer, pressed on like fire swallowing houses and he speared
an elephant to the ground so that its tusks shattered like a
mountain

where thunder and lightning has struck. But then they charged
and attacked him and he took a grave wound. The healers
saw this and their eyes flooded. O greatness! That courtyard
in Vañci had become a field of victory! You had that land
of the west trampled flat, destroying the stacks of men
who had been warriors free of fear! May the broad field
glow where your royal drum resounds! The great poets say
that they go to every field where there are highborn,
resplendent kings, to glorify them and there win elephants
with spotted faces! Though I have little skill, I also drum
on my black kiṇai drum with its handsome eye and with love
I sing your praises, for there are no others like you in this world,
O greatness! and I have come to win gifts that you have gained
from the strong walls of your opponents! You are a lord
whose virility is exalted even by your enemies! And you have
the virtue of giving flawless help to those who are your friends!
You who are the master of the field of terrifying breadth where
a pack of foxes wanders together with demons
and is joined by the red-eared eagle that has tasted human fat!

Kōvūrkiḻār sings Cōḻaṉ Kuḷamuṟṟattut Tuñciya Kiḻḻivaḷavaṉ Karuvūreṟintāṉ.
Tiṇai: vākai. Tuṟai: maṟakkaḷa vaḻi and/or *ērkkaḷa uruvakam.*

374

It was the hour before dawn when the cool dew collects and I had
    just
arranged my tangled hair glowing with gold, which had seemed like
the forehead of an antelope that grazes through the forest and then
    lingers
in the broad fields, and I was sitting in a courtyard by the huge trunk
of a jackfruit tree, beating out a rhythm on my dark kiṇai drum
with its clear eye, and beautifully then some large stags came
up close to hear me playing and singing of the hillsides
overgrown with the black branches of the kuṟiñci, when our king
gave away what he thought he should give to his guests: rich pieces

of meat from the porcupines, brought down by bows at the great water holes
by the husbands of women with eyes like deer who have borne children
with heads easily hurt and tigers' teeth necklaces, and he gave away
sandalwood from trees with branches ripened on the slopes of hills
where there are caves and crevices and he gave away the tusks
from elephants with spotted heads. He heaped up these three things
on the striped skin of a brightly colored tiger! O sun! You
should be as generous as Āy Aṇṭiraṉ
who wears loose bracelets! You are of no use just shining in the sky!

Uṟaiyūr Ēṇiccēri Muṭamōciyār sings Āy Aṇṭiraṉ. *Tiṇai: pāṭāṇṭiṇai. Tuṟai: pūvainilai.*

375

A corner of unkempt common ground for my bed where there are many
sagging posts so that it looks like a dirty pond with blades
of wavering grass, I pack up my kiṇai drum and the fibers
and shoots of long sharp-edged leaves from a palmyra tree
with the base of its trunk like a kettledrum and go off
to enter one after another the houses of those who live
by the plow. I was wondering who were the noble men who might
be willing to take upon themselves the weight of supporting
this miserable life I live of begging and of eating. O lord
of a fine land with gardens that make the mountains lovely
and yield their crops without end, where the honeycombs
hang, Āy who wears loose bracelets, of unfailing magnanimity!
Since there was no one else for whom to play my drum, just as
a huge cloud moves toward the sea, so I, thinking of you
who are one of a kind, have not stayed away but have come here!
May you live long in this world as a refuge for poets! Without
doubt, if you were not in this world, it would be empty
and poets would not endure! And even if they did, my people

would not sing of kings who have no stature or greatness, who have nothing
but their enormous wealth and no matter how much
you may say to them will never understand the slightest thing!

Uṟaiyūr Ēṇiccēri Muṭamōciyār sings Āy Aṇṭiraṉ. *Tiṇai: pāṭāṇṭiṇai. Tuṟai: vāḻttiyal.*

376

In the evening, during the brief twilight, as the sun that had crossed
the ocean of the sky was withdrawing its golden rays and turning
red and curving down, I held my drum close, the taṭāri that is tightly
laced with old leather thongs, and I stood by a bin of rice
near his fine, flourishing palace, as the bards were stuffing themselves
with food. In only the time it takes to blink an eye,
the moon flashed up in the east and dissolved the dense presence
of the dark. No one would ever know who I was by the way
I looked then! The garment around my waist showed frayed fringes,
unraveling threads and old holes. That man who is of such
great worth saw this and he said, "Here is a guest, newly
arrived, and he as well is deserving of our compassion."
He took the cymbals from my hand and he gave me roasted meat
and he gave me clear toddy to drink so strong it was like a snake's
rage! Then and there he made the hell of my poverty vanish
away! O lord, on that very night! He is a boat that can carry you
beyond misery, and so I who have this wondrous skill for understanding whatever
exists within the minds of others, from then and forever after, I would never
consider begging! Instead I will be as happy as the channel
through which the water pours from a brim-full reservoir!
Before the entrance gates of men who are generous and who always
grant their gifts to the needy, my small
kiṇai drum need never appear, repeating and repeating praises!

Pu<u>r</u>attiṇai Na<u>n</u><u>n</u>āka<u>n</u>ār sings Ōymā<u>n</u> Nalliyak Kōṭa<u>n</u>. *Tiṇai: pāṭāṇṭiṇai. Tu<u>r</u>ai: iya<u>n</u>mo<u>l</u>i.*

377

My tangled hair is soaked from sleeping
through all the dew of the many stretches
of night, and to relieve my poverty in some home
of wealth where they sleep sweetly I went out beating upon
my kiṇai drum and while the gods who consume
their offerings of boiled rice protected me,
I said, "May he whose heart is inclined
toward Righteousness live many days" and he,
hearing it, welcomed me. Because he is
generous without end, his hand ready
to give, he cannot be compared with others
for whom poets have wished long life
nor can others be compared with him. I was
deep in thought of his majesty when he said,
"You with your kiṇai which has traveled across
distant lands are in my care!" and he gave me sapphires from the
    mountains,
gold from the forests and shining pearls
from the sea and a varied range of clothes and vessels filled full
of toddy as he saw me standing there, as I stood there
free of grief. What one sees in dreams that loving lord gave me
while I was wide awake! Those who would choose the best country
choose his country. Those who name the best king utter his name.
May that lord last long who is hungry for killing
with his army that has the roar of the ocean
passionately gathered together, with his men
who ride elephants with spotted foreheads,
and gold-encased tusks, horsemen on fine saddled horses
traveling with various gaits, men on fine chariots with lofty banners
and curving wheels with sharply sounding bells,

and men who are fast, famed, fierce warriors who live by the sword!

Ulōccaṉār sings Cōḻaṉ Irāyacūyam Vēṭṭa Perunaṟkiḷḷi. *Tiṇai: pāṭāṇṭiṇai. Tuṟai: vāḻttiyal.*

378

At the palace of the Chola king who reduced
the strength of the coastal people of the south
and drove away the swords of the Andhra people of the north, he whose
chaplet is elegantly fastened, whose powerful hand holds a straight spear,
who wears spurs to goad his swift horse and dons a handsome garland
and is rich in liquor, I was standing with the great mansion before me
like a cool pond, its upper story glowing white with its plaster so that
it resembled the new moon, and I was drumming so hard on my black kiṇai drum
with its sharp sound that it nearly broke as I sang a song in the Vañci mode
that praises unrestrained attack. Then he poured out precious gems
before me, a wealth of them so that I could barely endure it, of such
supreme excellence, of such number! and they were in no way jewels
relegated only for the likes of us! When they saw that, my large family,
burned dark under the sun, suffering, and in need, took up the ornaments
meant for the fingers and put them on their ears, and those that were meant
for ears they squeezed onto their fingers, those meant for the waist
they made fit the neck, and those meant for the neck they tried to fasten

around their waists! It was like the time when a huge family of monkeys,
their red mouths gaping open, shone in splendor as they scooped up
the beautiful ornaments fallen to the ground the day the mighty demon
snatched away Sītā, the wife of Rāma who has the ferocious power of destruction,
and we were so happy that I was laughing and I couldn't stop my laughing,
free of anguish and freed from the suffering
that is my due because I stand at the head of a numerous family!

Ūṉpoti Pacuṅkuṭaiyār sings Cōḻaṉ Ceruppāḻiyeṟinta Iḷañcēṭceṉṉi. *Tiṇai: pāṭāṇṭiṇai. Tuṟai: iyaṉmoḻi.*

379

I heard one of your kiṇai drummers, whose work is to come to you at dawn
and praise you, singing of you: "May I gain a life shaded by his feet!
May he receive, from my tongue, the accounting of his glory! We
are the kiṇai drummers of Villiyātaṉ, the overlord of Ilaṅkai!
There the fields are thick with paddy and the men who harvest it,
when their sharp sickles go dull, look around for a stone, because they want
to keep on vigorously reaping, and they wind up whetting the blades
on the humped backs of tortoises lying in the marshes! My lord,
O greatness! is well able to relieve our hunger, for in the morning
he passes out rice and the fine white meat running with juice
of a short-legged pig, all of it with fragrant melted ghee!" Because
I heard those words, I did not restrain my desires and behind me I left
the mountains whose summits touch the sky, and like a child
that runs to suck his mother's flawless breast, eagerness
drawing me on, I came to the city with its bulwarks and its long
walls and its moat where the fragrant smoke softly rising
from an elegant and prosperous mansion covers

the whole street, as if it were a cloud coming there to grant rain!

Puṟattiṇai Naṉṉākaṉār sings Ōymāṉ Villiyātaṉ. *Tiṇai: pāṭāṇṭiṇai. Tuṟai: paricilṟṟuṟai.*

380

He is wearing pearls that come from the ocean in the south
and he is smeared with sandalwood from the northern mountains
. . . . the powerful warrior
of the Pandyas, with his army
like the sea, victorious in sweet-famed war!
Water raining down from above spreads through the ocean and turns
to pearls! Nightshade and the fragrant petals of wild jasmine
flourish. . . . . The king of Nāñcil
where jackfruit grows with its honeyed pulp! He is so far above those
who raise their strength against him that they cannot even contain him
within their minds! To those friends who stand by him, he is closer than
the palms of their hands, the glory of Cāttaṉ of the strong bow . . .
. . . . lovely children wearing their garlands that seem
like rainbows! Because he is the kind of man he is, even though
in the world it has become a season . . .
of want, the deprivation of my family, now well off, is over!

Karuvūrk Katap Piḷḷai sings Nāñcil Vaḷḷuvaṉ. *Tiṇai: pāṭāṇṭiṇai. Tuṟai: iyaṉmoḻi.*

381

When we had more than enough of eating rice and meat, leisurely we drank
a drink mixed with milk and ate a sweet made with sugar syrup, all of it

perfectly measured and mingled for taste and when we had finished the feast
and satisfied our hunger, we lingered and I said to him "Lord, since we wish
to be there to celebrate a festival, may we ask your leave to return
to our own country?" Fearful that we would be separated and moved
by his great love, he, my lord, said, "If you make an appearance
in the opulent courts of those kings who will give no gifts and if you
drum there on taṭāri drums, on the clear eyes surrounded with bits of flesh
not scraped away, the drums with their sides worn down and their binding cords
frayed, and you perform your songs that are without flaw, their rhythms
faster than fingers snapping, you will be like the rain that pours down
to fall upon an immemorial wilderness where the thickets of tangled plants
serve no purpose, where fruits maturing in clusters are not gathered!
In such a place, what relief can there be for your need? But I relieve
the anguish felt after your long and painful wanderings! And so
in the season of summer, when all across the vast earth, the grains
perish and the rains that had appeared have vanished away to the music
of the thunder, whether you are here with me or whether you are far
away from me, consider, drummer! the things that I have just said!
Only think a little while about them but think hard!" These are the words
my lord spoke, he who reigns over Vēṅkaṭam where resounding waterfalls
of white foam fall, he who is the beloved son of the overlord of Karumpaṉūr!
And he is like a boat that carries the great and the lowly alike in charity
between the shores! So he showed his unyielding
determination to cling to his noble principles and never to forget them!

Naṉṉākaṉār sings Karumpaṉūrkiḻāṉ. *Tiṇai: pāṭāṇṭiṇai. Tuṟai: iyaṉmoḻi.*

382

Your bards, my lord, are singing:
"The warrior lord of the cool country
of the Cholas, who has gained his spoils through
his mighty efforts of the utmost bravery,
killing with the ocean of his army, Nalaṅkiḷḷi
whose horses' manes bear waving plumes! We are
his bards who love him! We want nothing
through praising others! May his deeds
long endure! To drive away the pain
of your hunger, he will grant you,
if you go to him, dishes of rice
and meat seasoned with ghee and also many other succulent foods"
and so these humble people, hearing the bards, knowing how you gave in the past,
have come and so have I! O lord of swift horses!
Grant us gifts, so that we may cast off our poverty
like the skin of the brightly colored snake with glowing spots
and its forked tongue, its eyes for ears, and its uplifted jewel, so that we
too may be able to give gifts! Everyone knows that this wide world
surrounded by the ocean is yours! Everyone knows that this dark kiṇai drum
with its clear eye, light as a sola pith stick, is mine! In the courts
of other kings, I will sing of the chariots you conquered
so that every time they hear of it your enemies will begin to tremble,
just as every time the small stick lashed within my drum
rattles and makes its sharp, subtle sound, the eye of my kiṇai drum quivers!

Kōvūrkiḻār sings Cōḻaṉ Nalaṅkiḷḷi. *Tiṇai: pāṭāṇṭiṇai. Tuṟai: kaṭainilai.*

383

It was not yet dawn but I had already been woken from my bed
by the cock with brightly spotted feathers as the cool dew
settled in. And I was standing by his high gate, beating
my small kiṇai drum so that its slender sounding-sticks
resonated as I praised his many plowing oxen and lauded
his glory! Driving away the pain of my poverty that has made
my body so thin, he showed a desire for us to approach
his well-guarded palace and to have me drink from a cup of fine
fragrance, the toddy topped with honey so it seemed like a waterlily
unfolding a closed, tender bud. He dressed me in silken clothes sewn
with ornaments past all price, so well embroidered with gleaming flowers
it seemed a single flow, like the inner sheath of a stalk of bamboo
or a snakeskin, and then he laid himself down on a soft bed
while his loyal woman hugged him from behind, her curving waist
adorned with elegant ornaments, her navel lovely and round . . .
leaving me . . . . looking . . . .
. . . . I am a man who has died and who has then been
reborn and so I have no intention of going off to sing the fame
of other kings whom the bards praise in song! He is the only one
for me, Aviyaṉ, the master of swift chariots, overlord of the forests
where there are many hills rising up . . . .
. . . where a white lamb circles around the small teats of its mother,
drinks her milk, and then goes off frisking with a white-faced monkey!
He will never fail me! Why should I be afraid,
even if as an ill omen the Silver Planet should rise in the south?

Māṟōkkattu Nappacalaiyār sings. . . . *Tiṇai: pāṭāṇṭiṇai. Tuṟai: kaṭainilai.*

384

In the rice paddy land around the city of the lord
of Karumpaṉūr, cranes who have fed together sleep

on the branches of vañci trees and then they
pick off the blossoms of the ripened sugarcane
and on the land strewn with rocks, quails chase after rats that live
near the lopped-off roots of black-stemmed millet and they frighten
the little rabbits while blossoms with black stalks are falling
nearby from the iruppai trees, and though there is no festival,
there is toddy with flowers floating in it and the meat from big
keṭiṟu fish for the bowls of farm laborers!
And we are his drummers, O greatness!
What is rice to us? What is gold,
or the liquor that heats the body?
Though I may lack them in my house,
he has great quantities! He has spread
his fame so wide that the earth
seems small! He pours ghee
more freely than water on my rice juicy
with abundant fat! He who protects us! What need do we have
now to suffer? With such a patron, let the Silver Planet rise where it will,
though it promises drought! I will know no days other than those
on which the fine leaves we have eaten from are folded and flung
away still filled with food!
And we are left to wedge out the bits then that stick between our teeth!

Puṟattiṇai Naṉṉākaṉār sings Karumpaṉūr Kiḻāṉ. *Tiṇai: pāṭāṇṭiṇai. Tuṟai: kaṭainilai.*

385

As the Silver Planet appeared and the calls of the birds were heard
at the break of dawn, I did not appear at his gateway to praise
his many plowing oxen! But when he heard the music of my taṭāri drum
with its broad eye sounding at the doorways of other kings, he felt
kindness toward me and wishing my poverty to vanish, he stripped me
of the threadbare garment around my waist that the dust of the earth

was consuming and he clothed me in white and he banished my hunger!
May the overlord of Ampar where the fields grow their paddy and the water
of the Kāviri River laps into the low-lying land of the gardens,
may that good man Aruvantai live for more years than there might be
drops of rain falling from the heights
of the sky upon Palli's hill of Vēṅkaṭam, the mountain of victory!

Kallāṭaṉār sings Amparkiḻāṉ Aruvantai. *Tiṇai: pāṭāṇṭiṇai. Tuṟai: vāḻttiyal.*

386

We took what he offered us, the fried meat
dripping with ghee as when drops of rain
shower down on a lake of water and we ate
the roasted meat pierced through by the skewers!
And into white cups where there was already meat,
he had cow's milk poured for us to fill them
to the top! Other than the sweat from eating
this heated food, we knew nothing of the sweat of work!
My lord was generous so that he would thereby gain fame!
His fields are full of many blossoming flowers that grow
among the stretches of tall sugarcane that enclose his rice paddies.
On his meadows where his many herds of cows graze on the grass,
fierce fortresses rise with their bowmen.
From his ocean, branches of mastwood are washed into gardens
where people stand and count the ships brought by the wind.
His salt pans swarm with the salt merchants who leave for a fine country
with tall mountains, there to shout the price of their white,
small-grained salt. Such is the good land that is ours,we
called "Fighters" by caste but we do not fight!
Let the Silver Planet rise in the east and then move westward
or let it rise in the west and then move toward the east
or let it appear in the north and then move toward the south

or let it rise in the south and remain there without moving!
Let the Silver Planet stand anywhere it wishes!
But may his projects prosper, he who knows what we need!

Kōvūrkiḻār sings Cōḻaṉ Kuḷamuṟṟattut Tuñciya Kiḷḷi Vaḷavaṉ. *Tiṇai: pāṭāṇṭiṇai. Tuṟai: vāḻttiyal.*

387

I will play on my black kiṇai drum that has
its clear eye and its new full cover stretched
tightly around it and wrapped with straps
so that it looks like the white belly of a sharp-clawed tortoise
and this is what I will sing: "You drove away poverty
from your musicians who bring you joy,
giving them the tribute humbly offered
by kings who opposed you and who own many elephants
skilled at their work of war, always
breaking down enemy walls, their fragrant
temples coated with powdered lime, their giant necks
adorned with ornaments marked with flowers, who move dispersed
in various formations, who with their lofty tusks and their dark
huge, harsh trunks were stationed near the guarded forests
of the great kings! May his worthy feet glow!" And the king of those men
there who acclaimed this and the many other ways I praised. . . . .
In the large courtyard of the palace which is
a delight to approach, he wanted me to advance toward his worthy feet
in their excellent anklets, he who owns the royal drum
of victory that is beaten after conquests!
Not despising my low status, thinking only
of his stature and his worth, didn't he give me
elephants like mountains? Didn't he give me horses
with cropped manes? Didn't he give me herds
of cattle filling his courtyard? Didn't he give me
fields with farmers who are part of the property,

and all so quickly it seemed a waking dream? He is that lord
filled with love, the great overlord of the Pūḻiyar! If one only
mentions the name of Celvak Kaṭuṅkō Vāḻiyātaṉ who has elephants
with their tusks and rough trunks, he whose energies are imposing
in battle, then his enemies will dip their lofty umbrellas and without
a moment's hesitation they will send their tribute to him here!
And so may he live on for more aeons than the grains of sand by the resounding
Porunai River that washes the city of Vañci named for the tree
with dull-colored leaves, more than the grains
of rice that grow in all the fields around the many cities of that land!

Kuṉṟukaṭpāliyātaṉār sings Cēramāṉ Cikkaṟpaḷḷit Tuñciya Celvak Kaṭuṅkō Vāḻiyātaṉ. *Tiṇai: pāṭāṇṭiṇai. Tuṟai: vāḻttiyal.*

388

At a time when the Silver Planet was seen in the south and the fields
where things grow yielded nothing and the irrigation canals were dry,
a drummer with a big paṟai drum went traveling to seek out the presence
of his Cṟukuṭikiḻāṉ Paṇṇaṉ and to let him know how poorly
he stood. My lord then gave whatever he had so as to make
that suffering vanish away. Our chieftain, our overlord,
he who is supreme in generosity! Hear me then sing of Paṇṇaṉ
who gives away fields where the rice grows to poets who own
the elephant of true victorious speech, whose mighty trunk is compositions
of penetrating art, whose tusks are their tongues. . . . .
If I do not exalt the high quality of his plowing oxen
as I beat my kiṇai drum, if I don't sing each and every day,
may he who is descended from Teṉṉavaṉ, he in whose courtyard
a bell is always hung to be rung by those in need, may Vaḻuti
of the vast army with a resounding, well-strapped
royal drum and massive elephants protect my large family no longer!

Maturai Aḷakkarñāḻalār Makaṉār Maḷvaṉār sings Ciṟukuṭikiḻāṉ Paṇṇaṉ.
Tiṇai: pāṭāṇṭiṇai. Tuṟai: iyaṉmoḻi.

389

Even though it was the season of heat when the moist
seed of the palmyra fruit dries out and the green fruits
of the forest margosa shrivel and the reservoirs turn
to sludge, the time when the Silver Planet turns south
in ill omen, he still said "Remember us as well, young musician!"
and that man of worth whose fame is great was generous to me!
Today he is nowhere you can go and reach him, nor anywhere
you can see him, Ātaṉuṅkaṉ who was the overlord of Vēṅkaṭam
with its roaring waterfall, where they would capture an elephant calf
and tie it up in the courtyard of a fine home within a city
that encloses a hill! And its innocent mother whose head is so tender
would grieve for it! Nallēr Mutiyaṉ, you who control yourself
and do not simply go where desire draws you! You too, like Ātaṉuṅkaṉ,
should give us the finest of jewels, to lift away the suffering
of my hungry family! Greatness! May your women
with their broad, soft zones of love
never hear funeral drums while they stand at their lofty gates!

Kaḷḷil Āttiraiyaṉār sings Nallēr Mutiyaṉ. *Tiṇai: pāṭāṇṭiṇai. Tuṟai: iyaṉmoḻi.*

390

I was in the broad, well-protected city that enemy kings cannot even
approach in their dreams but anyone who comes there in need
may enter! In a courtyard that was like a great field decorated
for a festival, fragrant with the blooming flowers of the gold-blossomed
pear tree from a forest inhabited by cowherds of upright mind and others

with great valor swelling up in their hearts, I drummed
on my sharp-toned taṭāri drum hard enough to shatter it,
so that the buildings resounded around me like mountain ranges
and I sang! There was no need for me to remain there many days
but on that very day I arrived, at the onset of the night,
he said, because I had come to him, "The musician with little hair
on his head who is standing at the high gate is in a sorry state!"
He asked me to approach him and from my waist he removed the garment
that was like moss in stagnant water and he replaced it with a new one
that was like a splendid flower and he gave me the toddy that brings joy
and he fed me rice with pieces of meat like amṛta in a vessel of white
silver! And then to soothe the anguish of my large family burned dark
under the sun, so weak they could barely move, as they waited for me
in the public field before the city, he gave me a whole heap
of fine paddy the color of the vēṅkai flower filled with nectar,
grown with the help of plowing oxen, and he said, "Accept this!
Take it from me!"—that man from a land with the best water, where
the springs people visit are adorned with mountain flowers! If you
should see him, he will take you into his home and there
as you sing the praises of his handsome feet. . . . .
Those who say, "The clouds ignore our suffering!" do not know the king
who commands the best of elephants
and who drives away murderous hunger or else they have not seen him!

Auvaiyār sings Atiyamāṉ Neṭumāṉ Añci. *Tiṇai: pāṭāṇtiṇai. Tuṟai: iyaṉmoḻi.*

391

In the north, along Vēṅkaṭam Mountain, where they used to drink
their toddy and slice entire cuts of meat into pieces for eating
and joyfully welcome what they received, singing the praises
of the great wealth of paddy raised with plowing oxen and piled up
in stacks that towered so high they scraped the sky as if forming

some mountain where the cool drops of rain spill down
from roaring clouds, everyone goes hungry now and so my family,
large and burned dark under the sun, has come here and here they still
remain in this fine city whose ancient clans are of such worth
that we never think of leaving, since you ask. . . . .
Aware of me, those wise men who understand you spoke to you,
saying "This is the same man who came here once before. He is poor
and he is a musician still worth your pity!" And so I have come,
to see you, greatness! you who reside in your opulent mansion
surrounded by your flourishing mastwood trees, where a crane
with its tight-packed feathers eats the fish that enter
the dark waters of a vast tidal pool and then goes to sleep. May it be
that you sleep sweetly at home, with your beloved whose heart is full
with love for you! And as the rain drops drift down, knowing
the right time to nourish the crops,
may your thousands of vēlis of fields offer their rich harvest!

Kallāṭaṉār sings Poṟaiyāṟṟukiḻāṉ. *Tiṇai: pāṭāṇṭiṇai. Tuṟai: kaṭainilai.*

392

I stood at the high gate of Eḻiṉi who wears a curving ornament,
the king of the Atiyar, he whose white umbrella is like the moon!
It was dawn and under the pale moonlight the dew was settling in.
Like the foot of a war elephant was the dark, one-eyed kiṇai drum
I held in my hand, and I drummed out a rhythm upon it and I sang,
"You have beaten down the formidable walls of fearsome kings
who refused you tribute and on every one of your great
battlefields where demonic spirits roam and the ground is
soaked through with blood and fat, you have yoked
a vile herd of white-mouthed donkeys and planted horsegram
and common white millet and you plow new fields every day! May
your life be a long one!" As I had come to him and was standing
right there, at once, he stripped off my tattered garment
that looked like the roots of duckweed with its large leaves

growing in a pond from which a town will drink and he dressed me
in fine cloth of costly thread with a wonderfully elegant border
and told me to eat, pouring aged toddy as strong as the sting
of a scorpion into a dish as golden as the planets in the sky
and gave me foods, one after another, and more! a seat and a feast
for us to enjoy! That great man whose ancestor
brought us the sugarcane, as hard to gain as amṛta, from the land beyond!

Auvaiyār sings Atiyamāṉ Makaṉ Pokuṭṭeḻiṉi [Atiyamāṉ's son Pokuṭṭeḻiṉi].
Tiṇai: pāṭāṇṭiṇai. Tuṟai: kaṭainilai.

393

From the time it began my life has been filled with suffering though I
have never been able to accept it, and now the sharpness of my mind
has gone and so has that of my young wife who has been with me a long time,
and my pain is great as I sing my songs for the clans one after another
in due order of their rank. Hero! You who wear a garland of flowers!
Since in other lands no one exists who is aware of the responsibility
to turn our cooking pot right side up even though it has forgotten its will
to cook, and with our minds wondering who will be properly generous to us,
the goad of desire impelling me, I think of your noble reputation, you
for whom it seems the whole wealth of the world has been gathered together!
Lifting away the fierce suffering from my large family burned dark by sun,
who have forgotten how it feels to have their hands moist with food,
you should tear juicy, fat meat into pieces and offer them those chunks

white with fat like the cotton of summer carded and packed into dense
bundles! And you should strip me of my old ragged garment that is split
like the tongue of a serpent that has laid its eggs at its time to breed,
and you should clothe me then in a broad garment with folds like the petals
of newly blossoming pakaṉṟai flowers that have sprung open their buds!
And you should give away wealth without holding anything back,
O greatness! O lord of a good land where the Kāviri spreads its water
without fail even in the season of the heat when everything withers
like the yoni of a dancing girl when the dance is done! We will drum
clear notes on the dark kiṇai drum that is like the full moon and we'll
chant, "Long life to Vaḷavaṉ, whose sword never fails!"
and again and again we will sing of your great and strenuous achievements!

Nalliṟaiyaṉār sings Cōḻaṉ Kuḷamuṟṟattut Tuñciya Kiḷḷivaḷavaṉ. *Tiṇai: pāṭāṇṭiṇai. Tuṟai: kaṭainilai.*

394

Though all the world may praise the generosity of Kuṭṭuvaṉ,
the lord of Veṇkuṭai whose fields are filled with luxuriant grain,
whose chest smeared with sandal paste is burly from drawing the bow,
in whose hands strength rests, whose sword never fails,
yet give up your thoughts of going to him, poets of lofty speech!
I as well, at dawn, when the darkness and the moonlight were over,
played softly for him on my black kiṇai drum with its single eye
and in honor of his father who rode a fine chariot, whose royal drum
had roared, I sang for him a Vañci song of invasions.
Happiness filled his heart and he showed desire for me to approach him

and he gave me an elephant not yet calmed down after a kill,
sending out a stench from its tusks covered with blood, tossing
its body in anger! In terror I refused it, and he, ashamed, thinking
I felt it was too little, ordered an elephant brought to me that was
yet more immense! And so, because of that, even if my large family,
which has been burned dark under the sun, may suffer, I have realized
the gifts that he gives you cannot approach!
and I have never gone back to that land of his, with its hills.

Kōṉāṭṭu Eṟiccilūr Māṭalaṉ Maturaik Kumaraṉār sings Cōḻiya Ēṉāti Tirukkuṭṭuvaṉ. *Tiṇai: pāṭāṇṭiṇai. Tuṟai: kaṭainilai.* All *kaṭainilai's* are *pāṭāṇṭiṇai.*

395

Lord! We are Cāttaṉ's drummers,
he who is famous for Righteousness and hails
from Piṭavūr, ruled by his father
Vēṇmāṉ of the long arms, which is guarded well
and lies to the east of Uṟantai, that city
nobly, endlessly famed, and ruled
by Tittaṉ, master of small-eyed elephants,
he whose favor is hard to gain, he whose
worth is so high. In Piṭavūr, a tame hen
calls softly and a cock of the forest
seductively answers and a water hen
chimes in and when women as gently beautiful
as peacocks, their arms willowy as bamboo,
chase the parrots from the mountain fields,
birds throughout vast marshes
flee in fear. And that city is adorned with many
fine fields with plowmen who farm the fertile soil,
letting their oxen loose to graze over
rougher ground, and then they dine on a stew of well-cooked pieces
of small rabbit and long scabbard fish and yesterday's rice,
and deck themselves with jasmine from a bush,
and play sharp-toned drums that frighten off birds and drink strained
toddy

made from the raw rice! Yesterday, at midday, I was
wandering the forest, suffering the heat. Then at evening, the sun gone,
darkness massing, with my sweet-voiced . . . . . sharp-toned
taṭāri drum I appeared at his door,
announcing my worries and without a moment's
hesitation when he saw me standing there, without a lot of words
he told me to enter and he gave me precious ornaments and full
of goodwill, with gentle language, he showed me to the woman
of his house, as lovely as Lakṣmī, and he said to her,
"Treat him as you would me!" Therefore I will not forget him
nor will I think of others! May his efforts endure, dedicated
to giving, unconcerned if the omens
are good or evil, so that should
the wide world wither away or many blazing stars flash across
the sky or the constellation of the reservoir smoke with a comet,
the people will still eat green pieces of fried vegetables
and meat and boiled rice grains long
as the claws of cranes and they will shout, "May the harvest come flooding in!"

Maturai Nakkīrar sings Cōḻanāṭṭup Piṭavūrkiḻāṉ Makaṉ Peruñ Cāttaṉ. *Tiṇai: pāṭāṇṭiṇai. Tuṟai: kaṭainilai.*

396

Lord! He rules Vaṭṭāṟu
of the rich waters where they frighten the birds with drums
sharply beaten in the growing fields
that are circled by the tidal pools
where the fish dart under the water
and the flowers blossom on the surface
like so many eyes and from the sand
heaped up by the great waters, birds
fly off on soft wings in cool wind,
where warrior Kōcars, who store flower wine
in their homes, drink strained sweet toddy
and are delighted! And the honeyed sound

is heard of the kuravai dance! We are
his drummers! He who is strength to those
without determination, kin to those who have
no kin, a Vēḷir with a victorious spear
in battle! He! E̲li̲ni Āta̲n!
Should I sing of his cooked meat, its
succulent pieces, or his rich flower wine?
Should I sing of his fragrant rice,
with ghee and the fat of a small rabbit
poured upon it? Should I sing of food
taken from a bin left open and forgotten
for us to eat at will! Many, many things!
. . . .
Happy to do it, my lord gave to us graciously
so that my large family burned dark under the sun
and in pain could eat in happiness and have food left over!
Is there any limit to the
wealth he has given my people?
May his flawless good name shine like the white moon that spreads
    its rays
in the midst of the sky filled with rain! And as he grants
every day long strings of fine gems,
we and others praising him, may his glory grow though a rich wealth
    of song!

Māṅkuṭi Ki̲lār sings Vāṭṭāṟṟeḻiniyātaṉ. *Tiṇai: pāṭāṇṭiṇai. Tuṟai: kaṭainilai.*

397

The Silver Planet was rising in the vast sky, and the birds
in their nests on the high branches were beginning to sing.
The ponds were opening their eyes of flowers and the moon
slowly was lessening its light. The music sounded—an ascent
of conches that spiral to the right and the roaring royal drum!
In that time when you see the night fleeing, I appeared
at the guarded camp and as the darkness was shrinking away,
I drummed on my black kiṇai drum with its clear-sounding eye,
and it resounded as I sang, "You on whose chest rests a garland,

of many plaits, listen to the sounds of the morning! Awaken
from your sleep!" And so I stood there at his towering gate!
And that pleased him. He said, "Here is someone who has thought of me
and come to me in his need," and magnanimous as a shower of rain,
he poured out masses of fried meat, well seasoned and full of ghee,
and fragrant toddy that filled a jeweled vessel to the top,
and he gave me a garment with beautifully embroidered flowers,
colorful as a snake's skin, and he gave me precious gems to free me
of anguish that burned like the season of the heat. He comes
from a land where lotuses with their red petals blossoming
in a marsh shine alongside the fires kindled for the sake of
Righteousness by Brahmins who fulfil the six duties. Vaḷavaṉ
who wears ornaments of gold taken from those islands conquered
with his unswerving sword! Even if the end should dawn for the great sea
heaving with its waves or the sun of blazing rays appears in the sky
of the south, we will not fear and wonder what to do! He has power
to win victories with his conquering spear in hard battle!
We rest in the cool shade of his mighty feet with their handsome anklets!

Erukkāṭṭūrt Tāyaṅkaṇṇaṉār sings Cōḻaṉ Kuḷamuṟṟattut Tuñciya Kiḻḻivaḷavaṉ.
Tiṇai: pāṭāṇṭiṇai. Tuṟai: paricilviṭai and/or *kaṭainilai viṭai.*

398

As the moonlight was waning and the Silver Planet rising,
and in many varied, handsome houses . . . .
the cock with spotted feathers, aware of the dawn, was crowing,
when the buds opened in the ponds and bards with their skilled hands,
knowing their art, were playing their small yāḻs at the auspicious
moment of daybreak that sees the night fleeing, I was drumming
on my sharp-toned taṭāri drum that is like the moon, its long straps
resonating with their message of pleading in the ancient city of great name
where under a pavilion with a never-ending fragrance sat Vañcaṉ

whose words are always true, who pays his debts according to the merit
of those who come to him in need, a city that cannot be approached
by enemies though those who come laughing may approach it, just like
a cave hollowed in stone where a family of tigers is sleeping!
I was singing, "May you fill the bowls of those who have come
thinking of you! May you be for us a shelter that will never disappear!"
He knew I had come and for the little I had done he showed
his joy and his face filled with love. He stripped
the torn and tattered garment from my waist and he dressed me
in the fine garment that spread like smoke around his own waist.
And into my drinking dish, which had been hard put to receive
anything and had seemed only to spew up fire, he poured toddy to the top,
so clear that you could see your face reflected in it.
And not only for me but to my family he gave fried venison to eat
and elephant yams and rice with grains as long as a crane's claws,
the same to be seen on the plates he dined from and then, to spread his fame,
he gave me the necklace formed like a snake—glowing with manifold gems,
esteemed by the whole world—that lay on his mountainous chest and he gave
to me the garment embroidered with flowers clothing
his august body, the king of Pāyal where waterfalls resound like drums!

Tiruttāmaṉār sings Cēramāṉ Vañcaṉ. *Tiṇai: pāṭāṇṭiṇai. Tuṟai: kaṭainilai.*

399

We were on our way to him, he who is the lord of the Kāviri River,
where the fields murmur with water and laborers working among the stacks
of grain grow groggy with drink and fill their plates with yesterday's rice,

whole grains cooked soft—each grain, the husk removed, looking as if the petals
of the ripening bud of a trumpet flower had been spread open—with already cooked
rice . . . .
and rice water poured in to mix with the fruit of the small pākal vine,
with vaḻḻai leaves from the marshes and juicy pieces of horned fish and big black
murrel fish and the sour fragrant juice of sweet mangoes grown on high branches
casting shadows, ...
all boiled in a white pot with more rice from the inexhaustible paddy a large ring-bearing pestle
has pounded, rice brought them by a woman cook.
We were on our way to Kiḻḻi Vaḷavaṉ whose noble fame is never-ending!
He it was whom I thought of! Nor would I ever go off anywhere else!
I would not go! I would not look into the faces of others! As my food,
at the wrong times for dining, I ate thin gruel made from tamarind
cooked by my drummer woman after she sold the fish she had caught
with a long bamboo pole! In my despair, I was standing to one side. And then
I was told, "Why are you standing there? He who is the most righteous
of the righteous, he who is the foremost hero among heroes, he who has
the greatest Martial Courage among those of Martial Courage, whose descent
is from the ancients, he wishes you to come to him because of your fame
so that you may eat the amṛta you desire!" I thought of what I must
do next and I went off and cleaned my strong poet's stick and took
my black kiṇai drum with its clear-sounding eye which had been lying

dilapidated with its thongs cut and I tied it up with fresh strings,
drummed a rhythm on a new strong skin fit for music so that its thongs,
like an endless garland, resounded, and fearing it might delay the food,
I did not worship the god in the drum. And before I could express
my wish for anything, before I could say I had come with a desire
for strong-necked oxen who would never tire even dragging a cart
like a swift chariot through the mud, he responded at once! He gave me
many rows of cattle, their bodies as lovely as the stars that blossom
in the sky and many carriages for them to pull, that king of Tōṉṟi
mountain whose towering summit scrapes
against the sky and down which a waterfall descends, roaring in rhythm!

Aiyūr Muṭavaṉār sings Tāmāṉ Tōṉṟikkōṉ. *Tiṇai: pāṭāṇṭiṇai. Tuṟai: Paricilviṭai.*

400

I was beating my drum that had
the look of the moon grown full
after fifteen days, set in the midst
of the dark sea. And I proclaimed
his majesty, appearing at dawn
at his door. Though many were asleep,
he was not sleeping, but my lord
of lofty principles, he who is the protector of the world
heard the voice of my clear-toned kiṇai drum and so,
with undiminished desire he stripped me of the old,
torn clothes that encircled my waist . . . and fine, precious stones
. . . . looking
at my waist, he gave me a garment of the highest quality!
And I was filled with joy as I drank liquor that had been
strained through fiber and I don't even
know how much time I passed in that village! Not only can he

drive away his enemies but he can also drive away that enemy,
hunger! from those who come to him. Full of warriors,
. . . . . that wealthy country sweet to live in, with prosperous
cities where the river running with clear water is maintained
at every harbor so that oceangoing ships may come up through
the dark tidal channels and dock, where
sacrificial posts are attended by learned Brahmins—the land he rules!

Kōvūrkiḻār sings Cōḻaṉ Nalaṅkiḷḷi. *Tiṇai: pāṭāṇṭiṇai. Tuṟai: iyaṉmoḻi.*

NOTES TO THE *PUṞANĀṈŪṞU*

1

This is a *kaṭavuḷ vāḻttu*, or "invocation to God." It was customary to begin all long works in India in this way. This initial poem was written centuries later than the poems that comprise the *Puṟanāṉūṟu*.

1: Laburnam is *koṉṟai*.

5: "Poison" is literally "a scar." This refers to the myth that during the churning of the ocean, Śiva drank the Hālāhala poison, which would have destroyed all living things had he not consumed it. The poison left a blue scar on Śiva's throat, and for that reason, he is called *nīlakaṇṭha*, "he whose throat is dark blue."

10: "His followers" is added for clarity. The Gaṇas are Śiva's attendants.

13: Tapas (Tamil *tavam*) comes from the Sanskrit root *tap*, "to burn or suffer." The word is sometimes translated as "penance" or "austerities," but there is no good English equivalent. It refers to self-denial and austerities, which are believed to give one power and to produce a positive result in the future. In the Purāṇas and epics, it often means the magic heat or power gained by ascetic practices and hence refers to the performance of any ascetic practice, usually with the aim of forcing some divine agency to do what one wishes.

2

9–10: The Chera king, to whom this poem is addressed, traditionally ruled Kerala. The fact that he is described as ruling from ocean to ocean—a land much larger than Kerala—is, of course, a form of flattery.

12: "You are bounded by the sky" refers to the fact that the land ruled by the Chera king included the western Ghats.

14: The hundred are the Kauravas, the villains of the *Mahābhārata.*

15: *Tumpai* was used for "a garland of flowers worn by warriors when engaged in battle as a mark of their valour" (Lexicon). It could be translated as "white dead nettle." We have not translated the names of Tamil flowers and plants unless the English equivalent sounds felicitous and unforced.

16: "The five" are the five Pāṇḍavas, the heroes of the *Mahābhārata.* This poem has been used to suggest that some of the Tamil kings were contemporaneous with that great epic, but clearly this is simply a way of enhancing the status of the lineage of the Chera king, much as the *Aeneid* served to enhance the status of Emperor Augustus.

17: The text reads *pāal puḷippiṉum,* which could mean "even if milk becomes sour." However, since that is an ordinary occurrence, it would hardly fit the meaning the poet obviously intends here. According to the OC's gloss, it is "Even if milk loses its sweetness and becomes [something] sour," that is, becomes something quite different from what it usually is. Our translation attempts to convey this meaning.

19: "On and on" is *muḻutu cēṇ viḷaṅki,* literally, "shining far for a long time."

20: "Himālaya" is *imayam.* We have used the singular to reflect the Tamil usage, although occasionally we say "the Himālayas" when the singular would be awkward.

22: "Faint dawn" is *anti,* a name for the morning or evening twilight. It could be either here, but it must be morning, as it would be inauspicious to invoke the evening twilight.

24: "Offer ghee" is added at the suggestion of OC.

3

6: "Stainless purity" is literally chastity—*kaṟpu.* See the notes to 361.15.

13: The bells were intended to warn of the approach of the elephant, especially if he is in rut.

6: "Infallible arrow after arrow" is the translation of *cen toṭai piḻaiyāa. Toṭai* probably means a succession of bow shots; hence the literal meaning is "not failing in their excellent rounds of shots."

20: "From the sun" has been added for clarity.

24: "Those who are in need" is *iravalar,* literally, suppliants.

26: "What they want in their hearts" is added for clarity.

4

1–2: Literally, "swords are spotted (*maṟuppaṭṭaṉa*) [with blood]." This brings to mind the famous verse from Kālidāsa's *Kumārasaṃbhava,* 8:54: "'As the rest of the sun's radiance has passed, / the sky in the west wears the red stripe / of twilight like a battlefield on which a curving sword, / soaked in blood, has been planted aslant'" (trans. Hank Heifetz).

2: "Evening" is added for clarity.

7: "Riders" is added for clarity.

8: For "forward" (*iṭam kāṭṭa*), OC says to the right or left.

5

D. says the king was renowned for having "bodily brilliance." When the poet, who suffered from a deformity, went to see the king, his own body was made whole by the sight of the king's brilliant body. It is difficult to see any connection between this story and the poem.

8: *Aḷitō tāṉē atu, peṟal aruṅku uraittu,* literally, "it [protection] is something that should be bestowed, and it is hard to get."

6

1: Eternally is implied by *paṉi paṭu.*

3: This is apparently a reference to the story of Sagara who, when his sacrificial horse was stolen by Indra and carried down to Pātāla, had his sixty thousand sons search for it. In trying to find the horse, they dug down into the earth, thereby increasing the boundaries of the ocean, which is therefore called *sāgara.* "Of the earth" is added for clarity.

6: "Universe" and "earth" are supplied for clarity.

7: "Holy" is supplied to give "realm of the cows" its proper tone; "highest sphere" is supplied for clarity.

15: "Near their cities" is the translation of *paṭappai,* one of whose meanings is "vicinity or outskirts of a town" (the Lexicon). According to OC, this line means "hard-to-take walled fortifications that are near green fields that grow [grain]."

16: *Varicaiyiṉ,* here translated as "by rank," could also mean "by worth."

17: *Valam cey* means to "circumambulate keeping to the right."

18: The word for "Brahmins" is *muṉivar.* This is from Sanskrit *muni,* but it has a Tamil folk etymology from the root *muṉi,* "hate"—they who hate [the world and are therefore ascetics].

27–29: It is common to compare the gracious and generous aspects of a king to the moon, and the fierce character he shows in war and in punishing evildoers to the sun.

7

9: Here Tamil has *ākaliṉ,* "because of this," which has been omitted to make the translation flow better.

13: This is OC's suggestion. The literal meaning is "to block the [widely] spread noise of cool water." According to OC, this means "to block *uṭaippu*"—breaches in a tank or in ridges around a paddy field.

8

1: Or just "habitually praise him."

2: According to OC, *pōkam* (from Sanskrit *bhoga* and translated as "pleasures") means "happiness that one enjoys." D. adds: "Because kings praise him and act, there is no mischief or trouble or enmity or anything else [like that] in his land, and so he engages in the experience of enjoyment."

4: Literally, his generosity is such that he does not hoard (his wealth).

6: So OC. This could also mean "his army that kills in victory."

7: "To the moon" is added at OC's suggestion.

8: "You advance from various directions" is literally "you come changing." According to OC, this means the sun goes north or south at different times of the year.

9–10: Literally, "And in the day you shine, spreading your many rays in the vast, broad sky."

9

1: "Share the holiness of cows" is literally "have the nature of cows"—*āṉ iyal*.

4: The dead were believed to live in the south.

6: For "Righteousness," see the notes to 44.11–12.

7: For "Martial Courage," see the notes to 39.10.

10: Literally, "whose waters are good."

11: Literally, "Neṭiyōṉ who was his king" (and hence his forefather).

12: "Musicians" is *vayiriyar.* "Reddish yellow gold" is *cennīr pacum poṉ*—literally, *pacum poṉ* whose nature is reddish. The Lexicon says *pacum poṉ* is either fine gold or a kind of gold.

10

1: "Favor" is *aṟiti,* literally, "you know."

4: "Search out": according to OC, you look through the books on *nīti* (statecraft, proper conduct for a king) and do what they say. "As is right" is literally "what is fitting [for that evil]."

6: "Esteem them more than before"—*paṇṭaiyiṟ peritu*— is elliptical and unclear in Tamil; the translation follows OC.

9: "Guests" is the suggestion of OC for the literal "those who come."

7: "This far" is added for clarity.

10: *Amṛta* is the drink that makes one immortal. In these poems, it is often used to signify food or drink that is very precious, life-giving, or sweet. *Amṛta* is the Sanskrit source word for the Tamil *amiḻtam.* Some translations from classical Indian languages use the word *ambrosia* (which has a similar etymology in Greek). We chose not to because of its overuse in neoromantic diction and translations that use such diction.

13: "Many virtues" is added at suggestion of oc.

11

The king being sung here is a famous poet in his own right, having written many *akam* poems, usually in the *tiṇai* of *pālai*—hence his name, "the great ferocious Chera king who sang *pālai.*" The poet's name means "Iḷaveyiṉi who was a female ghoul." D. says that there was a story current at the time of oc that a female ghoul took on a human body and sang in praise of this king. Probably, he suggests, Iḷaveyiṉi was a poetess who took the pseudonym "female ghoul" because she sang many poems about the female ghouls who frequent the battlefield and eat the flesh of the fallen.

5: "Bright" is *vāl,* "pure" or "white." oc says this means "pure" (*tūya*).

11: For "Martial Courage," see the notes to 39.10.

14: "Heavy" is literally "of [many] excellent *kaḻañcus.*" A *kaḻañcu* is a weight, equal to 1/6 oz. troy, according to the Lexicon.

15: Literally, "skilled in song with rhythm (*cīr*) that goes [i.e., starts?] with the base note of the rāga." The base note of the rāga is *kural,* "first note of the Indian gamut" (the Lexicon).

12

1: "Of gold" is added for clarity.

5: "Those who ask you for favor" is *ārvalar,* plural of *ārvalaṉ,* "one who seeks a present from a prince or patron."

13

D. says that the Chola king Kōperunaṟkiḷḷi was besieging the Chera king's city of Karuvūr. One day when the Chola king was approaching Karuvūr, the elephant he was riding went into rut. At that time, the poet was on the roof of the palace with the Chera king. When the Chera king remarked that the Chola king was on an elephant and that the elephant was rampaging wildly and that it couldn't be controlled by the mahouts, the poet sang this song.

14

11: "Those who seek your favor" is *paricilar,* literally, "suppliants."

12: "In your skills" is added for clarity. For Murugan, see the notes to 55.18.

17: "Rice and curry and chunks of meat" is *ūṉ tuvai kaṟi cōṟu,* literally, "flesh (*ūn̲*), thick curry (*tuvai*), spiced food [*kar̲i* could be meat or vegetables] and cooked rice."

15

1: "Torn up" is *kul̲itta*, literally, "pitted."

12: *Nacai tara vantōr nacai pir̲akku ol̲iya*, literally, "they who came impelled by their desire [and were disgraced] so that desire was left behind."

23: "Odes that praise invasions" is *vañci*. The Lexicon defines *vañci* as a "theme describing the decision of a king to wear the vañci flowers on his head and to advance against his enemies, with a view to annexing their territories."

25: Drums were smeared with paste to create a black resonant "eye" on the head of the drum.

16

The king's name means "the Chola Perunar̲kiḷḷi who sacrificed the Rājasūya." The Rājasūya is a Vedic sacrifice.

1: "Advances" is added for clarity.

11: "Chest" and "reeks" are added for clarity.

12: For Murugan, see the notes to 55.18.

14: "Wide and lovely fields" is literally "wide, cool fields."

17

1: Cape Kumari is Kanyākumari, the southernmost point of India.

7: Literally, "rolling pleasantly." The wheel is the wheel of law (Sanskrit *dharmacakra*). In these poems, it stands for the power and authority of the king.

8: *Kōl tirutti*—that is, ruling justly.

18: "So that it cannot be used again" is literally "so its state is destroyed."

20–22: This section is literally "So, through your irresistible strength, you escaped (*pir̲itu cen̲r̲u*), [overcoming—added at suggestion of oc] the great weakness you had experienced, so many rejoiced." For *pir̲itu cen̲r̲u*, oc says "you went with another strategem." We take it as "having escaped." The colophon suggests that the Chera king being addressed escaped from jail.

23–24: "A multitude of nobles of exalted family" is *malar tāyattu palar*, literally, "many of broad share [or inheritance]."

40: In Tamil literary convention, thunder is supposed to attack cobras and shatter their hoods.

18

10: "Kāñci" could be translated as "river portia."

11: "At the surface of the water" is *nīr tāl̲nta*. The oc glosses this by *nīrin̲ kaṇṇe ur̲a tāl̲nta*, which apparently means "they are low on the water."

18: According to the Lexicon, the word *yākkai* means "body, as compacted together." It is from the root *yā*, which means "bind, tie." We have translated *yākkai* as "bodies woven of their parts" because we believe that the etymology of the word is important to this poem.

20: "The body massed together of food" is *uṇaviṉ piṇṭam*, literally, "balls [or masses] of food."

22–23: "Create the means for bodies to exist . . . for life to be" is *uṭampum uyirum paṭaitticiṉōr*—literally, "they create body and life" A basic Tamil notion is that body and life go together and are very close to each other. The two are often used as a figure for two things that are inseparable.

30: "Glory" is added for clarity. The words for "make a dam" and "get glory" are the same—*taṭṭōr*, from *taṭṭu*, whose primary meaning is to "knock or beat." The idea is apparently to amass water/glory.

19

4: *Īṇṭu*, literally, "put together," is translated as "broad mass." According to OC, it is "put together of atoms."

5: "Weeping in their anguish" is *kacintu aḻa*, literally, "weep being distressed." According to OC, this means they weep from joy; apparently, he is taking the other meaning of *kaci*, "to ooze out," like moisture from a wall, and so (presumably) (to weep) with copious tears.

7: "Agonizing" is *arum puṇ*, literally, "which has a grievous wound."

10–11: "Who were not old enough to wear their hair groomed and oiled" is the translation of *puṉ talai*, literally, "dull-headed." This refers to the fact that they are too young to oil and take care of their hair properly. For the same reason, it could also mean "tawny-haired" (since untended black hair can turn tawny).

18: The syntax of this poem is quite remarkable—and difficult to reproduce: "O Ceḻiyaṉ! Thinking it like the stone . . . I embraced, didn't I, O you who defeated the might of the seven on the field where Death felt shame . . . , your chest." The last word of the poem, "chest," brings the poem together and gives it meaning and closure.

20

1–5: The five great elements (*mahābhūtas* in Sanskrit) are water, earth, fire, air (wind), and ether or, to use a more modern term, space. In this poem, fire has been omitted.

17: For "Righteousness," see the notes to 44.11–12.

18: "Even if the evil omen is seen" is added for clarity.

21: Literally, "are fearful for you."

21

10: The Lexicon defines *tumpai* as follows: "a garland of flowers worn by warriors when engaged in battle, as a mark of their valour." It defines *tumpait tiṇai* as "major theme of a king or warrior heroically fighting against his enemy."

11: "As you triumph in battle" is added for clarity.

12: "The themes poets sing" is *tuṟai*. These are the major subdivisions of both *akam* and *puram* poems—see the introduction.

14: "With black hands" is *karum kai*, which can also mean "with strong hands," which is how OC takes it.

22

12: The heads of the elephants ooze pus because they have been struck with a goad.

18–19: According to the Lexicon, "finest paddy" is *cennel*, "a kind of superior paddy of yellowish hue."

22: The Lexicon defines *kuravai* as "1. dance in a circle prevalent among the women of sylvan or hill tracts. 2. chorus of shrill sound made by woman by wagging the tongue, uttered on festive occasions."

23: According to OC, the petals are actually made of gold among the green leaves.

25: "Rustling" was added at the suggestion of OC.

30: For Murugan, see the notes to 55.18.

31: Literally, "May your immeasurable wealth live long!" We have interpreted it in accordance with D.'s suggestion.

23

1–2: Literally, "tired of standing in their sheds that have strong posts that have no fault [or weakness]"—*veḷiṟil nōṉ kāḻp paṇai nilai muṉaii.*

4: According to OC, this means the followers who are Kūḷis, which the Lexicon defines as "dwarfish, malformed race of goblins, constituting the army of Śiva," that is, the Gaṇas in Sanskrit. For Murugan, see the notes to 55.18.

5: "Kaṭampu" could be translated as "cadamba oak."

8–9: *Koḷ patam oḻiya vīciya pulaṉ*, literally, "fields [are laid waste]—in them warriors have taken what they want and thrown away whatever was left so it couldn't become cooked food (*patam*) that was of use [to enemies]."

9: "Trees guarded in honor of kings" is *kaṭi maram*, usually translated as "tutelary tree." This tree (or grove of trees) was zealously protected, and the *muracu* (war drum) was made from the wood of an enemy king's tutelary tree, which in battle a king would try to capture and cut down. King Naṉṉaṉ was infamous because he had killed a young girl who unwittingly ate a fruit from his mango tutelary tree (*Kuṟuntokai 292*). See Hart 1975, pp. 16–17.

10–12: The OC interprets this differently: "raging fire roars so that the fire [people] desire (*vev*) [i.e., cooking fire] is destroyed in fine, well-built houses."

19: "Leaping" is *teṟi naṭai. Teṟi* has the sense of both jumping and moving swiftly.

24

3: "You have taken" is added for clarity.

4: "Bursting with people past counting" is *tāṅkā uṟaiyuḷ nal ūr,* literally, "a good city whose population [is so numerous] that it can't be borne [by the earth]."

5–6: Literally, "brawny plowmen who cut paddy grow tired of the burning sun."

9: For *kuravai,* see the notes to 22.22.

15: Muṇṭakam could be translated as "water thorn."

12–13: *talaikkai tarūuntu.* Lexicon: "To show one's great love by taking into one's arms."

20: *Munnīr uṇṭu munnīr pāyum*—both "beverage of three flavors" and "water" are the same word, *munnīr,* which the Lexicon defines as "the three kinds of liquids, viz., milk of tender coconut, sugared water and juice of sugarcane" and "sea, as having the three qualities of forming, protecting and destroying the earth, or as consisting of three waters, viz., river water, spring water and rain water."

25: "Stars" is literally *nāṇ mīṉ,* "lunar asterism." "Given over to destruction" is *patāac celīiyar,* literally, "may it fall and go."

36: "To spread and firmly ground their fame" is *tol icai cela,* literally, "so their ancient fame spreads." The sense is that the fame can be ancient only if it is firmly grounded.

25

1: "Swollen" is *tirukiya,* literally, "twisted, intense."

6: "The battlefield where pain is endured" is *aṇaṅkarum paṟantalai.* According to OC, it is "the battlefield that is hard to vex," but that doesn't make sense. Thus our translation, based on the literal interpretation, "the battlefield that is hard to endure [because it causes] pain."

12: Literally, "hitting so they pained their chests on which breasts glistened."

14: "Dark sand" is *aṟal,* which the Lexicon defines as "black sand found on the seashore."

26

6: "Quickened" is *ulakki*—literally, "disturbed," "stirred up."

9–15: The war sacrifice was undertaken after battle. It involved some sort of ritual cannibalism, the point of which, I have argued, is not merely to partake of the enemy's heroism but to create a bond between the victor and the dead enemies so that the spirits of the dead will not take vengeance on their killers. See Hart 1975, pp. 33–36. See also *Puṟ*. 372.

10: An oven was (and still is) traditionally made by putting three stones in a triangular configuration, kindling a fire inside them, and putting a pot on top of them.

13: "Calm through the breadth of their knowledge" is *āṉṟa kēḷvi*. According to OC, this means *amainta kēḷvi*, "of tranquil (or suitable) learning." The Lexicon says that *āṉṟa* can mean "wide" and "excellent" and that it refers to "one who has grown calm through deep learning." *Kēḷvi* is apparently a translation of the Sanskrit *śruti*.

16: For "tapas," see 1.13.

27

1: "Carefree in their majesty" is *vīṟṟiruntōr*, literally, "who sat in majesty." This may also mean "they who were carefree," which is how UVS takes it.

2: "Equally noble" is OC's suggestion for *vēṟṟumai illā*, whose literal meaning is "which have no difference." The point of the comparison is that when people are born they are without difference, just like the lotuses, that only what they do afterward distinguishes them. Note that a flower is worthy only if it is worn. Literally, "When I think of those who sat enthroned, after being born in an excellent line with no difference [between them] just like a row of 100-petaled lotuses." The 100 petals seem to suggest the exalted quality of their families.

7: "Everything they must do" is *cey viṉai*. This could also mean "the karma they do."

16–17: Literally, "may they be able not to give."

28

1: "Monstrous" is *eccam*, literally, "defect." This word may also be used as a technical term for any of the eight possible defects at birth.

3: "Whom no one favors" is *ciṟappu il*, literally, "without excellence."

11: For "Righteousness," see the notes to 44.11–12.

15: "Three aims of life" is added for clarity. In Sanskrit, the three aims of life are called *trivarga*. They are *dharma* (Tamil *aṟam*), *artha* (Tamil *poruḷ*), and *kāma* (Tamil *kāmam* or *iṉpam*). These signify, roughly, "duty," "attainment of riches or worldly prosperity," and "sexual enjoyment." See also the notes to 362.10 and 44.11–12.

29

3: D. points out that garlands of gold are not fragrant and that the attribution of fragrance to them is simply conventional.

14: *Peṟṟu*—this is land the king has given them.

24: Literally, "as is the *nīrmai* of actors." *Nīrmai* usually means "nature or wont"; hence, our translation. According to OC, this means "costume." The idea is that just as an actor at a festival takes a role for only a short time, so do men in life.

26: Literally, "may the wealth you protect be a place of your fame"; that is, may you act so that people don't criticize you for your wealth, or may you be generous.

30

3: "Pace of movement" is OC's suggestion for *parippu*.

3–4: "The sphere of the earth around which the sun moves" is *parippuc cūḻnta maṇṭilam*, literally, "the sphere enclosed by its moving." According to OC, "sphere" (*maṇṭilam*) here means *pār vaṭṭam*, the "globe of the earth."

31

1–2: For Prosperity, Pleasure, and Righteousness, see the notes to 28.15 and 44.11–12.

4: Two umbrellas refers to the umbrellas of the Chera and Pandya kings. Like other Indian kings, Tamil kings would have an umbrella or parasol that was held above them on royal occasions. The umbrella was white and was often compared to the moon, whose light is cool and life-giving. It was said to shield from the sun (which, in South India, is hot and destructive), and it was a bad omen for its pole to snap (*Puṟ*. 229).

10: Literally, "They don't say, 'We won't go.'"

15: "Circle" is *valam muṟai varutal*—"to circle it keeping one's right side toward it." This is the ceremonial way of circling things (e.g., deities in temples) in India—Sanskrit *pradakṣiṇaṃ kṛ*.

32

3: "Women of the caste of bards" are *viṟaliyār*, female bards (Pāṇaṉs). These women would sell flowers to warriors to wear into battle.

3–4: "Their arms / swaying like bamboo" is literally "with bamboo arms with bending joints."

6: "People in need" is *paricil mākkaḷ*. This refers to "suppliants," specifically those low castes that ask the king for gifts.

33

11–12: "Odes that praise invasions" are *vañci* songs. See the notes to 15.23.

15: D. says these are garlands of jasmine.

20: "No man strolls alone at night"—presumably because he would feel lonely there without a woman, since the place is so lovely.

21–22: "Dancing puppets" is *allip pāvai. Alli* puppets are both male and female. D. says that they do not talk, and that is what is stressed here. According to the commentary of Aṭiyārkkunallār on the *Cilappatikāram,* the *alliyam* dance portrays Krishna breaking the tusks of the elephant sent by Kaṃsa to kill him.

34

1: For "Righteousness," see the notes to 44.11–12.

3: That the women wear ornaments shows they are in an auspicious (married) state.

4: "Brahmins," *pārppār.* D. reads *kuravar,* "elders," but does not give satisfactory evidence for abandoning the usual reading (and the reading of OC). D. claims the reading was changed in the time of Parimēlaḻakar, the greatest of the commentators on the *Tirukkuṟaḷ,* who probably lived in the thirteenth century of the common era.

17–18: This is a puzzle. According to OC, the millet is from before they met the king, the rice from after, but it's not clear where they get the milk and honey.

22: "Noble men" is *cāṉṟōr. Cāṉṟōṉ* (the singular) is defined by the Lexicon as "a wise, learned and respectable man." *Puṟ.* 191 uses the phrase "*āṉṟu avintu aṭaṅkiya koḷkaic cāṉṟōr,*" about which OC says "they have become calm through their good virtues, they do service to high ones [i.e., noble people] whom one should serve, and they [live by the] principle of restraining their five senses." The OC further remarks that this may mean "filled with learning, and accordingly suppressing the sense perceptions that follow taste etc., and being restrained in mind, speech, and body."

35

D. says that the people have failed to pay taxes for a few years. In this poem, the poet persuades the king to forgive those taxes.

1–2: "That the wind cannot penetrate" is literally "where the wind does not go." By its position, it modifies "sky," but D. says it modifies "earth."

15: For "Righteousness," see the notes to 44.11–12.

31–32: "Those weighed down with dependents, those who care for the oxen that plow" is literally "the burden (*pāram*—by extension, families) of those who care for the plowing oxen."

34: "The castes" is *kuṭi,* which may mean communities, clans, and families as well as castes. "Enemies" is *aṭaṅkātōr,* literally, "those who do not submit to you."

36

1–2: This is D.'s interpretation of *aṭunai āyiṉum viṭunai āyiṉum nī aḷantu aṟiti niṉ puraimai,* literally, "Whether you kill or whether you release, you measure and know your greatness."

4–5: See the notes to 23.9. The point of this is that the king, even though his tutelary trees are being cut down outside his city and even though he can hear them being cut down, sits in his fortress with his women and doesn't go out to war.

10: "Exquisitely turned" is *vār kōl,* glossed by OC as *nīṇṭa kōl toḻilāl ceyyappaṭṭa,* "made with long stick work." This must have something to do with how bracelets (or anklets) were made. The Lexicon says it means "[made with] exquisite workmanship." By its position, this should modify anklets, but OC has it modify bracelet, perhaps because *vār kōl* is usually applied to bracelets.

11: "A dais" is teṟṟi. According to OC, this is a raised place that resembles an altar.

12: "To bother fighting against him" is *malaittaṉai eṉpatu,* literally, "to say that you have fought."

37

1: Cempiyaṉ is apparently the same as King Śibi in Sanskrit, who, according to Apte, "is said to have saved Agni in the form of a dove from Indra in the form of a hawk by offering an equal quantity of his own flesh weighed in a balance."

2–6: Lightning is considered the traditional enemy of the cobra, whose hood it is supposed to shatter.

3: "Where a cobra lives" is *nākam pukkeṉa,* literally, "because a cobra has entered [there]."

6: "Had the force in battle" is *vallai,* literally, "you were able."

12–13: "You did not consider how wondrous all this was" is *nalla eṉṉātu*—literally, "not thinking [these things] good."

14: "Harnessed elephant" is *vampu aṇi yāṉai,* literally, "an elephant that wears a girth band."

38

11: "How far may my mind go" is *eṉ aḷavu evaṉō,* literally, "what is my measure." We have followed OC, which construes this as *eṉ niṉaivellai colla vēṇṭumō,* "is it necessary to speak of the limit of my thinking."

13: In Sanskrit, the trees with flowers of gold are called *kalpaka* trees. They exist in the world of the gods and are supposed to have the power to give any object one desires.

15: "Something is missing" is *kaiyaṟavu uṭaittu. Kaiyaṟavu* means destitution of power, inability, faintheartedness, deficiency in good manners (Winslow). According to OC, *ceyalaṟavu* can also mean deficiency in ritual action.

16: "Can be found" is *kūṭaliṉ,* which can also mean "are possible."

39

1–5: See the notes to 37.1 for the story of Cempiyaṉ.

8: For "Righteousness," see the notes to 44.11–12.

10: "Martial Courage" is our translation for *maṟam,* the glorification of courage in war and the militarism that characterized Tamil society during the Sangam age. We capitalize it to remind the reader of its special meaning. See also the notes to 44.11–12.

12: "Kindled by courage" is D.'s suggestion for *maṟam mikku.*

14: Vañci was the Chera capital. Since the Vañci referred to here is not the *vañci* plant, it is called "Unwithering Vañci."

16–18: This calls to mind the story of the *Cilappatikāram,* in which the Chera king moves to the Himālayas with his armies, conquering everyone on the way, and erects there a stone for the heroine Kaṇṇaki.

17: "Immeasurable" is literally "which cannot be measured and known."

40

2: For "Martial Courage," see the notes to 39.10.

8: "Flourish" is *polivu tōṉṟa.* D. says this means they stand straight.

11: D. says this poem is the utterance of the poet after he was unable to see the king for a long time and then finally obtained an audience.

41

4–5: "While awake and in dreams, men see sights that are hard to endure" (*kaṉaviṉ ariyaṉa kāṇā naṉaviṉ*) can also mean "Men see things waking that are as hard to bear as [bad] dreams."

5 ff: According to OC, the first four things are seen while awake, the rest in dreams.

11: "Boars"—*kaḷiṟu*—can also mean bull elephants.

12: "The color of silver"—*veḷḷi*—can also mean "colored white" or "made of silver."

42

5: "What you do is never wrong" is *purai tīrntaṉṟu*—"it [antecedent uncertain] is without fault." According to OC, this may also mean "This has no highness [i.e., is no great thing], since it is not new for you."

13–14: "Rich fields" is the translation of *meṉpulam;* "arid lands" is the translation of *vaṉpulam.* According to OC, *meṉpulam* consists of the tracts of *marutam* (paddy land) and *neytal* (seashore), whereas *vaṉpulam* consists of *kuṟiñci* (mountainous land) and *mullai* (forest or meadowland).

21–24: According to OC, the reason the king goes out to conquer is to win booty so that he may continue to be munificent.

43

The Lexicon defines *vaṭṭu* as "(1) small spheroidal pawn, dice, draught; (2) roundness; (3) anything round; (4) a water-squirt; (5) a circular piece used in *pāṇṭi* game; (6) a game-piece." Tāmaṟpalkaṇṇaṉ is obviously a Brahmin.

1–5: For the story of "Cempiyaṉ," see 39.1.

5–9: It is not quite clear what this means. According to OC, the sages may be the *vēṇāviyōr,* "a band of *ṛṣis* who accompany the sun obstructing its heat from affecting the earth fully and thus prevent suffering" (Lexicon), or *munis* (sages) who do tapas, going where the sun goes. D. says these *munis* are referred to in *Murukāṟṟuppaṭai* 107 (*miṉ celal marapiṉ aiyar*). He says that these *munis* are amazed to see someone who has even more disinterested love (*aruḷ*)—that is, is even more willing to suffer in order to help others—than they do.

14: "As to your origins" is added for clarity. The poet is accusing the king of being a bastard.

20: "Clan" is *kuṭi,* which may also mean "caste."

44

6–7: It is inauspicious for married women not to have flowers in their hair.

11–12: "Righteousness" is *aṟam,* which we have sometimes translated as "Order of the World," another possible meaning. *Aṟam* is often contrasted with *maṟam,* the ethic of killing and war associated with the periodic wars in South India through the centuries. The Hindu "order of the world," which included rule by the upper-caste landholders in alliance with the Brahmins, is in contrast with such endemic warfare. See also the notes to 39.10 and 28.15.

45

1–4: The Great Kings were the Cēra (usually written Chera in English), Cōḻa (Chola), and Pāṇṭiya (Pandya). Of these three, the Chera kings would wear the palmyra leaf, and the Pandya king would wear a margosa (*vēmpu*) garland. The poet makes the point that both kings who are fighting are Cholas, who wear the laburnum (*ār*).

46

1–2: For the story of Cempiyaṉ, see the notes to 37.1.

2: "Descend" is supplied at the suggestion of OC. Clearly, the word *marukaṉ,* "descendant," which applies to "you," is meant also to carry over to "these."

4–5: They who eat by plowing the fields of knowledge (*pulaṉ uḻutu uṇmār*) are poets.

5–6: "Hair unoiled" is *puṉ talai,* literally, "dull heads." This refers to the fact that they are too young to oil and take care of their hair properly. It can also mean "tawny-haired" (since untended black hair can turn tawny), for the same reason.

6–8: According to OC earlier, this means that young and afraid, they were weeping; now, apparently, they are delighted at the sight of the elephant who, in reality, is coming to kill them, but this changes the order of the poem. "Terror they never imagined" is *viruntiṉ puṉkaṇ,* literally, "a suffering that is new." This poem has a power and economy of expression that is very difficult to convey in English.

47

1–2: "Life of a bard in need . . . as he grows lean in search of reward" is the translation of *varicaikku varuntum ipparicil vāḻkkai,* literally, "this suppliant's life in which one suffers for dignity."

3: "Like a bird"—looking for a tree with ripe fruit, according to OC.

6: "Eating without saving." In the modern Malayalam novel *Chemmeen* (by Thakazhi Sivasankara Pillai), it is said that fishermen are not allowed to save money because they live by killing fish, the idea being that since they make their living by killing living creatures, they must not profit inordinately from that activity.

8: "The shame it causes rivals in the disciplines of songs" is the translation of *tiṟappaṭa naṇṇār nāṇa.* The exact meaning of *tiṟappaṭa* is not clear. According to OC, this means *kūṟuppaṭa,* "according to each category." Thus our translation.

48

1–4: The first two lines of this poem in Tamil contain a play on the word *kōtai,* which also means "garland": *kōtai mārpil kōtaiyāṉum / kōtaiyaip puṇarntōr kōtaiyāṉum.*

4: D. says the salt pans are dark because of the mire.

49

1: "Mountain king" is *nāṭaṉ,* "king of the plains" is *ūraṉ,* and "king of lands by the sea" is *cērppaṉ.* These correspond to the tracts of *kuṟiñci, marutam,* and *neytal.* See the introduction, n. 41, for more on the five major *tiṇais.*

5: "Are swept by wind" is *alamaru,* literally, "whirl."

50

1: The royal drum (*muracu*) was beaten during battle and was supposed to confer title to a kingdom. It was made of the wood of an enemy's tutelary tree and the skin of a bull that fought another bull and won in a staged contest. See Hart 1975, pp. 15–16; n. 25 of the introduction to this book; and also the notes to 58.11.

13: The OC suggests he would fan the poet with a *cāmara* (yak's tail), one of the insignia of royalty.

15: "Is that why you just did this?" is a translation of the interrogative particle *kol.*

51

8: "To be pitied" is *aḷiyar.* This word has a rich set of meanings and resonances. By itself, *aḷi* means "grace," "kindness." As a verb, it means "to give," "to protect," "to be gracious."

52

1: *Vayamāṉ* can also mean "lion."

7: "War" and "kings" have been added for clarity.

14: "Pieces slammed down in play" is *iṭa,* literally, "as they put down their pieces." "Pieces" is *nāy,* whose usual meaning is "dog."

15: "Public squares" is the translation of *poti.* This meaning is not given in the Lexicon; instead, we followed OC, which glosses *poti* as *ampalam,* which the Lexicon defines as "open space for the use of the public."

17: The word for "pillars" is *kantam,* evidently from Sanskrit *skandha.* In Sanskrit, the word means the "trunk of a tree." Our translation follows OC. Gods were (and are) thought to inhabit a great number of objects—a drum, a memorial stone, columns. A Kannada poem by the tenth-century poet Basavaṇṇa says,

> The pot is a god. The winnowing
> fan is a god. The stone in the
> street is a god. The comb is a
> god. The bowstring is also a
> god. The bushel is a god and the
> spouted cup is a god . . . (Ramanujan 1973, p. 84).

53

3: "Stage of sand" is *teṟṟi,* literally, "elevated mound."

9–10: Literally, "But we can't refuse to live in this great world where eminent [poets] have been born."

11: Kapilaṉ is the renowned poet. See *Puṟ.* 105 through 124.

54

6: "Joint resolutions" is *neṭumoḻi,* literally, "long words." The Lexicon defines this as "(1) eulogy, encomium, praise; (2) boast, as of a victorious hero; (3) vow; (4) puranic story; (5) well-known fact."

55

1: "Two kings" is *vēntu*—"two" is added because of the context. These two are the Pandya and Chera monarchs; the king addressed is a Chola.

2: The eye in Śiva's forehead is above his other two eyes, just as the king addressed is superior to his two rivals.

3–5: The Three Cities (Sanskrit Tripura) were built by Maya for the Asuras, who lived in them. They were destroyed by the arrow of Śiva. For the detailed story, see Mani 1975, pp. 793–794.

6–7: The four divisions of an Indian army are chariots, elephants, horses, and infantry.

10: For "Righteousness" see the notes to 44.11–12.

11–12: The king would hold a rod (*kōl*) as emblem of his office. When he was doing his proper duty, this was said to be straight (literally, red—*ceṅ kōl*); when he strayed from justice, it would be bent (see canto 20 of the *Cilappatikāram,* in which when the king is shown to have been unjust, his scepter bends).

11–13: Literally, "Therefore do not allow your scepter to be bent, thinking of some, 'They are ours,' and do not destroy the virtue of others thinking, 'They are foreign.'" This last part could also mean "do not destroy your own virtue [by hurting others] thinking, 'They are foreign.'"

18: Neṭu Vēḷ is Murugan, commonly called Kumāra, Skanda, and Subrahmaṇya in Sanskrit. Murugan was an indigenous Tamil deity often invoked for his fierceness in battle. He came to be identified with Kumāra, the second son of Śiva and Pārvatī. He is the most popular deity in Tamil Nadu. His slaying of the demon Cūr (Sanskrit Śūrapadma) is celebrated to this day at his temple in Centil.

56

1: The "god whose neck is the color of [blue] sapphire" is Śiva.

3–4: The "god whose body is white as a conch" is Balarāma, the elder brother of Krishna. "Twisting upward" is *vaḷar,* literally, "which grows."

5–7: The "god . . . who is the color of lovely blue sapphire" is Viṣṇu.

7–8: The "Red God" (*ceyyōṉ*) is Murugan—see the notes to 55.18.

10: "You are to be ranked" is added for clarity.

11: Śiva is identified with Death (*kūṟṟu*), evidently because he is the god who presides over the destruction of the world.

13: For Murugan, see the notes to 55.18.

18: "Wine" is *tēṟal,* whose usual meaning is "pure, clarified toddy."

19: "Greeks" is *yavaṉar,* from "Ionians." This could also refer to the Romans—the ancient Indians called all white-skinned foreigners *yavaṉar.*

57

10: For tutelary tree, see the notes to 23.9.

11: According to OC, the trees cannot serve as hitching posts because they are young trees. He says the purpose of the poem is conciliation—if the king being attacked is so weak and unworthy, why bother attacking him?

58

1: That is, the Chola king.

7: "Pandyas" is OC's suggestion for *pañcavar,* literally, "the five." This usually refers to the five Pāṇḍavas, but that would not make sense here.

7–8: Thunder is thought to attack cobras and shatter their hoods.

9: For "Righteousness," see the notes to 44.11–12.

10: Literally, "Madurai that has Tamil"—*tamiḻ keḻu maturai.* Madurai has always been famous for its association with Tamil. Some would see this as a reference to the legend of the sangams, but they are mentioned nowhere before medieval times.

11: For "royal drum," see the notes to 50.1. According to OC, these drums are the drum of valor *(vīram),* the drum of justice (*niyāyam*), and the drum of renunciation. It also suggests they may be the marriage drum and "the other two," which D. says are the drum of victory and of giving.

19: "Grow and" is added for clarity.

20–21: *Oruvīr oruvīrkku āṟṟutir,* literally, "may each of you be strong [or encouraging] for the other."

24–25: "Paying attention to" is *pōlavum,* literally, "according to."

27: "Strangers" is *ētil mākkaḷ.* The primary meaning of this is "strangers," with the secondary meaning of "enemies."

31–32: The tiger is the symbol of the Cholas, and the carp the symbol of the Pandyas.

59

1: "As befits you" is *takai māṇ,* literally, "of fitting handsomeness."

60

3: The Lexicon defines *viṟali* as "(1) female dancer who exhibits the various emotions and sentiments in her dance; (2) woman of the *pāṇ* caste." The word *viṟali* comes from *viṟal,* "victory."

61

3: "Harrow" is *taḷampu,* "a machine that plows up the mud, breaks the clods, and makes the earth ready," according to D.

5–6: "Too young to dress their hair" is *puṉ talai.* This can also mean "tawny-haired."

7: "Growing stacks" is *kuṟai kaṇ,* "whose spaces are incomplete," that is, which are still not complete.

16–17: Literally, "We have never seen any live who contend without mistake against his strong crossbar-like arms."

62

1: *Varu tār tāṅki amar mikal yāvatu,* literally, "how can war rage now, in which [warriors] hold back advancing ranks?" According to OC, this means "how can there be excess in war where one says to the other, 'We will conquer' as [men] hold back the advancing ranks?"

2: Demonesses is *"pēeyp peṇṭir."* According to the Lexicon, *pēy* is a "devil, goblin, fiend." "Plunge into" is *toṭṭu,* literally, "touch," a word that has a much broader range of meanings than its English equivalent.

4: "Sad throb of the *paṟai* drums beaten in slowed pain" is *eṭuttu eṟi aṉantal paṟaic cīr.* Here, *aṉantal* means "soft sound," "mournfully beaten drum" (Lexicon). According to OC, the drum is beaten slowly because the drummers' hands have grown sore from beating.

6: For "Righteousness," see the notes to 44.11–12.

9–10: "Men speaking in various languages" is *vēṟupaṭu paiññilam,* literally, "the various human race." According to OC, this means "people of the eighteen languages." The Lexicon says these are "the eighteen languages mentioned in Tamil literature, other than Sanskrit, viz., '*ciṅkaḻam, cōṉakam, cāvakam, cīṉam, tuḷuvam, kuṭakam, koṅkaṇam, kaṉṉaṭam, kollam, teluṅku, kaliṅkam, vaṅkam, kaṅkam, makatam, kaṭāram, kavuṭam, kōcalam, tamiḻ.*'"

12: "That silence" is added for clarity.

13: D. says that eating green leaves and bathing is what new widows do but that these women don't yet even do the things widows do, but just hold their dead husbands.

15–17: The gods are thought to have unblinking eyes and unfading garlands.

19: "Of both of you" is added for clarity.

63

1–2: "Unable . . . to charge on in battle" is *viḷaikkum viṉai iṉṟi,* literally, "without any acts that [they can] perform."

4: "Noble warriors" is *cāṉṟōr*—see the notes to 34.22. D. says the warriors are *cāṉṟōr* because they fight a righteous war. For "Martial Courage," see the notes to 39.10.

6–7: For "royal drum," see the notes to 50.1. D. says this could mean drums with eyes made of pelts that still retain their original hair.

8: "Have been abandoned" is *iruntu,* literally, "having stayed," "having sat."

64

1: For "dancing woman" (*viṟali*), see the notes to 60.3.

2: The *yāḻ* was a sort of lute played by Pāṇaṉs. The Lexicon says that they are "stringed musical instruments, of which there are four kinds, viz., *pēriyāḻ, cakōṭayāḻ, makarayāḻ, veṇkōṭṭiyāḻ.*"

5: "White-headed, red-bodied vultures" is *eruvai*. According to OC, this vulture has a white head and a red body, and so we have added the description, as the name must have evoked this image for an ancient Tamil.

6–7: Literally, "shall we go and see Kuṭumi . . . so that we can come [back] no longer needing to eat gruel."

65

1: "Drums" here is *muḻā*. This was probably the same as—or very similar to—the modern *mṛdaṅgam*. It was apparently then, as now, a concert drum. For the *yāḻ*, see the notes to 64.2. "Rāgas" is *paṇ* in Tamil—clearly, a system of music very similar to modern Indian classical music was practiced in ancient Tamilnad. The fact that the practitioners of this art were the lowest castes and that all the musical terms are indigenous Dravidian words suggests that classical Indian music had its origin in South India (although the contemporary northern classical style shows significant Persian influence as well).

3: "Pure toddy" is *tēṟal*, toddy that has been filtered or clarified.

10: For "Martial Courage," see the notes to 39.10.

11: "Facing the north" is *vaṭakkiruttal*, a rite in which a king who felt he had been dishonored would sit facing north, surrounded by those who felt close enough to him to share his fate. All would fast until they starved to death. The *Puṟanāṉūṟu* describes two kings who performed this rite. One was Cēramāṉ Peruñcēralātaṉ (see also *Puṟ*. 66 and *Ak*. 55), who was so ashamed of his back wound that he decided to commit ritual suicide; the other was Kōpperuñcōḻaṉ, whose sons came against him in battle to take his kingdom (*Puṟ*. 213; *Puṟ*. 218–222).

66

1–2: D. says this refers to the monsoon winds, and OC interprets it according to a mythological story—"he who is in the line of Valiyōṉ [or the strong one] who summoned the wind and commanded him when his ship[s?] would not move because there was no wind to wage war."

7: According to OC, *mikap pukaḻ ulakam eyti* is "gaining great fame across the world." This can also mean "gaining the world of great fame."

8: For sitting facing north, see the notes to 65.11.

67

1: This is one of the earliest examples of a messenger poem, a genre made famous by Kālidāsa's *Meghadūta*. George Hart argues that this sort of poem originated in the south and was borrowed into Sanskrit. See Hart 1975, pp. 244–246.

5: "Triumphant" is *aṭu koḷ veṉṟi*, literally, "of victory that has killing." "Killing" here is omitted in the translation, as it is repeated in the next part of the description.

7: "Mountain of the far north" is Himālaya, which the poems often envision as one mountain rather than a range.

11: The Tamil for "your humble servant" is *aṭiyuṟai,* defined by the Lexicon as "'Your obedient servant,' as flourishing beneath your feet, an ancient term of humble respect."

68

8: D. takes the fact that the king is wearing his ornaments as a sign that he is spending pleasant hours with his women.

9: "Locks away" is *piṇikkum,* literally, "ties up," "binds." According to OC, *akapaṭukkum* is "catches," "entraps."

11: For "Martial Courage," see the notes to 39.10.

12: "Here" is added for clarity.

13: "Drum" is *paṟai,* which is usually the drum beaten by the Kiṇaiyaṉ.

15: "Although no one rides on their heads" is *vaṟum talai,* literally, "empty-headed."

69

1: "Accustomed to the playing of a master" is *kaṭaṉ niṟai,* "filled with [proper] order." According to OC, this means "abounding in the proper use of convention."

5: "Lest you rip open the new seams" is added for clarity.

7: "Burned black under the sun" is *irum.* According to OC, this is just a second word for "large," but one of the meanings of *irum* is "black." This phrase occurs often, and we have consistently translated it as we have here. This is the suggestion of Ramasubramaniam, who taught George Hart Tamil in India.

9: "I will tell you" is added for clarity.

19: "Gives away chariots in the middle of the day"—see poem 123, which describes how a particular king is able to give away chariots even before he gets drunk.

21: "Though . . . flowers" is a conjectured meaning for *pūviṉ āṭum,* which OC says means "which search for the nectar of flowers."

70

1: "You who travel seeking gifts" is added for clarity.

4: "Big drum" is *mā kiṇai,* which OC glosses as "large *uṭukkai.*" The *uṭukkai* is a drum shaped like an hourglass. Since its middle is very slender, it probably needs thin sticks running from one end to the other for extra support. "Balanced" is *takaitta,* literally, "bound," "fastened."

7–8: "Two healers of hunger, rice and water." The literal meaning is simply *iru maruntu,* "two medicines."

12: "Moist month of" is added for clarity.

13: "Dancing woman" is *viṟali*—see the notes to 60.3.

71

1–2: These lines have extraordinary alliteration: **maṭaṅkaliṉ**: *ciṉaiiya,* **maṭaṅkā**: *uḷḷattu,* **aṭaṅkāt**: *tāṉai vēntar,* **uṭaṅku**: *iyaintu*. We have attempted to render something of this effect by the repetition of l's and r's.

7: "Worthy of her face" is the translation of *amar,* literally, "suitable." We have followed OC.

19: "Foreigners" is *piṟar,* literally, "others."

72

5–6: "Well skilled in the handling of their weapons" is literally "suited to their weapons." According to OC, this means they are suited to the business of (using) weapons.

10: These are the royal drums (*muracu*) that give title to a kingdom. See the notes to 50.1.

73

11: "Fierce" is *maintu,* which can also mean "mad" or "rutting."

12–14: "Embraces of . . . women . . . who do not respond to me" is *makaḷir ollā muyakkiṭai,* literally, "in the unresponsive embraces of women." According to OC, these are prostitutes.

74

1–3: The literal meaning is "They did not fail [to cut it] with the sword on the grounds that it was not a person"—*āḷ aṉṟu eṉṟu vāḷiṉ tappār.* According to OC, this means "Not thinking it was not a person, they did not fail [to cut it with] the sword." We have followed OC here. The idea, according to D., is that men of a great family are not taken by death but by other heroes—that is, it is better to die on the battlefield than in bed. By cutting the deformed with a sword, the family of the king shows that even deformed or stillborn fetuses are considered "human" and so are cut by the sword so they they at least formally die the death of a warrior. D. quotes the beginning of *Akanāṉūṟu* 61: "They who are fortunate (*nōṟṟōr*) do not die carried away by Death, but they die at the hands of others."

6: "People without generosity" is the translation of *kēḷal kēḷir,* literally, "kinsmen who are not kinsmen."

75

4: "Towers over other men" is the translation of *eytiṉam ciṟappu eṉa,* "thinking, 'we have gained excellence [or preeminence].'"

6: "Heavy burden" is the translation of *ciṟantatu*. One of the meanings of this verb is "to be unbearably heavy." According to OC, this means "that inheritance will be so heavy that he can't be parted from it"—that is, he won't give anything.

7–8: "Near-weightless cork tree" is the translation of *kiṭai*. This is the sola tree, whose pith is used for making light hats and the like.

10: The poem could also mean "for him, the wealth that goes with a kingdom of kings who have umbrellas . . . and royal drums . . . is light." In English, "wealth" has to be repeated twice for the poem to make sense, whereas in Tamil, the word is used only once, at the end.

76

5: "Chaplet and garland" are *kaṇṇi* and *oliyal mālai,* both of which usually mean "chaplet."

13: The actual syntax of this poem is impossible to reproduce. It is roughly "[Yet] we have never heard before today [of something like this]: his fighting and killing on the field, suppressing the victory of the seven who came . . . not realizing the majesty and greatness of Ceḻiyaṉ who. . . ."

77

1–2: "Support / formed in the shape of a lotus" is the translation of *koṭiñci,* defined by the Lexicon as "ornamental staff in the form of a lotus, fixed in front of the seat in a chariot and held by the hand as support."

7: "Amulet of childhood" is the translation of *tāli*. According to OC, this is the *aimpaṭaittāli,* defined in the Lexicon as "a gold pendant worn by children in a necklace bearing in relief the five weapons of Viṣṇu, as an amulet."

8: Even given the fact that in India, mothers often nurse their children until quite late (five or six), this is clearly hyperbole!

13: The theme of precocious children is a common one in Tamil. For example, Ñāṉacampantar is supposed to have begun singing his songs to Śiva when he was three.

78

5: "Curving joints" is the translation of *toṭai,* which usually means "thigh." Here, we have followed OC. "Do not retreat in battle" is OC's interpretation of *nōṉ,* which literally means "strong" or "which endures."

8: "Without worth" is the translation of *vampa,* the meaning given by the Lexicon; OC says it means "who do not abide."

12: The drum is also beaten at the funeral ceremony. The drum is beaten by a Kiṇaiyaṉ—apparently, the modern Paṟaiyaṉ (pariah).

79

2: "Inner meadow" is the translation of *maṉṟa[m]*, which the Lexicon defines as "(1) hall assembly; (2) court; (3) meeting place under a tree, in a village; (4) open place used for riding horses; (5) plain, open space; (6) central place in a battlefield."

4: "Without worth" is the translation of *vampa*. This is the meaning given by the Lexicon; OC says it means "who do not abide."

3: According to OC, both an elephant and a king would be preceded by a *kiṇai*.

80

3–4: "The other leg . . . free" is the translation of *oru kāl varu tār tāṅkip piṉ otuṅkiṉṟu*. *Tār* means "trick" or "tactical move," literally, "one leg restrains his back, preventing his tactical move [to break free]."

8: "Twists and snaps the body" is the translation of *iru talai ociya eṟṟi*, literally, "strikes so both ends break."

9: According to OC, Tittaṉ is his father, and father and son have become estranged.

81

4: "Whose hand is a cup for giving gifts" is the translation of *kavi kai*, "who has a cupped hand." This generally means either that his hand is cupped for giving or for pulling arrows from his quiver and fitting them to his bow. We have followed OC.

82

1: "Low-caste leather worker" is the translation of *iḻiciṉaṉ*, literally, "low one," "despised one." This shows that in Sangam times, as now, leather workers were one of the lowest castes.

1–4: The untouchable leather worker has to help out at the festival and at his wife's labor. The setting sun makes his stitching more hurried and more difficult. The fact that he is a leather worker by caste means that he is very skilled at stitching and can do it very fast.

83

The author of this poem is a woman. Her name means "Nakkaṇṇaiyār, daughter of Peruṇkōḻi Nāykaṉ."

1–6: The woman who ostensibly narrates this poem is in love with the young king. If she doesn't say anything and merely wastes away, she is afraid of the reaction of her mother, who will rant at her and think she is possessed. If she accepts him, she fears the assembly (which apparently convened to discuss important issues) because they may not allow her to marry him. Thus, she is unable to choose between remaining silent about her love—and incurring her mother's anger—and revealing it—and maybe not being allowed to marry the man she loves.

84

1: He lives on gruel, according to OC, because he's not in his own city. See the next poem.

2: "By his house" is the translation of *puṟañciṟai*. For *ciṟaippuṟam* (the same, but with the words reversed), the Lexicon says "a hedge-side near a mansion from which a lover can watch unseen what passes between his sweetheart and her maid." "I . . . am pale as gold" is literally "I . . . am like gold."

5: "Blithely" is the translation of *ēmuṟṟu,* which OC says suggests that they brag about their strength.

86

D. remarks, "Her name is Kātaṟpeṇṭu in some manuscripts. It was the custom to call the foster mother (*cevilittāy*) *kāvaṟpeṇṭu*. Here, it comes as her given name (*iyaṟpeyar*)." *Kāvaṟpeṇṭu* means "woman of protection," and *kātaṟpeṇṭu* means "woman who is the object of one's romantic love."

1: D. says the pillar is called "fine" because it holds up the roof of the hut.

87

4: "Craftsman" is the translation of *taccaṉ,* a carpenter or member of the carpenter caste.

88

2: "Vanguard and the rest of his army" is the translation of *kūḻai tār,* literally, "rear ranks [and] front ranks."

6: D. says that "glitter" means the spears have been sharpened, oiled with ghee, and put into skin scabbards.

89

1: "Woman of the caste of bards" is the translation of *viṟali*—see the notes to 60.3.

6–9: D. writes, "Just as, when one hears the sound of the bells on an elephant in the distance, he says, 'This is an elephant,' so when [the king] hears the sound of the drum created by the wind he says 'It is war.'"

90

2: "White lilies" is the translation of *kāntaḷ,* the malabar glory lily, red or white species, *gloriosa superba.*

5: "Tangled sky" is the translation of *maruḷiṉa*. D. says this means cloudy, or "clouds, spreading like smoke, and covering the blue sky."

10: The hands reaching down to the knees is one of the supposed characteristics of a king or great hero—such a man is called *ājānubāhu* in Sanskrit. The Tamil here is actually "hand that reaches to the foot [or leg—*tāḷ*]," but OC says this must mean knee.

10–11: Literally, "O lord of warriors, whose strong hand is faultless, whose strong hand that reaches to your knees is like a crossbar." This could also be interpreted as "O lord of warriors with strong, faultless hands, you whose strong hand that reaches to your knees is like a crossbar."

91

7: "Without considering how difficult it is to obtain" is the translation of *kuṟiyātu,* literally, "not considering." Here, we follow OC's suggestion for meaning.

11: D. writes: "Once, Atiyamāṉ went to hunt to a mountain in his land. On that mountain was a crevice. In it, a difficult-to-reach *nelli* (myrobolan) tree held its sweet fruit. It was said that anyone who ate that fruit would live long. He took a fruit and returned. Then he gave it to Auvaiyār, and when she had eaten it, he told the poetess of its powers. She then sang this song."

92

3: "Love" is the translation of *aruḷ,* which the Lexicon defines as "grace, mercy, favour, benevolence." There are three types of love in Tamil: *kātal,* romantic love; *aṉpu,* the love one feels for those one is familiar with; and *aruḷ,* the disinterested love that ascetics feel toward everyone. Here, *aruḷ* signifies the paternal love a father feels for a child.

93

7: For "Righteousness," see the notes to 44.11–12.

16: It is difficult to capture in English the bizarre logic of this. The idea is that because the king fought so hard he received a wound, he was able to dispatch all the enemy kings, and so those enemy kings didn't have to undergo the disgrace of dying a natural death in bed and undergoing the shameful rite described.

95

4: D. says the joint is the part of the shaft that holds the leaflike blade.

96

9: "The cities he visits" is the translation of *avaṉ cellum ūr,* literally, "the cities he goes to." According to OC, this means he takes his army and goes there; D. says this means he besieges them, but the text does not justify these interpretations.

D. says both these "enemies" are actually good points, showing that he is skilled and practiced at love and at battle, but that seems far-fetched. There is no reason to think he is besieging the cities mentioned in the second part. We thus have translated this according to the literal meaning.

97

1: "Swept forward" is the translation of *uṟaii* and is based on D.'s convincing comments. The Lexicon says this means "worn down."

6–7: D. says it was usual to hollow out (the shaft of the spear), put in that a smaller shaft, put a nail (crosswise) on that, and drive it in to hold the blade.

13: "With blood" is added for clarity.

16: "That leave marks" is interpretive. The text is *kaḻaṟ pāṇṭiṟ kaṇai,* which D. says means "arrows whose heads (*vāy*) are in the shape of legrings or small bowls."

24–25: This is unclear. The commentator says the hair style is *paṉiccai,* one of the five styles of hair that women wore. Apparently, the hair was parted before curling it with an instrument called a *kaḻal maṇi.* According to OC, this means "the fruit (*kaṉi*) of a jewel (*maṇi*) from an anklet (*kaḻal*)," perhaps a jewel shaped like a small fruit taken from an anklet.

98

5: "Thoroughbred" is the translation of *iṉa naṉ,* literally, "of good stock."

8: "Forked stakes" is the translation of *kavai muḷ.* According to OC, this means *kavaitta vēla muḷ,* but *vēla* is not clear. *Muḷ* usually means "thorn."

11–12: Literally, "When they saw the strength of your soldiers who have martial courage."

17–20: Literally, "as those who do not praise you are plunged into grief, will not their far-flung territories . . . be spoiled?"

99

1–2: We do not know the details of the story referred to here.

3: "Of their power" is added for clarity. The wheel (Sanskrit *cakra*) is an Indian symbol of sovereignty. In these poems, the symbol of rolling the wheel (presumably the wheels of a chariot) is used to indicate a king's establishing his rule over new land.

7: It is not certain what the "seven symbols" are. D. quotes the invocation of the *Kaliṅkattup Paraṇi* and says they are a boar, a plow, a stag, an *āḷi,* a veena, a bow, and a *keṇṭai* fish.

9–10: According to OC, "eager for war" modifies the seven kings, not "you." The line could be construed either way.

100

1: D. writes, "When the first son was born to a family, it was the custom among the old Tamils for the father to put on war dress a few days after the birth and to go and see the son while eminent men surrounded the event. The intention was that when a son first saw his father after being born into this world, the costume and valor of war should be well imprinted on his heart." He says that this describes the ceremony at which Atiyamāṉ first saw his first son, Pokuṭṭeḻiṉi.

5: The vēṅkai is the East Indian kino tree.

8: In old Tamil literature, the heart is often personified and is said to think.

101

8: Literally, "that will not be false [i.e., will not fail to happen.]"

10: "Efforts" is the translation of *tāḷ,* which can also mean feet.

102

6: This line apparently means that Pokuṭṭeḻiṉi, to whom this poem is addressed, is there to help his father Atiyamāṉ.

103

1: "Woman of the caste of bards" is the translation of *viṟali*—see the notes to 60.3.

11–12: "Meal cakes" is the translation of *aṭai.* Meal cakes made of wax are, of course, pure fantasy.

12: "Efforts" is the translation of *tāḷ,* which can also mean "feet."

104

4: The king is supposed to be merciless to his enemies but full of kindness toward those who honor him.

105

Poems 105 through 120 and 200 through 202 concern the story of the great poet Kapilar and his patron Vēḷ Pāri. The poet was a Brahmin and Pāri was a chieftain renowned for his generosity who ruled over a mountain called Paṟampu. The three great kings (the Chera, Chola, and Pandya) became jealous of Pāri and laid siege to his hill. In the end, they prevailed through the treachery of some of Pāri's men. They killed Pāri, and Kapilar took Pāri's unmarried daughters to various kings to try to marry them. All the kings refused, and Pāri is supposed to have ultimately married them to other Brahmins and then to have taken his life in the rite of *vaṭakkiruttal* (see the notes to 65.11).

1: "Woman of the caste of bards" is the translation of *viṟali*—see the notes to 60.3.

7: "Grace" is the translation of *cāyal,* which OC glosses as "sweetness."

8: "Crimson ornament," or just "a fine ornament," is the translation of *cēyiḻai.*

106

2: D. says that because the *erukkam* has no fragrance, it is not a good flower, but because gods wear it, it is not bad either.

5: Literally, "he will do his duty with regard to his generosity."

107

4: *Māri,* here translated as "monsoons," can also mean "clouds." Clouds are the prototypical examples of generosity, since they give their rain, are diminished, and expect nothing in return.

108

1–3: D. suggests that the point of this simile is that just as the fragrant smoke spreads, so the fame of Pāri has spread, eclipsing the fame of the three kings, who therefore became jealous and attacked him.

4–6: For "Righteousness," see the notes to 44.11–12. Literally, "If suppliants ask him (or beg him), Pāri, who wears Virtue (*aṟam*), will not say 'I won't come' but will be right next to them [to give them what they want]."

109

1: "A miserable place" is the translation of *aḷitō tāṉē,* literally, "is indeed to be pitied." This is often used ironically, as here.

7–8: This is difficult. When honey is mature, it turns a dark color, called *ōri.* "Because the dark lovely color of [honey] gushes out, the heavy, tall mountain, the [dense creepers, according to OC] on its summit destroyed [i.e., their color destroyed?], flows with honey."

15: "Tensed and polished" is the translation of *cukir puri,* literally, "polished and twisted."

16: "Women of the caste of bards"—for *viṟali,* see the notes to 60.3.

110

5–6: D. says this means you will get us (i.e., the poet, Kapilar), Pāri, and what is left of his mountain after most of it has been given away.

111

1: The text is the translation of *aḷitō tāṉē,* which has the connotation of "wretched," "pitiful," said ironically.

3: "Woman with a drum" is literally "woman from the caste of drummers"—*kiṇai makaḷ.*

113

D. says that Kapilar wished to leave Pāri's daughters with Brahmins, as he could be sure they would not harm them. His intention was to leave them in a safe place while he went looking for worthy kings who would accept them in marriage.

2: "Stewed meat" is the translation of *koḻun tuvai. Koḻum* means "rich," "luxuriant." One meaning the Lexicon gives for *tuvai* is "thick, liquid curry." "Fried meat" is the translation of *ūṉ*.

9: "Engraved" is the translation of *kōl,* literally, "stick." Apparently, fine sticks were used to engrave designs on bangles.

114

4: This could also refer to some kind of flower or other part of a plant from which a liquid was extracted to be fermented into an intoxicating drink. According to OC, it is fiber from which *matu* has been pressed. The Lexicon defines *matu* as "intoxicating drink distilled from mahua flowers, etc."

5: "Balls" is the translation of *kavaḷam,* defined by the Lexicon as "ball of rice or other food for an elephant."

6: *Vīcu,* used here for "give," means also "throw." Thus it has a sense of profligate, almost irresponsible giving. The Lexicon says "give liberally"; thus our translation of "freely give away."

115

2–3: The poet is engaging in hyperbole to describe the large amounts of toddy available to bards in Pāri's kingdom.

5: "Kindly" is the translation of *iṉiyōṉ*—literally, "sweet," and "ferocious" is the translation of *iṉṉāṉ*—literally, "not sweet."

117

1: *Maimmīṉ* means "the Black Planet," that is, Saturn. *Pukaiyiṉum* can mean "become smoky" or "be unfavorable."

1–2: All these are bad omens. The Silver Planet (*veḷḷi*) is Venus.

9–10: D. interprets as "but that land is now barren, where jasmine with its green leaves bloomed like the sharp teeth of a kitten when the father of the girls with fine bangles ruled there." The Tamil is *peyal piḻaippu aṟiyāp puṉ pulattatuvē . . . tantai nāṭē,* literally, "The land of their father is in the dry zone which does not know the failure of rains." D. would like to take *puṉ pulattatuvē* as "is barren [now]," which is possible, but makes it difficult to construe "which does not know the failure of rains."

118

1: The reservoirs (or tanks) supplied water and allowed Pāri's land to hold out indefinitely against the three great kings. One of the first acts of the enemy kings after they defeated Pāri through treachery was to destroy them so that the territory could have never have the resources to resist them again.

120

13: It is customary in South Indian cooking to "season" a preparation by frying mustard seeds and urid dahl in some oil and pouring it over the food.

16: For Murugan, see the notes to 55.18.

122

9: Arundhatī was the wife of the sage Vasiṣṭha. Apte writes, "She is regarded as the highest pattern of conjugal excellence and wifely devotion" (p. 219). She is considered to be the morning star.

10: "You are the greater" is the translation of *perumitattai.* According to OC, this means "you are proud," but *perumitam* can also mean "greatness."

124

5: "Evenly descending" is the translation of *neṟi koḷa,* "keeping to the [right] path." The OC glosses this with *oḻuṅkupaṭa,* which has the sense of good or proper behavior. Perhaps the phrase suggests that the waterfalls neither swell out of bounds, flooding the lowlands, nor totally dry up, leaving the lowlands without water.

125

The poet is apparently a Brahmin of the Vaṭama subcaste.

18–20: The idea is that both your enemies and friends praise you (though in different ways), just as both enemies and friends praise Murugan. According to OC, *niṉ peṟṟiciṉōrkku,* which we have translated "whoever has any stake in you," means "those who have you either as friend or enemy."

8: *Amṛta* is the drink that makes one immortal. In these poems, it is often used to signify food or drink that is very precious, life-giving, or sweet.

18: For Murugan, see the notes to 55.18.

126

4: "Golden" is added to make the meaning clear.

7: "Kapilar" is added for clarity.

16–17: "So that no other vessels dare / to travel those waters" has been added for clarity.

20: Thunder is conventionally said to be the enemy of cobras and to shatter their hoods.

127

3: We have omitted "whose sides are empty."

5: "Their marriage *tālis* / which cannot be given as gifts" is literally "the ornament that cannot be given." In straitened circumstances, Indian women might give away their ornaments to be sold or for other purposes, but they can never give away the *tāli,* which is tied by the groom around the neck of the bride during the wedding ceremony and is the mark of their married state.

128

1: "Sliding bracelets" is the translation of *kaḻal toṭi.* It was considered a sign of virility for a man to wear loose anklets and bracelets, perhaps because they signified that he was lithe and strong.

6: "A woman . . . dancing" is the translation of *āṭumakaḷ,* literally, "a dancing woman."

129

3: "Aged liquor" is the translation of *tēṟal,* which the Lexicon defines as "pure, clarified toddy." According to OC, this is *matu,* which the Lexicon defines as "intoxicating drink distilled from mahua flowers, etc."

5. For *kuravai,* see the notes to 22.22.

8: "Would at the least bear some resemblance" is the translation of *piḻaiyātu maṉṉē,* literally, "it would not be in error."

130

6: Literally, "that were thrown down as the Koṅkaṉs fled."

132

1: Literally, "I thought afterward of him I should have thought of first."

3: "Deserted city" is the translation of *pāḻ ūr. Pāḻ* implies desolation or barren land. Probably the sense is that in a deserted village, the wells are not maintained and so become clogged.

9: "Slide loose" is added to capture the effect of the Tamil phrase *piṟaḻvatu maṉṉō.* According to the Lexicon, *piṟaḻ* means "to flop," "to be dislocated."

133

1: "Dancing woman" is the translation of *viṟali*—see the notes to 60.3.

134

3–4: Literally, "But because it is the way other good men [have followed], his generosity is what it is."

135

1: "My wife" is added for clarity. "The dancer" is the translation of *viṟali*—see the notes to 60.3.

4: "Taking only short steps because she has already walked too much" is the translation of *taṭavaral koṇṭa.* The meaning of this is not clear; this is OC's suggestion.

8: "Tightened" is conjectural for *aṭaṅkiya.* "Full of singing melody" is the translation of *vari navil paṉuval,* whose exact meaning is unclear.

9: For *paṭumalai,* the Lexicon says "a secondary melody-type of the *pālai* class."

13: According to OC, this means "feet that have scars."

16: "Golden" is added at the suggestion of OC.

136

5: "Where the strings hang down" is added (suggestion by Ramasubramaniam).

7: "Pursue" is the translation of *alaikkum,* literally, "afflict," "make wander back and forth."

10: According to OC, they seize or steal, just as monkeys frequently steal things.

137

9–10: "Flowing of the river," literally, "water."

10: *Maṇi* can mean a sapphire, a ruby, or a pearl.

138

5–6: "Of leaving to seek out the king" is added for clarity.

8: The OC interprets this as "like a large ear [of millet] put in the hollow of a tree on a wide field where parrots stay." This is reminiscent of the proverb "like what is kept (*īṭu*) by a parrot," meaning a treasure.

139

2: *Cillōti* means literally "a few braids." Ramasubramaniam suggests that it means "two braids."

4: "Dancing women" are *viṟalis*—see the notes to 60.3.

7: Literally, "of the *nāñcil* which does not plow." This is a way of saying that the *nāñcil* meant is not the word that means "plow" but the word that is the name of a mountain.

9–10: This could also be taken with the speaker: "There is no time to wait for the right occasion [to give to me who came] desiring (*uṉṉi*) a gift with a heart (*uḷḷam*) that was unrelenting (*māyā*) [in its desire]." This is how OC interprets it.

13–15: According to OC, it is "Therefore before battle comes, you should give me a present."

15: Literally: turned upside down—*miḷirnticiṉ āṅku.*

140

6: "But he knew of my value" is the translation of *tāṉ piṟa varicai aṟitaliṉ. Varicai* literally means "worth," "rank," "excellence." According to OC, this means "he knew the excellence of giving," but *varicai* is usually used by poets to indicate their worth as poets. Here, *varicai* is preceded by the word *piṟa,* which usually means "other." D. remarks that this is an *acai,* a particle that conveys an emotional tone.

10: Literally, "Don't great men do their duty?" This verse is of a type called in Sanskrit *nindāstuti*—"praise in the form of blame." The poet appears to be insulting the king while he actually is praising him.

141

2: "Burned black under the sun" is the translation of *kār eṉ okkal.* This can also mean "lackluster," "dull," which is how OC takes it.

3–4: The idea is that the bard being addressed has become so rich that he can be as comfortable in the wasteland as he can at home.

10–11: Pēkaṉ gave a garment to a peacock because of his great generosity.

142

5: That is, he gives to people whether or not they are worthy of his generosity.

6: Literally, "He has no ignorance with regard to an army if an enemy army comes together with him." In Tamil, lines 5 and 6 read *koṭai maṭam paṭutal allatu / paṭai maṭam paṭāṉ piṟar paṭai mayakkuṟiṉē.*

143

1–2: This could also mean "the best of sacrifice" (*uyar pali*).

8: Literally, "because my grieving family was hungry."

15: Pēkaṉ has left his wife alone to go off with a courtesan. Here, Kapilar addresses this poem to him to make him feel sorry for her.

144

1: Literally, "That you have no compassion is cruel!"

2: "Of longing" has been added. According to the Lexicon, *cevvaḻi* is a primary melody-type of the *mullai* class.

8: *Em kēḷ veyyōṟku,* literally, "to him who desires a relationship with us."

9: "Red" has been added. *Kāntaḷ* is *gloriosa superba;* its flower is white with red coloring and resembles a group of fingers.

12: The OC and D. suggest that Kaṇṇaki implies that the courtesan that Pēkaṉ loves is no more beautiful than she is.

12–13: "*Olleṉa olikkum*" has the sense that the chariot is making noise (probably because it has bells on it) for everyone to hear. For the bells on Pēkaṉ's chariot, see the next poem.

146

1: Literally, "Let your wealth of precious jewels be [whatever they will]—we don't want them!"

3: "Of longing" has been added. According to the Lexicon, *cevvaḻi* is a primary melody-type of the *mullai* class.

4: "Mountainous" is the translation of *vaṉ pulam,* which the Lexicon defines as "hard soil," "hilly tract," "jungle tract."

8: "They" has been added for clarity. The original is impersonal: "so that the hair may be perfumed . . . and adorned."

11: D. points out that women separated from their husbands do not adorn themselves.

147

3: "Of longing" has been added. According to the Lexicon, *cevvaḻi* is a primary melody-type of the *mullai* class. Literally, "the gift for my coming is if you set out."

7: "Left dry" is the translation of *neyyoṭu tuṟanta,* literally, "which has abandoned ghee also."

148

1: *Piṟaṅku,* the word translated as "glowing," may also mean "high."

3: "To those who have come to you in need" is added for clarity.

4: "Rice bins" is the translation of *nēr kūṭu,* literally, "storage receptacles for grain." D. says these were (and are) set up on the streets near the houses.

5: "You have been magnanimous" is the translation of *muṟṟu aḷippa,* literally, "you give copiously."

6–8: Literally, "our small eloquent tongues do not have to express themselves, desiring to praise insignificant kings, saying things they did not do."

149

1–2: "With the soft lilt of low notes in the evening" is the interpretion of *naḷ eṉ mālai.* The Lexicon says that *naḷ eṉ* signifies a subdued noise.

2: "Of unfaithful love" is added for clarity. *Marutam* is the category (*tuṟai*) of *akam* poems in which the hero forsakes his wife and associates with a courtesan (*parattai*).

4: "Where lovers yearn for their lovers in the evening" is added for clarity.

5: Literally, "Because you have generosity as a part of your protecting and ruling your people." *Marutam* songs, which talk of the man's infidelities and his relationship with courtesans, were apparently meant to be sung in the day, whereas *cevvaḻi* songs, which belong to the *mullai* category, talk of romantic love and were appropriate to the evening.

15: *Amṛta* is the drink that makes one immortal. In these poems, it is often used to signify food or drink that is very precious, life-giving, or sweet.

150

3: "Wet" has been added for clarity.

6–7: "On his head . . . rays" is the translation of *vāṉ katirt tirumaṇi viḷaṅkum ceṉṉi,* literally, "his head that shone with a lovely blue sapphire whose rays are pure."

14: "Burned black under the sun" (*irum*) could also be translated as "big."

19: "I am a man of the forest"—Tamil kings were supposed to hunt, thereby proving their manliness and linking themselves with the dangerous spirits and powers that live in the forest (*kāṭu*).

26: Literally, *tōṭṭi* that was not fashioned of iron. The normal meaning of *tōṭṭi* is elephant goad. The poet wishes to clarify that *tōṭṭi* here is the name of the hill, not of the implement.

151

10: Naṉṉaṉ had a young girl executed because she ate a mango fruit that fell from his royal guarded tree into the water near where she was swimming. For this, he earned undying ignominy.

152

2: "Aimed with utmost precision" is the translation of *viluttoṭai,* literally, "of excellent shooting."

6: Literally, "a killer whose excellence is famed."

13: The *mṛdaṅgam* drum is the translation of *muḻā* in the text. The eye of the drum was polished with clay.

15: *Kaṇ viṭu tūmpil kaḷiṟṟu uyir toṭumiṉ.* We have followed OC in interpreting this.

19: "The twenty-one themes" is the translation of *mūvēḻ tuṟai.* According to OC, this refers to themes in three pitches (high, low, and medium) that end on each one of the seven notes for each pitch (his meaning is unclear). He says it can also mean the *yāḻ* that has twenty-one strings.

20–21: The point of this is apparently that they were not sure who the lord before them was. Nonetheless, since they knew it was a lord, they sang the twenty-one themes and addressed him as "King." It happens that the person there was actually the king, Valvilōri, and when he heard himself addressed properly, he felt ashamed at the poverty of those who had come to see him and immediately was generous to them.

25: *Pul̲ukku* can mean flesh, boiled rice, and dahl. This interpretation is based on the meaning of *pul̲ukkal,* "anything slightly boiled."

28: *Maṇi,* which we have translated as "sapphire," can also mean ruby or pearl.

153

6: "Family of dancers" is the translation of *kaṇṇuḷam kaṭumpu,* which OC glosses as *kūtta cur̲r̲am.*

154

3: "Wise men"—*pulavar*—can also mean "poets."

4: "Seek out" is the translation of *paṭar,* which can mean either "think of" or "go to."

10: "War" is the translation of *vel pōr,* "the fight you win," that is, not the *pōr* that means "haystack."

11: The text is Koṇperuṅkāṉam, but the place is usually called Koṇkāṉam. Perum means "great." The name thus means the forest (*kāṉam*) of Koṇ or the great forest (*peruṅ kāṉam*) of Koṇ. "Mountain" is supplied because the place is clearly a mountain.

155

3: "Caring people" is the translation of *uṇarvōr,* literally, "those who have realized," "those who know." The OC glosses as *ar̲ivōr.*

7: Note that "whose fame glows" can also modify Koṇkāṉam.

8: "Blossom" is the translation of *malar,* for which the Lexicon gives the following meanings: "(1) to open, as a flower; to bloom; (2) to be expanded, extended or spread; (3) to be cheerful; to beam with joy; (4) to appear; to rise to view; (5) to happen, befall; (6) to be wide open, as a gate; (7) to abound, become full."

156

3–4: "For the food they expect to receive" is added at the suggestion of OC.

157

4: D. says that only those who have knowledge, manliness, and an army can stride proudly in the courts of kings. Here, "kings" is the translation of *vēntu,* often used to refer to the three great kings (the Cēraṉ, Cōḻaṉ, and Pāṇṭiyaṉ).

5: According to OC, "your people" (*nummōr*) means "the chieftains (*talaivarkaḷ*) who are revered by you."

158

8: "Stallion mountain" is literally "the *kutirai* that is not ridden," that is, Kutirai mountain, not *kutirai* meaning "horse."

23: *Curapuṉṉai* is what the commentary gives for the original *vaḻai*. For *curapuṉṉai,* the Lexicon gives "long-leaved two-sepalled gamboge, *ochrocarpus longifolius.*"

159

3: "Many small steps" is the translation of *kuṟum pala*. We have added "steps" for clarity.

5: "Wears her one meager, filthy garment" is the translation of *mācoṭu kuṟainta uṭukkaiyal,* literally, "wearing a scanty, filthy garment." Ramasubramaniam suggests that *kuṟainta* implies that she has no other; hence, our translation.

9: According to OC, the plant has grown of its own accord, without being planted by anyone.

13: For "Order of the World," see the notes to 44.11–12.

19: "Burned over . . . field" is unclear; the Tamil is *kāṉavar kari puṉam mayakkiya akaṉ kaṇ kollai.*

23: "If it is offered without goodwill" is the translation of *tavirntu viṭu paricil.* According to OC, this means a gift given with an unhappy face.

28: Literally, "I ask you to be gracious in this way!"

160

7: We have added "around the silver salver" because otherwise the comparison does not make sense.

8: Literally, the lunar asterism (*nāṇ mīṉ*).

17–18: "A sparse topknot" is the translation of *pul uḷai kuṭumi.* According to OC, this means "a sparse topknot like a horse's plume," but *uḷai* can also mean a man's hair.

23: "To frighten him" has been added at OC's suggestion that she tells her son a ferocious tiger is coming.

26: That is, not just in her dreams. Grief is especially sharp at night, as there are no other activities then to distract one; here, the poet suggests it is so powerful that the wife suffers in the day as well.

161

16: "The wealth you have gained," that is, the wealth you gained by fighting in battle and then gave to me.

17: "My life is gone" is V. S. Rajam's translation for *yāṇṭu talaip peyara.* The literal meaning seems to be "the years go," but oc takes this as an optative: "May the years go."

162

Presumably, this poem was sung after 161.

6: For "tutelary tree," see the notes to 23.9.

7: This may be ironic, as *kaṭu māṉ,* "swift horse," can also mean "cruel animal." In this poem, the poet uses the respective plural for himself, the nonrespective singular for the king.

163

1: The gender of the "friends" is indeterminate—"woman" is supplied because of context and oc.

3: "Purity" is the translation of *kaṟpu,* literally, "chastity." See the notes to 361.15.

3–4: "Who gave . . . expecting repayment only whenever we could" is the translation of *niṉ neṭum kuṟi etirppai nalkiyōrkku.* According to the Lexicon, *etirppai* means "an equivalent given for a thing borrowed."

9: According to oc, this is jackfruit.

164

The younger brother of Kumaṇaṉ is jealous, so Kumaṇaṉ gives his kingdom to him and goes to the forest. The younger brother puts a price on his head. The poet, not knowing this, approaches Kumaṇaṉ in the forest.

1–2: "It has never been worn down! It stands as high as ever!" is the translation of *kōṭu uyar aṭuppiṉ,* literally, "oven with high sides." An *aṭuppu* was (and is), in its simplest form, simply three stones arranged in a triangle, with a pot on top and wood fuel between the stones. The oven here is obviously more elaborate; thus, we have supplied "clay."

6: "Ugly" is the translation of *pollā,* literally, "bad," vicious," "evil."

7: "The skin dry as leather" is the translation of *tōloṭu tiraṅki.* This could simply mean "dried up with the skin," but oc suggests that *tōl* here might mean "leather."

11: "Dancers" is the translation of *vayiriyar.*

165

4: "Have failed to create an awareness" is the translation of *aṟiyār,* literally, "failed to know." According to oc, this means they did not know any lasting connection (with earth, i.e., fame) as these ancient ones did (through their generosity).

15: "Your elder brother" is the translation of *kiḻamaiyōṉ*. It can also mean "your lord."

166

This poem is addressed to a Brahmin.

2: "Renowned for their superb learning" is the translation of *urai cāl ciṟappiṉ uravōr,* following the suggestion of OC. This could also mean "men of strength who have the excellence of fame."

9: "Focused on Righteousness" is added at the suggestion of OC, which says it is what is meant by *oṉṟu purinta,* "which concerns [only] one thing [i.e., Righteousness]." For "Righteousness," see the notes to 44.11–12.

11: The primal being (*mutu mutalvaṉ*) is Śiva.

15: Swaminathaier suggests that at some sacrifices, the priest must have at least three wives.

17: According to the Lexicon, the *valai* is the "ornament worn on the forehead by the wife of the chief sacrificer." According to OC, this is the *cālakam* (Sanskrit *jālaka*). Probably, the Lexicon intends "the wife of the chief priest," as the sacrificer is the *yajamāna,* who sponsors and pays for the ceremony.

20: According to OC, the sacrifice must be performed for seven days in the forest and seven days on cultivated land.

21: According to OC, "not omitting the seven forest sacrificial animals or the seven sacrificial animals from settled lands" is the translation of *kāṭṭuḷ eḻuvaikaippaṭṭa pacuvāṉum nāṭṭuḷ eḻuvakaippaṭṭa pacuvāṉum muṭṭātu.* The translation given here is literal—there is nothing in the text that would appear to support OC's interpretation.

22: Literally, "pour so much ghee that water is ashamed."

25: This is at the suggestion of OC, literally, "at the great time of the difficult worship."

168

1: "Stallion mountain" is literally "the *kutirai* that is not ridden," that is, Kutirai mountain, not *kutirai* meaning "horse."

11: "Nightshade" is the translation of *kūtaḷam.*

169

7: "Power"—*valaṉ*—may also mean "victory."

170

4: "Berry seeds" is the translation of *paral.* This could also mean "gravel," but D. remarks that when wild cows eat gooseberries, they spit out the pits.

5: The *tuṭi* is a small drum shaped like an hourglass. It would be played by low-caste men called Tuṭiyaṉs, who lived in wild country. "Lowborn drummer" is the translation of *iḻi piṟappāḷaṉ,* literally, "one of low [or despised] birth."

10–11: It is a Tamil belief that one of the sources of pearls is elephants' tusks (in Sanskrit literature, they are supposed to come from the elephants' temples—see Hart 1975, p. 250).

171

7: "Difficult labor of combat" is literally "his difficult occupation." According to OC, this means fighting.

11–12: "This worth of his raised on Righteousness" is the translation of *piṟarkkum aṉṉa aṟat takaiyaṉ,* literally, "a worthy man of similar Righteousness even to others." For "Righteousness," see the notes to 44.11–12.

172

7: "During the night" has been added at OC's suggestion.

9: "Jewels" is the translation of *maṇi;* according to OC, these are rubies.

11: Kōtai is the king for whom Piṭṭaṉ is a general. As long as there are enemy kings, he can defeat them, take booty, and distribute it.

173

The poet is a king and a friend of Paṇṇaṉ, to whom this is addressed.

174

D. adds, "a king of the Chola country fought with his enemies, lost the strength to prevail, became afraid and ran, and hid in Muḷḷūr, which belonged to Malaiyamāṉ. The Chola country, just like the world when it had lost the sun, suffered. Malaiyamāṉ, when he found out about that, went to Muḷḷūr, brought the Chola, made him the king of the Chola country, and established his white umbrella and kingship. Because he is in the line of such great ones [i.e., Malaiyamāṉ], he [the king addressed here] became king and did good to the people when they suffered without splendor because Tirumuṭikkāri had died." A variant of the poet's name is Malaiyamāṉ Cōḻiyavēṉāti Tirukkiḷḷi.

1–5: The story, apparently, is that the Asuras and gods fought, and the gods won in the day, the Asuras at night. Thus, the Asuras took the sun and hid it behind a mountain, but Krishna got it back.

4: According to OC, this is Krishna.

12: "Field for training horses" is OC's suggestion for *muṟṟam,* which the Lexicon defines as "(1) courtyard of a house; (2) inner yard of a house; (3) esplanade, open space; (4) expanse."

29: This poem manages to put an extremely complex series of connections into one sentence in Tamil. In English, it can't be understood without being unpacked. At the beginning, there is an implicit comparison between the sun rescued by Krishna and the moonlike umbrella of the Chola king rescued by Malaiyamāṉ. At the end, the first figure is paralleled by the figure comparing the present king to a cloud. This makes for a very intricate and dense structure.

175

8: The wheel was a symbol of rule; thus, a universal emperor was called Cakravartin, "he who rolls the wheel." The wheel of law is on the flag of modern India. D. remarks, "When [the Mauryas] took an army toward the southern part of their country intent on fighting, a mountain blocked their path. They cut one side of it, made a way, and made their wagons carrying implements of war and other things go through it easily. This information is referred to by Māmūlaṉār and Paraṅkoṟṟaṉār."

176

D. explains, "While Nalliyakkōṭaṉ was staying in Māvilaṅkai and ruling, a poet named Puṟattiṇai Naṉṉākaṉār went to see him. Before, he had gone to Karumpaṉūr, which is in the land that surrounds Vēṅkaṭam, sung Karumpaṉūr Kiḻāṉ who had gotten gifts, and stayed in his house without thinking of begging. Nalliyakkōṭaṉ, who saw him coming to him, gave him many gifts and welcomed him."

2: According to Ramasubramaniam, the girls are playing a game named *ōri*, in which one person buries something and the others try to find it.

9–12: That is, familiarity breeds contempt.

177

3: It was customary to reward a bard with an elephant.

6: According to D., this means the forests are filled with thick brush.

8: This can also mean paths or entrances.

180

1: "The wealth that every day he would lavish on others" is the translation of *nirappātu koṭukkum celvam*. D. comments, "[Wealth] given in such a way that people don't reproach him saying, 'He doesn't have [much].'"

3: The OC says the troubles that have befallen him are because of war.

13: The king will demand a spear so that he can immediately go out and fight to gain booty that he can give as presents to the poet.

181

D. says, "The town has extensive fortifications, including a protective forest. A *viḷā* tree stands in the city's open space and ripens. The fruit falls into the yard of a house, and the children of the warrior's wife who lives there run to get the fruit, as does the cub of a cow elephant that lives in the guarded forest."

2: "Mountain woman" is the translation of *eyiṟṟi,* literally, woman of the *eyiṉ* caste, a group that inhabits the desert tract. According to OC, this is *maṟatti,* which can also be a woman from the hills, which is obviously what is meant here.

8–10: Literally, "Go now, before he moves against his enemies, and having gone, show [your poverty] so that you may win a gift that is the enemy of hunger."

182

The poet's name means "Iḷamperuvaḻuti who perished in the ocean."

7: "Men who have no regrets," according to D. and apparently OC. The Tamil is *ayarvu ilar*—"who don't have forgetfulness."

9: The poems ends with the word *uṇmaiyāṉē,* "by their existence." "Is" is the only verb in the poem except for the first word, *uṇṭu,* "it exists." Thus the poem frames the means of existence of the world between two words meaning "be," "exist."

183

The poet's name means "Pāṇṭiyaṉ Neṭuñceḻiyaṉ who defeated the Aryan army."

5: "Joint family" is *kuṭi,* which can also mean "family" or "caste."

8: These are the four *varṇas,* enumerated as far back as the Ṛg Veda—Brahmin, Kṣatriya, Vaiśya, and Śūdra. In Old Tamil, in place of the Śūdra, we have the Vēḷāḷaṉ, which is a strange change. The Śūdra was supposed to be a servant, and the Vēḷāḷaṉs were (and still are) the highest caste in many senses. They own the land and control most of the other castes, except the Brahmins, who are, ritually at least, superior to them. In fact, it is difficult to say whether they or the Brahmins have higher status—it depends on what criteria one adopts. There have never really been any Kṣatriyas or Vaiśyas in the Tamil country, and so the whole notion of *varṇa* is quite inapplicable (as I believe it was in all of India—no foreigner has ever seen "four *varṇas,*" and *jāti*—caste—is the unit by which society has always been organized, except perhaps among the Aryans in Vedic times). D. remarks, "This is a division of the Northern Aryans. In the Tamil country, this division is not seen today, and never existed previously. . . . If the Vēḷāḷaṉs were low, then Tiruvaḷḷuvar and other eminent men would not have exalted their occupation, which is farming by means of the plow." Indeed, by the laws of Manu, Vēḷāḷaṉs should be Vaiśyas.

184

The poet Picirāntaiyār lived in the Pandya country. He became a close friend of the Chola king Kōpperuñcōḻaṉ, whom he had never seen. D. suggests that he loved a king in a foreign country because his own Pandya king, addressed in this poem, was unworthy of his affection. See poems 212 through 223 and also 191.

4: Literally, a hundred *ce̲rus.* Ramasubramaniam claims that ten *mās* make one *ce̲ru,* but D. says *ce̲ru* just means a bounded paddy field and is equal to a *mā.*

7: "Without a backbone" is the translation of *mel iyal,* literally, "one of a soft character." According to OC, this is the result of not having correct knowledge.

9: "Corrupt" is the translation of *varicai a̲riyā,* literally, "who do not know what is proper," "who do not know what is befitting rank or accomplishment," and therefore corrupt.

185

1: This is the Tamil ship of state. The cart is usually said to be hauling salt from the seashore to the mountains.

2: "With wheels and shaft joined" is the translation of *kāl pār kōttu;* presumably, the shaft and wheels are joined by an axle.

186

1: "Of the world" is added for clarity.

187

1: "Whether you grow rice" is the translation of *nāṭu ākin̲r̲ō.* A *nāṭu* is an agricultural tract. "Forest" is the translation of *kāṭu,* an uninhabited jungle or forest where nothing is cultivated. This word often means the cremation ground or ground where pots with the bones of the dead are put.

4: According to OC, it does not matter whether the land is good or useless; its excellence is determined by the men who live on it, not by the crops it can or cannot grow.

189

1: "That lord of tenacious purpose" is the translation of *orumayōr,* which OC glosses as *oru tan̲maiyai uṭaiyōr.* This can also mean "that unique one." It is notable that this is plural/respective and that *tuñcān̲,* "he who doesn't sleep," is singular/nonrespective.

8: D. suggests that things will go wrong for everyone, the poor as well as the wealthy.

190

1: "Men without soul" is the translation of *uḷam ilāḷar.* According to OC, *uḷam* means *uḷḷa mikuti,* "liberality of spirit."

2: "Closed fists" is implied by *vali u̲rukkum.* "To be closefisted" is one of the definitions of this phrase given by the Lexicon.

7: "Undiminishing resolution" is the translation of *melivu il uḷḷattu,* literally, "with hearts that are not small."

12: It is not clear whether it is a bad omen for an animal to fall on the left or whether it is a mark of the pride of the tiger that he will eat only an animal brought down on the right.

191

Picirāntaiyār had never seen his great friend, Kōpperuñcōḻaṉ. He came after the king had started starving himself to death in the rite of *vaṭakkiruttal.* See the notes to 65.11.

3: "My children have gone far in learning" is the translation of *makkaḷum nirampiṉar,* literally, "my children are fulfilled," which OC glosses as *putalvarum aṟivu nirampiṉār,* "my sons are fulfilled in knowledge."

4: "Do what I wish" is literally "see things as I see them," which OC glosses as "they consider things in the same terms that I consider them." "Who shuns corruption" is the translation of *allavai ceyyāṉ,* "does not do what he should not."

6–7: This is a very famous formulation; the Tamil is *āṉṟu avintu aṭaṅkiya koḷkaic cāṉṟōr.* According to OC, "they have become calm through their good virtues, they do service to high ones [i.e., noble people] whom one should serve, and they [live by the] principle of restraining their five senses." The OC further remarks that this may mean "filled with learning, and accordingly suppressing the sense perceptions that follow taste etc., and being restrained in mind, speech, and body." In our translation, we have attempted to be as literal as we could and still make good sense but have added "through their deep knowledge" to reflect OC.

192

1: This line is one of the most famous in Tamil: *yātum ūrē yāvarum kēḷir.*

2: "Failure and prosperity" are OC's interpretation of *tītum naṉṟum,* which can also mean "evil and good."

6: "If something unwanted happens" is the translation of *muṉiviṉ,* "if it produces dislike," which OC glosses as "when a displeasure [or loathing] comes."

7: "Those who have understood" is the translation of *tiṟavōr,* which the Lexicon translates as "person[s] of strength or capability" or "person[s] of discernment or discrimination." Here, we have followed OC, "Those who know the nature [or distinction] of what is good."

13: "The weak" is the translation of *ciṟiyōr,* literally, "the small."

193

2–3: "A flayed skin thrown down to dry" is the translation of *ataḷ eṟintu.* D., glossing OC, says this means "flaying a skin and turning it upside down."

194

2: "Wedding music" is the translation of *pāṇi,* which can also mean "[musical] beat." "Wedding" is added for clarity. "Booms out pleasure" is the translation of *tatumpa,* which means "increase, be full, resound." "A concert drum" is the translation of *īrntaṇ muḻavu,* "the pleasurable cool concert drum." We have translated these connotations with other words in the line.

4: Literally, "the pale, blackened [with collyrium] eyes of [women] separated [from their men] pour down dripping [cool] water (*paṉi*)."

5: "God" is added at the suggestion of the OC. It is justified because the being described is masculine.

5: "A god who has no virtues" is the translation of *paṇpilāḷaṉ*—"one who is without *paṇpu*" (decency, civilized conduct). According to OC, this is Brahmā.

196

9: "Seeing it here for the first time" is the translation of *itu eṉaittum cēyttuk kāṇātu kaṇṭaṉam,* "we, not having seen this at all at a distance, see it." We have added "those of our clan" at OC's suggestion.

13: "Who shows her purity only in her modesty" is the translation of *nāṇ alatu illāk kaṟpu,* literally, "chastity (*kaṟpu*) that knows nothing but shame." Perhaps the idea is that "chastity" involves keeping a decent house and living a decent life. The wife of the poet is so poor that she is denied such things, and so her chastity can express itself only through her modesty or shame. See the notes to 361.15.

14: That is, a house that has no roof.

197

7–8: "Shaded by" is added for clarity.

15: "If that man only shows the virtue" is the translation of *paṇpiṉōr,* literally, "if he is a man who has decency [dignity, civility]."

16–18: "Who are utterly without awareness" is the translation of *eṉaittum uṇarcci illōr.* According to OC, *uṇarcci,* which may mean "feeling" or "awareness," means "knowledge." This is to contrast it with "those who are truly aware"—*nal aṟivuṭaiyōr,* literally, "they who have good knowledge." We have translated this as "awareness" because we feel the words here have that connotation.

198

3: "With divine purity" is the translation of *kaṭavuḷ cāṉṟa kaṟpiṉ,* "whose chastity [is so perfect that it] possesses a god," that is, is the locus of a spirit or divine power such that the woman who possesses it has special power and fitness. See the notes to 361.15.

5: "Who desires you" is the translation of *taṇṭā,* which OC interprets as "whose [desire] does not diminish."

9: According to OC, the god who rests in the banyan tree is Vishnu.

17: "Filled your great city already bulging with gold" is literally "filled your city that had gold."

23: "Your grandchildren" is literally "the children whom these [children of yours] get."

24–25: "A bird craving drops of water." According to OC, this is the Indian skylark (*vāṉampāṭi*).

199

3: "The sacred banyan tree" is the translation of *kaṭavuḷ ālam,* "the banyan tree [that has a] god." D. remarks that it is common to suppose that gods live in banyan trees.

5–7: Literally, "The wealth of the men of noble acts who undertake to protect [those suppliants] is [those suppliants'] wealth; [those suppliants'] need is the need [of those noble men]." In other words, the wealth of noble men is also the wealth of the suppliants they support, since those noble men give it to them, and the need of the suppliants is also the need of the noble men, since it makes the noble men feel they must attempt to fill it.

200

This and the next poem continue the story of Kapilar. See the notes to 105.

5: According to OC, the point of this image is that the king should marry Pāri's daughters and live happily like the monkeys.

11: "So that it might climb up" is added for clarity—all Tamils know this story.

12: The convention is that a poet's tongue literally gets scarred because he sings the praises of his patron so lavishly.

13: "Firmly respectable" is the translation of *maṉṉum,* literally, "firmly established." Kapilar means that he can be trusted not to have corrupted the girls.

14: "In due and right order" is the translation of *varicaiyil,* which OC glosses as "you make enemies bow, having fought them in the proper way of doing battle."

201

4: "To climb" has been added for clarity.

6–7: By describing himself as a Brahmin (*antaṇaṉ*) and a poet (*pulavaṉ*), Kapilar stresses the fact that he is a decent man and would not have corrupted the girls.

8: This is an attempt to capture the double sense of Vēḷir, which means both the caste of Vēḷirs and a generous person. Literally, "you are a Vēḷir among Vēḷirs." "Caste" is added for clarity.

10: Tuvarai is apparently Tuvarāpati in Karnataka. Swaminathaier hyphothesizes that the northern sage might be Śambumuni.

16: "Girls" is added for clarity.

202

Kapilar to Iruṅkōvēḷ when he would not accept Pāri's daughters; the poem is an indirect insult to the king.

1: Araiyam is a city in Iruṅkōvēḷ's domain. The idea is that the great city of Pulikaṭimāl's ancestors was destroyed because one of them scorned the words of a poet—which is just what Pulikaṭimāl is doing.

2: Literally, "to you (pl.)."

4: Ciṟṟaraiyam and Pēraraiyam, little and big Araiyam, according to OC.

7: "Leaving traces of her flight" is added for clarity.

9: According to OC, the implication of this is that Pulikaṭimāl did not earn his own wealth but merely inherited it.

13–14: "The destruction of his city" is added for clarity.

203

3: "Being that draws a breath" is the translation of *uyir,* since that word means both "breath" and "life."

7–8: The literal is (following OC) "Even more than those who are unable to fill suppliants' [wants] with what they don't have [i.e., because they don't have anything], those [benefactors] whom suppliants think of and approach [desiring a gift] disappoint the desire [of those suppliants]." That is, look at you: everyone came to you thinking you'd give, but you disappointed them—you're worse than those who don't give because they don't have anything.

204

1: Literally, "begging saying 'give' is low."

3: Literally, "it is high," contrasting with "low" in the preceding lines.

9–10: "Of kings and go to them" is added for clarity.

205

1: The Cēra, Cōḻa, and Pāṇṭiya—the three great kings of the Tamil country.

2: The word for "love" is *peṭpu,* which may also mean "desire."

4–5: Literally, "whose rage is cooled [only by] victory."

7: According to OC, this is jasmine. D. points out that Kōṭai mountain was known for its jasmine.

8: "That block their way" is the translation of *puḻai keṭa vilaṅkiya,* literally, "that go athwart [their way] so their path is blocked."

206

2–6: This probably refers to the caste of bards (Pāṇaṉs), who were proud of their skill with words.

8–9: Literally, "this is no world that is empty because all the wise and famous men have died."

207

6: Literally, "without [any of the] desire (*vēṭkai*) [that should come to someone who gives—just as when] one drinks [things in with the eyes]."

9: An *āḷi* can be either a fabulous animal or a lion, according to the Lexicon. It is probably the same as a *yāḷi*, which the Lexicon defines as "a mythological lion-faced animal with elephantine proboscis and tusks."

9–11: "Who" is supplied at OC's suggestion, as otherwise this section cannot be construed. The OC's interpretation is as follows: "[Get up] without your spirit inside being restrained or suppressed, [get up] like a *yāḷi* whose strength is fierce. Who (*yārō*) would be confused for a strong fruit, still not ripened, shriveling up before someone who, in front of everyone, does not have sympathy [*nōvātōṉ*—literally, who doesn't suffer]?"

208

It is highly insulting in Tamil to say "go" rather than "go and come."

3: "Saying to his men" has been added for clarity. This could also simply mean "thinking."

4: "My true worth" is the translation of *tuṇai aḷavu,* literally, "the measure of my extent." *Tuṇai* has many meanings, the primary one being "companion, help, friend."

209

4: "Herons" is the translation of *nārai.* This could also be a pelican, crane, or stork.

6: "White waterlilies" is the translation of *neytal.* These might also be blue or red.

7: "Winging through their home in the empty air" is the translation of *alku vicumpu ukantu,* literally, "ascending in the sky where they stay."

13: "May you be well" or a similar phrase is often said sarcastically, as a sort of curse. For Murugan, see the notes to 55.18.

19: This, apparently, is meant to be sarcastic. The OC seems puzzled by this and suggests it means, "May those other than your court not know of the cruelty you did to me." D. believes that it is demeaning for a poet to go to a king and receive nothing and that therefore the poet is suggesting that only the court should know what happened.

210

2–4: The Tamil is *maṉpatai kākkum niṉ puraimai nōkkātu aṉpu kaṇ māṟiya aṟaṉ il kāṭciyoṭu,* literally, "with an outlook devoid of compassion (*aṟaṉ*), renouncing love, not thinking of your greatness [which is to] protect mankind." "Compassion" can also be translated as "justice"—see the note to line 8.

8: "That knows no order" is the translation of *aṟaṉ il,* "which is without *aṟam.*" *Aṟam* is the "Order of the World," the Tamil equivalent of *dharma.*

211

5: *Aṇaṅkuṭai. Aṇaṅku* is often used to denote a fearful power or spirit that can afflict people.

7: The poet, Peruṅkuṉṟūrkiḻār, is, judging by his name (which ends in *-kiḻār*), a Vēḷāḷaṉ, a high, landowning caste. Many of these poems are put into the mouths of low-caste bards or drummers. If that is intended here, then the "high status" (*ōṅku nilai*) means "high status among bards."

9: Literally, "would bow (to me)."

13: "Even so I spun my language to make you feel ashamed" is the translation of *nāṇāy āyiṉum nāṇak kūṟi,* literally, "Even though you were not ashamed, I spoke to make you ashamed."

17: "Chest, ever more famous as I sing and sing of it till its fame draws forth renewed singing" is the translation of *pāṭap pāṭap pāṭu pukaḻ koṇṭa niṉ . . . mārpu.* The translation here is based on oc's interpretation.

18: It is disrespectful to say "I am going" rather than "I will go and come." "She lingers, a pauper, in our house" is based on oc's interpretation of *maṉait tolaintu irunta.*

22: "Glowing face" is the translation of *vāḷ nutal,* literally, "bright forehead."

212

6: Literally, "their usual (*vaiku*) occupation."

7: The poet here uses Kōḻi, an alternative name of the more common Uṟaiyūr.

11: "Poet" (*pulavaṉ*) is added at oc's suggestion.

213

Poems 213 through 223 are about the king Kōpperuñcōḻaṉ, whose sons rose against him in battle to take his kingdom. Unwilling to fight his own sons, the king renounced his kingdom and faced north to starve himself along with those who were close to him (see the notes to 65.11).

6: "Straining for the sight of battle" is the translation of *amar veṅ kāṭciyoṭu,* literally, "with sight hot for battle."

6–7: "They've changed their ways" is the translation of *māṟu,* which, according to OC, means *pakaiyāy vēṟupaṭṭu,* "changed into enemies." *Māṟu* can also mean merely "enmity."

8: "Elephants" is OC's suggestion for *māṉ,* literally, "beasts."

9: "Title" is the translation of *tāyam.* The Lexicon says this means "patrimony, inheritance, wealth of an ancestor capable of inheritance and partition."

14: "Thoughtless designs" is the translation of *eṇṇil kāṭci.* According to OC, this means "knowledge devoid of planning."

19: For "Martial Courage," see the notes to 39.10.

21: "Not lose respect" is the translation of *mayaṅkātu,* literally, "not be ruined, not be mixed up, not be unclear." According to OC, this means "you must live so that no evil comes to you." "Evil" apparently means a bad reputation.

214

7: "The world where the good and the bad karma no longer accumulate" is the translation of *toyyā ulakattu,* whose literal meaning is apparently "where one need not work," "one need not be wearied [by doing action]." According to OC, this means "the world where the two actions [good and bad] are not done." D. says "where one need not engage in action." While on earth, one cannot refrain from engaging in action, and the *vāsanās* (unconscious impressions) of that karma remain with one. At death, a person's fate is determined by the *vāsanās* that he has accumulated, as each unconscious impression must necessarily result in a fruit (*phalam*) that is experienced and everyone who dies inevitably has *vāsanās* that have not yet produced their fruit. Here, the poet hypothesizes that if one's karma is pure enough, a person will either go to a world where there are no actions to leave their insidious *vāsanās* or that he may not have to be reborn at all.

12: "A purified body" is the translation of *tītil yākkai,* literally, "a body without evil." The OC adds, "However it may be, it is a desirable thing (*aḻakitu*) to do good action."

215

1–6: D. describes how this tamarind gruel (*puḷiṅkūḻ*) was made: put *vēḷai* flowers with salt, boil them, mix with yogurt, knead it well, put black pepper powder in, then season it (with mustard seed), and add it to a gruel of millet and tamarind.

5: D. points out that pounded millet was considered superior to unpounded millet.

7: Literally, "he keeps my life [from going]."

216

4: "He has the right to sit beside you, as your familiar friend, of faultless conduct" is the translation of *vaḻu iṉṟu paḻakiya kiḻamaiyar,* literally, "he has the right of having grown close without fault." We have added "to sit beside you" for clarity.

9: D. remarks, "He says his name is Cōḻaṉ, not Āntai, and so is without a sense of distinction in his heart that he is different and the name of Cōḻaṉ is different. Thus he feels that he [and Cōḻaṉ] share the same life."

9–10: Literally, "he has the right [given by] excellent love."

217

2: "Starving" is added for clarity. The OC takes *ciṟappu,* here translated as "magnificent qualities," as "excellent things" and suggests this line means he is abandoning all of them. *Ciṟappu* means "excellence."

218

3: "Immovable" is the translation of *maṉṉiya,* literally, "permanent." According to D., gold is produced by the river, coral and pearls by the ocean, and rubies by the mountain.

7: "Noble" is the translation of *cāṉṟōr,* from *cāl,* "to excel in moral worth." "Vile" is the translation of *cālār,* the negative of *cāl.* The point of this is that the people surrounding Kōpperuñcōḻaṉ and fasting to death are from different places (see the preceding poem), yet they all are of excellent character. For *cāṉṟōṉ,* see the notes to 34.22.

220

2: "Sumptuous food" is the translation of *peruñcōṟu,* which the Lexicon defines as "sumptuous feast given by a king to the generals of his army."

3: "Mournful" is the translation of *aḻuṅkal,* which can also mean "noisy," in which case it means "which used to be noisy [because the elephant was there]."

5: "Public square" is the translation of *maṉṟam,* which OC says means *ceṇṭu veḷi.* According to the Lexicon, *ceṇṭu* means "place for training, exercising or running horses, etc.; race-course."

6: Or "the public square from which he is gone now."

221

6: *Kēḷvi* is the Sanskrit *śruti.*

11: This is a literal translation of *tūṅka,* which can also mean "abound in." For this line, OC says, "As this world with its good places becomes (filled with) pain."

222

D. clarifies, "Pottiyār wished to join Kōpperuñcōḻaṉ in the rite of *vaṭakkiruttal,* but since his wife was pregnant, the king told him to come back after a child was born. Pottiyār does so, finds that the king has died, and asks the memorial stone to give him a place to sit facing north and starve himself."

2: "Of your body" is added for clarification.

4: "You were heartless" is the translation of *aṉpilāḷa,* literally, "O you who are without love."

5: Literally, "You do not sit without thinking (of me)." The OC construes this as we have translated it.

6: "You who long" is the translation of *veyyōy,* literally, "you who are hot for," "you who strongly desire." "Beloved wife" in line 1 is the translation of *veyyōḷ,* "she who is hot for (you)," "she who strongly desires (you)."

223

Note that the memorial stone (*naṭu kal*) was supposed actually to house the hero's spirit.

2: Literally, "because it could not reach an end"—*talaip pōkaṉmaiyiṉ*. According to OC, "because, when he thinks of his next birth, there is no way to bring to a conclusion his role (*taṉmai*) of ruling"; that is, because the king realizes he cannot successfully fulfill his role of king, he decides to leave this world and go to his next birth.

224

6: The OC says "court of Brahmins." For "Righteousness," see the notes to 44.11–12.

6–9: Literally, "After those conversant with proper custom stand up and show their knowledge in the court of Righteousness . . . he, surrounded by . . . [his women], performed the Vedic sacrifices that have the towering post . . . within the circling many-layered wall."

9: Apparently, this is an image or representation of a kite (*eruvai*—"a kite whose head is white and whose body is brown," according to the Lexicon) set up to receive the sacrifice. Swaminathaier cites the commentary to *Takkayākapparaṇi* 507, which glosses a "false kite" as a "kite made for a sacrifice."

225

1: "What has become of" is the translation of *tōṟṟam,* literally, "appearance, origin, splendor." We have followed OC's suggestion here. "Majesty" is the translation of *āṟṟal,* literally, "strength."

3: "Circled" is the translation of *vala muṟai vaḷaii*—"circled it, keeping it to the right." This is the proper way to circle a god or temple.

6: "Matured so it split open" is a conjectured meaning for *viṭu vāy,* "with its mouth open." D. suggests that since there is no fruit left, the end of the army must eat the tuber.

7: "Forest" is the translation of *kāṭu,* which may also mean any place where people are burned or buried.

8: "Conches of war"—*valampuri.* These are the rare right-curving conches that are supposed to be auspicious and that announce victory. Right-curving is connected to circumambulating to the right, which, as pointed out earlier, is how a god or temple is circled.

8–14: These lines are quite difficult. We have followed UVS's suggestion. He says that before this, all the kings around were afraid to beat their drums and blow their conches in the morning, lest Nalaṅkiḷḷi hear and decide to attack them for their pride. Now, Nalaṅkiḷḷi is dead, and those kings can blow their conches in the morning. It was a custom to wake up kings in the morning with auspicious sounds.

226

2: "Touched" is the translation of *uṟṟaṉṟu,* about which OC says "if he had stood near, touched his body with his hand, and hurt him."

227

1: "Who show no mercy" is the translation of *nayaṉil,* which can also mean "unscrupulous."

8–10: The syntax is as follows: through the daily slaughter of victories so that horses, elephants, men perish on the field where water is rich red with blood.

228

5: "How can you do what you must do" is the translation of *yāṅku ākuvai,* literally, "how will you be?" According to OC, this means "what distress you will experience!" D. says, "Doing a task that is impossible gives someone great pain, and thus he says, '*yāṅku ākuvai!*'" We have followed D.'s sense here.

7: For the story of Cempiyaṉ, see the notes to 37.1.

13: "Great Mount Meru" is only "The Great Mountain" in the text. We have added Meru at OC's suggestion.

13: It was a custom to leave the body out to be stripped by birds (excarnated) and then to collect the bones in a pot which was put in a "burial" ground. It is not clear whether they were buried. Cremation was also an option.

229

D. says that the poet, an expert in astrology, sees omens in the sky indicating that a king will die in seven days. Subsequently, when the king actually does die as predicted, he sings this song. This poem is extremely difficult. We have relied on OC as much as possible.

10: It is worth translating OC's gloss for this section. We have given Sanskrit equivalents wherever possible (e.g., Mēṣarāśi for Mēṭavirāci): "At midnight filled with darkness, in the first quarter of the day when Kārttikā was in conjunction with Mēṣarāśi, in the first fifteen [days] of the month of Phalguni (Paṅkuṉi), when

Venus appeared after (*mutalā*) being at the foot in the lunar asterism of Anuṣa [Aṉuṭam] whose shape is like that of a bent palmyra, to being at the end of Punarpūsam, which has the form of a tank that is a pond, when Uttara that was at the zenith (*uccam*) descended from the zenith, and when Mūla, which is the eighth lunar asterism from that rose opposite it, and the lunar asterism of Mṛgaśīrṣa, which is the eighth asterism that does not go before that Uttara, descended in the tuṟai [? watering place, category]." Perhaps a specialist in the history of Indian astrology could make better sense of this than we have. It is significant that almost all the words used for technical astrological terms in this poem are of Dravidian, not Sanskritic, origin.

20–21: "Stand stock still" is the translation of *kati iṉṟi vaikavum,* literally, "stayed without *kati.*" *Kati* is from the Sanskrit word *gati,* the gait or pace of a horse. It can also mean "path."

25: "And killed them" is added at oc's suggestion.

14–15: "May he live without illness" is literally "it will be good if that lord is without disease."

230

The king's name means "Atiyamāṉ Eḻiṉi who fought at Takaṭūr and fell."

1: "Dazzling feats" is the translation of *vayaṅku viṉai,* literally, "dazzling acts." "Of war" is added at oc's suggestion.

2: "Never trembled" is the translation of *kalaṅkā,* literally, "didn't become mixed or confused," meaning that it didn't stray from justice. The rod of justice is the translation of *ceṅ kōl.*

8: "The people he loved" is the translation of *taṉ amar cuṟṟam.* These are the people who would surround him, his family and friends and others dependent on him.

15–16: "You would have grown fat" is the translation of *ārkuvai maṉṉō.* The latter word is a particle that has the sense of "it won't happen now" or "it is gone and vanished." It gives a plaintive and sad tone to the verb.

231

2: The Kuṟavaṉ gathers and uses already-burned wood. The cremation fire is also made of such wood, according to D. The Kuṟavaṉ is an inhabitant of the hilly tract (*kuṟiñci*), and he may also belong to a caste of snake charmers and basket makers.

5: D. says the point of this is "let Atiyamāṉ's body burn and blacken, or let it not burn and go directly to paradise (*viṇṇulaku*). The fame that he has attained will never go away."

232

1–2: For morning and evening, the Tamil uses the existential negative *il;* for the days of life, it uses the attributive negative *al.* Literally, "may the days I live not be (anything)."

5: It was customary to offer toddy to memorial stones, which were erected to house the spirits of dead heroes and *satīs.* The memorial stone (*naṭu kal,* literally, "erected stone," "planted stone") was put up to house the spirits of dead warriors and of *satīs* (young women who had taken their lives when their husbands died). Such stones were worshiped with offerings of toddy and blood. They were often carved into a likeness of the dead person, and sometimes the exploits of that person were engraved on it. Such stones were also erected to house the spirits of the dogs of dead heroes.

6: D. says "when enemies offered their whole country to him, he had such great valor that he would not accept it."

233

1–4: D. says that Akutai is supposed to have had an iron discus and to have been invincible on that account. In the end, he was defeated and killed by an enemy, and the iron discus was shown to have been a myth.

3: "Who performed strong and noble feats" is literally "whose efforts were strong and noble"—*cīr keḻu nōṉ tāḷ.*

8: "Insistent" is added to bring across the connotations of the verb *iyampiya* ("proclaims").

234

1: "May the duration of my life end" is the translation of *tēyka mā kālai,* literally, "may [my] long time be over."

2: "Accept" is literally "eat" (*uṇṭaṉaṉ*).

3: "Memorial ball" is the translation of *piṇṭam.*

4: It is still the custom to clean the area where one is going to eat with dried cow dung dissolved in water.

6: "Who took" is literally "who was accustomed to take."

235

1: "But now no longer" is the translation of *maṉṉē,* a particle that gives a sense of finality or disappearance.

5: That is, he would share the food he had, whether or not it was abundant.

6–7: "Wherever" in both these lines is the translation of *vaḻi ellām,* literally, "all places."

8–9: "Meat," *pulavu,* also gives a sense of impurity. The fact that he would dirty his clean hand by touching the bard's hair shows his generosity, kindness, and grace. The bard is low caste and hence ritually impure.

236

1: According to OC, this is a jackfruit.

9–10: "I could not be as near you as my love for you could reach" is the translation of *niṉakku yāṉ mēyiṉēṉ aṉmaiyāṉ* . . . , "I was not one who loved (reached, desired) you, and so. . . ."

12: "Some great destiny" is the translation of *uyarnta pāl,* literally, "a high fate."

237

3: "Song" is the translation of *paṉuval.* D. says this means "good words uttered by the good."

6–7: "Empty" and "it now has no value" are added for clarity. D. says that "fire blazing up in a cooking pot" was a proverb and that it suggests that the poet, searching for Veḷimāṉ and finding that he has died, is like someone who wishes for rice, looks in the pot, and finds only fire instead.

8: "Death has been brazen enough to take life without making any distinctions" is the translation of *tiṟaṉ iṉṟu tuṇiya,* which OC glosses as *kūṟupāṭiṉṟāki avaṉ uyiraik koḷḷat tuṇiya*—"he is bold to take life without distinction." The idea is that the king gives to the poor, and by killing the king, Death deprives the poor.

9: "Without any rest . . . beat their breasts in pain" is the translation of *ūḻiṉ uruppa erukkiya,* literally, "beat [themselves] so they pain steadily (*ūḻiṉ,* or "as is proper")."

10: Women's bangles are broken when they are widowed.

14–15: "May there be a curse on Death" is literally "may he [Death] be without disease." It is common to curse someone by saying, "may he live without disease," or words to that effect. See 209.13. The idea, apparently, is that the good words attract the evil eye. Accordingly, in modern South India, it is considered wrong to praise the attributes of a child, for fear it may harm him.

15–17: Here, apparently, the poet is the tiger, Veḷimāṉ is the elephant, and Iḷaveḷimāṉ is the rat.

238

2: No one seems to know exactly what kind of bird the *pokuval* was.

11–12: Literally, "that Death of hot strength was causing great pain and my lord had died because of it."

19: "It would be just" is the translation of *takutiyum atuvē,* literally, "and that would be fitting."

239

D. says this king has died of sickness, not in battle. The custom was to cut such people with swords and either bury them or burn them. The poet says it doesn't matter what you do with him.

2: "Guarded forest" is the translation of *kaṭi kā*. *Kaṭi* can mean a garden or protected, and *kā* can mean a garden or a forest. According to OC, *kāvalaiyuṭaiya iḷaiyamarakkākkaḷil,* "in protected groves of young trees."

5: "He praised to the skies" is the translation of *uyarpu kūṟiṉaṉ,* literally, "he praised highly."

10: "Kings" is the translation of *vēntu*. This usually refers to one of the three great crowned kings, the Chera, the Chola, and the Pandya. D. says that Neṭuñceḻiyaṉ, who is addressed in this poem, was clearly a smaller king (*kuṟunilamaṉṉaṉ*) and not one of these three and that the Pandya king gave him the Pandya title (Ceḻiyaṉ) as a mark of honor and respect.

11: "Armies bent on invasion" is the translation of *varu paṭai,* literally, "armies which came."

16: "Toddy" is added at OC's suggestion. Clearly, "thick and sweet" can refer only to drink.

18: According to OC, this means words that are opposed to the ideal of impartiality.

20: "Cut off and fling away" is OC's suggestion for *iṭuka*. D. says this means "bury."

240

1: "Gaits of various rhythms" is the translation of *āṭu naṭai,* which OC says are such that they move walking to a *tāḷam* (musical rhythm).

5: "Mounds of love" is the translation of *alkul.*

241

3: Drum is the translation of "*muracu,*" the royal drum that gives title to the kingdom. Indra is here envisioned as a king.

5: "Lightning bolt" is the translation of *vacciram,* from the Sanskrit *vajra.*

242

5: "And was a man" is the translation of *āṇmai tōṉṟa,* literally, "So that his manliness appeared."

243

The poet has taken his name from the central image of the poem—"he of the strong cane with a metal knob."

3–4: "A doll they had made of mud" is the translation of *vaṇṭaṟ pāvai.* The Lexicon says this means "toy made of mud."

10–11: "I dove" is the translation of *taṭum eṉap pāyntu kuḷittu,* "I jumped and dove with the sound '*taṭum.*'"

12: "Where is it gone"—*aḷitō tāṉē yāṇṭu uṇṭu kollō* means, literally, "It is pitiful, where is it?" It is conventional to describe in these terms something about which one feels sad.

13: "Strong" is the translation of *viḻu,* literally, "excellent." "A metal knob" is the translation of *toṭi,* which the Lexicon defines as "ferrule" and for which OC gives *pūṇ,* "an ornament." The point of this is that now the poet is rich enough to afford a fine cane, whereas in his youth all he had was sand.

245

7: "What kind of a place is this world?" is the translation of *eṉ itaṉ paṇpē,* literally, "what is the *paṇpu* of this?" *Paṇpu* is defined by the Lexicon as "(1) quality of four kinds, viz., *vaṇṇam, vaṭivu, aḷavu, cuvai;* (2) nature; property; (3) disposition, temper; (4) good quality, courtesy; (5) mode, state, manner; (6) noun denoting a quality; (7) beauty; (8) usage according to Shastras, customs, manners; (9) action, deed."

246

2–3: "You who do not allow me to put an end to my life!" is, literally, "who, not saying 'Go!' prevent me, saying 'Stop!'"

4: "A ball of boiled rice" is the translation of *piṇṭam.* According to OC, this is rice cooked and left (in water) overnight (*nīrccōṟu*) and then squeezed out in the hand, but it can also mean a ball of seeds squeezed in the hand from between (lily) leaves (cf. poem 248). "Left lying overnight" is our attempt to get OC's meaning into the poem. In modern Tamil, "food" (*cāppāṭu*) refers to a meal with fresh rice. It is considered demeaning to eat old rice or a rice substitute (such as lily seeds).

6: The text has merely "curved (unripe) fruit." According to OC, this is a cucumber (*veḷḷarik kāy*).

14: "Lake" is the translation of *poykai,* literally, "a natural spring or pond."

247

1: "Spirits" is the translation of *aṇaṅku,* a vexing, afflicting spirit. Such spirits were thought to inhabit wild places and also places of the dead. *Aṇaṅku* may also mean a goddess who has the power to do harm, which is how OC takes it. D. says that Pūtapāṇṭiyaṉ's wife takes her life before the temple of the goddess of the forest (*kāṭukiḻāḷ*). "Zone" is the translation of *muṉṟil,* which the Lexicon defines as "front of a house" or "space."

3: "Digs" is the translation of *cīkkum,* defined by the Lexicon as "(1) to scratch, as fowls; to tear up earth, as pigs; to scrape; (2) to sweep off, brush away, wipe off; (3) to expel, remove, root out; (4) to cleanse, purify; (5) to sharpen." It is possible that here, the monkey rouses the deer and then scratches up the earth. According to OC, *tūrkkum* means "sweeps."

6: It is still considered inauspicious to see a woman with her hair spread out, especially if it is wet.

8: "Never is silent" is the translation of *tuyilā,* literally, "does not sleep." According to OC, this means "never gets dry," but that meaning is not attested anywhere. D. says of this "because the drum is played without ceasing, the paste is put on so it's never dry so that the drum won't rip." In any case, OC says it means the drum is continually beaten.

10: Literally, "she shows her back to her youth [which is such that] her sweet life trembles."

248

2: "We wore them" is the translation of *ta<u>l</u>ai āyi<u>n</u>a,* literally, "they were our *ta<u>l</u>ai* [dress]."

5: Widows were required to eat unappetizing food at the wrong time of day.

249

4: "Weaver's spindle" is the translation of *katir,* which can also mean a spear of grass.

4–5: "Whiskered" is literally "with dense protuberances" (*kaṇai kōṭu*). D. says this refers to the fish's moustache.

5: "Is overturned" is the translation of *miḷira,* which can also mean "shines," but the context seems to demand the meaning "overturned."

6: D. says this means "whose sound is like that of a quail."

12: "Exalted being" is the translation of *uyar nilai,* literally, "of high state."

14: Before a wife serves her husband, she customarily cleans his eating place with dried cow dung dissolved in water.

250

3: In South India, it is customary to "season" food by frying mustard seeds (which pop), urid dahl, and other spices and then pouring the mixture on top of the food before eating it.

3: "Pavilion" is the translation of *pantar,* a pandal (a structure that usually consists of four columns and a roof).

5: "You have lost everything" is the translation of *pul e<u>n</u><u>r</u>a<u>n</u>ai,* literally, "you have lost your splendor," "you have become dull."

252

1: "Matted hair" is the translation of *caṭai*—Sanskrit *jaṭā,* the matted hair that ascetics wear. For "new leaves of a *tillai* tree," the original has just "*tillai.*" According to OC, this refers to the shoots of the tree.

2–3: "He plucks the leaves from a dense growth of *tāḷi* bushes" is literally "he plucks the dense-leafed *tāḷi.*" Presumably, he plucks the leaves for his food—which, now that he is an ascetic, are supposed to be unappetizing. The *tāḷi* can be a palmyra palm or several other plants, including bindweed. It is not clear which is meant here.

3–4: "The woman . . . peacock" is literally "the peacock who lives in his house."

253

A woman's husband has fallen on the battlefield. Here, she addresses her dead husband, asking him to tell her what to do and suggesting that she is not strong enough to do her duty, which is to go tell his relatives of his death. A woman's bangles would be broken and discarded when she was widowed (a custom still quite prevalent).

254

5: Apparently, this is how a young widow would go to tell everyone of the death of her husband, her bare arms (which have no bangles anymore) indicating her widowed status. See the previous poem.

11: "You should feel deep pity for her" is the conventional *aḷiyaḷ tāṉē,* literally, "she is pitiful indeed."

255

1: "If I start to scream" is literally "If I say 'help!'" or "If I say 'alas!'"—*aiyō eṉiṉ.*

6: As in the previous two poems, a woman addresses the body of her husband who has fallen on the battlefield. The fact that her hand is still "dense with bangles" shows that she has not yet assumed the marks and condition of a widow.

256

2: "Caught on the spoke of a turning wagon wheel" is literally "on the spoke of a wagon that has an axle." According to OC, the axle implies turning.

7: She means that the potter should make the pot large enough for her also, as she will become a *satī* and join her husband in death.

257

2–3: "His beard the deep shade of *kucci* grass" is literally "a beard whose hair is lustrous like arrayed *kucci* grass."

6: Apparently, the idea here is that even though he rarely leaves his city, he is able to fight and bring back the cows—he isn't one who always has to be prowling around looking for a fight.

11: The poet seems to mean that the hero gives away the cows he takes even before the next day, and as a result, there is no milk to put in his pot or to churn.

12: "With milk" is added for clarity.

258

1: "Liquor" is the translation of *teem,* which may be toddy or, according to OC, *matu,* which may also be an intoxicating drink distilled from mahua flowers. We have used "liquor" here to avoid repeating "toddy."

3: Presumably, the fermented toddy (*matu*) tastes like the *kārai* fruit.

3–4: "He traded them for toddy, which he drank" is the translation of *talaic ceṉṟu uṇṭu.* We have relied on OC's gloss to make sense of this.

4–5: "Hand still moist with spit" is the translation of *eccil īrṅkai*—his hand is still moist from the food that he had been eating.

7: The Lexicon says *pullaṇal* means "down on the chin." "These warriors" is added for clarity, at the suggestion of OC.

259

5: "Low-caste woman" is the translation of *pulaitti.* People of low caste were (and are) thought to have powers over the spirit world; hence, they often are mediums, prophesying while possessed.

6: "A god" is the translation of *muruku.* This could also mean Murugan.

260

2: "Mode of grief" is added for clarity.

3–4: It is a bad omen to see a woman with her hair spread out to dry.

8: Literally, "will I not see him."

8–9: "Fields he has granted you" is the translation of *puravu,* land given free of rent by a king.

11: "At once" is the translation of *kaṭitu aṇmaiyavē,* literally, "it is very close." The OC takes this with "city"—the city that is very (*kaṭitu*) close. If this interpretation is correct, the poet is emphasizing the boldness of the enemies who stole the cattle from right next to the hero's city.

15: "War drum" is the translation of *tuṭi.* This drum, shaped like an hourglass, was played by low-caste men called Tuṭiyaṉs. Tuṭiyaṉs are usually said to reside in villages in the wilderness.

16: The serpent who devours the moon (when it is eclipsed) is Rāhu, one of the nine planets.

26: "Cloth" is the translation of *paṭam*—the Lexicon says this may mean painted or printed cloth or a cloth for wearing. According to OC, it is a sari.

27: It was customary to erect a memorial stone (see the notes to 232.5) to a fallen hero that would supposedly house his spirit.

261

2: "Raised verandah with its worn floor" is OC's interpretation of *muri vāy muṟṟam*. "The finest of rice" is the translation of *peruñcōṟu*, which, according to the Lexicon, is "sumptuous feast given by a king to the generals of his army." It means literally "great rice."

10: "Raiders" is supplied at D.'s suggestion.

11–12: "His kin of other owls to a feast on the dead" is added for clarification at D.'s suggestion.

12: "Fragrant basil" is the translation of *karantai*. It was the custom to wear *veṭci* when going off on a raid and *karantai* when returning.

18: Literally, "you have grown dim, having lost your many ornaments."

262

1: "Male goat" is the translation of *viṭai*. The Lexicon says this may be a bull, a male buffalo, a male bison, or a ram. According to OC, *āṭṭu viṭai* is "a male goat (or ram)." "Pavilion" is the translation of *pantar*, a pandal.

2: "Pale" is the translation of *puṉ*, which means "dull" or "empty."

263

3: "Memorial" is added for clarity.

4: D. says that if the suppliant bows to it, the spirit in the stone will make it rain. It is a belief held even today that a good king (or leader) can keep away drought.

6: "Ignorant" is the translation of *kallā*, which can also mean "unlearned."

265

1: "Worn down" is the translation of *mutir*, literally, "old."

4: After "to your stone," the original has "and adorn it with a garland of green leaves and flowers"—*paṭalai cūṭṭa*. We have omitted this, as it simply repeats what went before.

266

7: According to OC, "The sense of the snail mating in the day with a conch is as follows: through pride, they pay no attention to their *jāti* [caste or species] and mate with other species, thereby showing the excessive nature of [things in] his land. Thus, his excessive wealth is indicated."

13: These are especially powerful words in a land where hospitality is the greatest of virtues and guests are considered as God incarnate (*atithiḥ svayaṃ viṣṇuḥ*).

269

Before going on a cattle raid, the king and his men drink some filtered toddy. Suddenly, when the Tuṭiyaṉ comes and beats his drum to announce the beginning of hostilities, the king refuses to drink more but picks up his sword instead and sets out on the raid.

4: "As amber as" is added at D.'s suggestion.

5: A man of very low caste" —giving to such people was a sign of a king's true generosity.

6: "Drumming the call to battle on his drum" is added at D.'s suggestion.

11: For fragrant basil (*karantai*), see the notes to 261.

270

1: For the wheel of law, see the notes to 99.3.

2: The royal drum (*muracu*) is the most important of drums for a king. It is carefully guarded and is said to confer title to his kingdom. See the notes to 50.1.

9: The *taṇṇumai* drum was a large kettle drum beaten by Pāṇaṉs to summon men to battle.

271

The name of the poetess means "Kāmakkāṇiyār who sang of frenzy."

1: "Garments" is the translation of *taḻai,* a dress of leaves that young women would wear around their waist.

4: "Filigreed" is, literally, "delicate" (*mel*). D. says that this adjective should be taken with "women."

6: *Oṟuvāyppaṭṭa* is, if anything, stronger than "torn." *Oṟuvāy* by itself means "the broken edge of a pot."

6: "All changed" is literally "its [true] form concealed"—*uruvu karantu.*

272

8: "Before the fortified wall" is the translation of *kāppuṭaiya puricai pukku,* literally, "having entered the fortified wall." D. says this means "standing at the fortified wall."

273

D. says this is spoken by the man's wife—its power rests on the fact that she doesn't mention the possibility that her husband has fallen.

274

4–5: "Had caught" can also be translated as "has caught."

5–6: "Caught in his hands the javelins that enemies hurled at him from ranging horses" is the translation of *oṉṉalar eḥkuṭai valattar māvoṭu parattara kaiyiṉ vāṅki,* literally, "as the men, with javelins in their right hands, spread out with horses [or elephants], he caught [them] in his hands." It is not certain whether they ride the horses (or elephants) or merely accompany them. D. says *mā* means "elephants."

275

1: "For his hair" is added for clarity.

8: "Cow" here is *kaṟavai,* a milch cow.

276

3: "Fruit of an ironwood tree" is the translation of *iṟaṅkāḻ.* This is not given in the Lexicon. D. says it means *iravamarattiṉ vitai,* the "seed of the ironwood tree." *Kāḻ* means both the seed and skin of a fruit, rind; hence our translation as "fruit."

6: "He pervades the enemy's army with pain" is the translation of *paṭaikku nōy ellām tāṉ āyiṉaṉē,* literally, "He is entirely a sickness (or pain) to the army."

277

3: "Heron" is the translation of *kokku.* The Lexicon says this means crane, stork, or paddy bird; we have used "heron," as most English-speaking people envision that bird standing in the water and eating fish. *Nārai* can mean either crane or heron.

6: "Bamboo" is the translation of *vetiram,* which could also be the name of a mountain; thus, this line could also mean "which hang on strong bamboo [*kaḻai* can mean both bamboo and shaft of bamboo] on Mount Vetiram after collecting there in the rain."

278

2: "Dry, veined arms where the soft flesh hangs down" is the translation of *narampu eḻuntu ulaṟiya nirampā meṉ tōḷ,* literally, "soft arms, not full [i.e., firm], dried, with raised veins."

3: "Wrinkled like a lotus leaf"—according to D., this refers to the fact that her stomach no longer is soft and fresh but has grown wrinkled and has veins raised on it.

8–9: Ramasubramaniam suggests that she had to put the pieces of her son's body together before she could recognize him.

279

1: "May her will be broken" is the translation of *keṭuka cintai,* literally, "may her thought perish."

3: "Her father" (*taṉṉai*) can also mean "her elder brother."

280

8: "Bodiless voice of an oracle" is the translation of *viricci,* which the Lexicon defines as "utterance of an invisible speaker."

8–9: The Tuṭi drummer and the bard (*pāṇaṉ*) belong to different castes. The dancing woman (*viṟali*) is probably a female bard; see the notes to 60.3, and for the Tuṭiyan, see 260.15.

12–15: Continual tonsure, removal of ornaments, and eating unappetizing food are some of the acts of mortification that widows performed.

281

1: "Branches" is added for clarification.

5–6: Kāñci is defined as follows by the Lexicon: "(4) theme describing the defence of a fortress on the approach of an enemy by a king decked with *kāñci* flowers appropriate to the occasion; (5) instability, transiency." The fifth meaning is probably meant here. This song is classified by Nacciṉārkkiṉiyar as *toṭākkāñci,* which is summarized by D. as follows: "A wife protects a warrior who has fallen and is wounded, to make ghosts go away, afraid they may infect (*toṭu*) him."

9: "Threat" is the translation of *viḻumam,* literally, "affliction."

282

12: "Which has lost its power" is D.'s suggestion for *alakai pōki,* whose meaning is uncertain.

283

4: This whole sequence is somewhat problematic. We have followed D., who suggests that the point of the image is that just as the otter gets his prey at first and then, not content, continues to search for prey before leaving, so the hero wins his victory and then continues to fight before retiring.

5–7: This is unclear because of the text that has been lost. It seems corrupt as well.

9: The Lexicon says of *tumpai,* "a garland of flowers worn by warriors when engaged in battle, as a mark of their valour."

11: "His own" is added for clarity. It is not clear whether the friend puts the *tumpai* garland on his own head or on the head of his dying friend. Most probably, the friend puts the *tumpai* on his own head and sets out to battle.

284

2: "Royal messengers of noble birth" is D.'s interpretation of *viḻut tūtu.* The people who announced the king's decrees and summons to battle were usually of low caste. Perhaps these messengers are Brahmins. The word "travel" is added to convey the sense of "here and there" (*āṅku āṅku*).

4: That is, he doesn't take time to find his horse or gather others to come with him.

5: "Turns the difficult battle around" is the translation of *arum camam tāṅki,* literally, "wards off the difficult battle."

285

2: "The drummer" is the translation of *tuṭiyaṉ*—the tuṭi drummer.

2–4: Apparently, the hero has generously given his shield and spear to his drummer and bard, since he will not need them anymore.

5: "Filled with new rice" is added, as a *mūṭai* (sack) is generally filled with paddy. This probably is an image for corpses, but it is impossible to tell, as part of the poem has been lost.

12: The fat is on his anklets because he is walking over corpses. "Human" is added for clarity.

17: The hero, though dying, still is modest and self-effacing.

286

1: A version of the old commentary, which has been preserved for this poem, says that this means "like the *veṭci* garland on the pure, spotless goat, which is the cause of its death." This would apparently mean that the cup given to the warrior should lead to his death in battle, just as the *veṭci* garland is a sign that the goat is about to be sacrificed. In the poem, the mother goes on to describe how her son, who was given the cup, did *not* die, even though he should have—presumably, she is expressing her joy that he survived. This interpretation makes sense of the image of the goat. *Ceccai* may mean *veṭci* (garland of scarlet ixora), but may also mean a male goat. D. takes the latter meaning. In his subcommentary, R. Teyvacikāmaṇi Kavuṇṭar says that a black goat is called "white" (*veḷḷāṭu*) as a euphemism. D. suggests that in this poem, the mother feels ashamed that her son, distinguished by being the recipient of the cup, did not die in the fight but, rather, returned alive.

287

1: A Pulaiyaṉ is an untouchable—a person contaminated with dangerous power (*pulai*), the same sort of power inherent in a menstruating woman or in meat. For the *tuṭi* drum, see the notes to 260.15.

2: *Iḻiciṉaṉ,* "one who is despised."

4: "Shoot down" is literally "pierce" (*taippiṉum*). "Fly through the air" is literally "leap" (*piṟaliṉum*).

11: "They will have" is the translation of *maṉṟal,* which can mean either "marry" or "copulate with."

13: "Coming, rampaging" is the translation of *vampa,* which literally means "mischievous."

288

1: "The drum" is the translation of the *muracam,* the royal drum that gives a king title to his kingdom. Elsewhere, it is said that the wood of this drum is often made from an enemy's tutelary tree. For the royal drum, see the notes to 50.1.

2: "Unfinished skin"—that is, without scraping off the hair.

7: "Around him" is the translation of *aruku uṟai.* It is difficult to construe this because part of the poem is missing. It could also be *aru kuṟai,* "a hard-to-bear fault or defect."

289

7: "Do not be surprised at it!" is conjectured. It is either *maṉṟiciṉē* or *aṉṟiciṉē.* This interpretation is D.'s.

9: The *taṇṇumai,* a large drum, one of whose uses was to be beaten to summon men to battle.

10: "Its mouth covered" is the translation of *maṭi vāy,* literally, "wrinkled or bent mouth." D. says its mouth was covered with skin bent around it. This might also refer to the drummer, whose mouth may be wrinkled. "Low-caste drummer" is the translation of *iḻiciṉaṉ,* "low one." Ritual drummers are still low caste. The English word "pariah" comes from the Tamil *paṟaiyaṉ,* "drummer." Low-caste people were supposed to cover their mouths when they spoke to people of the upper castes.

290

4: "The hub . . . wheel," according to D. for *taccaṉ aṭuttu eṟi kuṟaṭṭiṉ.* The spears are probably meant to be compared to the spokes coming out of the hub.

291

D. says this is spoken by the dead hero's wife, but it may also be spoken by a low-caste bard of some sort.

1: *Ciṟāar*—literally, "little ones." D. takes this as "children," but low-caste people are also called "little ones." In *Puṟam* 381.23, *ciṟuvar,* "little ones," is contrasted with *uṟuvar,* "great ones." George Hart has collected a modern folk song in which a low-caste leather worker is called "*ciṉṉāṉ,*" "little one." See also poem

382. "Drummers" is the translation of *tuṭiyar*—ones who play the *tuṭi* drum. See the notes to 260.15.

2: It was apparently the custom of men to wear a pure white cloth when going into battle. See *Puṟam* 279.

4: The Lexicon defines *viḷari* as "melody-type of the *neytal* class, suited for mourning."

4–8: D. says that the hero's garland was given him by his wife, something he suggests was an old custom.

292

1–2: Apparently, this describes the ceremony of *uṇṭāṭṭu,* in which a drink is passed around to the men before they went out to fight. The hero addressed has refused to take his drink in the proper order—probably because he feels he deserves a higher place in the order of precedence. Instead, he has drawn his sword at the perceived insult, thus angering those around him. The *Ayottiyākkāṇṭam* of the Kampaṉ's *Rāmāyaṇa* has an *Uṇṭāṭṭuppaṭalam,* an erotic section before the marriage of Rāma and Sītā that describes men and women drinking before they make love.

293

Before going to battle, men must buy flowers to wear. Here, since the war has started, there are no warriors left at home to buy flowers, so the girl who sells flowers has gone to the houses of noncombatants to try to sell flowers there. D. suggests these are Brahmins, the sick, the childless, and the like. The poet here pities her because there is no one left to whom she can sell flowers easily.

2: The drum here is the *taṇṇumai,* the large drum beaten by an untouchable (usually a Pāṇaṉ) to summon men to battle. "Local chieftains" are *kuṟumpar.*

3: Presumably they are ashamed because they do not go to battle. This probably means those who are left after the fighting men have gone out to fight.

4: *Eḻil* usually means "beauty." Here, we conjecture it means "things of beauty," that is, treasure. D. says it means *eḻucci,* "motivation to act," and takes the phrase as meaning "having lost her motivation (to sell flowers here)."

6: "You should feel compassion for her" is the translation of *aḷiyaḷ tāṉē,* literally, "she is pitiful indeed."

294

D. writes, "One day the poet happened to see a battle incident. The chief of the army who had stayed in the camp at night stood on the battlefield in the day. Warriors from the two sides opposed each other and fought so that you couldn't tell who was friend and who was enemy in the fierce battle. The army chief went into the battle, looked at the enemies, and said, 'Showing your fame and the excellence of your king, the days of your life gone, come here to fight with us,' and he defeated many of the great opposing warriors and stood to one side. The enemies who saw his valor in battle feared to approach him just as people fear to approach a jewel dropped by a snake [cobra]. Peruntalaiccāttaṉār [the poet], amazed at seeing this, after the battle had finished and when that chief was staying at home, went and told his deeds so his wife would hear and made her happy. That speech is reported in this song."

6: Literally, "camp like an ocean where they gathered all together." Clearly, this means that the army in the camp was as large as an ocean (a common comparison).

7: This could mean "like [the king's] white umbrella." D. says that by comparing it to the moon, the poet is suggesting the king's umbrella is even more impressive than the moon.

7–8: Cobras are supposed to have a jewel in the middle of their hoods, which they occasionally drop. Obviously, no one wants to pick it up, even though it has great value, as the cobra may return to retrieve it.

295

8: "Overcome by love" is the translation of *aruḷi.* The verb *aruḷ* means "be gracious to," "rejoice." We have followed D. in expressing the connotations of the noun *aruḷ,* "grace" or "love," here.

296

There has been a battle, and in all the houses, wounded men are being tended. All the ritual activities described at the beginning of the poem are to that end. The hero of the poem, however, has not returned, and so the poet supposes he surely must be defeating the enemy king.

2: The *tiṇai* of Kāñci is defined by the Lexicon as "(1) major theme inculcating a belief in the instability of earthly things as a necessary preliminary to attain liberation, (2) major theme describing a warrior defending his position." We have assumed the first meaning is meant here. In the *Puṟanāṉūṟu,* poems assigned to the *tiṇai* of *kāñci,* describe men who have been wounded, a woman selling flowers for war (*Puṟ.* 293), and a girl who has come of age and for whom various enemy kings are about to fight (*Puṟ.* 336–355), all themes of the insubstantiality and vanity of existence. There are in addition several poems assigned to *kāñci* (355–360) in which the evanescence of things is the literal theme of the poem.

297

1: "Reward" is the translation of *puravu,* "land given free of rent by a king."

5: "And refuse" is supplied at D.'s suggestion—"When refusing something that has been given, it was the custom of ancient warriors to praise and drink toddy."

5–6: "The sweetly aged liquor strained through fiber and afloat with flowers" is the translation of *nār ari naṉai mutir cāṭi naṟavu,* literally, "aged toddy in cups with flowers strewn on top and filtered through fiber."

8: "The fords" is the translation of *tuṟai.* This word means "harbor," "bathing place," "sea," "river." D. says it is the equivalent of *nīrttuṟai,* which means (according to the Lexicon) "ghat, a path of descent to a tank or river; ford, ferry; watering-place for cattle; place for bathing or washing clothes."

298

2: Mixed toddy is more intoxicating and is considered better than the clear kind.

5: The speaker says the king appears to be a generous and self-sacrificing person, taking the inferior toddy while others drink the better toddy at the drinking ceremony before the battle. Why should such a king, who appears to be so courteous, not allow his warriors to attack before he does? By not allowing them to attack first, he is taking the preeminent place and is not showing a self-sacrificing attitude. Of course, this all is meant as praise couched in an ironic form.

299

2: Literally, "horses with halting walks that ate black gram." The obvious sense is that the horses walk haltingly because of their deficient, poor diet (though it's hard not to feel that black gram would be healthier than paddy mixed with ghee).

5: *Miti,* which the Lexicon defines as "food trampled and formed into a ball." Probably paddy is meant. D. suggests that the best oil for horses is supposed to be pork lard. It is possible that *ney,* translated as "ghee" (its usual meaning) actually means "lard" here.

7: "In their time of the month" is added for clarity. Hindu women do not enter temples or cook or eat from their usual dishes when they are menstruating. "Avenging" is the translation of *aṇaṅkuṭai*—who has *aṇaṅku,* afflicting dangerous power. George Hart has written at length on this intriguing and important word (see Hart 1975, pp. 81 ff). For Murugan, see the notes to 55.18.

301

1: "All you many noble men" is the translation of *pal cāṉṟīrē.* This is a conventional and formulaic way of showing disrespect for the people addressed. It is spoken by a representative of the opposing army, who scorns his enemies because their king stays inside his camp and will not fight. For *cāṉṟōṉ,* see the notes to 34.22.

2–3: "Hair of virgins"; that is, no one can touch them.

9: Presumably, he considers them all unworthy to fight with him except for the enemy king himself. "He" is our king.

302

4: "Poor land" is the translation of *karampai,* which may mean either wasteland or land with a surface layer of alluvium. "Where roads barely exist" is the translation of *nirampā iyaviṉ.* A variant reading is *nirampā iyalpiṉ,* "whose nature is not full." The fact that the king can give away only villages in poor land means that he is not a great king but a marginal chieftain. The poet wishes to contrast his low status as a chief of a poor area with his extraordinary valor in battle.

5: "Bitter orange" is the translation of *narantam,* which can also mean "a fragrant grass."

303

2: "With the hooves cutting" is the translation of *kuḷampu kaṭaiyū,* literally, "churning or mashing the hooves."

3: "Torments and destroys" is literally "making a wound and tormenting" (*vaṭu viḷaippa āṭṭi*).

5: D. says this implies "so that the enemy king could see."

9: "Tender" is the translation of *kayam,* which can also mean "large." Presumably, "tender-headed" signifies their vulnerability and youth.

304

4: "Outruns the wind" is literally "which destroys [i.e., surpasses] the action of the wind."

5: Presumably, he has made a vow not to eat until he has killed his brother's killer.

10: This is the *muracu,* the royal drum.

305

The Brahmin comes as an envoy to try to avoid war and is successful.

1: "Walking on the tips of his toes" is the translation of *uyaval ūrti,* literally, "with distressed creeping along." Pērāciriyar says this means going on tiptoe.

4–6: D. says that because the elephants have bells, they are the king's elephants. Presumably, the ladders are to scale the opposing king's walls, the stakes to protect one's own walls.

306

3: "Reservoirs" is the translation of *kūval,* which usually means "well." Here it means a place on the bank of a river or reservoir where people go to get water.

4: "Huge, immovable stone" is the translation of *naṭu kal,* literally, "a planted stone." See the notes to 232.5.

307

1: "My king" is the translation of *entai,* literally, "my lord." This apparently refers to the king who, in the latter half of the poem, decides to become immortal through fighting and dying.

3–6: D. suggests the hero is hard to recognize because of the flowers on his head.

6–9: D. suggests that just as when the bull is left with no food, he will eat whatever grass he can find, the hero will kill any enemies he can find around him.

14: According to D., "without any wish to continue in life" is the translation of *neñcu aṟa,* "without the heart [to live]." He remarks that "he fell without making his heart his own, but rather making it belong to the one [the hero in the earlier part of the poem] who gave his life for him."

308

2: "With its strings like twisted gold drawn out into wires" is the translation of *poṉ vārntaṉṉa puri aṭaṅku narampiṉ,* literally, "with strings that are subjected to twisting, like gold drawn out."

5: "Has pierced" is literally "is in."

11: "Whose heads are tender" is the translation of *puṉ talai.* This is difficult to translate. The Lexicon gives the following meanings for the noun form of the adjective *puṉ:* "(1) meanness, lowness, vileness; (2) uncleanness; (3) smallness; (4) affliction, suffering; (5) poverty; (6) fault; (7) murkiness, tawny colour; (8) dimness of vision; (9) forgetfulness, oblivion."

309

7: The word for "flashing fame" is the translation of *oḷi,* whose main meaning is "light." According to UVS, it is the respect one has from striking fear into others. Parimēlaḻakar, commenting on *Kuṟaḷ* 698, says *oḷi* is "the divine quality of a king through which, even when he is asleep, he protects the earth." It would be nice to take this as "light is in his eye (*kaṇṇatu*) that causes fear," but this would probably be wrong.

310

4: "Descendant" is literally "son." D. suggests that "strong men who fell in earlier days" includes his brothers and ancestors.

6–8: The tuft (*kuṭumi*) of hair and the straggling beard are signs that he is scarcely more than a child.

311

3: "Washerwoman" is the translation of *pulaitti,* literally, "an untouchable woman."

6: "Blazing" is literally "smoking."

7: "Weapons" is added at D.'s suggestion.

312

2: "Noble man" is the translation of *cāṉṟōṉ;* see the notes to 34.22.

5–6: "To fight indomitably" is literally "to kill in difficult battle."

313

1: "Rough roads" is the translation of *attam*. The Lexicon says *attam* is a "way," "rough path," "difficult course." D. says this means "with many roads," but that would not seem to fit the impoverished nature of the chieftain addressed. D. supposes the warrior is from a rich land, but that does not seem to fit the poem.

4–7: Literally, "Like a hill eroded (*muri*) by a salt-pan [or shallow seawaters] in the forest [way] of merchants with wagons bearing salt." This image is unclear. D. says, "Even though the hill next to the salt pan which is the source of income for the salt merchants is in a land that produces salt, it is excellent because it does not diminish [even though it is eroded], just as the king, even though he is in a state of having no wealth, because of his intention to be generous, should not be belittled." Apparently, his point is that just as the salt merchants underestimate the difficulty of the hill, which is very hard for them to get past, even though it appears to be undermined by the salt pan, so it would be easy to underestimate the commitment of the impoverished king to giving.

7: "His goodwill" is literally "the goal he intends" (*avaṉ uḷḷiya poruḷē*).

314

4: "Dun-colored seeds" is the translation of *puṉ kāḻ*. One of the meanings of *puṉ* is "murky, dim colored." It can also mean "small."

315

1: "If he has much food, some will be left for himself" is literally "If he has, he is able to eat."

3: "Relishes dining" is added at D.'s suggestion. "Ordinary people" is the translation of *maṭavar*—"foolish, unlearned people."

7: Literally, "He is able to appear when he (must) appear."

316

1: "Liquor" is literally "toddy" (*kaḷ*).

6: "To back up the truth of my words" has been added for clarity at D.'s suggestion.

11: "From the drinking" has been added for clarity. The literal is "And, having gone, come afterward with your mouth red." This is a Tamil idiom.

12: The idea apparently is that since the king being addressed has won in battle, he will have something to give to bards. D. connects this with the beginning of the poem: "Because an (enemy) king died, he praised liquor [i.e., drank] and then went to sleep." But this involves radically changing the order of the elements of the poem.

317

Not enough of this poem has survived to make much sense of it.

318

5: "In the eaves" is supplied at D.'s suggestion.

7: "Shavings" is the translation of *cukir.* D. thinks this means the refuse that resembles the tiny pieces of strings that bards cut off when they tune (or fix) their *yāḻs.*

8: "Frayed" has been supplied. D. says that this is hair that has grown old and mangy and fallen off the lions which, having begun to split and soften, resembles peacock feathers.

319

1: "Flaking mouth" is literally an old mouth or lip.

4: "Ravine" is the translation of *paṭu,* which usually means "a tank," "a pond," "a pool."

11: "To a toy chariot" is added at D.'s suggestion.

11–13: The point of this, as with the description of the water in the old pot at the beginning of the poem, is that the hero addressed comes from a poor village. Here, there are no ordinary calves for the children to play with, and so they must play with a wild calf instead.

14: D. says "with a golden garland."

15: "Your wife" is added for clarity. Once the hero has returned from battle, he will bring sufficient booty to be very generous to the bard and his wife.

320

1: "Pavilion" is the translation of *pantar,* a pandal.

4: "Set out to entice him" is the translation of *pārvai.* A *pārvaimāṉ* is a tame animal set out as a decoy to attract its wild counterparts—in D's words, "a young doe trained to catch other deer."

8: "Cackling loudly" is the translation of *kal eṉa olittu,* literally, "making a loud noise."

10: D. suggests they come because everything is so quiet. This is indicated by the syntax of the poem, which has "*vaḻaṅkāmaiyiṉ,*" "because she is motionless."

10: "She catches them and prepares them" is added at D.'s suggestion.

11: Here, we take the meaning of *irum* as "black." It can also mean "large," in which case it merely repeats the meaning of *pēr.*

321

3–4: D. says that just as cocks are trained to fight in ancient times, quails also were trained.

7: "Field rat" is the translation of *kōṭṭu eli. Kōṭu* means the ridge at the boundary of paddy fields.

7–8: "The inner petals of a *kōṅku*" is literally "the pericarp that is in the flower of the *kōṅku.*"

10: "Fruit that is wolfed down" is the translation of *tiṉ paḻam pacīi.* It is not clear what the last word here means. The last part (in Tamil) is fragmentary and cannot be construed. D. says the lost lines must have described what the bard would get if he went to the king.

322

1: "Prickly pear" is the translation of *kaḷḷi,* which can also mean "spurge."

3: "Whose heads are easily hurt" is the translation of *puṉ talai*—heads that are dull colored or tender.

323

2: "Slain" is literally "caught."

3–4: Presumably, the lost lines say that the city of the spearman is in a wasteland.

324

4: "Foul-mouthed" is the translation of *veḷ vāy.* D. says this can also mean "mouths which do not take betelnut [and are white and unstained]." *Veḷ* can mean "white" or "ignorant."

325

1: "Defended by forests" is the translation of *miḷai,* a forest that serves as a defense.

1–2: "Men whose words can be trusted" is the translation of *muḻuc col āṭavar,* literally, "men whose words are whole." D. suggests this means men who can be taken at their word.

7: "Lizard" is the translation of *uṭumpu*—the Lexicon says "big lizard found all over India, and growing to 3 ft. in length."

11: "Jujube" is the translation of *iratti*, which can also be a fig tree.

12: "Bows and" is added for clarity.

15: D. says "kings."

326

1: "Defended by forests" is the translation of *miḷai*—a forest that serves as a defense.

4–5: "Clucks so loud it seems to tear the flesh inside her throat" is the translation of *pulā viṭṭu ararra*, literally, crows leaving her flesh. D. says this means "crows opening the flesh of her throat."

6–7: "To clean off the area with its piles of seeds" is literally "to clean (*puṭai*—or dust) the area (*ciṟai*) and the bushes (*ceṟṟai*)." D. says this means to clean up the cotton seeds and debris left from carding the cotton.

9: "Woman" is literally "wife"; we have translated it as "woman," since "wife" would have no referent and the proper meaning is conveyed by "her husband" in the last line.

10: The *uṭumpu* is defined by the Lexicon as follows: "big lizard found all over India, and growing to 3 ft. in length, *varamus bengalensis*."

14: D. takes "elephant" as plural and says the husband will give away ornaments of gold that were worn by lordly elephants.

327

7: "Low men" is the translation of *ciṟu pullāḷar*, or "little, mean men." D. says this means men who, even though they have little, act as if they have a lot.

328

2: "Forest tracts" is the translation of *puṟavu*, *mullai* lands. These are the lands of forests and meadows where jasmine grows.

3: The two kinds of millet are *varaku* and *tiṉai*.

329

1: "Set the offerings" is literally "feed sacrifices" (*pali ūṭṭi*).

1–2: For "stones memorializing heroes" (*naṭu kal*), see the notes to 232.5.

4–5: This is how D. construes this passage. Literally, "the streets are fragrant from the dark [or abundant] cloud-smoke from lighting the ghee *naṟai*." *Naṟai* usually means "incense," but here it is apparently used figuratively for a lamp, since there is no such thing as ghee incense.

5: "Secure and dominating" is the translation of *aru muṉai*, literally, "which has hard [-to-approach] eminence [or superiority]." *Muṉai* can also mean "battle," in which case this would mean "which has hard battle."

6–9: That is, he makes other kings suffer by attacking them and obtaining booty to distribute to his suppliants, but he does not pay heed to their suffering, being intent on generosity instead.

330

5: "Ruler" is literally "he who comes from," but in this context, this means he is the chieftain of the village.

331

1–2: This is a figure of speech meaning they earn their livelihood through their bows, not by plowing, as do men of a more prosperous area.

4–6: Just as the cowherd can make something he doesn't have—fire—so the hero can somehow come up with what he doesn't have in order to be generous.

7: "He does not worry"—Swaminathaier has *eṉṉāḷ* instead of *eṉṉāṉ*. If one accepts this reading, it goes with the woman: "like a woman who does not worry about there being many who come to her."

11: "The white rice of sacrifice" is the translation of *pōkupali*. D. says this means "the best of sacrifices." *Pōku* is not given in the Lexicon.

332

6: "Virtuous women" is the translation of *maṅkala makaḷir*. This probably means women who are *cumaṅkaḷis*, that is, who are not widows.

8: "Of the enemy" is added for clarity.

333

4: "Pitted" is the translation of *toḻḻai*. D. says it means full of holes made by rats etc.

8–9: The two kinds of millet are *varaku* and *tiṉai*, respectively.

11: "For your visit to the city" is added for clarity. "Recompense" is the translation of *kuṟiyetirppai*, which means (according to the Lexicon), "exact return of things borrowed."

14: "Empty" is added at D.'s suggestion.

16–19: D. suggests that this means he would feed kings the same as he would suppliants, but *uṇpatu* means "what is eaten," not "what is fed." No doubt, the meaning of these lines would be clarified by the parts of the poem that have been lost.

334

2: "Reservoirs" is the translation of *pal̲an̲am,* which can also mean "agricultural fields." "Lovely" is the translation of *kāmaru,* which can also be separated as *kā maru,* "fragrant from [or near] a garden [or grove]."

335

This poem has often been misinterpreted and used to show that there were only four castes (or groups) in ancient Tamil Nadu. In order to dispel this misconception, we quote what D. says about it: "Māṅkuṭikil̲ār describes in this poem the divisions of life of people who live in a certain town in the forest (*mullai*) land—the flowers they wear, the food they eat, the kinds of castes found among them, and the way they worship gods." As with the other poems in this section, this poem deals with life in a marginal village, one that is far removed from the rich paddy country of the riverine valleys. All these plants, food, castes, and gods are typically those found in such marginal areas. In a version of the Maduraivīran̲ story that George Hart collected (with the help of Mr. Sundaram), a leather worker's wife goes to the forest to collect beans from the bean plant (*avarai*). It is interesting to see the same plant described as typical of a forested area.

4–5: "Common millet" is the translation of *varaku;* "large-eared millet" is the translation of *tin̲ai.*

6–7: All these are groups that are marginal and are considered Harijans (untouchables). The Tuṭiyan̲s play a small drum shaped like an hourglass, and they often are said to live in wild, remote, forested places. The Pāṇan̲ is the bard so often encountered in these poems. The Par̲aiyan̲ is apparently the same as the Kiṇaiyan̲, the man who announces the king's commands and who drums at funerals. The last poems of the *Pur̲anān̲ūr̲u* concern the life of this drummer, who, it appears, was not allowed to enter people's houses. The Kaṭampan̲ is perhaps the same as the Vēlan̲. He wears the *kaṭampu* flower sacred to Murugan and becomes possessed by the god. Vēlan̲s, a very low caste, still exist in Kerala, where their religious practices emphasize possession by various spirits.

9: Memorial stones: see the notes to 232.5.

336

4: "Have been unleashed from the sacred tree" is the translation of *kaṭimaram cērā.* The *kaṭimaram,* or "guarded tree," was a tree that was sacred to the king and was guarded by his men so it could not come to harm. For "tutelary tree," see the notes to 23.9.

5: "Of both factions" is the translation of *cērnta,* "who belong." "Both factions" has been added at D.'s suggestions, as otherwise *cērnta* would make no sense.

5–6: Literally, "Warriors who have gleaming swords have shut their mouths."

Our translation is justified by the sense of the poem, which is clearly that the swords are about to be used.

8: "Evil" is the translation of *paṇpu il*—without *paṇpu* ("manners, good qualities, decency, civilized tendency," according to the Lexicon).

9: "Principles" is the translation of *aṟaṉ*, the Tamil word for *dharma*.

10: "Until they reached their present beauty" is the translation of *takai vaḷartta*, literally, "who raised [caused to grow] the excellence [or beauty]."

11: "Red cotton tree" is the translation of *kōṅku*, which can also be the common caung or the ironwood.

337

2: Literally, "even though he possesses wealth from ruling the earth, he does not consider it."

4–5: This passage is difficult to construe. We have followed what seemed the best of D.'s suggestions. It could also mean "when men approach him as bards would, singing of his hand that is cupped [to give]."

8–9: "Girl with a glowing face, a glory among women" is the translation of *māṇṭa peṇmai niṟainta polivoṭu*, literally, "with a glowing filled with excellent womanhood."

8–10: Not only is she beautiful, she is impossible to reach. Pāri's mountain was besieged by the three great kings but was captured only through treachery. Kapilar was the poet who made Pāri immortal through his famous cycle of songs. See the notes to 105.

9: D. says the incense has stained the walls of the mansion brown.

12–15: This whole section is problematic. It could also mean "not only are there people who take care of the elephants . . . spread in every grove; kings don't stop coming." "While everyone watches them attend to their animals" is the translation of *teṟṟeṉa ōmpi;* the sense is not clear, and our translation is conjectural.

19: For "Martial Courage," see the notes to 39.10.

22: "Spots of puberty" is the translation of *cuṇaṅku,* defined by the Lexicon as "(1) yellow spreading spots on the body of women, regarded as beautiful; (2) sallow complexion of a love-lorn woman; (3) a spreading skin-disease, especially of animals; (4) pollen-dust." Obviously, it is challenging to translate this. It seems that this condition is related to hormonal changes that happen at puberty, and that is why we have translated it as we have. In all the descriptions, it is applied only to young women who are just becoming adults.

338

1: "Their bows tensed" or just "bearing their bows"—*aṇinta villar.*

1–3: The three great Tamil kings, the Chera, Chola, and Pandya.

339

10: "The fields," *ceṟu,* can mean either a field or a reservoir. D. takes it as "field"; presumably, they come to the fields after they have finished playing on the water.

10: "Ornament" is the translation of *kalam.* This could also mean cooking vessel or ship—there is no context to determine which meaning is intended.

11: "She must steadily continue to grow" is unclear. D. says the people of the town continually desire her growth.

340

5: The pronouns are omitted in Tamil, and since there is no context, it is impossible to determine whether the subjects of "take up" conjectured here are correct.

9: "Fragrant basil" is the translation of *karantai,* worn by warriors when recovering cows seized by the enemy.

341

1: "Sloping" is literally "which has raised sides" (*ēntu kōṭṭu*).

8: "He is spoiling for a fight," literally, "he has anger such that he [wants to] fight."

9: These are preparations undertaken before a battle.

11: "Marriage," *maṇam,* means both marriage and sexual union.

13: "Yielding by nature" is literally "of a soft nature" (*melliyal*). For "spots of puberty" (*cuṇaṅku*), see the notes to 337.22.

15: For "Martial Courage," see the notes to 39.10.

342

2: D. says that *mayilai* flowers bloom at night.

3: "Flowing" is the translation of *kali,* "luxuriant," "dense."

4: "Daughter of anyone other than a warrior" is literally "the daughter of others." As D. points out, context demands that this mean "other than warriors."

15: "For threshing the harvest" has been added for clarity.

343

1: "Drums" is the translation of *muḻavu,* "concert drum." This could also mean "Muciṟi, which has the roaring ocean for its drums"—*muḻaṅku kaṭal muḻaviṉ muciṟi.*

2–3: This apparently means the paddy is stacked on the boats. D. says that old unseaworthy boats were left on shore and that paddy would be stacked on them.

4–5: Perhaps the shore is full of sacks, and so there is no place for the pepper except next to the houses, which therefore resemble the shore.

7: That is, by the boats that bring goods from shore from the larger vessels anchored further out.

14–17: This meaning is conjectured. D. says, "Will the ladders that have been thrown up by men who have come to force their way in come to grief in the tall city where. . . ." Our interpretation is that the kite is meant as a bad omen, and the men with weapons on the roads belong to the enemy king. The end of poem 345, in which the military strength of the city is described, seems to support this reading.

344

5: For "Martial Courage," see the notes to 39.10.

7: Probably, like the *cuṇaṅku* (rash on the skin—see the notes to 337.22), the lines on her mons (*alkul av vari*) is a sign of puberty. Part of the poem has been lost, and it is possible that the "lines . . . on her mons" does not refer to the cause of either wealth or destruction but is, rather, connected with some other meaning by the words that have been lost.

8: D. says "young girls would want very much to smear on the fine pollen of *vēṅkai* when the sandal paste they had put all over their breasts had dried." However, the Lexicon does not give any such meaning for *kaṇi,* which we, following D., have translated as "*vēṅkai* pollen."

345

5: "Fords," *tuṟai,* could mean any tank, watering place, ford, or other place where water is accessible and used.

8–10: This is difficult to construe. The problem is the meaning of what UVS splits into *nōvuṟal irum puṟam* (D. splits *ōvuṟal irum puṟam*). D. says *ōvu* means "painting" and here means "door that is painted." But *ō* can mean a shutter, and that may be what is meant: "great space [i.e., underground way?] blocked by a shutter [i.e., a door]." If one splits the words as UVS does, it could mean the great space that is like (or blocked by) pain, which is how we have translated it.

15–16: "Woven of strips" is the translation of *kaḻi,* for which the Lexicon gives two possible meanings: "lath, strip put across the rafters to support tiles; knot, tie, string, thread."

19: "Hedges of cotton" is the translation of *paṉṉal vēli.* This could also be broken as *pal nal vēli,* "many fine hedges."

346

This is a difficult poem. The point of the first half seems to be that the family is extremely proud of their daughter and is highly accomplished (the young boy is learned, the father is brave in battle). Because of this, they will not give her to those who come to ask her hand.

1: "Former nurse" is the *cevilittāy.* She is of lower class, serves as the heroine's wet nurse, and is often the mother of the heroine's best friend (*tōḻi*). "Former nurse" is supplied (and is implied by the use of "real mother"—*īṉṟa tāy*—in the next line). "Daughter" is also added for clarity.

2–3: Presumably, the mother would normally object because her daughter is grown up. But she is so attached to her daughter that she says nothing.

4: "Father" is supplied at D.'s suggestion. D. uses the reading *oḷ vēl nallaṉ,* and UVS has the reading *olvēṉallaṉ,* which could be broken into *olvēṉ allaṉ,* but it is not possible to construe this.

6: This is at variance with D.'s interpretation, but it is less problematic. D. says, "Since those perish who must, he protects the families of those who are left," but this means supplying "he protects."

347

2–3: "Whose chest is smeared with sandalwood paste" is literally "whose chest smells with fragrance." D. says this means that his chest smells of the sandalwood paste that was smeared on it.

6–8: D. says the tongue grows red as it is rubbed raw trying to dislodge the pieces of ginger, dried meat, and fish that he has eaten along with his toddy.

11: "Can be seen from far away" is the translation of *naṉṟum viḷaṅkuṟu,* literally, "are readily apparent," " shine out well."

348

2: "Street" is the translation of *cēri.* Today, this word usually means the quarters of the pariahs and other very low castes in a village.

2: "Catch" is the translation of *cīvum,* which usually means "pare" or "scrape off." D. says this word refers to the act of catching fish in a little net.

4: D. says that in ancient times, it was customary to beat the *taṇṇumai* drum before harvesting paddy so that any birds that had nested there could leave without harm.

7: "Darkened eyes" is the translation of *uṇ kaṇ,* literally, "eyes that have eaten [collyrium]." This is a conventional way of saying "collyriumed eyes."

10: This is a translation of D.'s reading, *varuntiṉa.* Note that UVS has *varuntala,* in which case the poem means: "If her mother had never given birth to this girl . . . , then the trees of our large harbor would not have to suffer without respite long chariots standing wherever there is shade and elephants with red-painted foreheads tied up everywhere." *Āṉātu* can mean either "without respite" or "it wouldn't have happened."

349

In his commentary on the *Tolkāppiyam,* Iḷampūraṇar says that in this poem, Peruñcikkalkiḻāṉ refuses to give his daughter [in marriage]. (*Puṟattiṇai, cūttiram* 19).

6–7: Or "like a small fire kindled in a tree."

7: Just as the stick of wood destroys the whole pile of wood, she destroys the town. D. also points out that the stick of wood was produced by a tree and destroys that tree, just as she destroys the town that produced her.

350

2: "Walls" is the translation of *iñci*—according to the Lexicon, the ramparts of a fort. D. says this just means "walls."

9: "Darkened"—that is, collyriumed. *Mai uṇṭa kaṇ.*

11: "Spots of puberty" is the translation of *cuṇaṅku.* See the notes to 337.22.

352

3: "Sagging" is the translation of *aval,* literally, "made so it is a shallow depression" (i.e., concave?). According to D., this umbrella is a palmyra umbrella.

13: For the spots of puberty, see the notes to 337.22.

353

1: "Eyes half closed with desire" is the translation of *viḷartta kaṇ,* literally, your eyes white (or ashamed). D. says this means he didn't look with wide-open (*malarnta*) eyes but, rather, with eyes [narrow] with infatuation.

2–3: "Sand swept in by the ocean" is the translation of *taru maṇal,* literally, "sand that has been brought." This can also mean sand that has been brought from the shore and spread in a courtyard or similar place.

4: "Studded with many jewels" is the translation of *pal kācu aṇinta,* literally, "adorned by many *kācus.*" For *kācu,* the *Lexicon* gives "(1) gold; (2) necklace of gold coins; (3) an ancient gold coin = 28 gr. troy; (4) a small copper coin; (5) coin, cash, money; (6) gem, crystal bead; (7) girdle strung with gems."

354

1: "Heavy shaft" is the translation of *niṟai kāl,* literally, "full shaft."

3: "So that he may bathe" is added for clarity at D.'s suggestion. According to D., here two ceremonies were performed: *vāṇ maṅkalam,* "giving the spear a bath," and *maṇṇumaṅkalam,* "the king's taking a bath."

8: "Graceful" is added for clarity.

10: For "spots of puberty," see the notes to 337.22.

355

5: Since Kiḷḷi is a Chola, D. suggests this chaplet is of *atti,* whose English name is the country fig tree.

356

1: "Jungle" is the translation of *kaḷari,* which can also mean "barren earth," "salty earth."

3: "Demon women open their mouths wide" is UVS's reading. D. reads "there are demon women with wide mouths."

8: "And go away" is added to complete the metaphor of warriors fleeing in defeat while the burning ground always triumphs.

357

The poet's name is evidently from Sanskrit Brahma (or Brahmā), meaning either the substratum of the universe or the creator god.

358

The poet's name is evidently from the Sanskrit Vālmīki, who wrote the Vālmīki Rāmāyaṇam. The *tuṟai* is "the *dharma* of the house[holder], the *dharma* of renunciation [i.e., of the ascetic]."

3: Tapas is a Sanskrit word that comes from the root *tap,* "to burn." It denotes the austerities one performs in order to gain some end. Here, it refers to the life of hardship and deprivation lived by ascetics who have renounced the world. For "tapas," see the notes to 1.13.

5: "Of liberation" is added at UVS's (and D.'s) suggestion.

6: "The goddess of good fortune" is the translation of *tiru,* that is, Śrī.

359

2: D. says *māṟu* means "dry thorn," but this meaning is not given in the Lexicon, which says "twig or branch without leaves."

3: Literally, "hot mouths," that is, mouths eager to eat.

8: "Bloodless" is the translation of *viḷar,* literally, "white."

11–13: D. says this means the king should not take bribes.

13: "Your words should be impartial" is literally "you should say what is good."

17: "All have seen" is the translation of *veḷḷeṉa,* literally, "clearly," that is, so everyone can see it.

360

The poet's name, Caṅkavaruṇar, means "he who is white as a conch" and is a name of Balarāma. D. says it is a Sanskrit translation of the original Tamil Vaḷaivaṇṇaṉ.

3: "Sensitive feelings" is the translation of *nuṇ uṇarvu,* "subtle feeling," and thus sensitivity. This could also mean subtle knowledge or awareness, which is how D. apparently takes it when he says that this quality arises from much listening.

5: "Seasoned with spices" is the translation of *kuy* (modern *tāḷittal*). Mustard seeds and (sometimes) urid dahl are fried until they pop, along with curry leaves and (in modern times) dry red chili, and then the whole is poured over a dish of meat or vegetables.

12: "Their wealth is unstable" is literally "even now, such is its nature."

13: Literally, "always, you should not be deficient in your proper conduct."

17–18: "Site of what is other than life" is the translation of *māṟu taka,* literally, "fit for change [or otherness]." "Death" is one of the many meanings of *māṟu.*

18: Darbha grass is laid out, and the body is put on top of that.

19: "Outcaste" is added for clarity. *Puṟanāṉūṟu* 363 says that the Pulaiyaṉ would actually put food in the corpse's mouth, something that is extremely revolting for a traditional upper-caste person, who does not even eat in the presence of an outcaste. This stresses the repulsiveness of death.

21: "For many of those who ate and grew fat"—our translation is based on UVS's reading *paruttuṇṭōr;* D's reading, *pakuttuṇṭōr,* would mean "they who shared and ate have not flourished," which doesn't make sense. The word "fame" has been added at D.'s suggestion.

361

4: The pouring of water solemnized a gift.

8: "Crisply gaited," literally, "horses with clear gaits." D. says that since the horses have practiced and learned various gaits and steps, they move very surely.

15: "Purity" is the translation of *kaṟpu*. This word is often translated as "chastity." It comes from the root *kal,* "to learn," and it denotes not merely chastity but also the self-denial and extreme modesty that are supposed to be exhibited by women toward their husbands and elders. The Tamil says "of purity that is increased by patience."

17: *Amṛta* is the drink that makes one immortal. In these poems, it is often used to signify food or drink that is very precious, life-giving, or sweet.

20–21: "Because he has studied all of it" is the translation of *muḻutuṇar kēḷviyaṉ,* literally, "He possesses the sacred learning that he has realized entirely." The word *kēḷvi* is evidently a translation of the Sanskrit *śruti,* but it is often used to mean "sacred or technical learning." "All that he already knew" is the translation of *muntaṟinta*. D. suggests that he has learned of the evanescence of things from his own experience but in addition he has also studied the sacred books.

362

3: The royal drum (*muracu*) was treated as an extremely sacred object, and sacrifices were made to it with blood and liquor. D. says that kings would sacrifice to the royal drum before going into battle—see the notes to 50.1.

5: "As if a god had been provoked" is the translation of *aṇaṅku uruttaṉṉa. Aṇaṅku* refers to a malevolent god who causes pain and suffering and also to the deity that inhabits certain drums (including the *muracu*).

7–8: "The uproar produced by the assault" is the translation of *tākkural,* literally, "the voice of attack."

10: "Mercy" is the translation of *aruḷ:* "grace," "mercy," "kindness." "Righteousness" is the translation of *aṟam,* the Tamil equivalent of Sanskrit *dharma,* and "acquisition" is the translation of *poruḷ,* the equivalent of *artha. Dharma* and *artha* are two of the three aims of life (the third being *kāma,* "sexual fulfillment"). See the notes to 28.15 and 44.11–12. This passage points up an opposition that plays an important part in Tamil culture to the present day and that is fully articulated in the *Kamparāmāyaṇa,* the greatest work of Tamil (and, perhaps, Indian) literature. On the one hand, it concerns the warrior's ethos (often called *maṟam*)—the mentality that is revealed by many of these poems—and, on the other hand, the Hindu notion of a stable, divinely ordained society (*aṟam*).

12–13: D. says this means they are given to Brahmins.

20: "To escape from home" is literally "thinking there is no place for them in the house."

21: According to D., *iṭam ciṟitu otuṅkal añci* means "afraid of being confined in a small place." This could also refer to their houses.

22: D. adds "And go off to battle" at the beginning of this line. "Heaven" is the translation of *uyarntōr nāṭu,* literally, "the country of the high ones." In light of the next poem, which has the same *tiṇai* and *tuṟai,* one would expect the end of this poem to be about renouncing the world and becoming an ascetic, not about fighting. Thus, D's addition here does not seem justified.

363

1: "Blissful" is the translation of *ēmam,* which can also mean "strong."

4: "Final" is added at D.'s suggestion.

11–12: "Of a caste that is despised" is the translation of *iḻi piṟappiṉōṉ,* literally, he who is of despised (or low) birth. To eat food from the hand of a person of a very low caste is conventionally extremely distasteful for a person of higher caste.

18: That is, renounce the world and find peace through being an ascetic.

364

10–13: One method of disposing of the dead was to excarnate the body, collect the bones, and put them into an urn, which would then be put in a special place in the "forest." It is not clear whether this same place was also a burning ground. *Kāṭu,* whose normal meaning is "forest," can mean both burning ground and burial ground.

11–12: This image has given the poet his name: Kūkaikkōḻiyār means "he of the male owl."

13: "In the wind" is added because it is implied by "sway."

365

1: "Marked with the immense confusion" is literally "the sky with the great [or black] clouds that are mixed [or confused] [with lightning, rain, etc.]."

4: "Kings" is added for clarity.

5–8: This could also mean (D.'s interpretation) "they [have died and] gone to the deep [i.e., "ether" or—to use a more modern translation—"space"], so difficult to go to, where the shifting wind does not go." It could, even less plausibly, have this meaning and go with the wheels: "they have rolled their wheels across the deep [ether]." There are problems with all these interpretations. First, *nīttam* usually means "ocean" or "flood," but there is no mention of an ocean where the wind does not go. On the other hand, there is no mention of people dying and going to the "ether" or "space" (the fifth element). Nor does it seem plausible that kings would roll their wheels of law across an "element."

9: Traditionally, the earth was thought to be a consort of the king. The imagery, then, is that the earth has one man after another and so is like a whore.

10: "Of grief and mourning" has been added.

366

3–4: The Tamil folk belief is that thunder shatters the hoods of cobras.

4: "To heroic warriors" is the translation of *oḻukkuṭai maruṅkiṉ,* literally, "in the place which has proper [martial] conduct."

6: "Son of a righteous man, chieftain among those men who are courageous" is the translation of *aṟavōṉ makaṉē maṟavōr cemmāl.* This is a play between *aṟam*—*dharma* or proper conduct (often associated with Brahmins and Brahminical ideals)—and *maṟam,* the war ethic that is described so eloquently in these poems. See the note to 362.10.

14–15: D. suggests that unfiltered, "mixed" toddy (*kalaṅkal*) is considered to be better than filtered toddy (*tēṟal*) and that the king here becomes angry at his women because they give him an inferior kind. This interpretation seems excessively pedantic.

18: "Oblation" is the translation of *maṭai,* which can mean "boiled rice" and "oblation of food to a deity." D. says, "Just as an oblation was put in teak leaves and offered to deities, they wished to be given meat and boiled rice in leaves as if it were an oblation."

18: "Boiled rice" is the translation of *avil̲*. According to UVS, this means *cōr̲r̲up-parukkai*, "boiled grains of rice." The exact difference between *avil̲* and *maṭai* is unclear.

20: "For sacrifice" is added for clarity. At the sacrifice described, apparently the belief was that every single goat had to be slaughtered.

367

1: D. takes *pāku* as "part, district" rather than "sugarcane syrup." Thus he says "which has good parts."

2: "The world of the Nāgas"—the Lexicon says this is Indra's heaven, *svarga* (a meaning not given in Apte's *Practical Sanskrit Dictionary*).

4: "Flowers and gold"—D. says this means gold flowers and gold coins and that Brahmins call the golden flower *suvarṇa puṣpa*.

15: D. says this will is for liberation.

16–18: The syntax in the original permits both the drops and the stars to be compared to both the loftiness of the king's days and their number.

368

The Chera king is almost dead. The poet says this to celebrate his generosity—since he gives even when he's almost dead.

3–4: "On which glowing clouds are caught" is literally "hills that obstruct clouds."

5: "Lotus-shaped support for one's balance" is the translation of *koṭiñci*. We have unpacked this word, since just "support" would not mean much.

11–12: The corpses that are piled up after being trampled are like stacks of straw that are piled up after being threshed by buffaloes.

15: The actual word here is *teṭāri*, a variant of *taṭāri*.

18: "Dancers" is the translation of *kōṭiyar*, for which the Lexicon gives "professional dancers." These people probably get their name from the *kōṭu*, a brass instrument they must have played. The concert drum is the translation of the *mul̲avu*, the modern *mṛdaṅgam*. "Armlets" has been added at D.'s suggestion.

369

6–7: Literally, "when those snakes . . . feel deep anguish." It is a Tamil belief that thunder attacks cobras and shatters their hoods.

1–17: This an extended agricultural image. The grain grows heavy and its heads bend down, just as men with broken necks have their heads bent down. In addition, the corpses are stacked, just as the harvest is put into haystacks. Then the grain is threshed by buffaloes. Usually, this is compared to elephants or horses trampling the corpses. Here, it says demons and foxes do the threshing (*paṭuppa*), an idea that occurs nowhere else. Perhaps this is why D. takes *paṭuppa* as "seize" and suggests that they snatch and eat parts of the dead bodies.

18: D. says he sits in state to hear the songs of the singers.

20: "Flawlessly" is the translation of *vēyvai kāṇā,* literally, "which does not see *vēyvai,*" which D. says is a frayed or decayed condition found in the skin or strings of musical instruments. "Sandalwood powder" is the translation of *tēyvu*—"fragrant unguent from sandalwood, formed by trituration" (Lexicon).

28: "As you should be" attempts to catch the connotation of *takai* in *tāḻā īkait takai veyyōy.*

370

2: "From my troubles" is added.

2–3: "I pack my things and carry the fiber and soft shoots of palmyra" is D.'s interpretation. It says literally, "I make fiber and pieces [*pōḻ* or a leather strap]." D. gives an identical usage in poem 375, in which *nār* and *pōḻ* are used: *mā maṭal nārum pōḻum kiṇaiyoṭu curukki,* "I pack up my kiṇai drum and the fibers / and shoots of long sharp-edged leaves from a palmyra tree." It is not certain what these are for.

4: "A wealth of food" follows D. for *ārpatam kaṇ eṉa.* The exact meaning of this is not certain, but the context demands something similar to what D. says.

6: "Dried out from the sweat of fatigue" is the translation of *vēr uḻantu ulaṟi.* It is difficult to interpret *uḻantu.* D. says it means "running down," a meaning not supported by the Lexicon (which says instead "to suffer, to experience pain or fatigue"). Thus D. believes it means "with sweat running down and drying." We have taken it to mean "with sweat drying [because I have] experienced fatigue."

10: This tree is not given in the Lexicon.

12: "Fruit" is added at D.'s suggestion.

13: "Bat" is D's interpretation of *paṟavai,* which can also mean "bird."

15–19: This is the standard comparison of battle to harvest. See the notes to 369.1–17.

25: "Axe" is D's meaning for *eḵkam*—any weapon of steel. "Weeps from exhaustion" is the translation of *aḻukural ayara.* D. says this means "she sings songs in a weeping voice and dances," taking *ayar* in its meaning as "play," but the usual meaning of the verb is "to be exhausted," which is how we have taken it. (See, however, poem 371, line 22, where it definitely means "dance.")

25–26: Literally, "she surrounds herself with the lined intestines of fearless men that are mixed with her legs."

371

2: D. says the tree here is the margosa tree referred to in line 9.

5: "Carrying bag" is the translation of *kalappai:* "hold-all for keeping musical instruments and other articles" (Lexicon).

12: "Drum" is the translation of *muraicu,* a variant of *muracu,* "royal drum."

14: "I beating" is added for clarity.

18: "Kettledrums" is the translation of *paṇai,* a drum used in farming areas.

19: "Are stacked" is literally "are opposite," "are there in front [of one]."

22: "Boar" is the translation of *kaḷiṟu,* which can also mean a bull elephant.

23: "Weaves" is added for clarity.

24: "Dances and sings" is the translation of *ayara,* defined by the Lexicon as "perform."

372

The structure of this poem is remarkable. It starts out "The whole reason I came . . . beating . . . my drum." This is followed by a vocative that spans ten lines. Then after the vocative, the poem ends "is to take home your necklace." This gives the poem a tension that is not resolved until the very end.

6: "Flesh" is the translation of *pulavu,* a word whose etymology probably connects it with *pulai,* "impurity," "pollution," and *pulaiyaṉ,* an untouchable.

9: "Sacrificial priestess" is the translation of *vēṇmāḷ.* This usually means a woman of the Vēḷir clan, but here it must come from *vēḷ,* "to sacrifice," even though the meaning "sacrificial priestess" is not mentioned in the Lexicon.

12: "Fresh water" is the translation of *putu nīr,* but UVS reads *pūta nīr,* "spirit water," for this.

3–12: This is the war sacrifice. D. says it is offered by demons to the goddess Kālī, but the poem does not indicate that. It is not at all clear why the sacrifice is compared to a wedding. The water poured at the wedding seals the contract between the two families, but the meaning of "burning mouth" is not clear. I (George Hart) have elsewhere hypothesized that the ceremony solemnizes a sort of wedding between the victorious king and his dead enemies and that its purpose is to unite the souls of the two so that the enemy spirits do not come back to haunt the living king (Hart 1975, p. 36).

373

7–8: "At the touch of earth" is added for clarity.

12: "To take their own lives" is added at D.'s suggestion. He says that as young widows, they would die voluntarily in the rite of suttee. His interpretation seems justified, as otherwise their not going into the courtyard does not make sense.

17: "Fathers and elder brothers" is the translation of *tamar,* literally, "their own people."

18: "He did not charge with the sword" is not in UVS's edition. It may be corrupt, or its meaning may be clarified by the lines lost immediately before it. D. says that since he is fighting an elephant, he does not attack with a sword but, rather, uses a spear.

17–23: This part apparently concerns a hero in the army that opposed the Cōḻa king and whom the Cōḻa king wounded. D. says he has become enraged when his own king has fled and that he is wounded by the Cōḻa king.

24–26: This is the standard image: piles of corpses are like haystacks that are then destroyed so that the grain can be threshed. The word for "trampled flat" usually means "threshed."

27: "Poets" is added for clarity. It is possible that this refers not only to poets but to others as well who receive booty from the battle. Technically, one should distinguish among drummers (*kiṇaiyar*), bards, (*pāṇar*) and poets (*pulavar*). The first two were low caste, and the poets were upper-caste people who wrote imitations of the works of the drummers and bards. The poems of the *Puṟanāṉūṟu* are such imitations by poets. All three groups probably received booty from battle.

29: "Glorify" is literally "saying 'may they glow.'" The same word was used earlier ("May the broad field glow.")

374

7–8: That is, he was singing *kuṟiñci* songs. These are love songs that take place in the mountains (where *kuṟiñci* grows) and deal with a hidden love.

11: "Who have borne" is added at D.'s suggestion.

16–18: Literally, "Are you as generous as Āy Aṇṭiraṉ? You shine uselessly in the sky."

375

2: "Sagging posts" is the translation of *olku nilaip pal kāl*. D. connects *olku nilai* with "common ground," meaning "whose state is in disrepair." This is more or less what the other adjectives applied here to "common ground" mean.

4: "Sharp-edged" is literally "with rasplike edge," *ara vāy*.

6: "One after another" is the translation of *ūḻ muṟai*. This may also imply an order of precedence: "in due order of status."

18: "And even if they did" is added for clarity.

376

3: The drum is here called a *teṭāri* rather than a *taṭāri*. We have kept *taṭāri* for clarity.

7: "Presence" is added for clarity.

11: "Guest," *viruntiṉaṉ*, may also mean "newcomer."

12: "Deserving of our compassion" is the translation of *aḷiyaṉ*. It can also mean "to be pitied."

16: Literally, "on that very night, he gave."

18–19: "I would never consider begging" is added for clarity.

19: "Channel" can also mean "sluice."

21–22: Literally, the voice of my small *kiṇai* drum.

377

6: "Offerings of boiled rice" is *avi,* from the Sanskrit *havis,* "(1) offerings made to the gods in sacrificial fire; (2) food; (3) boiled rice" (Lexicon).

10–11: "Ready to give," literally, "cupped." The idea is that his hand is cupped to hold the gifts he will bestow.

12: "Poets" is added for clarity.

25–30: This is the Indian four-part army (Sanskrit *caturaṅga*): elephants, cavalry, chariots, and infantry.

378

2: "Coastal people of the south" is the translation of *teṉ paratavar.* According to the Lexicon, *paratavar* can refer to either the name of a Tamil dynasty or the inhabitants of the maritime tract. D. says they live on the shore of the Pandya country in the south.

5: "Spurs" is the translation of *pari vaṭimpu. Pari* means "horse." For *vaṭimpu,* the Lexicon gives "(1) border; edge, as of garment; blade, as of a knife; (2) extremity, as of the foot; (3) eaves, edge of a roof; (4) lever; (5) mark, scar; (6) reproach, blame." D. says this means spurs: "An iron (implement) worn on the foot to make a horse go fast."

8: For "Righteousness," see the notes to 44.11–12.

9: "That it almost broke" is the translation of *iriya,* "so it spoiled." D. says this means its eye is torn. For "Vañci," see the notes to 15.23.

10: "Unrestrained attack" is an interpretation of *eñcā marapiṉ,* literally, "whose nature (*marapu*) is [of] unrestrained [strength]."

19: "Scooped up" is literally "saw."

21: This story, although in keeping with the spirit of several passages in the *Rāmāyaṇa* concerning the amusing ignorance of the monkeys, does not appear in that work. It is, of course, a variant on the episode, found in the *Vālmīki Rāmāyaṇa* and elsewhere, of the monkeys recovering Sīta's jewelry, perhaps influenced by a little bit of monkey business in which Hanumān takes Sītā's *śiromaṇi,* her hair ornament, as a token and puts it on his little finger. Our thanks to Robert Goldman for this information.

379

2: "And praise you" is added for clarity.

4: According to the Lexicon, this is not Sri Lanka (often called Ilaṅkai in Tamil) but a town in the Tamil country of India.

6–8: Literally, "[they,] wishing to go on vigorously reaping, think the humped back of a tortoise . . . is a stone, and they whet the blades on that."

14: "Runs to suck" is D.'s suggestion for *tūum*. The exact meaning of this is unclear. It is, literally, a child who comes (? *tūu*) to where his faultless mother is." D. suggests that since the mother is faultless, her breast flows with milk spontaneously, without the child's even asking for it. But UVS has a different reading: *tāyil tūvāk kuḻavi pōla,* a phrase also found in poem 4.18. It means "like a motherless child that has not eaten" (according to the old commentary). Even though D.'s reading is problematic, it seems to fit the poem much better than UVS's. It should be kept in mind that D. had the advantage of several manuscripts unavailable to UVS.

16: "Softly" is the translation of *aitu tōṉṟum,* literally, "fine," "attenuated," "soft."

380

4: "Pāṇṭiyaṉs" is the translation of *teṉṉavar*—"the southern ones," a name of the Pandyas.

16: Because so much of this poem has been lost, its overall meaning is unclear.

381

1–3: Here we follow D. He says the milk concoction is something resembling *pāyasam* (milk mixed with sugar or honey, rice, raisins, and cardomom), and the sweet is made of treacle.

3: "Perfectly measured and mingled for taste" is the translation of *aḷavupu kalantu.*

11–12: "Their rhythms faster than fingers snapping" is D.'s interpretation of *viral vicai tavirkkum aralaiyil pāṇiyiṉ.*

21: "Only think a little while about them but think hard" is D.'s interpretation of *ciṟu naṉi oru vaḻip paṭarka.* One could also take *paṭarka* as meaning "go," in which case it would mean something like "just go on your way." In other words, "Realize what I say, and then go."

26: We have translated "*irum kōḷ*" as "noble principles." D. apparently understands this as "great grasp" and takes the whole as "he who had a great grasp (*kaippiṭi*) and unshakable resolve." This makes no sense, especially as "grasp" is not given as a meaning in the Lexicon for "*kōḷ*" but "principle" is.

382

1: Here, "bards" is the translation of *porunar,* for which the Lexicon says, "(1) one who dances and sings on the battlefield and on the threshing-floor; (2) actor, dancer." The word can also mean a warrior, hero, king, and it is used in that way in line 2 of the poem ("The warrior lord . . .").

2–12: This actually contains a quotation within a quotation: "Your bards . . . are singing, 'We sing him saying, "the warrior . . . may his deeds long endure!" To drive . . . foods.'"

5: D. suggests that this is an "ocean army," that is, one that goes abroad and gathers booty. But the comparison of an army to an ocean is commonplace in these poems.

8: "Deeds" is the translation of *tāḷ*, literally, "efforts"; this can also mean "feet."

12: "Humble people" is the translation of *ciṟār*—"small people," probably with a connotation of low caste. In a modern folk song that I (George Hart) have collected, *ciṉṉāṉ*, "the little one" is used to refer to a leather worker. Bards and drummers were low caste. This word usually means "children." See also poem 291.

15: "Grant us gifts" is the translation of *viṭumati*. This may also mean "give us your leave [to go after giving us gifts]." "Gifts" is added for clarity.

16: "The skin of" is added for clarity at D.'s suggestion.

17: The belief is that snakes hear through their eyes. Cobras are said to have a jewel on their heads.

18–19: "Knows" is the translation of *aṟiya*. D. says the implied subject of "know" is "good men." We have taken it as "everyone."

20: The sola pith is usually invoked because it is so insubstantial and weighs so little. We have taken a slight liberty here with the syntax in order to make the simile understandable. The Tamil says, "Everyone knows this dark *kiṇai* whose clear-sounding eye is [as insubstantial] as a twig of sola pith is mine. I will sing, in the courts of other kings, of the chariots you have vanquished, and make your enemies tremble every time they hear me, just as when I strike with the slender little stick that reverberates and is tied next to the eye [the drum trembles]."

23: "Lashed within my drum" is the translation of *kaṇ akattu yātta*, literally, "lashed inside the eye." Presumably, the stick was lashed to the top of the drum.

383

9–10: According to D., the point of this image is that the cup is shaped like the opening waterlily bud.

11: "So well embroidered with gleaming flowers it seemed a single flow" is the translation of *iḻai aṇi vārā oṇ pūṅ kaliṅkam*, which D. says means *neyyappaṭṭa iḻaikaḷiṉ varicai aṟiya iyalāta oḷḷiya pūvēlai ceyyappaṭṭa āṭai*, "A garment made with bright flower designs in which you could not distinguish the rows of sewn-on ornaments [since they looked as if they were an integral part of the garment and not sewn on]."

14: "Loyal" is the translation of *kaṟpuṭai*, "possessing *kaṟpu* (chastity)." See the notes to 361.15.

24–25: Literally, "Why should I be troubled about the position of Venus [*veḷḷi* means both Venus and silver]?" Venus rising in the south was thought to be an evil omen.

384

The situation of this poem is not entirely clear. Apparently, the drummer is addressing some other king and telling him how supportive the ruler of Karumpa-ṉūr is. D. says he is addressing "good men," but that does not fit the use of "O greatness" (*peruma*) in line 11.

4: "Strewn with rocks" is the translation of *vaṉpāl,* defined by the Lexicon as "(1) hard, rocky soil; (2) desert tract, barren and sterile ground; (3) hilly tract; (4) rising ground, mound."

9: According to D., *pūṅkaḷ* means "with flowers floating in it." But in his comments, he says it was a custom for the ancients to make a garland of ginger and other flowers and to put it around the pot of toddy.

14–15: Literally, "even though I lack those many things, which are not established in my house, he does not lack them."

22: "The fine leaves we have eaten from are folded and flung away still filled with food" is D.'s translation of *uṇta naṉkalam peytu nuṭakkavum. Kalam* usually means "vessel." *Nuṭakku* can mean "bend, fold." It is customary after eating to fold one's leaf (which serves as a plate) and have it discarded.

386

10–17: In this section, some of the major landscapes of the Tamil country are invoked: the paddy land (*marutam*), the forest/meadow land (*mullai*), and the ocean tract (*neytal*). A king had to be especially powerful for his kingdom to include many kinds of landscapes.

15: D. says these people are women.

19: Porunaṉ has two meanings: warrior or hero, and a caste of actors and dancers. Here, the singer plays on the two meanings. "By caste" has been added for clarity. Literally, "we are *porunaṉs* of such a good land, we who are *porunaṉs* who do not fight (*porāa*)."

23: Literally, "let it stay in the south, not staying there for a short while (*kuṟu-kātu*) but remaining there long." Venus rising in the south was thought to be a harbinger of drought.

25: "Projects" is the translation of *tāḷ,* literally, "efforts" or "feet."

387

4: "Tortoise" is the translation of *vayal āmai:* "field turtle or tortoise." The "field" seems to indicate that the animal is a tortoise, not a turtle, and so we have not translated it separately.

6: "Musicians" is the translation of *vāṇar,* which the Lexicon defines as "resident, one who pursues a profession or calling." D. says that here it refers to the poets, bards, performers, and the like who amuse the king.

11: "Powdered lime" (*nīṟu*) can also mean "dust."

12: "Ornaments marked with flowers" is the translation of *pūm poṟi.* D. says this means a *paṭṭam* with flowers inscribed on it. A *paṭṭam* is an ornament usually worn on the forehead. Among its many meanings, *poṟi* can mean a "sign" or "badge."

12–13: "Who move dispersed in various formations" is literally "are spread variously and move."

16: This sentence may be corrupt in the manuscripts—it does not seem to fit the poem. It occurs immediately before a section that has been lost.

26: "Fields with farmers who form part of the property" is the translation of *maṉaik kaḷamaroṭu kaḷam.* The exact meaning of this is unclear. Perhaps the "house" is the house of the landlord, and the farmers are attached to that.

27: Literally, "he gave in waking, quickly, so I was confused and thought it a dream."

29: "The name of" is added for clarity at D.'s suggestion.

31–32: "Without a moment's hesitation, they will send their tribute here to him" is the translation of *ivaṉ viṭuvar mātō neṭitē nillā.* D. says this means that if someone says the name of Celvak Kaṭuṅkō Vāḻiyātaṉ, they will honor that person and, without delay, give him leave to come here (to where the king is). This seems forced. *Viṭu* can mean both "give leave to go" and "give." "Tribute" is supplied for clarity in our translation.

33: "May he live on for more eons" is displaced in the poem, coming in the sentence "He is that lord filled with love." It is meant to be construed as we have translated it.

34: "The city of Vañci named for the tree" is the translation of *pul ilai vañci.* Here we follow UVS. D. says this means "the Vañci that is not (*pul*) the leaf." The Lexicon shows no such usage for *pul.*

388

1: Venus rising in the south was an omen of drought.

3: D. says this is a Porunaṉ playing a *taṭāri* drum. The Tamil says it is a Kiṇaimakaṉ playing a *paṟai* (a generic word for drum).

9–10: This is opaque. At D.'s suggestion, we have supplied "elephant." Probably the poets are compared with kings (as in poem 47), and their contests with one another are compared with the battles presided over by kings. Just as the king has an elephant to help him fight, the poets have an "elephant"—their true words. And the trunk and tusks of that "elephant" are the penetrating books of the poets and their tongues.

13: Teṉṉavaṉ ("the southern one") is a name of the Pandya king.

14: "To be rung by those in need" is added for clarity. Vaḻuti is a title of the Pandya kings. The relationship between the second and first parts of this poem (which are separated by several lines that have been lost) is unclear. In the first part, the poet sings a chieftain named Paṇṇaṉ. In the second, he sings of the Pandyan king.

389

4–5: "Silver planet . . . in ill omen" is the translation of *ēlā veṇpoṉ*. *Veṇpoṉ* (silver iron or metal) means "Venus." D. says *ēlā veṇpoṉ* together means "Venus." But *ēlā* means "not suitable" and so would seem to mean "unfavorable." "Turns south" follows D.'s reading *pōku uṟu,* in which "to the south" must be supplied, and UVS reads "does battle (with other planets)"—*pōr uṟu*.

5: "Musician" is the translation of *porunaṉ*.

8: "Ātaṉuṅkaṉ" is added for clarity.

9–12: D. says the point of this image is that just as the elephant calf is taken from its mother, so Ātaṉuṅkaṉ has been taken by death from everyone who loves him.

12–13: "Who control yourself and" is added for clarity.

390

3: "Coming . . . in need" is the translation of *ārvalar.* D. takes this with its other meaning: "those with love," but UVS takes it as we have.

5: "Pear tree" is the translation of *cerunti,* which can also mean a kind of sedge and Indian houndsberry.

3–5: This section is problematic. It is not certain whether "where cowherds . . . live" modifies "courtyard," "festival," or "forest." The section translated "others . . ." (*vaḷarum maṟavai neñcattu āyilāḷar*—UVS reads *ayivāḷar* for the last word) is obscure. D. says it means "those who have carefully chosen houses (*āy il*) and in whose hearts valor is great." We have chosen to take *āy* in its most common meaning of "cowherd"; thus *āyilāḷar* means literally "those who are not cowherds" and so "others." V. S. Rajam suggests that *āy* may mean "protection" and that these two groups may go with "*arvalar*": "In the broad city, protected so that while virtuous-hearted cowherds and those who do not have any protectors with hearts in which valor increases and suppliants may enter, [enemy] kings cannot approach even in dreams." This interpretation is somewhat forced, since the section about the courtyard intervenes between "cowherds and those who do not have any protectors" and "suppliants."

7: "Hard enough to shatter it" is the translation of *iriya.* D. says this means "hard enough to tear it." See also line 9 of poem 378.

11: "Musician" is the translation of *porunaṉ*. "Little hair" is the translation of *pun̲ talai.* This is difficult to translate. When it refers to children and cow elephants, we have usually rendered it as "tender-headed." It denotes vulnerability.

12: "Is in a sorry state" is the translation of *aḷiyan̲,* literally, "is to be pitied."

15: "Splendid flower"—we have translated *tirumalar* literally. The Lexicon says it means "lotus" (probably because it is the tower where Śrī, Tamil Tiru, sits). D. and UVS say it means a *pakan̲r̲ai* flower, and UVS cites poem 393, lines 17–18: "you should clothe me then in a wide garment with folds like the petals of newly blossoming *pakan̲r̲ai* flowers."

16: "Anguish" is the translation of *pulampu.* One of the meanings the Lexicon gives for this is "grief, affliction." It can also mean loneliness, and that is how D. takes it: to dispel their loneliness as they waited in separation from me. *Amṛta* is the drink that makes one immortal. In these poems, it is often used to signify food or drink that is very precious, life-giving, or sweet.

20: "Fine paddy" is the translation of *cennel,* which the Lexicon defines as " a kind of superior paddy of yellowish hue." "The color of the *vēṅkai* flower filled with nectar" is literally "which looked like the flower of the *vēṅkai* (when) wet inside."

21: According to UVS and D., *pakaṭu taru* means "grown with the help of plowing oxen." It could also mean "brought by oxen."

22: D. says "best of waters"—*talai nīr*—refers to the fact that the water is still pure after coming down from a mountain, since this land is the first thing it touches. He translates it as "land that is rich because of the finest water where in the places where people get water, flowers that bloomed on the mountain are brought down and washed onto the banks."

26: It is commonplace to compare someone's generosity to a cloud, which rains down without thinking of recompense. Here, the poet suggests that even those who blame the clouds, which are usually paragons of generosity, can receive help from the king. He is, in other words, even more generous than the clouds.

391

2: "Slice entire cuts of meat into pieces for eating" is the translation of *tiruntā mūri parantu paṭak keṇṭi,* literally, "cut and eat, as it was spread out, unprepared (*tiruntā*) meat." D. says that "*mūri*" means "flesh, meat." But the Lexicon gives only "buffalo, ox" for that word, and so it may mean "who ate . . . buffalo (meat)."

4: "Raised with plowing oxen"—see the note to poem 390, line 21. This could also mean "brought by oxen."

5: "Scraped the sky" is the translation of *mukaṭu ur̲a,* literally, "so they touched the highest part." *Mukaṭu* means "highest part," "roof of the heavens."

9–10: Or "which has ancient clans and [also has] so many excellences (*paṇpin̲a*) that we never think of leaving."

11–12: "Aware of me . . . saying" is the translation of *nin̲ uṇarntu ar̲iyunar en̲ uṇarntu kūṟa*. D. says this means "they who who knew and understood you, understanding me, said [to me]," but this does not fit the quotation.

13: "Musician" is the translation of *porunaṉ*.

16: In his text, D. has *nuḻai*, "enter," but in the gloss he has "*tuḻaii*," and he says it means "search" (*tuḻavi*), taking it with the crane. The order, however, shows that the verb goes with "fish," in which case only *nuḻai* makes sense. These lines are lost in UVS's manuscripts.

17: "Tidal pool" is the translation of *kaḻi:* "(1) backwater, shallow seawaters, salt river, marsh; (2) salt-pan" (Lexicon).

17: "Goes to sleep," *cēkkum,* can also mean "stay," which is how D. takes it. But it seems clearly meant to go with the next lines, the crane's sleeping happily after eating being compared to that of the king.

18: "At home" added for clarity.

21: A *vēli* is 6.74 acres.

392

1: "Curving ornament" is UVS's suggestion for *koṭum pūṇ*. D. says this means a "curving garland," but *pūṇ* usually means "ornament"; its meaning as "garland" is not given in the Lexicon. UVS cites poem 200, *viḷaṅku maṇik koṭum pūṇ,* "who wears curving ornaments that bear radiant jewels!"

4: D. says this means it is round like the footprint of an elephant. Obviously, the size is also a factor in the comparison.

5: Literally, "I beat [it], saying. . . ."

8: "Demonic spirits" is the translation of *aṇaṅku. Aṇaṅku* can mean a malevolent spirit or simply the quality of inflicting pain. Often, as probably here, it means a spirit or spirits that cause anguish and suffering.

9: Literally, "a flood of blood and fat."

10–11: These are grains that grow in poorer areas, mainly mountains. D. says the point of this practice is to make the enemy's land into a wasteland. "New fields" is added for clarity. The idea is that the king wins victories every day and then ceremonially plants the fields where he has won his victories with the grains found in poor areas.

14: "Duckweed" is the translation of *pāci.* The Lexicon says this may mean "moss," "lichen," "duckweed," "seaweed," or "sola pith."

16: "Costly thread" is the translation of *nuṇ nūl,* literally, "subtle thread."

18: "The planets" are *kōḷ mīṉ,* literally, "stars that are planets." D. says that "since planets are bigger than stars, they are compared to the golden dish."

19: "One after another" is the translation of *ūṇ muṟai.* D. says this implies the proper order: he gave the proper foods for the first, middle, and last courses.

21: See poem 99 for this story. *Amṛta* is the drink that makes one immortal.

In these poems, it is often used to signify food or drink that is very precious, life-giving, or sweet.

393

1: "Beginning" is D.'s interpretation of *pati;* a meaning is not given in the Lexicon.

2: "Of my mind" is added at D.'s suggestion.

3: "Young wife who has been with me a long time" is D.'s suggestion for *kuṟum neṭum tuṇai,* literally, "short long companion."

4: "Clans" is the translation of *kuṭi.* D. says these clans or families are Vēḷāḷars, who live by agriculture. Vēḷāḷars are usually landowners.

5: "In due order of their rank" or "one after the other"—*muṟaiyē.*

9: "The goad of desire impelling me" is the translation of *ulai nacai tuṇaiyā,* literally, "with desire that causes pain as a companion [or help]."

10: "Wealth of" is added at D.'s suggestion.

12: "With food" is added for clarity. Then as now, Tamils ate with their hand.

13: "Meat" is the translation of *mūri,* which the Lexicon says means "buffalo."

15: "Is split" is added for clarity.

16: D. says the fork of the serpent's tongue is especially pronounced when it lays eggs.

21: "When the dance is done" is added for clarity at D.'s suggestion. D. has *olkal,* "becoming weak," for UVS's *alkul,* "yoni." His reading would be "when everything withers just as a dancing girl grows weak [after dancing]," and UVS's reading seems preferable.

394

Kaṭainilai, the name of the *tuṟai* for this poem, means literally "The state [or standing] at the outer entrance." The colophon apparently means that all the poems that have this theme belong to the *tiṇai* of *pāṭāṇṭiṇai.*

5: "Of going to him" is added for clarity.

7: According to D., "softly" is the translation of *teḷirppa.* The Lexicon says *teḷir* means "to sound" and says *teḷiral* is a loud sound or high pitch.

9: Literally, "I sang an unflowering *vañci* of his father." *Vañci* can either be a flower or a kind of ode. To indicate that the flower is not meant, the poet says "unflowering *vañci.*" See the notes to 15.23.

12–13: "Tossing its body in anger" is the translation of *veñciṉam,* literally, "hot rage."

14: D. says it is too small for the bard's status or excellence (in singing) (*varicai*).

395

1: "We are . . . drummers" is the translation of *kiṇaiyēm*—"we play the *kiṇai* drum."

2: For "Righteousness," see the notes to 44.11–12.

3: "His father" is added for clarity at D.'s suggestion.

5: Uṟantai was the Chola capital.

8: "He whose favor is hard to gain" is the translation of *peṟaṟku ariya,* "difficult to obtain." We have taken this to mean "difficult to obtain as a patron."

9–22: By position, all these descriptions of the countryside could modify either Piṭavūr or Uṟantai. Both UVS and D. say they should be applied to Piṭavūr.

12: All three of these birds are called "*kōḻi,*" which may mean either "hen" or "cock." We have taken the liberty of marking genders, as that is usually what is involved when one bird responds to the calling of another bird. The point of this is that the kingdom contains more than one kind of landscape. "Tame hen" in line 9 is literally "house *kōḻi.*"

14: "From mountain fields" is added for clarity. The women chase the parrots away so they will not eat the grain.

14–16: The parrots are on mountain fields (on the *kuṟiñci* tract), and the birds that fly up from marshes are near the seashore (the *neytal* tract). Again, the kingdom includes more than one landscape.

17: "Fine fields" is the translation of *meṉpulam*—soil of paddy land (*marutam*).

19: "Rougher ground" is the translation of *vaṉpulam.* D. says this means forest land (*mullai*). Once again, the poet stresses that the kingdom contains diverse landscapes.

20: "Scabbardfish" is the translation of *vāḷai,* which can also mean "shark." "Yesterday's rice" is the translation of *paḻañcōṟu,* which the Lexicon defines as "boiled rice preserved in water and kept overnight."

22: "Strained toddy made from raw rice" is the translation of *aviḻ nelliṉ ariyal. Ariyal* is strained toddy. *Aviḻ* means "boiled rice, grain of boiled rice," and *nel* means "paddy," that is, uncooked rice. *Aviḻ* as a verb means "become loose, fall." Perhaps the toddy is made of grains of paddy that have fallen down in the process of harvesting.

24: "The heat" is added for clarity.

25: It is not sure what "sweet voiced" modifies, since that part has been lost.

27: "My concerns" is the translation of *uṟavu.* This could also mean "love," "relationship."

30–31: "Woman . . . as lovely as Lakṣmī" is the translation of *poṉ pōl maṭantai,* which can also mean "woman like gold."

36–37: "Blazing stars flash across the sky" is the translation of *mika vāṉuḷ eri tōṉṟiṉum,* literally, "if much fire appears in the sky."

37: "The constellation of the reservoir smokes with a comet"—it is not certain what this means. The Tamil is *kuḷamīṉoṭu tāḷ pukaiyiṉum. Kuḷam* means a "tank" (or "reservoir") and is apparently a constellation. *Tāḷ* means "foot" but can also mean "comet." Perhaps it means a comet emits its smoky light in the constellation of *kuḷam.*

38: "Green pieces of fried vegetables and meat" is the translation of *pacuṅ kaṇ karuṉaic cūṭṭoṭu.* D. says that *karuṉai* ("any preparation that is fried," according to the Lexicon) is the same as *porikkaṟi* ("seasoned curry prepared without tamarind"). *Cūṭṭu* can be anything hot, but D. takes it as cooked meat.

396

2: "Drums" is the translation of *paṟai,* the generic word for drum.

10: "Flower wine" is D.'s suggestion for *naṉaikkaḷ.*

13: "Is heard" is the translation of *tāṅkuntu.* D. says this means "the melody is played (*icaikkappaṭum*)," but the Lexicon does not give this meaning. We have followed D., as there is no satisfactory meaning given by the Lexicon for this context. For *kuravai,* see the notes to 22.22.

16: "Vēḷir" is the translation of *vēḷ,* which can also mean "petty chieftain."

24: "For us" and "at will" are added for clarity.

32: "Rain" is the translation of *māri,* which can mean both "cloud" and "rain." The life-giving qualities of the rain are meant here, and that is how we have translated it. The poet means the sky is filled with rain clouds.

33: "Long strings of fine gems" is the translation of *nirai cāl naṉkalaṉ alki.* D. takes *nirai* as meaning "rows [of elephants]," but the primary meaning of this word is "row" or "series."

397

5: "That spiral to the right" is the translation of *valam puri.* Most conches spiral to the left; those that spiral to the right were (and are) considered extremely auspicious.

9–10: "A garland of many plaits" is the translation of *pala kōḷ cey tār.* D. says this indicates the garland was made with many various kinds of workmanship. The Lexicon gives neither of these meanings for *kōḷ.* We take our interpretation from the meaning "cluster," and D. apparently takes his from the meaning "nature."

20: D. says "like" for our "alongside." The original is *tīyōṭu,* "with the fires"; D.'s interpretation seems unjustified.

21: For "Righteousness," see the notes to 44.11–12.

22: *Tīvu,* "island," can also mean "distant country."

29: "Handsome" is literally "straight" (*tiruntu*). This may refer to the king's righteousness and straightforwardness.

398

5: "Knowing their art" is the translation of *kaṭaṉ aṟintu,* literally, "knowing their duty." D. glosses this as *muṟaimai aṟintu,* "knowing the proper way."

9: "Sat" is supplied. The literal syntax is "city of Vañcaṉ who, [beneath] a pavilion, pays."

15: Literally, "may you be a state [of being] for us which cannot be pushed away"—*emakkut taḻḻā nilaiyai ākiyar.*

16: "For the little I had done he showed his joy" is the translation of *ciṟitiṟkup peritu uvantu*—"being greatly happy for little." "Little" and "great" are contrasted in the Tamil.

23–24: "Fried venison . . . and elephant yams" is the translation of *māṉ vaṟai karuṇai.* D. says this is just "fried venison"—apparently, he takes *karuṇai* as "meat." This meaning is not given in the Lexicon, which says it means "elephant yam."

399

2–4: According to D., the laborers get drunk in the evening, pass out during the night, and then wake up in the morning and eat old rice. The point of this is apparently that here even old rice is considered delicious food because of the richness of the country.

5: "Fill their plates with yesterday's rice, whole grains cooked soft"—this is quite difficult to construe. The Tamil is *mūḻppap peyta muḻu aviḻp puḻukkal.*

6: "To mix with" is the translation of *iṉaṉoṭu viraii.* It is not certain what is meant by *iṉaṉ.*

11: "More rice"—it is unclear whether this is meant to be pounded rice that is added to the old rice or whether it is another dish. We have added "more" for clarity. "White pot" is the translation of *veḻḻulai,* which, according to D., means a pot in which rice is mixed with old rice water and is not put on the fire. The Lexicon does not have any such meaning. The original has only one lacuna; we have put in two because it is not clear what part of the description is missing.

16: "Thin" is D.'s suggestion for *pāval.* This usually means "balsam pear," and if so, it would be a "sour mix of tamarind and balsam pear."

17: "Drummer woman" is the translation of *kiṇaimakaḷ.*

19: "Why are you standing there" is the translation of *eṉṉē,* literally, "what." D. thinks it means, "What is your good fate!" that is, "lucky you."

20: "Hero among heroes"—the order here has been changed for effect in English; in the original, this is third in the list. D. says *maḻḻar maḻḻaṉ* means "agriculturalist of agriculturalists," but a more common meaning of *maḻḻaṉ* is "warrior."

21: For "Martial Courage," see the notes to 39.10.

23: *Amṛta* is the drink that makes one immortal. In these poems, it is often used to signify food or drink that is very precious, life-giving, or sweet.

34: "Many carriages" is the translation of *paṉṉirai ūrtiyoṭu,* literally, "many herds with vehicles." D. says this means "many herds of cattle together with bulls that are fit for being hitched [to vehicles]." The Lexicon gives only "vehicle" for *ūrti.*

400

1: "My drum," literally, "my instrument." The Kiṇaimakaṉ, who narrates this poem, plays a *taṭāri* drum, which is elsewhere compared to the moon (see poem 371).

4: "Dark" is added for clarity. V. S. Rajam suggests the drum may be covered by a light skin in the middle surrounded by a darker skin—hence the comparison to the full moon in the ocean; D. says the point of comparison is that the drum is round.

5: "Majesty," or "his lineage," is the translation of *marapu.*

10–13: D. changes the order and construes "He put on a new garment, and, looking at my waist [and seeing how glorious it looked now, gave] excellent, precious stones." There is only one lacuna here, but the sense in English is as if there were two.

23: "Brahmins" is added at D.'s suggestion. The original is "sacrificial posts filled with sacred lore [*kēḷvi* is probably a translation of Sanskrit *śruti*]."

APPENDIX A Guide to the Contents of the Puṟanāṉūṟu

At first glance, the poems of the *Puṟanāṉūṟu* seem to be arranged in an arbitrary way. On closer analysis, it is clear that the anthologizer put related poems together into different sections. He or she did not, however, adopt a coherent principle of organization: some poems are grouped together by theme, others by author, and some by story. The following outline shows how the poems are grouped.

Poem	Content
1	Invocation
Poems to or about kings of one of the three great dynasties (Chera, Chola, Pandyan)	
2–64	Praise of kings
65–66	Death of the king, facing north to die (see notes to 65.11)
67	Messenger poem
68–70	Sending a bard to a king
71–73	King bragging he will defeat the enemy
74	King complaining about his treatment as a captive
75	Good king contrasted with bad king
76–78	King overcoming insurmountable odds
79–82	Speed of fighting
83–85	Nakkaṇṇaiyār's love for the Chola king
Groups or cycles by particular poets, often for their patrons	
86	Mother describing her warrior son
87–104	Poems by the poetess Auvaiyār to her patron Atiyamāṉ

105–120	The story of the poet Kapilar and the king Vēḷ Pāri (see the notes to 105)
121–124	Kapilar singing other kings
125–126	On King Malaiyamāṉ
127–135	The poet Uṟaiyūr Ēṇiccēri Muṭamōciyār singing Āy
136	Tuṟaiyūr Ōṭaikiḻār singing Āy
137–140	Various poets singing Nāñcil Vaḷḷuvaṉ
141–147	Various poets singing Vaiyāvik Kōpperum Pēkaṉ, who abandoned his wife, Kaṇṇaki
148–150	Vaṉparaṇar singing Kaṇṭīrak Kōpperunaḷḷi
151	On Iḷaṅkaṇṭīrakkō, the son of Kaṇṭīrak Kōpperunaḷḷi
152–153	Vaṉparaṇar singing Valvilōri
154–156	Mōcikīraṉār singing Koṇkāṉaṅkiḻāṉ
157	The poetess Kuṟamakaḷ Iḷaveyiṉiyār singing Ēṟaikkōṉ
158–161	A famous cycle in which Peruñcittiraṉār, whose name means "the great painter," describes the poverty of the poet and asks the king to be generous
162–165	Poems to and about Kumaṇaṉ (see the notes to 164)
166–170	Praise of kings
171–173	On the generosity of kings to bards

Ethical and moral poems

182–195	A section containing ethical and moral poems, many among the most famous poems in Tamil

Kings who are not generous

196–199	To a king who is slow to give
200–202	Kapilar and Pāri's daughters (see the notes to 105)
203–211	To a king who is slow to give

Death, (mostly) the death of kings

213–223	The story of Kōpperuñcōḻaṉ (see the notes to poem 213)
224–242	On the death of a king
243	A famous poem contrasting youth and old age
244	On the death of a king
245	A king lamenting the death of his wife
246–250	Widowhood, suttee
251–252	About an ascetic
253–256	New widow; a mother who has lost her son
257–259	Cattle raids
260–261	On the death of a king

262–263	Cattle raids
264–265	Hero who has become a memorial stone (see the notes to 232.5)
266	A bard's poverty
269	Drinking before a cattle raid
270–271	On the death of a king
271–272	Poems about the *nocci* flower
273–275	Combat
276–279	Poems about the mother of a dead hero
280–282	King/hero who is wounded or dead

War/combat poems

283–314

King who rules a poor area; his generosity

315–335

The ephemeral nature of life

336–355	War breaking out over a young girl who has just reached puberty: various kings want to marry her, but her people will not give her in marriage
356–367	The insubstantiality of the world, the inevitability of death

Drummer poems

368–400	A low-caste drummer (Kiṇaiyaṉ) coming to a king, often at dawn, and asking him for gifts

ABBREVIATIONS AND EDITIONS USED

We used two major editions of the *Puṟanāṉūṟu*. The first was published by the South India Saiva Siddhanta Works Publishing Society and was edited and annotated by Auvai Cu. Turaicāmip Piḷḷai (anglicized as Duraisamy Pillai). The second was published by the Kapīr Accukkūṭam and was edited by Dr. U. Ve. Cāminataiyar (U. V. Swaminathaier). Most of the time, we relied on the first of these because Duraisamy Pillai had more manuscripts at his disposal than did Swaminathaier, whose work was done earlier. We indicated in the notes when we followed Swaminathaier's readings. To disentangle difficult passages, we depended mostly on the old commentary when it exists and on Duraisamy Pillai when it does not.

We used the following abbreviations throughout:

D.: Duraisamy Pillai
UVS: U. V. Swaminathaier
OC: old commentary
The Lexicon: *The Tamil Lexicon*

ANNOTATED BIBLIOGRAPHY

PRIMARY SOURCES

Encyclopaedia of Tamil Literature (in Ten Volumes). Vol. 1. Madras: Institute of Asian Studies, 1990. The first volume in a very ambitious project.

Kalaikkalañciyam, 1954–68. The standard Tamil encyclopedia, especially useful for finding details about Tamil literature.

Pu̱ranā̱nū̱ru Mūlamum Uraiyum. Edited by U. Ve. Cāminātaiyar. 6th ed. Chennai: Kabir Publishing House, 1963. One of the two major editions of the text.

Pu̱ranā̱nū̱ru: 1–200 Pāṭṭukkaḷ. Edited by Auvai Cu. Turaicāmip Piḷḷai. 4th ed., 2 vols. Vol. 1. Chennai: South India Saiva Siddhanta Works Publishing Society, 1964. One of the two major editions of the text.

Pu̱ranā̱nū̱ru: 201–400 Pāṭṭukkaḷ. Edited by Auvai Cu. Turaicāmip Piḷḷai. 3d ed., 2 vols. Vol. 2. Chennai: South India Saiva Siddhanta Works Publishing Society, 1962. One of the two major editions of the text.

Tamil Lexicon. Madras: University of Madras, 1982. The standard Tamil-English dictionary.

Tamil Lexicon. Supplement. Madras: University of Madras, 1982.

SECONDARY SOURCES

Apte, V. S. *The Practical Sanskrit-English Dictionary*. Vols. 1–3. Poona: Prasad Prakashan, 1957. The most usable Sanskrit-English dictionary.

Buck, David C., and K. Paramasivam. *The Study of Stolen Love: A Translation of Kaḷaviyal e̱ṉra I̱raiya̱nār Akapporuḷ with Commentary by Nakkīra̱nār*. Edited by Terry Godlove. American Academy of Religion: Texts and Translations Series. Vol. 18. Atlanta: Scholars Press, 1997. An excellent and exhaustive annotated translation of this important Tamil text on aesthetics.

Chelliah, J. V. *Pattupattu: Ten Tamil Idylls.* Colombo: General Publishers, 1947. A complete translation into Victorian poetic English of the *Pattuppāṭṭu,* part of Sangam literature.

Cutler, Norman, and Paula Richman. *A Gift of Tamil.* New Delhi: American Institute of Indian Studies, 1992. Contains translations of various classical Tamil works.

Hart, George L. "Early Evidence for Caste in South India." In *Dimensions of Social Life: Essays in Honor of David B. Mandelbaum.* Edited by Paul Hockings. Berlin: Mouton Gruyter, 1987.

Hart, George L. "The Maṇikkuṟavaṉ Story: From Ritual to Entertainment." In *Another Harmony.* Edited by Stuart H. Blackburn and A. K. Ramanujan. Berkeley and Los Angeles: University of California, 1986.

Hart, George L. *The Poems of Ancient Tamil, Their Milieu and Their Sanskrit Counterparts.* Berkeley and Los Angeles: University of California Press, 1975.

Hart, George L. *Poets of the Tamil Anthologies: Ancient Poems of Love and War.* Princeton, N.J.: Princeton University Press, 1979.

Hart, George L. "Woman and the Sacred in Ancient Tamil Nad." *Journal of Asian Studies* 32, no. 2 (1973): 233–250.

Ilakkuvanar, Singaravel. *Tholkappiyam in English; with Critical Studies.* Madurai: "Kural Neri" Publishing House, 1963. One of two translations of this oldest Tamil work, a treatise on grammar and poetics.

Ilankovatikal, and R. Parthasarathy. *The Cilappatikaram of Ilanko Atikal: An Epic of South India.* New York: Columbia University Press, 1993. The best translation of the most important Tamil epic.

Jesudasan, C., and Hephzibah Jesudasan. *A History of Tamil Literature.* Calcutta: Y.M.C.A. Publishing House, 1961.

Kailasapathy, K. *Tamil Heroic Poetry.* Oxford: Clarendon Press, 1968.

Kampar, George L. Hart, and Hank Heifetz. *The Forest Book of the Ramayana of Kampaṉ.* Berkeley and Los Angeles: University of California Press, 1989. Translation of a section of the greatest work of Tamil literature, dating from the twelfth century C.E.

Kavuṇṭar, Irā. Teyvacikāmaṇi. *Puṟappāṭṭurai.* Pollacci: Shanti Trust, 1976.

Lord, Albert Bates. *The Singer of Tales.* Harvard Studies in Comparative Literature no. 24. Cambridge, Mass.: Harvard University Press, 1960.

Mahadevan, Iravatham. "Tamil Brahmi Inscriptions of the Sangam Age." In *Proceedings of the Second International Conference Seminar of Tamil Studies.* Edited by R. E. Asher. Madras: International Association of Tamil Research, 1971.

Mani, Vettam. 1975. *Purāṇic Encyclopedia: A Comprehensive Dictionary with Special Reference to the Epic and Purāṇic Literature.* Vol. 7, p. 922. Delhi: Motilal Banarsidass.

Marr, John Ralston. *The Eight Anthologies: A Study in Early Tamil Literature.* Madras: Institute of Asian Studies, 1985. An analysis of themes and poetics.
Meenakshisundaram, T. P. *Aesthetics of the Tamils.* Madras: Dr. S. Radhakrishnan Institute for Advanced Study in Philosophy, University of Madras, 1977.
Meenakshisundaram, T. P. *A History of Tamil Literature.* Annamalainagar: Annamalai University, 1965.
Nilakanta Sastri, K. A. *Aryans and Dravidians.* Ajmer (India): Sachin Publications, 1979.
Nilakanta Sastri, K. A. *The Culture and History of the Tamils.* Calcutta: Firma K. L. Mukhopadhyay, 1964.
Nilakanta Sastri, K. A. *Development of Religion in South India.* Bombay: Orient Longmans, 1963.
Nilakanta Sastri, K. A. *A History of South India from Prehistoric Times to the Fall of Vijayanagar.* Madras: Oxford University Press, 1976.
Pope, G. U. *Tamil Heroic Poems.* Madras: South India Saiva Siddhanta Works Publishing Society, Tinnevelly, 1973. Some poems from the *Pur̲anān̲ūr̲u* translated into Victorian English.
Rajam, V. S. "Caṅka Ilakkiyap Pur̲appāṭalkaḷum Pur̲apporuḷ Ilakkaṇamum." *Vaiyai* 4 (1974–75): 53–72.
Rajam, V. S. *A Reference Grammar of Classical Tamil Poetry: 150 B.C.–Pre-Fifth/Sixth Century A.D.* Philadelphia: American Philosophical Society, 1992. A study of the grammatical forms of classical Tamil. This book also contains an exhaustive description of the meters of classical Tamil.
Ramanujan, A. K. *Poems of Love and War: From the Eight Anthologies and the Ten Long Poems of Classical Tamil.* New York: Columbia University Press, 1985. Ramanujan's excellent translations from the Sangam anthologies.
Ramanujan, A. K., comp. *Speaking of Siva.* Harmondsworth: Penguin, 1973.
Ramanujan, A. K., and Nammāl̲vār. *Hymns for the Drowning: Poems for Visnu.* Princeton, N.J.: Princeton University Press, 1981. Ramanujan's translations of selected poems from the *Tiruvāymol̲i,* one of the major devotional works of Tamil.
Shanmugam Pillai, M., and David E. Ludden. *Kuruntokai.* Madurai: Koodal Publishers, 1976. A translation of one of the Sangam works.
Shulman, David Dean. *Tamil Temple Myths: Sacrifice and Divine Marriage in the South Indian Saiva Tradition.* Princeton, N.J.: Princeton University Press, 1980.
Sivasankarapilla, Takazhi. *Chemmeen; a Novel.* New York: Harper Bros., 1962.
Stein, Burton. *Peasant, State, and Society in Medieval South India.* Delhi: Oxford University Press, 1980.
Subrahmanya Sastri, P. S. *Tolkappiyam: The Earliest Extant Tamil Grammar. Porulatikaram—Tamil Poetics.* Madras: Kuppuswami Sastri Research Institute, 1994.

One of two translations of the oldest work in Tamil. This translation is of the section on aesthetics.

Takahashi, Takanobu. *Tamil Love Poetry and Poetics.* Leiden: Brill, 1995. An excellent study of the conventions of *akam* poetry.

Tevaneyan, Na. *The Primary Classical Language of the World.* Ka[t]padi Extension, North Arcot Dt.: Nesamani Publishing House, 1966.

Vaiyapuri Pillai, S. *History of Tamil Language and Literature; Beginning to 1000 A.D.* Madras: New Century Book House, 1956.

Visswanathan, E. Sa. *A History of Tamil Literature.* Translated by Mu. Varadarajan. New Delhi: Sahitya Akademi, 1988.

Winslow, Miron, and Joseph Knight. *A Comprehensive Tamil and English Dictionary of High and Low Tamil.* Madras: P. R. Hunt, American Mission Press, 1862.

Zvelebil, Kamil. *Classical Tamil Prosody, an Introduction.* Madras: New Era Publications, 1989.

Zvelebil, Kamil. *The Smile of Murugan on Tamil Literature of South India.* Leiden: Brill, 1973.

Zvelebil, Kamil. *Tamil Literature.* Wiesbaden: Harrassowitz, 1974.

Zvelebil, Kamil. *Tamil Literature.* Leiden: Brill, 1975.

INDEX

178, 181, 182, 183, 184, 185, 186, 187, 188, 190, 192, 198, 205, 207, 217, 223, 224, 237, 322, 335. *See also* dancing woman; and kings, xvi; hair smells of meat, 146; king gives fortresses to bards, 129; life of bard described, 36; one of four castes in poor land, 191; oral literature of imitated by poets, xxiii–xxv
bark: of tree used by physician, 117
Basavaṇṇa, 259
bat: poet comes like, 212
bathe: ascetic bathes in waterfall, 154; before battle, 60, 194
battle: have to wear flowers for, 170
beard: of hero sparse as he lies on shield, 179
bee, 198; bees swarming during day bad omen, 166; voice of *yāḻ* like, 178
bell: helps guard wounded hero, 167; kings bell rung by those in need, 228
belt-string, 205; worn by beautiful woman, 201
Beowulf, xxiv
bhakti literature, xvi
bhoga, 246
bird: as omen, 33; drums frighten off birds, 235; eating fruit from tree, 125; frightened off by drums, 234; in banyan tree sign of prosperity, 155; man searching for elephant will get it, man searching for small bird will not, 135; seek fruit, 132
birth, 267; defects, 252; eight sorts of monstrous births, 23; king first sees new-born son, 70; ritual at birth of first son to a family, 271; stillbirth or mass of flesh still cut with sword, 57
blacksmith. *See* smith
blind man: enemy like blind man stumbling on tiger, 57
blind person, 148
blood: like water from rain in harvest image, 212; turns field muddy, 169; water in battle is rich red, 142
boar, 96, 114, 115, 186; female demon has teeth like boar's tusks, 213; not eaten by a tiger if it falls to left, 121
boat, 51, 82, 226, 263, 324, 325; bereaved poet like someone whose boat has overturned, 148; boat taking you to other world is good deeds, 209; carries goods from ship, 196; elephant like boat in battle, 22; filled with trade, 195; hero like boat sailing ocean, 176; horses in battle like ships on ocean, 174; horses lying in pools of blood like ships when there is no wind, 210; keep harbor clear so ocean-going ships can dock, 241; king is a boat that can carry you beyond misery, 217; king like a boat carrying great and lowly alike, 222; mansion of dead king like boat in dried-up river, 158; Mars like lantern on ship, 46; salt cart is Tamil ship of state, 287; ship unloaded in port, 25; single wall of city like ship dry on shore, 193
body, 140, 294; connection with life, 21, 249; does not matter whether you cremate or excarnate king, 144; good men reach other world with their very bodies, 206; must die with purified body, 136; supported by water, food, 16; *yākkai*, etymology, 249

possessed by a god, 157; man of despised caste feeds rice to corpse, 207; music players of lowest castes, 263; potters and bards live on different streets, 198; Pulaiyan̲ feeds rice to corpse, 204; *tuṭi* drummer called "low", 169
cat, 78
Cāttantaiyār, 61, 170
Cāttan̲, 115, 221. *See also* Cōl̲anāṭṭup Piṭavūrkil̲ān̲ Makan̲ Peruñ Cāttan̲, Pāṇṭiyan̲ Kīrañcāttan̲
caturaṅga. *See* army
cave, 132
Celvak Kaṭuṅkō Vāl̲iyātan̲. *See* Cēramān̲ Cikkar̲pal̲l̲it Tuñciya Celvak Kaṭuṅkō V āl̲iyātan̲
Cempiyan̲, 142; same as King Śibi in Sanskrit, 255; who saved a dove, 30, 31, 34, 36
Cen̲n̲i. *See* Cōl̲an̲ Ilavantikaip Pal̲l̲it Tuñciya Nalaṅkil̲l̲i Cēṭcen̲n̲i
Cēramān̲ Antuvañcēral Irumpor̲ai, 11
Cēramān̲ Celvak Kaṭuṅkō Vākiyātan̲, 12
Cēramān̲ Cikkar̲pal̲l̲it Tuñciya Celvak Kaṭuṅkō Vāl̲iyātan̲, 228
Cēramān̲ Kaṇaikkālirumpor̲ai, 57
Cēramān̲ Kaṭalōṭṭiya Vēlkel̲u Kuṭṭuvan̲, 211, 214
Cēramān̲ Kaṭuṅkō Vāl̲iyātan̲, 8
Cēramān̲ Karuvūrēr̲iya Oḷvāṭ Kōpperuñcēralirumpor̲ai, 6
Cēramān̲ Kōkkōtai Mārpan̲, 37, 38
Cēramān̲ Kōṭṭampalattut Tuñciya Mākkōtai, 151
Cēramān̲ Kuṭakkō Neṭuñcēralātan̲, 49
Cēramān̲ Kuṭakkōccēralirumpor̲ai, 133, 134
Cēramān̲ Kuṭakkōneṭuñ Cēralātan̲, 210
Cēramān̲ Kuṭṭuvan̲ Kōtai, 41
Cēramān̲ Māntarañcēral Irumpor̲ai, 40, 81
Cēramān̲ Māvaṇkō, 210
Cēramān̲ Pālai Pāṭiya Peruṅkaṭuṅkō, 10
Cēramān̲ Peruñ Cēralātan̲, 51
Cēramān̲ Peruñcōr̲r̲utiyañcēralātan̲, 4
Cēramān̲ Peruñcēralātan̲, 263
Cēramān̲ Takaṭūrer̲inta Peruñ Cēralirumpor̲ai, 38
Cēramān̲ Vañcan̲, 238
Cēramān̲ Yān̲aikkaṭcēy Māntarañcēralirumpor̲ai, 17, 19
cēri, 326
Cēṭcen̲n̲i Nalaṅkil̲l̲i, 141
cevilittāy. *See* mother
cevval̲i: a subcategory of *marutam* poems, contrasted with *mullai*, 279
cevval̲i paṇ, 92, 93; *paṇ* belonging to mullai class, 277; rāga of longing, 91
chariot, 59, 63, 80, 89, 91; are the plows in harvest image, 211; dead go in driverless chariot, 23; falling chariots like drops in harvest image, 214; given away by king, 54; given by Pāri to a jasmine vine, 126; has lotus-shaped support, 210, 266; of Mauryas, 114; Pāri gave to jasmine creeper, 127
chastity, 205. *See also* woman; *kar̲pu* defined, 329
Chemmeen, 258
Chera, 32, 75, 243; wear palmyra leaf, 257
chest: of king like tiger, 59; of king like trap, 16
child, 72; child king fearsome in war, 59; child of poet is hungry, 106; children fulfilled, 121; children make noise in courtyard, 190; children of carpenter, 130; children

child (*continued*)
of hunters make arrows with thorns, 185; children of hunters wear tigers' teeth necklaces, 216; children play with bows and arrows in poor land, 186; children search for wild rats in poor village, 184; children using play arrows, 214; hitch calf to toy chariot in poor land, 183; importance of children, 120; impoverished child of bard, 134; in poor land, harvest threshed by boys, not buffaloes, 187; king sweet to us like elephant to children, 66; "May your children be free of disease"—a curse, 123; mother would threaten child with stick to make him drink milk, 179; old man remembers life as a child, 150; people bereft like child abandoned by mother, 144; poet blesses children of king, 124; should wait to die until son is born, 139; son of hero has dull-colored topknot, 163; son of poet is starving, 102; unclear speech of, 65
Chola, 31, 35, 51, 75, 81, 113, 138, 192, 223; Chola king defeated coastal people of south, Andhras of north, 219; tiger symbol of, 261; wear laburnum, 257
Cilappatikāram, xvi, xxxiv, 254, 256, 260
cīr, metrical foot, xxvii
ciṟaippuṟam, 268
Ciṟukuṭikiḻāṉ Paṇṇaṉ, 112, 228, 229
Ciṟuveṇṭēraiyār, 206
city: is falling down, 202; single wall of city like ship dry on shore, 193
clothing, 86, 88, 94; dead hero covered with white cloth, 169; fallen man wears white clothing, 171; garment given by king like snake's skin, 237; hero wears white garment, 179; king dresses drummer in silken clothes so well embroidered with flowers it seemed a single flow, 224; king puts on drummer garment like smoke, 238; king removes old garment, replaces it, 230; king replaces threadbare garment of drummer with white, 225; king should give drummer new garment with folds like petals of *pakaṉṟai*, 233; king took off my tattered garment, like roots of duckweed, dressed me in fine cloth, 231; mother puts white garment on son going to war, 166; old clothing like moss in stagnant water, 230; old garment of drummer like tongue of serpent, 233; tattered garment of drummer, 217; women wear skirts of waterlilies, 76
cloud, 72, 80, 81, 85, 90, 97, 99, 102, 128, 161, 176; as figure for generosity, 342; collects water from ocean, 130; draws water from ocean, 103; elephants like, 210; generosity of, 73; king as generous as, 42; king should live more years than drops in a cloud, 28; king's generosity like, 41, 129; paradigm for generosity, 272; poet comes to king as cloud goes to sea, 216; smoke from cooking like cloud, 221; "The clouds ignore our suffering.", 230; umbrella like, 29;

Cūr, 260; demon slain by Murugan, 19
Curapuṉṉai, 281
curd: hero like a few drops of curd flicked into milk, 164

dam: king like mountain damming river, 110; king should construct, 16
dance, 132. *See also kuravai, alliyam.* ecstatic dancing, sacrifice of goats at festival, 209; of puppets, 29–30
dancer, 97, 139, 332
dancing woman, xxv, 46, 49, 54, 64, 71, 72, 74, 75, 83, 85, 88, 89, 111, 112, 151, 166, 183, 253; in summer things wither like *yoni* of dancing girl after dance, 233; Viṟali defined, 261
darbha grass, 329
date: of *Puṟanāṉūṟu*, xvi
daughter. *See* puberty
dawn, 115; *kiṇai* drummer sings king at dawn, 215, 220, 224, 231, 233, 236, 240
Death, 4, 6, 11, 16, 20, 32, 34, 43, 69, 123, 133, 139, 147, 148, 149, 172, 203, 205, 206, 300; cursed by widow of dead hero, 155; dead hero laid on legless bed, covered with white cloth, 169; has hurt self by taking king, 141; is real, not an illusion, 207, 209; like farmer who eats own seeds, 144; must have begged king for king's life, 141; Śiva identified with, 260; warrior should not die in bed, 265, 301
death ceremony. *See* funeral
Deccani culture: elements from entered North India, xxxvii
deer, 64, 94, 130; deer mate when hunter is asleep, 183; female deer set out by hunter as decoy, 183; one might escape relatives as a deer escapes hunter, 122; sambur deer sleep on cereal husks, 173
demon, 231; on battlefield, 211, 215; on burial ground, 148
demon woman, 211, 247, 262; dances on battlefield, 48; eats bloodless flesh of corpses, 203; on burning ground, 202; snatches severed arm on battlefield, 212; tangled in guts on battlefield, 212; teeth like boar's tusks, eats human flesh, 213
discus: false story of discus of Akutai, 145
dog, 57
doll, 168; girls make dolls of mud, 150
dove, 31, 34, 36
dream, 229; as omens, 33; what one sees in dreams he gave me while awake, 218
drink. *See* toddy
drum, 75. *See also ākuḷi* drum, *ellari* drum, *kiṇai* drum, *muḻavu, paṇai, patalai, taṇṇumai* drum, *tuṭi* drum, *uṭukkai*; bard's drum balanced on sticks, 54; drum (*paṟai*) like foot of an elephant, 159; drums announce victory, 141; drums frighten off birds, 234; drums have forgotten clay as king is dead, 50; eye of, 248; frightened off by drums, 235; in palace of Indra roars that (dead) king is coming, 150; king crossed flood of arrows using *tuṭi* drum as raft, 158; king's shoulders like drums, 63; like thunder, 82; may king's wives never hear funeral drums, 229; monkey beats eye of drum

hanging in tree, 83; mother hears sound of war drum, 166; *paṛai* drum beaten on battlefield, 48; smeared with paste and wrapped with leather strings, 13; waterfall like, 81, 143

elephant (*continued*)
drum like bottom of elephant's foot, 210; tied to tutelary tree, 196; wear golden forehead ornaments, gore with tusks, 169; with golden forehead ornament resembles Himālaya with golden peaks, 211
E̲li̲ṉi, 99. *See* Atiyamāṉ Makaṉ Pokuṭṭeliṉi
Eḻiṉi Ātaṉ. *See* Vāṭṭāṟṟeḻiṉiyātaṉ
ellari drum, 96
Ēṉāti Tirukkiḷḷi, 109
Ēṟaikkōṉ, 99
Erukkāṭṭūrt Tāyaṅkaṇṇaṉār, 237
erukkam flower, 73
Erumaiveḷiyaṉār, 163, 176
Evvi, 128, 145
execution: of children, 36; of enemy kings, 60
eye: eyes of girl who has reached puberty are like spear, 199; like crab's-eye seeds, 175; rabbits have eyeballs like buds, 189; waterflowers like, 235
Eyil: city of, 55
Eyiṉaṉ, 200

facing north, 50, 51, 121, 136, 137, 138, 139, 140, 263; Kapilar faces north after Pāri dies, 147; Kapilar supposed to have taken life by facing north, 271
fame: hero wants to establish fame by dying well, 178; important to die with fame, 136, 204
family: binds you, 122
father, 75, 197; and grandfathers fight, 171; has destined daughter for great kings, 194; his duty to make child into noble man, 180; of beautiful girl won't give her away, 202; of girl who has attained puberty, 199, 201; tries to keep nubile daughter from marrying, 191
festival, 18, 61, 62, 67, 134, 159, 222, 267; ecstatic dancing, sacrifice of goats at festival, 209; there is toddy even though there is no festival, 225; war sacrifice compared to wedding, 214; world like actors at a festival, 25
fire: hero like stick of kindling in eaves of house, 181; king in battle like fire swallowing houses, 214; lotus like flame, 207
fisherman: should not save for future in modern novel, 258
flag, 31, 181, 194, 199, 206; on fortress walls, 14
flower. *See* ornament; flowers in poor land, 191; flowers worn for battle, 194; meanings of *malar*, 280; woman sells flowers before battle, 172
flute, 90
food, 12, 27, 28, 67, 72, 75, 78, 81, 83, 89, 94, 96, 101, 102, 109, 112, 115, 119, 128, 130, 134, 136, 141, 153, 156, 158, 159, 183, 186, 187, 198, 204, 207, 208, 214, 216, 217, 220, 221, 223, 226, 230, 232, 234, 236, 238, 299; and children, 120; before king's death, food was shared, 153; crops that need no farmers, 74; Death like a man who eats his seeds, 141; gruel, 62; I will know no days except those when the leaves we have eaten from are flung away still filled with food, 225; king would eat with throngs, 145; king would share, 146; king's son eats meat even when no festival, 67;

lizard, 186; mouths of hunter children smell of birds they have eaten, 185; seasoning of, 303; Tamil conception of, 302
forest, xviii, 287. *See also* funeral; all have gone to ground where corpses burn, 206; as burial ground and burning ground, 331; burial ground, 141; burning ground, 149, 202, 206; chatter of relations obscures the existence of the burning ground, 206; even kings go to burning ground, 203; fertile land of enemy turned into forest, 39; it will be hard to enjoy after we have gone to burial ground, 207; must gain fame before you go to burning ground, 204; place of burial, burning ground, 147; place of burning or burial, 148; widow approaches burning ground, 152; wife has gone to burning ground, 151
forgiveness: as a virtue, 34
formulas: characteristic of oral poetry, xxiv
fortress, 115; carved with mark of tiger, 113; description of, 17; fortresses given to bards, 129
fox, 171; foxes on battlefield, 215
fragrant basil. *See* karantai
fruit: birds come for fruit on banyan tree, 155; fruit chewed by monkeys looks like torn up drum, 146; sought by birds, 132; unwilling gift compared to raw fruit, 131
funeral, 266. *See also* forest; can burn head of dead king or not, 149; contrasted with wedding, 122; cremation or excarnation, it doesn't matter, 144; dead hero lies on shield, 179; excarnation, 330; may king's wives never hear funeral drums, 229; widow immolates self, 152; would cut warriors who died in bed with sword, 66

Gajabāhu synchronism, xvi
gambling, 39
game: girls play *ōri*, 285
Gaṇas, 3; same as Kūḻis?, 250; Śiva's attendants, 243
gander. *See* goose
Ganges, 103
garland: bard gets garland of gold, 183; female demon makes garland of guts, 213; if king does not kill enemy, then may garland wither in embraces of women who don't love him, 57; king and hero exchange garlands, 171; king wears *tumpai* garland, 68; of gold, 89
garment. *See* clothing
gatekeeper, 130
generosity, 177; as source of immortality, 107; debased character of those who are not generous, 121; hero gives away villages, 169, 170; hide self when guests visit, 161; hospitality of rich relatives, 33; king gives fields and farmers in them to drummer, 227; king like a boat carrying great and lowly alike, 222; to feed guests, king pawned sword, 181; village given away by king, 173; villages given to bards, 175; work of hero is granting gifts, 191
ghee, 236; drips from meat like rain, 226; king pours ghee more freely than water, 225; widow does not eat, 151

sharpen sickles on backs of tortoises, 220
havis, 336
haystack: stacks of corpses like, 213
head: can burn head of dead king or not, 149; Peruntalaic Cāttaṉār offers his head to Kumaṇaṉ, 107
heaven. *See* rebirth
hell, 6, 217
heron, 165
Himālaya, xxxi, 4, 6, 14, 28, 32, 51, 84, 108, 136, 244, 264; elephant resembles, 211
honey, 74, 216, 272
horn: musical instrument, 332
horse, 49, 68, 69, 113, 116, 124, 227; all horses have died and lie in pools of blood like ships without wind, 210; fallen horse like tree fallen where rivers meet, 163; falling horses like drops in harvest image, 214; food of, 174; galloping horses like bent bamboo springing up, 175; horse of hero does not return, 163; horses in battle like ships on ocean, 174; like wind in harvest image, 211; outruns wind, 176; pained by small stick, 200; so swift it breaks spirit of those who watch it, 176; standing still a bad omen, 143; tuft of hair of hero sparse like mane of horse, 179
hospitality. *See* generosity
house: hero like stick of kindling in eaves of house, 181; king's enemies permitted to live only in mean houses, 24; mansion of king resembles cool pond with moon, 219
householder, 328
hunter, 94, 95, 115, 120, 122, 130; ascetic used to hunt with net of words, 154; children of hunters make arrows of thorns, 185; hunter of elephants is asleep, 183; hunters bring down porcupines, 216; lives in poor area, 190

Iḷampūraṇar, xxviii, xxx, 327
Ilaṅkai, 220, 336
Iḷaṅkaṇṭīrakkō, 95
Iḷaṅkumaṇaṉ, 107
Iḷantattaṉ, 37
Iḷaveḷimāṉ, 147
Iḷaviccikkō, 95
Iliad, xxiv
illness: "May you be free from illness" a curse, 130
incense: helps guard wounded hero, 167
Indra, 255, 332; dead king goes to place of, 150
ingratitude: worst of sins, 28
invocation, xxviii, 243
Ionians, 260
Iṟaiyaṉār, xxviii
Īrntūr Kiḻāṉ Tōyaṉ Māṟaṉ, 117
iron, 77, 111
irum: meaning of, 264
Irumpiṭart Talaiyār, 5
Iruṅkōvēḷ, 127, 128
island: rite of ritual suicide (facing north) on river island, 138
Iṭaikkāṭaṉār, 34
Iṭaikkuṉṟūrkiḻār, 58, 59, 60
Iyakkaṉ, 55

jackfruit, 74, 89, 94, 100, 126, 183, 215, 221
Jain, xxxi
jālaka, 283

Kiḻḻi. *See* Ēṉāti Tirukkiḻḻi
Kiḻḻi Vaḷavaṉ, 239. *See also* Cōḻaṉ Kuḷamuṟṟattut Tuñciya Kiḻḻivaḷavaṉ
kiṇai drum, 58, 215, 216, 217, 218, 219, 223, 224, 227, 228, 233, 236, 240; beats at execution, 60; has god in it, 239; king goes to battle behind the *kiṇai* drum, 60; like foot of elephant, 231
kiṇai drummer, 225, 322; beats drum at funeral, 266; wife sells fish, 239; work is to come at dawn and praise king, 220
Kiṇaiyaṉ. *See* kiṇai drummer
king, xvii–xx; duty to show how to behave, 180; how a good king should act, 204; ideal king shuns corruption, 121; is life of world, 119; divine quality of, 316; of poor land, 124; prosperous city will go hungry if king dies, 182; three kings, xvii, 74, 80, 87, 104, 130, 202; title of, 96; who rules whole earth, 206; "you surmount the two kings", 41
kīrai plant, 101
kite, 34, 94, 140, 148, 162, 196; made for sacrifice, 296
knee: king's hand reaches to, 64
Kōcars, 110, 168, 235
Kōccēramāṉ Yāṉaikaṭcēey Māntarañcēralirumpoṟai, 143
kokku, 308
kōlam, xxxiv
kōḷ, 337
Kōḻi, 51, 293
Kolli, 99
Kōṉāṭṭu Eṟiccilūr Māṭalaṉ Maturaik Kumaraṉār, 41, 48, 109, 117, 124, 234
Koṇkāṉaṅkiḻāṉ, 98
Koṇkāṉam, 98
Koṅkaṉs, 84
Kōpperuñcōḻaṉ, 52, 121, 134, 135, 136, 137, 138, 139, 140, 263, 293
Koṟṟaṉ. *See* Piṭṭaṅkoṟṟaṉ
Kōtai, 112. *See also* Cēramāṉ Kōkkōtai Mārpaṉ, Cēramāṉ Kuṭṭuvaṉ Kōtai
Kōṭai Mountain, 130
Kōṭaipāṭiya Perumpūtaṉār, 157
kōṭiyar, 332
Kōtamaṉār, 209
Kōvalūr: a city, 70
Kōvūrkiḻār, 26, 27, 33, 35, 36, 37, 53, 55, 178, 215, 223, 227, 241
Krishna, 254. *See also* Viṣṇu; got the sun back, 284
Kūkaikkōḻiyār, 207
Kuḷampantāyaṉār, 155
Kuḷamuṟṟattut Tuñciya Kiḻḻivaḷavaṉ, 33, 34, 36, 54, 55, 141, 142, 233, 237
Kūḷis: followers of Śiva, *gaṇas* in Sanskrit, 250
Kumaṇaṉ, 100, 101, 102, 103, 105, 106, 107; story of, 282
Kumārasaṃbhava, 244
Kumari, 14
Kumari river, 6
Kuṉṟukaṭpāliyātaṉār, 228
Kuṉṟūrkiḻār Makaṉār, 193
Kuṟamakaḷ Iḷaveyiṉiyār, 99
kuravai: a dance, 18, 20, 83, 236, 250
Kuṟavaṉ, 90, 99, 109, 144, 146, 298
Kuṟavar woman, 73
kuṟiñci, xxx, xxxvi, 215, 345; king rules more than one kind of tract, 37
kuṟiñci songs, 335
Kuṟṟuvaṉ Kīraṉār, 149

Mars, 46
martial courage, xvii, 9, 10, 32, 35, 49, 50, 52, 69, 135, 192, 195, 196, 239, 256, 257
marutam, xxxvi, 93, 339; a category of *akam* poems, contrasted with mullai, 279
marutam tree, 150, 196, 200
Marutaṉ Iḷanākaṉār, 39, 42, 88, 89, 199
Mūtūr: a city, 15
matu, 273, 305
Maturai Aḷakkarñāḻalār Makaṉār Maḷvaṉār, 229
Maturai Aṟuvai Vāṇikaṉ Iḷavēṭṭaṉār, 188
Maturai Iḷaṅkaṇṇik Kōcikaṉār, 179
Maturai Nakkīrar, 235
Maturai Vēḷācāṉ, 177
Maturaik Kaḷḷiṟ Kaṭaiyattaṉ Veṇṇākaṉār, 181
Maturaik Kaṇakkāyaṉār, 188
Maturaik Kaṇakkāyaṉār Makaṉār Nakkīraṉār, 43, 120
Maturaik Kaṭaikkaṇṇam Pukuttārāyattaṉār, 199
Maturaik Kūlavāṇikaṉ Cīttalaic Cāttaṉār, 46
Maturaik Paṭaimaṅka Maṉṉiyār, 200
Maturaip Pērālavāyār, 152, 159
Maturaip Pūtaṉilanākaṉār, 164
Maturait Tamiḻakkūttaṉār, 191
maṉṟam, 267
Mauryas, 114, 285
Māvaḷattāṉ, 35
Māvaṉ, 55
Māvilaṅkai, 114
Mayilainātar, xxviii
meat, 12, 156. *See also* food
Meghadūta, 263
memorial stone. *See* stone
Meru, 142, 297
Mēṣarāśi, 297
messenger, 168
meter: Sanskrit meters unlike Tamil meters, xxxii; Tamil meter not of North Indian origin, xxxi
meter and alliteration, xxv–xxviii
Miḻalai: a city, 20
milk, 4, 28, 35, 45, 52, 59, 102, 106, 109, 134, 154, 156, 164, 173, 179, 187, 197, 200, 221, 224, 226
millet, 24, 28, 78, 79, 88, 90, 101, 109, 112, 124, 131, 136, 182, 183, 184, 187, 190, 191, 225; common millet planted on battlefield, 231; kinds of in poor land, 191
Mōci, 100
Mōcicāttaṉār, 163
Mōcikīraṉār, 38, 98, 119
monkey, 77, 83, 86, 100, 126, 146, 152, 224; drummer's family puts ornaments on wrong places, like monkeys in the *Rāmāyaṇa*, 220
monsoon, 78, 93, 169. *See also* cloud
moon, 3, 4, 7, 8, 11, 18, 21, 23, 26, 31, 41, 42, 43, 46, 50, 65, 71, 75, 78, 102, 103, 113, 115, 144, 172, 213, 217, 219, 231, 233, 236, 240; eclipsed moon devoured by serpent, 158; light wanes at dawn, 237; like face of hero, 51; *taṭāri* drum like, 237; the lunar asterism, 281
moss: old clothing like moss in stagnant water, 230
mother, 62, 63; abortion of foetuses wrong, 27; blamed for giving birth to girl whom enemy kings want to marry, 198; cow adopts fawn of doe slain by tiger, 184; describes dead son laid out, 169; drummer came to king like child to mother's breast, 220; foster

Naṉṉaṉ, 95, 250; infamous king, 279
nārai, 292
Nariverūut Talaiyār, 6, 123
Nāyaṉmārs: imitated Sangam poets, xxxv
necklace, 84, 94, 205; hunter children wear tigers' teeth necklaces, 216; like a snake, 210, 238
nelli. *See* myrobolan plant
Neṭṭimaiyār, 9, 11, 13
Neṭumāṉ Añci, 130, 131, 181
Neṭumpalliyattaṉār, 50
Neṭuṅkaḷattupparaṇar, 171
Neṭuṅkiḷḷi, 35, 36
Neṭuvēḷātaṉ, 193
neytal, xxxvi, 339, 345; king rules more than one kind of tract, 37
Neytalaṅkāṉal: a city, 9
noble man. *See cāṉṟōṉ*
nocci: a *tiṇai*, xxix; *nocci* flower; compared before and after death of hero, 162; worn as dress by women and as garland by fighter, 163
Nocciniyamaṅkiḻār, 172
North India, xxxi–xxxii; and attitudes toward kingship, xvii

oath: king swears oath to marry beautiful woman who has reached puberty, 194, 199
oblation. *See* sacrifice
ocean, 97, 125, 147, 148, 189; cannot drink water of, 129; clouds take water from ocean, 130; dug out of earth, 7; even if ocean should end. . . ., 237; king blocks enemy like ocean shore, 188; poet comes to king as cloud goes to sea, 216; story of Sagara, 245; supplies water for clouds, 103; to east and west, 14
Odyssey, xxiv
oil: in hair bad omen, 33
Ōkkūr Mācāttaṉār, 153
Okkūr Mācāttiyār, 166
old age: old man remembers childhood, 150; old men who are foolish, 123; why do you not show old age?, 121
oḷi, 316
Ollaiyūr, 150
Ollaiyūr Kiḻāṉ Makaṉ Peruñcāttaṉ, 150, 151
Ollaiyūr Tanta Pūtappāṇṭiyaṉ, 55
omen, 52, 80, 129, 305; bees swarming during day, 166; birds, 17; detailed description of bad astrological omen, 142; does not matter whether omens are good or evil, 235; housewife spreading hair bad omen, 157; omens associated with movement of Venus, 226; omens indicate king will die in seven days, 297; sun appearing in south bad omen, 237; various bad omens, 33, 143; Venus in south is bad omen, 77, 224, 229; woman tells future by scattering water and rice, 166
oracle, 166
orality, xxiii–xxv
Ōrampōkiyār, 168
Order of the World, 101, 257, 293
Ōrēruḻavar, 122
Ōri, 99. *See also* Valvilōri
ōri: a game girls play, 285
ornament: composed of things from different places, 138; drummer's family puts ornaments on wrong places, 219; golden waterlily given to dancers, 97; king gives ornaments of gold, 102; king wears or-

puravu, 313
Pūtapāṇṭiyaṉ, 152

quail, 184, 225, 319

rabbit, 183, 187, 225, 234, 236; has eyeballs like bubbles in rain, 189; has hair like elephant grass, 190; eyeballs like buds, 189
raft: like life, 122; to go to other shore is righteous action, 203
rāga. *See paṇ*
Rāhu, 305
raid. *See* cow
rain, 77, 102, 103, 122, 125, 128. *See also* cloud; arrows compared to in harvest image, 211; arrows like, 169, 213; depends on Righteousness of king, 29; drops of rain would not suffice to count warriors killed by hero, 176; eyeballs of rabbit like bubbles in rain, 190; ghee dripping from meat like rain, 226; king will be like rain pouring down on wilderness, 222; your days should be more than raindrops, 209
rainbow: king's garland like, 47
Rajam, V. S., xxxvi, 282, 341, 348; on *tiṇais* in *Puṟanāṉūṟu*, xxx
Rājasūya, 248
Rāma, 220, 312
Ramachandran, M. G., xxxiii, xxxiv
Ramasubramaniam, 264, 276, 281, 285, 287, 308
Rāmāyaṇa, xxxv, 312, 328, 336; drummer's family puts ornaments on wrong places, like monkeys in the *Rāmāyaṇa*, 220; North Indian origin of, xxxi; of Kampaṉ, *maṟam* vs. *aṟam*, 330
rank. *See varicai*
rat, 147, 225; children search for wild rats in poor village, 184; hunted by children of hunters in poor land, 185; like someone who is not generous, 121; quail tries to kill, has ears like *kōṅku* flower, 184
rebirth, 85, 90, 204, 294; good men reach other world with their very bodies, 206; heroes have flawless wives in next world, 170; liberation from, 203; like a snake shedding skin, king has gone to other world, 158; north Indian origin of, xxxi; poet says he has figuratively died and been reborn, 224
renunciation: king should renounce world, 207
reservoir, 12, 13, 27, 35, 54, 58, 67, 78, 87, 90, 114, 132, 161, 167, 169, 170, 177, 189, 190, 193, 200, 201, 229, 315; dirtied by elephant, 195; enable country to withstand siege, 274; I will be as happy as the channel through which reservoir water pours, 217
rhythm: of drum faster than fingers snapping, 222
rice, 201, 345, 347. *See also* food; *aviḻ* vs. *maṭai*, 332; grains of look like petals of trumpet flower bud, 238; not life of world, 119; of sacrifice poured out in front of their doors by kings, 189; offering of boiled rice, 336; sacks filled with new rice, 168; unsalted rice fed to corpse, 207; rice bins, 93
rich land, 49, 134, 153, 161, 167, 174, 193, 195, 196, 200, 201, 220, 224, 230, 238; description of, 47; will become poor if king dies, 182

Rig Veda: varṇa in, xvii
righteous action: only thing that helps when you die, 203
Righteousness, 9, 17, 24, 25, 27, 28, 29, 31, 35, 41, 45, 48, 66, 74, 107, 111, 140, 206, 218, 234, 237, 257
river, 122; hero stops enemy like shore of river, 160; poets like many rivers flowing to sea, 34; rushing to sea, 147
rod. *See* scepter
Romans, 260
root: roots of tree on burning ground sway in wind, 207
royal drum, xvii, 4, 15, 21, 22, 24, 28, 38, 45, 47, 49, 58, 65, 70, 74, 75, 78, 87, 90, 99, 105, 113, 162, 199, 206, 213, 215, 227, 228, 233, 258, 334; beaten in morning, 236; drums of valor, justice, renunciation, 261; eyes torn on royal drums of dead king, 148; gives title to kingdom, 57; its eye bursting and rolling on ground a bad omen, 143; king will obliterate royal drums of enemies, 56; like thunder, 124; like thunder in harvest image, 214; like thunder killing snakes, 133, 208; made with skin of bull that defeated another, 170; power of, xxi; royal drum of defeated king is ruined, 48; sacrificed to with blood, 211; sacrificed to with blood and liquor, 330; sacrificed to, bathed, 38
royal umbrella. *See* umbrella

sacrifice, 13, 320, 331, 336. *See also* war sacrifice; at death you will accept a sacrifice you do not desire, 207; at some Vedic sacrifices, priest must have three wives, 283; ball of rice (*piṇḍam*) offered to dead king by wife, 145; by Brahmin, at fourteen sites, 108; king's widow offers dead husband food, 153; memorial stones worshipped in poor land, 191; performed to gods in pillars, 39; post of rises next to kite that is fed, 140; pour toddy on memorial stone, 144; royal drum sacrificed to with blood, 211; sacrifice male goats, 27; to memorial stone, 299; Tuvarai appeared in sacrificial pit, 127; twenty-one kinds of, 107; Vedic sacrifices, 140; white rice poured out in front of their doors by kings, 189
sacrificial priestess: stirs pot in war sacrifice, 214
Sagara: story of, 245
salt merchant, 62, 226; hero like buffalo bull abandoned by salt merchants, 178; king like a hill near where salt merchants get salt, 180; salt wagon, 47, 64, 71, 77; as Tamil ship of state, 119
Śambumuni, 290
sand: dark sand, *aṟal*, 251; more have died than sand heaped by waves, 206
sandal. *See* shoe
sandalpaste, 13, 24, 49, 96, 148
sandalwood, 73, 216; skin of *taṭāri* drum as white as a stick of sandalwood powder, 211
Sanskrit, xxxi; *mātrā* meters in, xxxvii; similarity of classical literature to Tamil, xxxii
Sanskritization, xviii
sapphire, 84, 128, 137, 210, 218; king's dark color like that of, 143

Sastri, K. A. Nilakanta, xxxvii
satī. *See* widow
Saturn, 77, 273
scale, 31, 34
scepter, 14, 17, 33, 42, 55, 137, 139, 143, 260; staff foretells future, 96
sea. *See* ocean
seed: Death like a man who eats his seeds, 141; Death like farmer eats seeds, 144; eyes like crab's-eye seeds, 175; millet seed adequate for gift if worth is recognized, 131; widows eat seeds of lily, 166; widows eat waterlily seeds, 152, 153; widows eats cucumber seeds, 151; world not worth weight of mustard seed, 203
servant: ideal, 121
seven symbols, 70, 270
shadow, 56, 105, 135, 139, 147; of king, 31
shepherd, 41
shield, 174, 179; covers eyes of fallen, 49; dead hero lies on, 179
ship. *See* boat
shoe: hero like pebble in sandals of enemies, 156
shore: hero stops enemy like shore of river, 160
Shulman, David Dean, xxxiii
sickle: sharpen on backs of tortoises, 220
siege, 177, 196; description of, 35
singer, 112, 139, 146
singers guard fallen hero, 171
singing woman, 205, 207
Sītā, 220, 312
Śiva, 7, 107, 266, 283; and Hālāhala poison, 243; army of; Kūḷis or Gaṇas, 250; arrow destroyed the Three Cities, 260; blue-throated, banner is bull, holds axe, 42; blue-throated, has Gaṅgā in hair, defeated cities, 41; Death identified with, 260; eye in forehead, 259; his son is Murugan, 260; invocatory verse to, 3; moon on head, dark throat, 65; north Indian origin of, xxxi
smith, 18, 111, 117, 201; blacksmith's duty to forge a spear, 180
smoke: from cooking like cloud, 220; king puts on drummer garment like smoke, 238
snail: mates with conch, 161
snake, 64, 167; supposed to hear through eyes, 338; bards want to cast poverty off as snake casts off skin, 223; camp of king like hole where cobra lurks, 179; cobra has jewel, which it may drop, 313; country of king like hole where snakes live, 188; destroyed by thunder, 15, 30, 82, 208, 211, 248; fork in tongue pronounced when laying eggs, 344; garment given by king like snake's skin, 237; has jewel, 223; head shattered by thunder, 133; like a snake shedding skin, king has gone to other world, 158; moon in eclipse devoured by serpent, 158; necklace like, 210, 238; old garment of drummer like tongue of serpent, 233; skin of compared to fine cloth, 224; snake drops jewel, which is dangerous, 172
sola tree, 266, 338
son. *See* child
south: land of dead in south, 9; sun appearing in south a bad omen, 237; Venus in south is bad omen, 77, 224, 229

spear, 68, 69, 70, 146, 270; bathed before battle, 201; ceremonies performed for, 327; contrast kings spears with those of enemy, 67; eats human fat, 126; garlanded, taken in procession, 189; like seeds in harvest image, 211; of king not like other spears, 189; on hero's chest like spokes on wheel hub, 168; scarred, 201
spurs, 336
squirrel, 178
Śrī, 8, 195, 342; king wears ornaments Śrī might envy, 116; must be renounced to attain liberation, 203
Sri Lanka, 336
śruti, 329, 348; *kēḷvi* translation of, 252
staff. *See* scepter
stag, 20, 96, 99, 104, 183
Stallion Mountain, 99, 109
star, 102; as omen, 21; bodies of cattle as lovely as stars, 240; elephants he has given like sky covered with, 83; falling star a bad omen, 33, 143; stars would not suffice to count warriors killed by hero, 176; your days should be more than, 209
Stein, Burton, xxxiii
sthalapurāṇas, xix, xxxiii
stone: customs regarding memorial stone, 299; dead in rite of facing north have become stones, 140; hero has become memorial stone worshipped with flowers by cowherds, 160; hero is memorial stone, 144; hero like pebble in sandals of enemies, 156; hero of cattle raid has become a memorial stone, 159; in desolate land, is bowed to, 159; king has died and become a stone, 139; memorial stone described, 158, 160; memorial stone only god in poor land, 191; memorial stone prayed to by woman, 177; memorial stones in wilderness, 180; offerings to memorial stone outside village, 188; will rain if you worship god in stone, 306
Śūdra: replaced by Vēḷāḷaṉ in Tamil, 286
sugarcane, 13, 18, 20, 24, 28, 34, 69, 76, 87, 184, 221, 225, 226; ancestor of Atiyamāṉ brought sugarcane, 232; world as sweet as, 209
summer, 114, 140, 147, 222, 229, 233; when no huge, bountiful cloud, 161
sun, 4, 5, 6, 7, 13, 17, 20, 21, 25, 28, 29, 31, 33, 34, 42, 43, 46, 50, 53, 61, 64, 87, 89, 94, 98, 99, 102, 113, 114, 123, 142, 144, 183, 203, 208, 212, 217, 219, 230, 231, 232, 234, 235, 236; appearing in south bad omen, 237; compared to king, 8; gems on necklace like suns, 205; god of many rays, 28; O sun, you are not as generous as king. . . . . , 216
Śūrapadma, 260
sword, 68; being wounded like being squeezed by sword, 214; is a palmyra whip in harvest image, 213; pawned by king to feed guests, 181; straighten sword on tusks of dead elephant, 168

Tai: month of, 54
Takkayākapparaṇi, 296
Talaiyālaṅkāṉam: place of battle, 16
tāli, 266; marriage *tāli*, 275
Taḻumpaṉ, 198

royal umbrella, xvii; umbrella of defeated king droops, 48; umbrella snapped is bad omen, 143
Ūṇ: city of, 198
universe: three-tiered, 7
Ūṉpoti Pacuṅkuṭaiyār, 10, 129, 212, 220
uṇṭāṭṭu, 312
Uṟaiyūr, 134, 138
Uṟaiyūr Ēṇiccēri Muṭamōciyār, 11, 83, 84, 85, 86, 150, 216, 217
Uṟaiyūr Iḷampoṉ Vāṇikaṉār, 160
Uṟaiyūr Maruttuvaṉ Tāmōtaraṉār, 47, 111, 184
Uṟaiyūr Mutukaṇṇaṉ Cāttaṉār, 23, 24, 25, 186
Uṟaiyūr Mutukūttaṉār, 189
Uṟantai, 31, 45, 53, 200, 234
urn: burial urn, 142, 148, 207; should be large enough for widow and dead hero, 156
Uttara, 298
uṭukkai drum, 264

vaṭimpu, 336
Vaiyai River, 55
Vaiyāvik Kōpperum Pēkaṉ, 90, 91, 92, 93
vajra, 301
vākai, 200; a *tiṇai*, xxix
Vaḷavaṉ, 113. *See also* Cōḻaṉ Kuḷamuṟṟattut Tuñciya Kiḷḷivaḷavaṉ
Vallār, 117
Vallārkiḻāṉ Paṇṇaṉ, 117
Vālmīki, 328
Valvilōri, 96, 97, 129
Vaḻuti, 228. *See also* Pāṇṭiyaṉ Cittiramāṭattut Tuñciya Naṉmāṟaṉ, Pāṇṭiyaṉ Kūṭakārattut Tuñciya Māṟaṉ Vaḻuti
vāṇar, 340
Vañcaṉ. *See* Cēramāṉ Vañcaṉ
Vañci, 228; a city, 10, 32; a *tiṇai*, xxix; Odes that Praise Invasions, 13, 27
vañci paṇ, 219, 233, 248
Vāṉmīkiyār, 203
vaṉpāl, 339
Vaṉparaṇar, 93, 94, 95, 97, 155
varicai, 277, 290
varṇa, 118, 286
Vasiṣṭha, 274
vaṭakkiruttal. *See* facing north
Vaṭama Vaṇṇakkaṉ Pēricāttaṉār, 125
Vaṭama Vaṇṇakkaṉ Peruñcāttaṉār, 81
Vaṭamavaṇṇakkaṉ Tāmōtaraṉār, 112
Vaṭamōtaṅkiḻār, 158
Vaṭaneṭuntattaṉār, 116
Vāṭṭāṟṟeḻiṉiyātaṉ, 236
Vaṭṭāṟu, 235
Vedas, 3, 4, 7, 12, 22, 66, 107, 139, 140, 206; north Indian origin of, xxxi–xxxii
Vedic sacrifice. *See* sacrifice
Vēḷ Evvi, 20, 145
Vēḷ Pāri, xxiii, xxvi, xxxv, 73, 74, 75, 76, 77, 78, 79, 99, 115, 146, 147; gave chariot to jasmine creeper, 127; girl as hard to see as spring on Pāri's Paṟampu, 192; story of, 271
Vēḷāḷars. *See* Veḷḷāḷaṉ
vēlaṉ, 322
Veḷimāṉ, 105, 131, 147, 148
Vēḷir, 21, 86, 127, 236, 290
Veḷḷaikkuṭi Nākaṉār, 29
Veḷḷaimāṟaṉār, 173
Veḷḷāḷaṉ, 344, 293
Veḷḷerukkilaiyār, 145
Vēmpaṟṟūrk Kumaraṉār, 182
vēṅkai, 70, 73, 78, 83, 87, 109, 128, 140, 160, 196, 200, 230, 271; girls would smear pollen of *vēṅkai* on their breasts, 325

terlily seeds, 152, 153; king's widow offers food to dead husband, 153; king's widow offers sacrificial food, 153; loses ornaments, hair, 159; may king's wives never hear funeral drums, 229; memorial stone for *satī*, 299; new widows do not yet take lives, but thrill at wounds of dead husbands, 214; of dead king immolates herself, 151, 152; of dead king must suffer as widow, 153; of dead king offers ball of rice, 145; of hero prays to a memorial stone in wilderness, 177; of king has gone to burning ground, 151; shed their ornaments, 140; shed ornaments, cut hair, eat waterlily seeds, 166; tries to lift up dead husband, 155; wants urn for husband large enough for her also, 156; widows kill selves, 334; widows of king lose bangles, 147; widows of war dead do not yet bathe, 48; wives of dead king die, 149; wives of dead king lose bangles, 148; women with men contrasted to widows, 122

wife, 105, 106, 139. *See also* widow; dark wife of king like peacock, 182; enemy kings will have to leave their women, 68; heroes have flawless wives in next world, 170; ideal, 121; impoverished wife of poet, 104; is light of house, 180; is very poor, 101; of bard, 133, 134; of bard, has waist as slender as a vine, 181; of drummer sells fish, 239; of drummer, her poverty, 232; of hero serves guests, 190; of hero serves poet millet kept as seed, 190; of hunter, 183; of king as lovely as Lakṣmī, 235; wife of king hugs him as he reclines, 224; of king sleeps with him, 231; poet's wife pure but impoverished, 123; wives of Brahmin, 107; wives of hunter, their children, 216; wives of king, 124, 132, 140, 143; wives of king serve toddy, 205

wildcat. *See also* cat; wildcat stalks hen, 186

wind: arrows like wind in harvest image, 214; horses compared to in harvest image, 211

wine, 235; king's women serve wine brought by Greeks, 43

winnowing fan, 153, 184; like elephant's ears, 194

woman, xix, xx–xxi. *See also* chastity, mother, puberty, widow, wife; fence like hair of virgins, 175; her chastity possesses a god, 289; importance of chastity (*kaṟpu*), xvii; is light of house, gives food, 189; *kaṟpu* (chastity) defined, 329; king may feel disturbed by women who pour out toddy, 208; menstruous woman should not touch food, enter temple, 314; purity of poet's wife, 123; tongues fear teeth, 205; when menstruous cannot touch dishes or enter temple, 174; women who love you, 105

womb, 63

world: as sweet as sugarcane, 209; exists because of good men, 117

worship. *See* sacrifice

wound, 51, 66, 70, 145, 166, 179, 184, 201, 215; chests wounded by spears like palmyra trees with jagged stems, 174; king ashamed at

Other Works in the

COLUMBIA ASIAN STUDIES SERIES

TRANSLATIONS FROM THE ASIAN CLASSICS

Major Plays of Chikamatsu, tr. Donald Keene 1961

Four Major Plays of Chikamatsu, tr. Donald Keene. Paperback ed. only. 1961; rev. ed. 1997

Records of the Grand Historian of China, translated from the Shih chi of Ssu-ma Ch'ien, tr. Burton Watson, 2 vols. 1961

Instructions for Practical Living and Other Neo-Confucian Writings by Wang Yang-ming, tr. Wing-tsit Chan 1963

Hsün Tzu: Basic Writings, tr. Burton Watson, paperback ed. only. 1963; rev. ed. 1996

Chuang Tzu: Basic Writings, tr. Burton Watson, paperback ed. only. 1964; rev. ed. 1996

The Mahābhārata, tr. Chakravarthi V. Narasimhan. Also in paperback ed. 1965; rev. ed. 1997

The Manyōshū, Nippon Gakujutsu Shinkōkai edition 1965

Su Tung-p'o: Selections from a Sung Dynasty Poet, tr. Burton Watson. Also in paperback ed. 1965

Bhartrihari: Poems, tr. Barbara Stoler Miller. Also in paperback ed. 1967

Basic Writings of Mo Tzu, Hsün Tzu, and Han Fei Tzu, tr. Burton Watson. Also in separate paperback eds. 1967

The Awakening of Faith, Attributed to Aśvaghosha, tr. Yoshito S. Hakeda. Also in paperback ed. 1967

Reflections on Things at Hand: The Neo-Confucian Anthology, comp. Chu Hsi and Lü Tsu-ch'ien, tr. Wing-tsit Chan 1967

The Platform Sutra of the Sixth Patriarch, tr. Philip B. Yampolsky. Also in paperback ed. 1967

Essays in Idleness: The Tsurezuregusa of Kenkō, tr. Donald Keene. Also in paperback ed. 1967

The Pillow Book of Sei Shōnagon, tr. Ivan Morris, 2 vols. 1967

Two Plays of Ancient India: The Little Clay Cart and the Minister's Seal, tr. J. A. B. van Buitenen 1968

The Complete Works of Chuang Tzu, tr. Burton Watson 1968

The Romance of the Western Chamber (Hsi Hsiang chi), tr. S. I. Hsiung. Also in paperback ed. 1968

The Manyōshū, Nippon Gakujutsu Shinkōkai edition. Paperback ed. only. 1969

Records of the Historian: Chapters from the Shih chi of Ssu-ma Ch'ien, tr. Burton Watson. Paperback ed. only. 1969

Cold Mountain: 100 Poems by the T'ang Poet Han-shan, tr. Burton Watson. Also in paperback ed. 1970

Twenty Plays of the Nō Theatre, ed. Donald Keene. Also in paperback ed. 1970

Chūshingura: The Treasury of Loyal Retainers, tr. Donald Keene. Also in paperback ed. 1971; rev. ed. 1997

The Zen Master Hakuin: Selected Writings, tr. Philip B. Yampolsky 1971

Chinese Rhyme-Prose: Poems in the Fu Form from the Han and Six Dynasties Periods, tr. Burton Watson. Also in paperback ed. 1971

Kūkai: Major Works, tr. Yoshito S. Hakeda. Also in paperback ed. 1972

The Old Man Who Does as He Pleases: Selections from the Poetry and Prose of Lu Yu, tr. Burton Watson 1973

The Lion's Roar of Queen Śrīmālā,tr. Alex and Hideko Wayman 1974

Courtier and Commoner in Ancient China: Selections from the History of the Former Han by Pan Ku, tr. Burton Watson. Also in paperback ed. 1974

Japanese Literature in Chinese, vol. 1: Poetry and Prose in Chinese by Japanese Writers of the Early Period, tr. Burton Watson 1975

Japanese Literature in Chinese, vol. 2: Poetry and Prose in Chinese by Japanese Writers of the Later Period, tr. Burton Watson 1976

Scripture of the Lotus Blossom of the Fine Dharma, tr. Leon Hurvitz. Also in paperback ed. 1976

Love Song of the Dark Lord: Jayadeva's Gītagovinda, tr. Barbara Stoler Miller. Also in paperback ed. Cloth ed. includes critical text of the Sanskrit. 1977; rev. ed. 1997

Ryōkan: Zen Monk-Poet of Japan, tr. Burton Watson 1977

Calming the Mind and Discerning the Real: From the Lam rim chen mo of Tsoṇ-kha-pa, tr. Alex Wayman 1978

The Hermit and the Love-Thief: Sanskrit Poems of Bhartrihari and Bilhaṇa, tr. Barbara Stoler Miller 1978

The Lute: Kao Ming's P'i-p'a chi, tr. Jean Mulligan. Also in paperback ed. 1980

A Chronicle of Gods and Sovereigns: Jinnō Shōtōki of Kitabatake Chikafusa, tr. H. Paul Varley. 1980

Among the Flowers: The Hua-chien chi, tr. Lois Fusek 1982
Grass Hill: Poems and Prose by the Japanese Monk Gensei, tr. Burton Watson 1983
Doctors, Diviners, and Magicians of Ancient China: Biographies of Fang-shih, tr. Kenneth J. DeWoskin. Also in paperback ed. 1983
Theater of Memory: The Plays of Kālidāsa, ed. Barbara Stoler Miller. Also in paperback ed. 1984
The Columbia Book of Chinese Poetry: From Early Times to the Thirteenth Century, ed. and tr. Burton Watson. Also in paperback ed. 1984
Poems of Love and War: From the Eight Anthologies and the Ten Long Poems of Classical Tamil, tr. A. K. Ramanujan. Also in paperback ed. 1985
The Bhagavad Gita: Krishna's Counsel in Time of War, tr. Barbara Stoler Miller 1986
The Columbia Book of Later Chinese Poetry, ed. and tr. Jonathan Chaves. Also in paperback ed. 1986
The Tso Chuan: Selections from China's Oldest Narrative History, tr. Burton Watson 1989
Waiting for the Wind: Thirty-six Poets of Japan's Late Medieval Age, tr. Steven Carter 1989
Selected Writings of Nichiren, ed. Philip B. Yampolsky 1990
Saigyō, Poems of a Mountain Home, tr. Burton Watson 1990
The Book of Lieh Tzu: A Classic of the Tao, tr. A. C. Graham. Morningside ed. 1990
The Tale of an Anklet: An Epic of South India—The Cilappatikāram of Iḷaṅkō Aṭikaḷ, tr. R. Parthasarathy 1993
Waiting for the Dawn: A Plan for the Prince, tr. and introduction by Wm. Theodore de Bary 1993
Yoshitsune and the Thousand Cherry Trees: A Masterpiece of the Eighteenth-Century Japanese Puppet Theater, tr., annotated, and with introduction by Stanleigh H. Jones, Jr. 1993
The Lotus Sutra, tr. Burton Watson. Also in paperback ed. 1993
The Classic of Changes: A New Translation of the I Ching as Interpreted by Wang Bi, tr. Richard John Lynn 1994
Beyond Spring: Tz'u Poems of the Sung Dynasty, tr. Julie Landau 1994
The Columbia Anthology of Traditional Chinese Literature, ed. Victor H. Mair 1994
Scenes for Mandarins: The Elite Theater of the Ming, tr. Cyril Birch 1995
Letters of Nichiren, ed. Philip B. Yampolsky; tr. Burton Watson et al. 1996
Unforgotten Dreams: Poems by the Zen Monk Shōtetsu, tr. Steven D. Carter 1997
The Vimalakirti Sutra, tr. Burton Watson 1997
Japanese and Chinese Poems to Sing: The Wakan rōei shū, tr. J. Thomas Rimer and Jonathan Chaves 1997
A Tower for the Summer Heat, Li Yu, tr. Patrick Hanan 1998
The Classic of the Way and Virtue: A New Translation of the Tao-te Ching of Laozi as Interpreted by Wang Bi, tr. Richard John Lynn 1999

Original Tao: Inward Training (Nei-yeh) *and the Foundations of Taoist Mysticism,* by Harold D. Roth 1999
Lao Tzu's Tao Te Ching: *A Translation of the Startling New Documents Found at Guodian,* Robert G. Henricks 2000
The Shorter Columbia Anthology of Traditional Chinese Literature, ed. Victor H. Mair 2000
Mistress and Maid (Jiaohongji) by Meng Chengshun, tr. Cyril Birch 2001
Chikamatsu: Five Late Plays, tr. and ed. C. Andrew Gerstle 2001
The Essential Lotus: Selections from the Lotus Sutra, tr. Burton Watson 2002
Early Modern Japanese Literature: An Anthology, 1600–1900, ed. Haruo Shirane 2002

MODERN ASIAN LITERATURE SERIES

Modern Japanese Drama: An Anthology, ed. and tr. Ted. Takaya. Also in paperback ed. 1979
Mask and Sword: Two Plays for the Contemporary Japanese Theater, by Yamazaki Masakazu, tr. J. Thomas Rimer 1980
Yokomitsu Riichi, Modernist, Dennis Keene 1980
Nepali Visions, Nepali Dreams: The Poetry of Laxmiprasad Devkota, tr. David Rubin 1980
Literature of the Hundred Flowers, vol. 1: Criticism and Polemics, ed. Hualing Nieh 1981
Literature of the Hundred Flowers, vol. 2: Poetry and Fiction, ed. Hualing Nieh 1981
Modern Chinese Stories and Novellas, 1919–1949, ed. Joseph S. M. Lau, C. T. Hsia, and Leo Ou-fan Lee. Also in paperback ed. 1984
A View by the Sea, by Yasuoka Shōtarō, tr. Kóren Wigen Lewis 1984
Other Worlds; Arishima Takeo and the Bounds of Modern Japanese Fiction, by Paul Anderer 1984
Selected Poems of Sō Chōngju, tr. with introduction by David R. McCann 1989
The Sting of Life: Four Contemporary Japanese Novelists, by Van C. Gessel 1989
Stories of Osaka Life, by Oda Sakunosuke, tr. Burton Watson 1990
The Bodhisattva, or Samantabhadra, by Ishikawa Jun, tr. with introduction by William Jefferson Tyler 1990
The Travels of Lao Ts'an, by Liu T'ieh-yün, tr. Harold Shadick. Morningside ed. 1990
Three Plays by Kōbō Abe, tr. with introduction by Donald Keene 1993
The Columbia Anthology of Modern Chinese Literature, ed. Joseph S. M. Lau and Howard Goldblatt 1995
Modern Japanese Tanka, ed. and tr. by Makoto Ueda 1996
Masaoka Shiki: Selected Poems, ed. and tr. by Burton Watson 1997
Writing Women in Modern China: An Anthology of Women's Literature from the Early Twentieth Century, ed. and tr. by Amy D. Dooling and Kristina M. Torgeson 1998

American Stories, by Nagai Kafū, tr. Mitsuko Iriye 2000
The Paper Door and Other Stories, by Shiga Naoya, tr. Lane Dunlop 2001
Grass for My Pillow, by Saiichi Maruya, tr. Dennis Keene 2002

STUDIES IN ASIAN CULTURE

The Ōnin War: History of Its Origins and Background, with a Selective Translation of the Chronicle of Ōnin, by H. Paul Varley 1967
Chinese Government in Ming Times: Seven Studies, ed. Charles O. Hucker 1969
The Actors' Analects (Yakusha Rongo), ed. and tr. by Charles J. Dunn and Bungō Torigoe 1969
Self and Society in Ming Thought, by Wm. Theodore de Bary and the Conference on Ming Thought. Also in paperback ed. 1970
A History of Islamic Philosophy, by Majid Fakhry, 2d ed. 1983
Phantasies of a Love Thief: The Caurapañatcāśikā Attributed to Bilhaṇa, by Barbara Stoler Miller 1971
Iqbal: Poet-Philosopher of Pakistan, ed. Hafeez Malik 1971
The Golden Tradition: An Anthology of Urdu Poetry, ed. and tr. Ahmed Ali. Also in paperback ed. 1973
Conquerors and Confucians: Aspects of Political Change in Late Yüan China, by John W. Dardess 1973
The Unfolding of Neo-Confucianism, by Wm. Theodore de Bary and the Conference on Seventeenth-Century Chinese Thought. Also in paperback ed. 1975
To Acquire Wisdom: The Way of Wang Yang-ming, by Julia Ching 1976
Gods, Priests, and Warriors: The Bhṛgus of the Mahābhārata, by Robert P. Goldman 1977
Mei Yao-ch'en and the Development of Early Sung Poetry, by Jonathan Chaves 1976
The Legend of Semimaru, Blind Musician of Japan, by Susan Matisoff 1977
Sir Sayyid Ahmad Khan and Muslim Modernization in India and Pakistan, by Hafeez Malik 1980
The Khilafat Movement: Religious Symbolism and Political Mobilization in India, by Gail Minault 1982
The World of K'ung Shang-jen: A Man of Letters in Early Ch'ing China, by Richard Strassberg 1983
The Lotus Boat: The Origins of Chinese Tz'u Poetry in T'ang Popular Culture, by Marsha L. Wagner 1984
Expressions of Self in Chinese Literature, ed. Robert E. Hegel and Richard C. Hessney 1985
Songs for the Bride: Women's Voices and Wedding Rites of Rural India, by W. G. Archer; eds. Barbara Stoler Miller and Mildred Archer 1986
A Heritage of Kings: One Man's Monarchy in the Confucian World, by JaHyun Kim Haboush 1988

The Confucian Kingship in Korea: Yŏngjo and the Politics of Sagacity, by JaHyun Kim Haboush 1988

COMPANIONS TO ASIAN STUDIES

Approaches to the Oriental Classics, ed. Wm. Theodore de Bary 1959

Early Chinese Literature, by Burton Watson. Also in paperback ed. 1962

Approaches to Asian Civilizations, eds. Wm. Theodore de Bary and Ainslie T. Embree 1964

The Classic Chinese Novel: A Critical Introduction, by C. T. Hsia. Also in paperback ed. 1968

Chinese Lyricism: Shih Poetry from the Second to the Twelfth Century, tr. Burton Watson. Also in paperback ed. 1971

A Syllabus of Indian Civilization, by Leonard A. Gordon and Barbara Stoler Miller 1971

Twentieth-Century Chinese Stories, ed. C. T. Hsia and Joseph S. M. Lau. Also in paperback ed. 1971

A Syllabus of Chinese Civilization, by J. Mason Gentzler, 2d ed. 1972

A Syllabus of Japanese Civilization, by H. Paul Varley, 2d ed. 1972

An Introduction to Chinese Civilization, ed. John Meskill, with the assistance of J. Mason Gentzler 1973

An Introduction to Japanese Civilization, ed. Arthur E. Tiedemann 1974

Ukifune: Love in the Tale of Genji, ed. Andrew Pekarik 1982

The Pleasures of Japanese Literature, by Donald Keene 1988

A Guide to Oriental Classics, eds. Wm. Theodore de Bary and Ainslie T. Embree; 3d edition ed. Amy Vladeck Heinrich, 2 vols. 1989

INTRODUCTION TO ASIAN CIVILIZATIONS
WM. THEODORE DE BARY, GENERAL EDITOR

Sources of Japanese Tradition, 1958; paperback ed., 2 vols., 1964

Sources of Indian Tradition, 1958; paperback ed., 2 vols., 1964; 2d ed., 2 vols., 1988

Sources of Chinese Tradition, 1960; paperback ed., 2 vols., 1964

Sources of Korean Tradition, ed. Peter H. Lee and Wm. Theodore de Bary; paperback ed., vol. 1, 1997

NEO-CONFUCIAN STUDIES

Instructions for Practical Living and Other Neo-Confucian Writings by Wang Yang-ming, tr. Wing-tsit Chan 1963

Reflections on Things at Hand: The Neo-Confucian Anthology, comp. Chu Hsi and Lü Tsu-ch'ien, tr. Wing-tsit Chan 1967

Self and Society in Ming Thought, by Wm. Theodore de Bary and the Conference on Ming Thought. Also in paperback ed. 1970

The Unfolding of Neo-Confucianism, by Wm. Theodore de Bary and the Conference on Seventeenth-Century Chinese Thought. Also in paperback ed. 1975

Principle and Practicality: Essays in Neo-Confucianism and Practical Learning, eds. Wm. Theodore de Bary and Irene Bloom. Also in paperback ed. 1979

The Syncretic Religion of Lin Chao-en, by Judith A. Berling 1980

The Renewal of Buddhism in China: Chu-hung and the Late Ming Synthesis, by Chün-fang Yü 1981

Neo-Confucian Orthodoxy and the Learning of the Mind-and-Heart, by Wm. Theodore de Bary 1981

Yüan Thought: Chinese Thought and Religion Under the Mongols, eds. Hok-lam Chan and Wm. Theodore de Bary 1982

The Liberal Tradition in China, by Wm. Theodore de Bary 1983

The Development and Decline of Chinese Cosmology, by John B. Henderson 1984

The Rise of Neo-Confucianism in Korea, by Wm. Theodore de Bary and JaHyun Kim Haboush 1985

Chiao Hung and the Restructuring of Neo-Confucianism in Late Ming, by Edward T. Ch'ien 1985

Neo-Confucian Terms Explained: Pei-hsi tzu-i, by Ch'en Ch'un, ed. and trans. Wing-tsit Chan 1986

Knowledge Painfully Acquired: K'un-chih chi, by Lo Ch'in-shun, ed. and trans. Irene Bloom 1987

To Become a Sage: The Ten Diagrams on Sage Learning, by Yi T'oegye, ed. and trans. Michael C. Kalton 1988

The Message of the Mind in Neo-Confucian Thought, by Wm. Theodore de Bary 1989

DATE DUE
